Community Structure
and Analysis

Community Structure and Analysis

✻ *Marvin B. Sussman, Editor*

Associate Professor of Sociology, Western Reserve University

Thomas Y. Crowell Company

Established 1834 · New York

Designed by Laurel Wagner

Manufactured in the United States of America by Vail-Ballou Press, Inc., Binghamton, N.Y.

Library of Congress Catalog Card Number 59-9401

* Foreword

*

$*$ THIS VOLUME is sponsored by the Society for the Study of
Social Problems (SSSP) and is recommended as a textbook for
courses in the community or as a supplement to the text for courses
in social problems. SSSP came into being in 1951 as "a non-profit
body for the promotion and protection, by means decided upon by
its membership, of sociological research and teaching on significant
problems of social life." It seeks, as its constitution and bylaws point
out, to "stimulate the application of scientific method and theory
to the study of vital social problems, encourage problem-centered
social research, and foster co-operative relations among persons and
organizations engaged in the application of scientific sociological
findings to the formulation of social policies." These purposes are
indirectly but effectively fostered in the college classroom; hence
this problem-oriented text on *Community Structure and Analysis*.

SSSP organized its Committee on Community Research and Development in 1953 with Marvin B. Sussman as its first chairman.
This committee has grown to include some seventy members and
has become one of the most active committees of the Society. The
present volume is but one of the fruits of this committee and represents a significant accomplishment of its able and hard-working
former chairman. The committee, following an SSSP policy, has
brought together a variety of social scientists, represented by the
authors of the selections in this volume, to analyze a given social
problem. While most members of SSSP are sociologists, and the

v

Society is affiliated with the American Sociological Society and the International Sociological Association, there are also members who identify themselves primarily as psychologists, psychiatrists, anthropologists, political scientists, social workers, and social action researchers. The special problems committee which produced this volume also includes non-members of the Society who are trained as city planners, urban economists, architects, community organizers, and human geographers. Thus, informally, as well as formally, SSSP has become a meeting ground for social science and social action.

Because of the broad scope of this book—as suggested by a glance at its table of contents—and because of the diverse specializations of its highly qualified contributors, the book should have a variety of uses. It should be invaluable as a text for college classroom use, since it brings together many of the best materials available on the community. Relevant courses are taught in sociology and in social welfare departments, and occasionally also in special institutes, which bring together the various disciplines interested in the urban community. Secondly, the volume should meet the needs of various persons engaged in community action who desire to understand their particular problems in a broad context. Such persons include city planners, architects, community organizers, welfare agency directors, recreational and public health specialists, religious and educational leaders, and—not least of all—practicing politicians. Needless to say, college students who are planning a career as one of the above-mentioned professionals will also find this volume invaluable for their occupational orientation. Thirdly, the "purer" types of social scientists will find some of the selections to be innovating contributions to their scientific disciplines.

The human community is not only a product of natural forces that reach an equilibrium. It also develops a number of conditions that its members recognize as social problems, and they seek to solve these problems by collective and individual action—thus contributing to the structure of the community. The college teacher will find that this volume offers his students a combination of materials which enable them to understand realistically the social forces and the social action which work together to form the community. The tools for studying and analyzing the community are also clearly presented.

While committees provide advice in the preparation of SSSP volumes, the main burden of selecting, stimulating, organizing, and editing falls on the respective editor. SSSP is deeply indebted to Marvin Sussman, one of its most energetic and loyal members. His reward is not only the gratitude of the members of the Society but also the recognition that will be derived from the publication of this excellent volume.

ARNOLD M. ROSE
Former President, Society for
the Study of Social Problems

University of Minnesota

✳ Contents

viii

Contents

Community Change

* General Introduction

Marvin B. Sussman

* I<small>N THIS INTRODUCTION</small> are described the meaningful areas of community study presented in each of the chapters which follow. In general, there is a close relationship between those chapters concerned with community theory and those with research. Some chapters cover methods for testing theory, while others suggest hypotheses which attempt to explain the complex phenomena and relationships found in the community. Still others describe community problems, many of which are still unsolved. The community has been studied for some time, but it has been only in the last two decades that serious efforts have been made to develop a community science. This book is an effort in this direction.

A starting point for describing the coverage of this book would be a definition of community. While most researchers agree that a precise and exact definition of a community is not possible or perhaps even desirable, there are, nevertheless, certain features common to what has been identified as the "community." Once these features are discerned it then becomes possible to define a community.

A community is said to exist when interaction between individuals has the purpose of meeting individual needs and obtaining group goals. In all societies physical, psychological, and social needs are met through the creation of social systems. Examples are the family, religious, government, welfare, and economic systems. Particular structures within systems are called institutions, and these

1

become basic features of a community. Thus a community will have varied institutions through which all types of needs are satisfied.

A limited geographical area is another feature of the community. It is difficult to determine the specific boundaries of a community, although for political and governmental purposes these have been arbitrarily established. Since populations move and institutions increase or decrease in number, expand or contract their activities over time, a fixed boundary to describe a community would ignore the dynamics of community growth and dissolution. Thus, the geographical area of community is that which contains the social structures which meet the physical, psychological, and social needs of the majority of residents.

The features of social interaction, structures for the gratification of physical, social and psychological needs, and limited geographical area are basic to a definition of community. One of the more interesting problems in the study of the community is how one may classify communities as to types using statistical indices and other measures. Typology is defined as the study of types and applied to the community it is the study of types of communities. In chapter 1, "Community Typology," Professor Christen T. Jonassen attempts just such an analysis using statistical indices. Every ten years (*e.g.*, in 1940 and 1950), the Bureau of the Census gathers and compiles a great deal of information about the American population, such as the number of persons employed, in what occupations and where; the number, type, and conditions of housing; the size and number of age and sex groupings; and mortality and fertility rates in the population. Data may be compiled in a variety of ways: by census tract, town, village, township, city, county, or metropolitan area. Professor Jonassen's suggested typology is based upon a comparison of the 88 counties of Ohio on 82 items from census reports relevant to community life. These items are grouped and ranked and then compared in terms of a "standard" population. The degree of community is determined by the "commuscale" devised by Professor Jonassen and its scoring procedures. This first chapter is a pioneering effort to order vast quantities of statistical data into meaningful groupings and then to use measures thus derived for determining community types and characteristics of county units.

A community typology may be developed without using statistical measurements. Frequently, more descriptive measures are used such as the functions a community performs and the spatial arrangement of residential, commercial, and industrial areas. Professor Allen D. Edward's contribution in chapter 2 to the section on typology is an analysis of pertinent factors in classifying rural communities. Some of these include economic system, religion, tradition, history of initial settlement, and the street or road patterns of the community. In his analyses he demonstrates how these factors are related to the development of community structures which clearly distinguish one community from another.

Smaller units sometimes called sub-communities or neighborhoods, especially those found in cities, can be classified as to their social characteristics. Comparative studies of neighborhoods usually measure the rate and direction of changes taking place within such areas. In this type of study the census tract is the basic unit of analysis and economic, family, and ethnic data are used to describe the small social worlds which together make up the larger area. Professor Wendell Bell in chapter 3 elaborates the theoretical and empirical development of "social area analysis," an advanced method for classifying small communities within the large metropolitan area and evaluating the changes in social characteristics of these communities between census years. His comparative analysis of neighborhoods ranked as to family, economic, and ethnic status permits the study of various problems ranging all the way from attitudes toward child rearing to the problems of voting behavior of racial groups.

An illustration of "social area analysis" methods is found in chapter 4, a study of social participation in Los Angeles by Professors Scott Greer and Ella Kube. Four areas which are similar in economic status and in the absence of large ethnic minorities but vary in "urbanization" (a broader term for family status) are studied for differences in social participation. The authors use the "urbanization index," which consists of scale values determined by the proportion of wives who have outside jobs, the proportion of population living in single family dwellings, and the fertility ratio for a given area. One might expect that the amount and type of participation in community and social life would vary according to high, low, or intermediate position on the urbanization index. But the findings are that the amount of social participation does not vary in a spectacular manner between the high and low areas, but high and low area residents do vary in the social groups and institutions they participate in. The conclusion is that classification of smaller communities is feasible with "social area analysis" methods. Once the typology is completed, it becomes possible to test a variety of hypotheses concerning social life and social structure of the urban community.

The academic social scientist is not the only person interested in the community. Probably, if one wishes to be accurate, one should say that all people who are members of a community are interested in it because a community could not continue if interest was lacking. However, the professional is referred to here, who until recently has been primarily concerned with factual analyses of community structures and processes and with doing an occasional experimental study involving evaluation of procedures. A new breed of professional, the community development expert, has appeared on the scene. His principal objective is to facilitate the growth of individual competence in community living. Less concern is given to description and more to action. Community betterment is the desired goal, and the community development expert helps to bring about the achievement of this objective. The next two chapters in the book are concerned with community development as providing models for action. Dr. William Biddle of Earlham College is a proponent of the "developmental concept"; he states the objectives of this approach and also offers case illustrations of community action. Professor Otto G. Hoiberg develops the educational and consulting roles of the community expert.

Development implies action: doing something and achieving something. Action unless carefully planned may lead to chaos and the opposite of accomplishment. Planning is not an abstract process, nor does it arise in a vacuum. It is the result of systematic thought tempered by the realities of conditions to be met and obstacles to overcome. Inherent in planning are values, and the values which dominate city planning are discussed by Dean Arthur Hillman in chapter 7.

The community is in a continuous process of change. What may be described as the "state of things" one day may be ancient history the next. Of course institutions do not change radically over night, and social relations are probably more stable than I have indicated. However, in some communities school population may have as high as a 50 per cent turnover in six months. This indicates high population movement and is so rapid a change that it shakes the very foundations of community institutions. Change means action. People come and go, and each new group changes the older institutions. Frequently, people in the midst of change are unaware that their actions have resulted in a way of life somewhat different from what it was previously. The change may be slow, not easily discernible to the participant, but perceptible to the outsider.

A fascinating tale of community change, the events and then the actions of members in the face of overwhelming disaster, is that of Riverville by Professor Robert Janes. For fifteen years the community has been under surveillance ever since it was stricken by a flood. Relocation of the community was one of its objectives. Who gave leadership to this effort? Who resisted this planned change? What factors affected attitudes and subsequent action by community members in this situation? Professor Janes gives some of the answers. Studies like this over a long period of time permit an intensive analysis of conditions effecting basic changes in community institutions.

Change and subsequent action is usually less perceptible, raw, and dramatic than in Janes's story. Within large metropolitan areas neighborhoods undergo changes of population. New migrants, usually of low income, find their way into the blighted or near-blighted areas of the city. Existing populations in such areas begin to leave, and this process of community change has been termed the invasion, concentration, and succession cycle. Several questions arise concerning this process. What can be done to avoid or reduce potential racial, ethnic, or class conflict in these areas? Also, in those areas where programs of urban renewal are imminent or underway, how can one help the community's residents to prepare for this change? This is Professor Mel J. Ravitz's topic. He analyzes this problem, and in addition gives ten suggestions for preparing neighborhoods for change. Here, once again the community expert has an important role in community action and change.

Communities today, large and small, are receiving a face lifting. The program is called urban renewal, and since 1949 the United States Government has spent millions of dollars in an effort to prevent the spread of urban decay. It is becoming evident that the program is only successful when it can arouse and hold the interest of community members. How is this accomplished? Several techniques and approaches have been tried. One is to obtain cooperation of individuals and group in a community. In chapter 10 Dr. Frank L. Sweetser suggests a model for citizen participation and demonstrates its use in two communities in the Boston area. One essential value of the model is that it indicates weaknesses in organization which may impede effective community action in urban renewal programs.

Models for community action are helpful, but ultimate success depends upon cooperation, especially on the grass roots level. In a neighborhood affected by an urban renewal program, a pressing question is, How do the people most affected feel about it? The study of Morton Rubin, Louis H. Orzack, and Ralph Thomlinson covers neighborhood residents' varied perceptions, evaluations, and reactions to intended redevelopment of their community. Age, length of residence, education, association membership, nationality background, and owner-tenant status of the respondent affects the pattern of response. Studies of this kind may make the difference between success and failure of community action programs.

The concept of community presented in the beginning of this chapter suggests that a community is a "vertical" structure with its own supporting social system and with patterned social interaction and "we-feelings" among members which set one community off from others. The vertical community as it is described here is the predominate form in any society. Another type of community without a specific geographical base, but with the basic features of heightened social relationships and in-group feelings of its members has been identified as a "horizontal" structure. The "Jewish Community" which cuts across geographical boundaries is in this category as are probably all socio-religious communities. Dr. Fred Massarik's study is of the Jewish Community of Los Angeles. Some Jews still reside in the central city, the area of initial settlement, but many, largely the newer generations, have migrated to the outlying suburbs. The factors producing intimate social relationships and strong identification are the commonly shared religion, a historic tradition, extensive social and welfare programs for members of their own group, and economic interdependence within the boundaries of the religious community. One point for speculation is how many other non-geographically based communities one can find in our society and how these support or conflict with the existing vertical community.

It is conceivable that a religious community in some instances may supercede in importance the vertical community located in a specific place. Besides the Jewish Community many religious denominations and sects like the Amish, Mennonites, and Jehovah's Witnesses are horizontal communities. Religion is important to the community in still another way. It divides the community. There are three major divisions, the Catholics, Jews, and Protestants, and the Protestants are themselves divided into 264 recognized denominations and sects in these United States. The differences between the three major groups and the competing sects and denominations appear to be theological in nature but probably reflect more the social differences of Americans in our communities. Each of these religious groups has its own cosmology, tradition, service, personnel, and belief that its way is *the* way to everlasting life. Professor Russell R. Dynes in chapter 13 discusses some of the social differences among religious groups as found in American communities. His analyses cover the relationship of community size and degree of urbanization to church type, religious participation, and religious affiliation. Religious activities reflect changes in community structure. The church and its functions can only be understood in relation to the population characteristics of a community.

Religious groupings are but one type of community structure. Voluntary associations are another type and engage in activities similar to the church, but their activities are social rather than religious in character. The principal function of voluntary associations is to integrate heterogeneous populations around special interests and needs. Thus, overweight persons from all walks of life interested in losing weight may come together and form a group and work together toward this objective. Voluntary associations are a necessary part of an age of specialization: they fill individual needs and give order and continuity to social relationships in what appears to be the jumbled mass of urban people. While one function of these associations is to integrate heterogeneous populations, it is probable that they are more successful in reinforcing and cementing the in-group sentiments of homogeneous populations. In this sense, like religious groups, they illustrate cleavage in a community. Persons of similar background in regards to race, ethnicity, religion, education are likely to belong to the same association. These associations have definite levels of prestige and are replicas of the social class system within the community. Dr. Mhyra S. Minnis discusses women's voluntary associations in New Haven, Connecticut. She gives four variables, race, religion, ethnic background, and social prestige, as the factors which differentiate voluntary associations from each other. She shows that participation in community affairs varies for different types of associations and that these variations reflect the social class differences of the organization's members.

Community betterment is a goal commonly desired by voluntary associations. Planning and action groups have been specifically organized. These are often called community councils and are composed of lay and professional representatives from civic, government, private and public social and welfare agencies. These councils work on problems such as recreation, health, education, safety, welfare, and community rehabilitation. Councils as structures for improvement are welcome additions to any community. One question usually raised is, How effective are the councils in achieving their goals? Do such conditions as the presence or absence of "high urbanization" have anything to do with their success or failure? Should community councils be organized in the matter-of-fact way we organize churches and schools? Dr. J. D. Mezirow answers some of these questions in his report on the Coordinating Councils of Los Angeles. Four variables, the size of community, its social rank, degree of organization, and rate of population mobility, are studied in relation to the failure or success of council programs. Studies of this type suggest what the scope of community organizations like the council should be and the probabilities of their success after being established.

Voluntary associations and community councils are structures in

which numerous individuals work towards some common objective.
Participating individuals are not representative of all social classes
or groups in a community. Studies like the one presented by Professor John M. Foskett in chapter 16 indicate that best educated
persons with relatively high income participate most in the community. Participation is not a necessary result of money or position.
It is rather that persons of high income and occupation are expected to be active in community life. Time, expectations, special
interests, and training are related to high and low community participation. Foskett in his empirical study points to the need for
wider community participation by members of all social classes in
American society. He presents some interesting techniques for increasing community activity. One of the more interesting problems
of community research is concerned with the relationship of social
class to community participation. Do working-class members always participate less than the middle-class persons?

The question of participation levels according to class is difficult to answer until we have more studies like Foskett's in various
communities. Another approach would be to study what people actually do in their non-working hours. Dr. Saxon Graham has made
such a study in Butler County, Pennsylvania. According to his
findings more joiners are found in the upper than lower classes, but
only 25 per cent of Butler's population belong to one or more organizations. Most persons are "bench sitters," spending a large
portion of their leisure time watching radio, television, and motion
pictures which are passive, non-creative, and commercially organized activities. The urban-rural differences in leisure-time patterns are also studied. Contrary to expectations more urbanites than
rural folk engage in recreational and religious activities, which are
most likely to produce warm and personal relationships and enriching experiences.

Religion and race are part of the urban scene. Church growth
has paralleled the growth of our communities. Since World War I,
rural non-whites in large numbers have migrated to Northern,
Midwestern, and Western cities. Settling in all-white communities
these newcomers pose problems for the already established
churches. Should the churches open their doors to the non-white
newcomers and develop a racially integrated church membership,

should they maintain themselves in Caucasian seclusion, or should they follow their white members to the suburbs? What factors affect decisions regarding church desegregation? This intriguing problem is the subject of Professor Lawrence K. Northwood's study of churches in Des Moines, Iowa. It is a problem every urbanized community faces and is a by-product of high population movement in American society today.

Mental illness, its ecology, incidence, prevalence, treatment, and the means of institutional care are of increasing concern to the student of the community. The complexity of community life with its concomitant social problems has paralleled increases in mental disorders. A valuable study is the relationship of stressful social conditions to high and low rates of psychotic disorders. Stress is difficult to define. Investigators suggest a stressful social condition exists when an individual is frustrated in his efforts at achieving a goal or when customary roles are inadequate in new or disruptive social situations. This definition is employed to classify communities as to high-low stress areas. Then analyses are made regarding the relationship of stress conditions to mental disorder. Some times a reverse of this research design is used. In chapter 19 by Professor E. Gartly Jaco, high and low rate areas for psychoses in Austin, Texas, are retrospectively determined by classifying by census tract all first admissions of diagnosed functional psychoses to the local state hospital for a given period. High admission areas are given a high rate designation and low admissions a low score. Random interviews were conducted covering interaction patterns and social conditions within the area. Jaco's findings indicate that conditions of community life are causally related to mental disorders. The specific role these conditions have in the origin of mental illness for an individual is yet to be studied. The fact that community structure and conditions of life are related to mental disorder suggests the need for more detailed studies on needed environmental conditions for reducing the incidence of mental disorders.

Throughout this introduction to *Community Structure and Analysis* is the recurring theme of social change and population movement with its attendant problems. Professor Vincent H. Whitney investigates in chapter 20 what happens to community institutions and social relations when a farm area becomes a limited-industry community and then a bedroom extension of a large city. His study of Smithfield covers this period of transition and the conditions under which conflict or varying degrees of cooperation are possible between the newcomers and oldtimers in a community. In this case study of community change, clarification is given to the reasons newcomers moved to Smithfield and their feelings about their location and services. The age of Smithfield's newcomers, their place of work, complaints, places for shopping, and sources for medical services are probably typical of a thousand new Smithfields growing up and developing from what was once a rural hinterland. In Whitney's report, Smithfield's community structure, people, and problems are presented clearly, and it is only with this type of analysis that understanding of community processes becomes possible.

As a community becomes increasingly urbanized, the nature of social relations and communication between its residents becomes a matter for study. Community theorists have speculated as to whether relationships between residents in the urban community become more secondary than primary. Secondary relations imply many contacts centering on special events or activities. A person knows many people, but very few of them are close or intimate friends. Primary relations involve a cohesiveness and "togetherness" of people, and another concern of the theorist is whether this intimacy increases or decreases with urbanization. One measure is the amount of "neighboring," a process of seeking and maintaining friendships within a neighborhood, usually a city block. In the concluding chapter, Professor Svend Riemer studies "neighboring" and indicates variations in this practice according to age, sex, location or residence, and family resources. His study explores the primary-secondary relationship concept and its efforts to explain the differences between urban and rural personality. The "tertiary group" is offered as a middle-road concept. Persons in the urban community need and do become loyal to some movement, trend, or institution in what Professor Riemer terms a "tertiary relationship." It then becomes possible for a dweller in the urban community to support a school expansion program (in the belief that education is good for everybody, especially for one's own kids) and be loyal to a food market, although he may not know intimately a single person in either institution. The attachments may not be conscious or rational, but emotional. The indi-

vidual need for identification is satisfied without the intimate relationship of the primary group. The individual is "free" from personal commitments while receiving some of the benefits derived
from the primary group relationship. This is an interesting concept
and its usefulness in explaining group relations in the urban community will be determined by future study. The tertiary group
concept fits in with the "identification" feature of our concept of the
community.

In this volume we have attempted to present the best in current
thinking and research on the community. We have also attempted to
cover the broad problem areas of the community. The materials presented represent an integration of community theory and research,
and they help to establish a base for building a community science.
As editor, the choice of chapters and commentaries are my own, as
well as the shortcomings of this book.

Community Typology

* 1. Community Typology

Christen T. Jonassen

Introduction We all speak about communities, and when we do, what do we really mean? Are they small, large, integrated, diverse, progressive or backward, in agreement or in conflict on common goals? This by no means exhausts the possible descriptions of a community. It is still a question of what we really mean.

In this first chapter Professor Jonassen helps our thinking about what a community is and how to describe it. He explores for us the theoretical and practical functions of a community typology and the varied problems involved in achieving such a system of classification. In doing this, he provides us with a typology that gives us a common understanding of the community and a common language for discussing it.

Classification implies order and the establishment of convenient categories into which observable or statistical data can be catalogued. To accomplish this requires some discussion of the nature of the community and the criteria for assigning communities to a particular classification.

A substantive definition of the community includes the following elements: a human population living in a given geographical area which has interdependence and often specialization of function and which shares a common culture. Individual members of the population group have a sense of identification with one another and act together to solve common problems. Dr. Jonassen uses "community" as a generic term; one is said to exist when some of the above dimensions are present. The kind of a community it is depends upon the presence or absence (sometimes degree of presence) of the various elements and their combinations.

Once the definition of a community is accepted how does one proceed to classify communities? There are many approaches, and Dr.

15

Jonassen succinctly describes the positions of the empirical-quantitative and philosophical-descriptive schools. The author's own is both brilliant and useful. Using the county as a basic unit, measures of community characteristics are normalized and are then compared in terms of a "standard" population. He employs a ranking procedure for 82 items relevant to community life and ranks each item for the 88 counties of Ohio. From this is evolved the *commuscale,* a set of standardized scores derived from a ranking of the 88 counties on 82 community characteristics. The commuscale permits a wide ordering of data. Types of communities can be described in terms of similarities and differences with others. Professor Jonassen provides students of the community with a useful community typology, which can serve as the base point for the analysis of community problems.

✳ THIS CHAPTER is concerned with the uses of a community typology, or a system of classification, and the problems involved in achieving a satisfactory one. Such a discussion could become highly abstract. To make it less so, the analysis will be illustrated by reference to a research project where these problems were met and resolved.

A fundamental contribution of social scientists to knowledge about the community consists in research on types. Simply stated, a primary purpose of a community typology is to provide a convenient and practical means by which persons interested in communities may know what they are talking about and others may understand them.

The teacher, the community organizer, welfare worker, the planner, and others in the field of community work depend on the social scientist for basic data on which to build a practical science of the community. That the science and arts of community have not developed further in spite of innumerable studies and thousands of man-hours and millions of dollars spent on them may be attributed in a large measure to failure to solve adequately the scientist's primary task, the development of an acceptable typology, or a system of concepts and classifications. Without generally accepted systems of guiding concepts and frames of reference, observation tends to be idiosyncratic and haphazard, and it impedes replication and verification necessary to the slow accumulation of tested hypotheses by which science grows.

Classification consists in arranging phenomena according to their characteristics in a system of categories and giving a name to each group thus established. If this task is to be accomplished two general problems must be solved: the nature of the phenomena must be determined, their constant features, their gradation, and variation ascertained; and the basis or principle which determines the category into which the thing classified is to be placed needs to be discovered. An examination of the extent to which these basic problems have been solved by students of the community should indicate the problems involved and whether a community typology is feasible at the present state of knowledge.

The plan is to discuss problems involved in community classification under these headings: "The Problem of the Nature of Community," "The Problem of Measurability," and "The Problem of a Taxonomic Principle." A solution to each of these problems is suggested at the end of each section. The solution offered is not the only nor a definitive one, but a suggestion and an example of how problems of community taxonomy or classification may be resolved.

THE PROBLEM OF THE NATURE OF COMMUNITY

A primary problem of taxonomy is to determine the essential nature of the thing classified. What is the essential character of the community; what qualities distinguish this from other phenomena?

It is obvious that taxonomy is closely related to definition-making and theory, if theory is defined as a simple statement of the relationship between phenomena which squares with empirical reality. Whether one is classifying, theorizing about, or defining the community, the number and character of its various components and their relationships to each other must be established. A community, for example, must be an area, or it must not be an area; or it must or must not be a psychological phenomenon. What is the consensus of social scientists with regard to the definition and nature of community? There is, unfortunately, a *lack* of consensus as to the nature of the community and the elements that comprise it. These disagreements constitute an important impediment, and some resolution of differences must be achieved before the process of classification may proceed.

The term "community" is used quite indiscriminately in common usage to mean anything from a neighborhood to a "world community," and it may be used to refer to a number of persons with like interests such as the "educational community," "the sporting community," or a "community of values."

Social scientists also differ in their conception of the term. Some think of the community essentially as the web of interrelationships between animals and plants in a habitat. Park saw "community" as the "biotic" and sub-social aspects and labeled the moral and evaluative aspects "society." [1] Galpin stressed the service and trade area aspects,[2] and Angell would use "ecological community" for spatial aspects and the term "moral community" for the socio-psychological unity.[3] MacIver emphasized the sharing of the basic conditions of common life in a territorial locality and held that a community need not be self-sufficient, yet declared that the mark of a community is that one's life *may* be lived wholly within it.[4] Davis agreed substantially with this definition and stated "the community is the smallest territorial group that can embrace all aspects of social life." [5]

Hillery's extensive analysis of definitions of *community* found in Social Science literature underscores the lack of consensus. There was complete agreement on only two points: namely, no author denied that area *could* be an element of community, and all definitions dealt with people.[6] It is thus apparent that there are important

[1] R. E. Park, "Human Ecology," *American Journal of Sociology*, vol. 42 (1936), p. 4.

[2] C. J. Galpin, *The Social Anatomy of an Agricultural Community*, Wisconsin Agricultural Experiment Station, Madison, Bulletin 34 (1915).

[3] Robert C. Angell, "The Moral Integration of American Cities," *American Journal of Sociology*, vol. 57 (1955), part 2 of no. 1.

[4] R. M. MacIver and C. H. Page, *Society* (New York: Rinehart & Company, Inc., 1949), pp. 9–10.

[5] Kingsley Davis, *Human Society* (New York: The Macmillan Co., 1949), p. 20.

[6] George A. Hillery, Jr., "Definitions of Community: Areas of Agreement," *Rural Sociology*, vol. 20 (1955), pp. 194–204. His detailed analysis is as fol-

and numerous divergencies both as to what the crucial variables are and how they combine in a community.

Many discrepancies in definition of the community and confusion as to its essential elements arise out of the spatial aspect of community phenomena. Such terms as "neighborhood," "local community," "community," "trade area," "region," "nation," and even "world" have been used to designate the spatial features of community phenomena. More often "community" is distinguished from neighborhood as being a larger territorial grouping within which the majority of a person's needs may be met and where secondary contacts tend to prevail; it is distinguished from nation and society as a smaller component of each of these. It would seem then that "community" is generally thought of as a *particular kind* of spatial grouping having specific characteristics which distinguish it from other spatial groupings not possessing such characteristics. On the other hand, the word "community" is often used by the same person preceded by an adjective such as "local community," "regional community," and "national community." In this sense it is used as a generic term. The use of the term "community" as both a particularistic and generic term at the same time makes for much confusion and is obviously false logic. Additional difficulty is created by the fact that more often than not it is not specified where one type of spatial grouping ends and another begins. It is most difficult to achieve such delineation because of the nature of community as a spatial phenomenon. A man is a member at one and the same time of the neighborhood, the community, the nation, the region, and the world, as is the area which he inhabits.

---

lows: "Of the 94 definitions, 69 are in accord that *social interaction, area,* and a *common tie* or *ties* are commonly found in community life. Seventy, or almost three-fourths mentioned area and social interaction as necessary elements of community. . . . Slightly more than two-thirds of the definitions maintain that social interaction and area are to be considered in studying the community. If the concept of area is omitted from consideration, the importance of interaction and common ties appearing jointly increases. One finds 73 of the 94 definitions (or excluding the rural formulations, 62 of the 78)—more than three-fourths—in which the community is considered a group of people in social interaction having some ties or bonds in common. Finally, all but three of the definitions stress social interaction as a necessary element of community life."

In other words, certain biotic, social, and cultural relations have significance for him at different loci and distance from him as the reference point.

Is there a way out of these difficulties? How can valid characteristics of the human community be determined and selected? Many of the problems involved would be resolved if it were assumed that a "community" exists where all or some of the community dimensions are present to a determinate degree. It is suggested that the concept "community" be used as a *generic* term to refer to all groups whose relations are spatially contingent, rather than to a specific form of spatial group. The kind of community it is may then be determined by the number, quality, degree, and combinations of factors present, and its delineation by the location of these factors in space.

The great store of empirical knowledge about the community can be utilized. While Hillery found social scientists defining "community" differently, he also discovered many agreements. He saw, for example, that a majority of the definitions he examined included as important elements: area, common ties, and social interaction; and that *all* authors, except two ecologists, would allow these three elements to be included in a definition of community.

Additional analysis of the attempts of social scientists to capture the essence of community, theorize about it, and define it shows that there is considerable agreement on the presence of all of these elements: (1) a population, (2) a territorial base, (3) interdependency of specialized parts and division of labor, (4) a common culture and social system which integrate activity, (5) a consciousness of unity or belonging among the inhabitants, and (6) an ability to act in a corporate fashion to solve problems.

The following definition of the community states the essential elements involved and their relationships to each other. *A community is a group integrated through a system of spatially contingent, interdependent biotic, cultural, and social relations and structures which have evolved in the process of mutual adjustment to environmental situations. It is a spatial group wherein the effects of interdependence and integration are made evident by the community's consciousness of unity and its ability to exercise adequate*

*ontrol over social, cultural, and biotic processes within it
boundaries.*

This definition may be elaborated in a list of community dimensions as follows:

1. Population
2. Spatial Structure
3. Systems of Environmental Exploitation
   a. Technology
   b. Organization
4. Systems of Integration
   a. Culture-values-folkways, mores, customs
   b. Social Organization—statics and dynamics, division of labor,
      social roles, institutions, groups, class, etc.
   c. Communication
   d. Social Control
   e. Ecological and Economic Systems of Integration
5. Processes of Change
6. Consciousness of Unity
7. Functional Efficiency—Ability to act in a corporate fashion to
   solve problems, secure and enhance life chances and standard of
   living
8. External Relations

The above list is, of course, an outline and each of the community dimensions might again be subdivided.

The list is, to an extent, tentative because it is based on scattered research where units of analysis were not strictly comparable
and where problems of measurement were not adequately solved.
Nevertheless, the great store of research data on communities is a
rich heritage which rewards those who dip into it with valuable
insights and hypotheses about community processes, characteristics,
and their interrelationships. A community typology should be
integrated with social scientific thought and empirical findings as
to the nature of the community and must be constructed by a
proper ordering of all constituent elements. The material from
earlier research and thought can guide researchers in selecting the
kinds of community elements for which valid and reliable measures
should be devised. Appropriate statistical techniques to determine

essential factors and to test relationships suggested by earlier theory
and research can then be undertaken. This task can not be successfully completed, however, before problems of measurability are
solved.

THE PROBLEM OF MEASURABILITY

The need for precise definition of characteristics or dimensions
of community is an obvious necessity. An acceptable typology cannot be created unless the meaning of the names used to describe
the determining criteria mean the same to all persons. The philosophic-descriptive typologists, using the ideal type approach, have
failed to meet this criterion as exemplified by the difference in
results achieved by Robert Redfield and later by Oscar Lewis in
their study of the Mexican village of Tepoztlán.[7]

Lewis points out that Redfield described Tepoztlán as a relatively homogeneous, isolated, smoothly functioning, and well-integrated cooperative society showing little or no evidence of poverty, violence, disruption, schisms, and maladjustment; while he
(Lewis) found individualism, lack of cooperation, tensions, and
a pervasive quality of fear, envy, and distrust in inter-personal
relations. Redfield's characterization emphasized unity, cooperation,
and integration; Lewis, looking at the same village, saw disunity,
maladjustment, schisms, and lack of cooperation.

The reason why many more such discrepancies are not reported
is probably that so few communities are ever restudied as rigorously
as was Tepoztlán. How could two well-trained and competent
anthropologists observing the same village achieve such divergent
results?

Both Lewis and Redfield minimize the effect of changes taking
place in the time interval between one study and the next, as the
cause of these fundamental differences and attribute them to differences between the two investigators, that is, between the theoret-

[7] Redfield, *Tepoztlán—A Mexican Village* (Chicago: University of Chicago
Press, 1930). Redfield, *The Folk Culture of Yucutan* (Chicago: University of
Chicago Press, 1941). Lewis, *Life in a Mexican Village: Tepoztlán Restudied*
(Urbana, Ill.: University of Illinois Press, 1951).

ical systems, concepts, and methods which each researcher used to guide the gathering of data and to formulate his analysis.

As Tomars suggests, there is a vast body of sociological, anthropological, and economic thought and research data compiled by social scientists demonstrating that there are real differences between rural and urban communities or "folk" and urban communities and that these differences are fundamental and pervasive.[8]

The "folk-urban" or "rural-urban" frame of reference has been very fruitful and may be even more valuable if used in quite a different way than it has usually been employed. Instead of the terms "folk," "rural," or "urban" being applied to combinations of community factors with the assumption that they all vary together in like directions as a community approaches the opposite ideal types, the terms should be applied to separate community elements. Furthermore, the character of each factor should be determined not by a vague qualitative designation in terms of ideal polar terms such as "folk-like" or "urban-like"; they might better be measured in terms of norms developed on the basis of "standard" population of communities. In other words, while the investigator must recognize the importance of differences between urban and non-urban communities, the poles of the continuum might be located at empirical rather than purely logical extremes.

But before the "folk-urban" continuum can be used to its fullest advantage, problems of operational definition of concepts and measurability must be solved, and it must be determined definitively by research which are "folk," "peasant," "rural," or "urban" characteristics. While it might seem obvious that this task has in most instances been achieved, it appears that as more comparable community data become available from other societies, there is less certainty. Contention that such qualities as secondary types of social control, dense population, heterogeneity, lack of isolation, disorganization, impersonal behavior, and market economy are essentially characteristic of urban communities everywhere seems to be challenged in one or more respects by Sjoberg's historical

[8] Adolph S. Tomars, "Rural Survivals in American Urban Life," *Rural Sociology,* vol. 8 (1943), pp. 378–386.

analysis [9] and by the studies of Guatamala communities by Sol Tax,[10] by Lewis' work in Mexico previously cited, by Miner's study of Timbuctoo in West Africa,[11] and by Bascom's analysis of the Yoruba settlements of Western Nigeria.[12]

In the work on a solution to this problem, the emphasis should be on achieving operational definitions of the variables suggested by earlier theorists and on refining instruments to measure them. Fortunately, considerable work has been done along this line, and many measures of community factors and instruments to measure them are available, but much more needs to be done. The problem is, however, that these measures of community dimensions are often not theoretically relevant or comparable from one community to another.

In a study of Ohio counties, the author, guided by the particular demands of this research project and aided by previous findings as to the nature of the community and its elements, used U. S. Census data and information gathered and published by other national, state, and municipal governmental units. From these data quantitative measures of 82 community dimensions were devised. These are shown in table 1.[13] This correlation table indicates also how relationships may be tested by probability statistics once measurements of variables have been achieved.

It is recognized, of course, that these dimensions represent only a few of many community factors that might be measured, and

[9] Gideon Sjoberg, "The Preindustrial City," *The American Journal of Sociology,* vol. 60 (1955), pp. 438–445.

[10] "World View and Social Relations in Guatemala," *American Anthropologist,* vol. 43 (1941), pp. 27–42.

[11] Horace Miner, *The Primitive City of Timbuctoo* (Princeton: Princeton University Press, 1953).

[12] William Bascom, "Urbanization Among the Yoruba," *American Journal of Sociology,* vol. 60 (1955), pp. 446–454.

[13] For definitions of the community dimensions shown in this table, see Christen T. Jonassen, "Cultural Variables in the Ecology of an Ethnic Group," *American Sociological Review,* vol. 14 (1949), pp. 32–41, and *The Measurement of Community Dimensions and Predictive Indices Significant for Administrators,* mimeographed report for the Center for Educational Administration, Ohio State University (1956). Revised edition, *The Measurement of Community Dimensions and Elements* (Columbus: Ohio State University Center for Educational Administration, 1958).

*Table 1. Coefficients of Correlation (r) Between the Percent of Population Urban * and Eighty-one Other Variables in Ohio Counties. (N = 88)*

DIMENSION	r	DIMENSION	r
1. Population size	.61	34. High school education	.50
2. Population density	.61	35. Educational expenditure	
3. Population urban	..	(total)	.49
4. Population stability	—.24	36. Educational self-suffi-	
5. Governmental complexity	.46	ciency	.69
6. Heterogeneity	.66	37. College education	.56
7. Social complexity	.74	38. Educational plant size	.73
8. Economic complexity	.84	39. High school enrollment	
9. Newspaper circulation	.81	I (14–17)	.33
10. Population over 21	.67	40. Educational wealth	.68
11. Productive population	.86	41. Educational expenditure	
12. Employed females	.71	(local)	.68
13. Dependent population	—.86	42. Educational status	.58
14. Farmers	—.82	43. Educational potential	.81
15. Unskilled workers	.04	44. Elementary school en-	
16. Craftsmen	.64	rollment	.05
17. Clerical and sales workers	.90	45. Population mobility	—.36
18. Professional workers	.80	46. Population increase	.43
19. White-collar workers	.86	47. Birth rate	.27
20. Economic base	.52	48. Population	.47
21. Retailing	.72	49. Infant deaths	.00
22. Wholesale trade	.44	50. Death rate	—.34
23. Services	.84	51. Accidental deaths	—.32
24. Commercial activity	.58	52. Morbidity	.17
25. Manufacturing	.80	53. Health index	.02
26. Industrialization	.76	54. Juvenile delinquency	.63
27. Agriculture	—.54	55. Crime	.31
28. School age population	—.72	56. Social control	—.65
29. Elementary school edu-		57. Child aid	—.35
cation	—.72	58. Welfare self-sufficiency	.40
30. Educational expenditure		59. Relief expenditure	.36
(state)	—.74	60. Welfare	.36
31. Educational effort	.08	61. Community efficiency	.24
32. High school enrollment		62. Socio-economic status	.68
II (16–17).	.31	63. Family income	.72
33. Technical illiteracy	.03	64. Home value	.70

*Table 1. Coefficients of Correlation (r) Between the Percent
of Population Urban * and Eighty-one Other Variables in Ohio Counties.* (N = 88) (*continued*)

DIMENSION	r	DIMENSION	r
65. Well-to-do	.70	75. Population change	
66. Wealth differential	.71	'50–56	.07
67. Extreme incomes	−.58	76. Retail sales gain '48–54	−.26
68. Poverty	−.70	77. Per capita retail sales '54	.45
69. Home ownership	−.43	78. Per capital local expend-	
70. Dwelling newness	.38	iture for education	.41
71. Dwelling modernity	.62	79. Educational sacrifice	−.07
72. Dwelling condition	.82	80. Unemployment index	−.51
73. Natural increase	.24	81. Insured labor force	.87
74. Migration pop. change		82. Mental illness	−.10
'50–56	.02		

.05 level of confidence = .20   .01 level of confidence = .27

* The percent of population living in urban places as defined by the 1950
U.S. Census. See Jonassen, *The Measurement of Community Dimensions and
Elements* (Columbus: Ohio State University Center for Educational Administra-
tion, 1958) and *Interrelationships among Dimensions of Community Systems:
A Factorial Analysis of Eighty-Two Variables* (Columbus: Ohio State Uni-
versity Press, 1959) for operational definitions of terms used in this table.

furthermore, that many important factors of community life are
difficult, if not impossible, to delineate with objectivity and exact-
itude. It is probable, however, that many community dimensions
which are now not measurable will become so as measuring techniques develop and improve. The difficulties involved in the rigorous
analysis of community should not be permitted to block the utilization of factors that *are now* amenable to measurement. It is necessary to establish some unmistakable reference points, and as these
become confirmed through replication, they may become useful
singly or in combination as indices or indirect measures of the
community factors which are difficult or impossible to measure
directly.

As this process continues the ambiguity attached to such
"sponge" concepts as "folk," "urban," *Gemeinschaft-Gesellschaft,*

and terms as homogeneity, isolation, well-integrated, maladjustment, individualism, spontaneous, rational, sentimental, secular,
and sacred will be removed and replication, verification, and
accumulation of tested scientific knowledge about communities
can proceed more quickly and with greater confidence.

The achievement of standard measures or norms is another
aspect of the measurement problem. Solving problems of measurability will do much to assure comparability of community studies,
but the raw measure by itself has little meaning unless it is compared to something within the universe of phenomena of which it
is a part. An animal may be classified according to whether it has
or does not have a backbone; in a community, a factor may be
present or not present, but when it is present, it exists to a degree.
The factor of *magnitude*, therefore, becomes very crucial.

Another problem of normalization that must be solved is that
of making units of measurement that are not comparable, comparable. For example, one unit of population is not equal, in its
significance and meaning, to one unit of murder, one unit of death
rate, or one of suicide, and any statistical manipulation of such
units would lead to erroneous conclusions.

If the degree to which a community possesses a given characteristic is to be determined, some points of reference must be established; without such guides questions as to "how far is up" or "how
far is down" cannot be answered. There are several ways in which
this problem might be solved. One could assume a theoretical scale
with zero at one end and infinity at the other. This technique
would run into the problem of differential meaning of value of units.
For example, the rise in one unit of birth rate has different meaning
and value from the rise in one unit of population. Another method
for determining degree of occurrence might be to determine variation in terms of standard deviation units from a measure of central
tendency. This method would, however, have to contend with the
assumption that the phenomenon under observation is distributed
within the universe of communities according to the theoretical
normal curve.

When a community is described as a "type" with reference to
an ordering variable, it can best be described in terms of its similarities and contrasts to other communities. In other words, the raw

measures of community characteristics may be normalized and compared in terms of a "standard" population of communities. In the study cited above, the 88 counties in Ohio were used as a "standard" population of communities to establish norms for each of the 82 community dimensions.[14] Counties were used because they constitute a type of community within which one might expect to find all factors or dimensions constituting community and within which they are to be found to a measurable degree. The use, for example, of cities only would immediately eliminate the rural factor and prohibit the measurement of the effect of the urban-rural factors within the community. Furthermore, the county was the formal fact-gathering unit for which the greatest amount of the kind of comparable data required in this study was available.

Measures for each county on every dimension were obtained, and each county was then ranked from 1 to 88, with the county achieving the highest magnitude in a given dimension ranked 1 and the lowest 88. Counties ranking 1 to 8 received a score of 11, those ranking 9 to 16 received a score of 10, and so on, with the lowest eight ranks receiving a score of 1. These standardized scores were called *commuscale scores*. The commuscale score of a given community on a given dimension essentially measures the degree to which this community approaches the highest or lowest magnitude to be found within the standard population of communities.

A great number of such commuscale scores covering all aspects of community life could be developed. In the study discussed commuscale scores for 82 dimensions were derived, and a table which converts raw measures of community dimensions to comparable commuscale scores was compiled.

If standardization of community dimensions is pursued vigorously, it should be possible to develop a system of norms for each community variable that will serve the same purpose in community

[14] The adequacy of Ohio counties as standard population must be tested by further research. It is quite possible that it is adequate for the United States since Ohio in many respects is like the United States. It is possible, however, that all counties in the United States might be better, and that neither Ohio nor all U.S. counties would serve for underdeveloped countries. These questions will have to be settled by further research attempting applications of these standards.

description as atomic weights do in physics, specific gravity in chemistry, and Greenwich in navigation.

THE PROBLEM OF A CLASSIFICATION PRINCIPLE

The types of communities an investigator establishes depend on the basis or principle used to categorize them. The implicit or explicit justification for the preference of one basis of classification over another is essentially that the classifier believes the principle he chooses represents the *crucial* element which will distinguish the thing he is describing. How shall he choose from community phenomena a principle which will order and integrate the vast complexity?

In zoology, for example, the oldest basis of classification was the mode of life, environmental adaptations, and association. In this system, whales were grouped with fishes, and bats with birds. This system was abandoned for the archetypal which grouped animals according to the number and kinds of common morphological characteristics; this principle of classification in turn gave way to the phylogenetic, by which a creature's classification depended on its character derived from common ancestors. The adoption of the latest system grew out of the theory of evolution which made it seem more natural, or empirically demonstrable, or pragmatically desirable.

With regard to communities, many bases of classification have been suggested. Principles of classification may be divided into two broad types and characterized as *empirical-quantitative* and *philosophic-descriptive*. The empirical-quantitative utilizes, as ordering principles, community dimensions on which quantitative data suitable for statistical manipulation may be obtained. Classification tends to be rigorous, systematic. Many have developed scales to measure the degree to which a given community possesses the ordering variable, and the limits of the scales are determined empirically rather than theoretically or philosophically. The number of ordering variables used is usually one or a few. Some typical bases of classification falling under this type are size (U.S. Census and most countries), "moral integration," occupational structure and status, function, "goodness," dominance, technological development, "social rank," "urbanization," and "segregation," urbanization, and *Gemeinschaft-Gesellschaft.*

The philosophic-descriptive principle of categorization is general and descriptive with the ordering variables, such as "folk," "urban," "sacred," and "secular," being composite characteristics composed of a great number of elements which are assumed to vary concomitantly as one or the other opposed ideal type of community is approached. Among the earlier bases of classification are kinship and territory, and status and contract, "mechanical" vs. "organic solidarity," and *Gemeinschaft-Gesellschaft.*

The urban-rural dichotomy has often been suggested as *the* ordering principle. Tomars states:

> Certainly there is a vast body of sociological analysis to attest to the reality of the rural as a type of society set off from the urban type, whether this be expressed in terms of primary group versus secondary group organization (Cooley, Brunner and Kolb), sentimental versus rational attitudes (Shaler and others), communal versus associational groupings (MacIver), or in terms of a host of other distinctions.[15]

The folk-urban basis of classification developed from the earlier conceptual schemes of Maine, Töennies, and Durkheim is probably most closely identified with Robert Redfield who has contributed most to its recent elaboration, research, and defense. The same author has suggested another basis of classification, orthogenetic vs. heterogenetic, which deals with the function of a community in the process of cultural development.[16] Other principles of classification are suggested by such dichotomies as sacred and secular, Apollonian and Dionysian, "universalistic-achievement" and "universalistic-ascription," and industrial-preindustrial city.

It is clear from the above discussion that there is no dearth of suggested bases or principles of classification. It is also evident that here, to an even greater extent, there is less consensus than with regard to the nature of the community, and, certainly, this discussion has not exhausted the possibilities in ideas concerning the bases for community classification. There seems to be an em-

[15] Tomars, *op. cit.,* p. 379.

[16] Redfield and Milton B. Singer, "The Cultural Role of Cities," *Economic Development and Cultural Change,* vol. 3 (1954), pp. 53–73.

barrassment of conceptual riches here, and one could easily get lost in a semantic fog.

It is evident that a salient feature of the community is its multidimensionality. This characteristic presents many difficulties and a dilemma for the typologist. On the one hand, he must encompass enough factors to include all essential community phenomena; on the other hand, he must studiously avoid the particularistic fallacy.

The focus is artificially narrowed and important differences between communities are lost by lumping together different communities under one category or a very limited number of categories. This difficulty is not satisfactorily solved by the majority of the empirical-quantitative typologies or by some "orthodox" ecologists.

While it is true that all science is a process of abstraction, if the very essence of the *human* community is abstracted, what is left is not a theoretically or empirically adequate description of community phenomena. Some ecologists, for example, by failing to include as integral parts of their conceptual formulations other variables besides what they called "biotic" and "subcultural" factors were left with fundamental theoretical inconsistencies and were led to evolve generalizations some of which were not supported by subsequent research.

If the investigator avoids the particularistic error, however, and includes a large number of factors, he is immediately confronted with the problem of multidimensionality. The more criteria he uses for classification, the more difficult and complex the process becomes because of all the combinations of community dimensions that are possible. If to this complexity is added the one induced by magnitude, additional types based on combinations of the degree to which a dimension is present are possible. The enormity of the problem may be gleaned by considering the number of theoretical community types that could be established on the basis of the 82 dimensions occurring in 11 degrees of magnitude. The number is astronomical, 11^{82}, one containing 86 digits.

It seems evident, therefore, that much effort must be devoted to reducing this complexity to manageable proportions. There seem to be two problems involved here: reducing the number of "essential" dimensions and minimizing the categories of magnitude.

One approach to the first of these problems is to seek an answer to this question: Can a small number of relatively independent factors be found that will account for variations in all the others? The author attempted to answer this question with relation to the 88 counties of Ohio. The data gathered in the study mentioned previously were subjected to additional analysis. An 82 × 82 correlation matrix was calculated, resulting in some 3,321 correlations. The baffling complex structure of interrelationships produced by 82 variables for 88 cases was reduced to simple structure by means of factor analysis.[17] Seven factors emerged which explained most of the variation between the counties. These factors cannot be fully described here, but their nature is indicated by the descriptive names given to them: urbanism, welfare, influx, poverty, magnicomplexity, educational effort, and proletarianism.[18]

If variations between communities can be explained in terms of these seven factors we have a valid basis of classification. A definitive "yes" cannot, unfortunately, be given. One only gets out of a factor analysis what one puts into it, and although an unusually large number of variables were included in the factorial matrix, some important ones may have been left out. Furthermore, the relationships established may be bound by time and place; that is, they may not be equally valid in another state or another country at different time periods.

Additional factorial studies which build on the relationships here established should be undertaken to determine if these seven factors are indeed the only essential ones and to discover if they will hold up as fundamental factors in other areas. Thus, after a number of studies that solve problems of measurability and

[17] Thurstone's group centroid method of factor analysis as modified by Wherry was used. (Robert J. Wherry, "Hierarchical Factor Solutions Without Rotation," *Psychometrica,* in preparation). The subject and its mathematical basis is excellently described in L. L. Thurstone, *Multiple Factor Analysis* (Chicago: University of Chicago Press, 1947) and K. J. Holzinger and Harry H. Harman, *Factor Analysis: A Synthesis of Factorial Methods* (Chicago: University of Chicago Press, 1941).

[18] For a complete description of factors, see Jonassen, *Interrelationships among Dimensions of Community Systems: A Factorial Analysis of Eighty-Two Variables* (Columbus: Ohio State University Press, 1959).

use equivalent units of measurement and similar data processing techniques have been made, there may emerge a *small number* of factors valid and reliable in a wide number of areas which can be used as criteria with which to build the analytical categories of a community typology.

The community typologist would not be "out of the woods," however, even though he were able to reduce the vast complexity of the community to seven essential factors. The number of combinations of seven factors with eleven degrees of magnitude would be 11^7 or approximately 19,486,000. High correlations among some dimensions will create redundancies; some types will appear to lack meaning and validity in the light of empirical research, and operational expediency would further reduce this number of theoretical community types, but the number of residual types would still be too large for practical use.

If essential elements could be satisfactorily chosen, the problem of reducing the number of categories of magnitude would have to be solved. What are the fewest categories of magnitude necessary to explain community phenomena? With regard to the dimension of size, are eleven categories of size required, or more; are ten sufficient, or five? What shall they be? It may be that there is no single answer, and that an answer can be given only in terms of the purpose for which the categories are to be used. It is obvious, at any rate, that much research needs to be done before these questions can be definitively answered.

The difficulties encountered in defining the community or in discovering a generally acceptable basis for its classification arise out of its great complexity and because it is composed of several orders of phenomena: physical and environmental, economic, social, cultural, and psychological. Some investigators see certain aspects of the total complex reality as the crucial variables; others, looking at the world through lenses ground to different theoretical and methodological specifications, judge different elements to be more important.

The lack of consensus as to a basis of classification, the nature of community phenomena, and the state of knowledge about them present formidable impediments; and the taxonomic experience of zoologists would suggest caution in attempting to specify at this stage of research a single principle of classification or a definitive community typology.

Can the functions of a typology be performed in some other way? It is suggested that the fundamental purposes of a community typology may be achieved by community profiles. These should be based on community dimensions properly chosen, measured, and standardized. Scales may be constructed by appropriate statistical techniques to measure the "essential" factors of community life. These "scales" which might be called *commuscales* constitute the combinations of dimensions in terms of which the community is to be measured and described. The utilization of standardized measures or *commuscale scores* permits the drawing on the same grid of community profiles based on many kinds of dimensions. The type of community under observation would thus be immediately apparent to the trained eye.

In the Ohio study, several commuscales were constructed. Figure 1 shows a portion of general ("G") profiles of actual rural and urban communities, figure 2 indicates a profile designed for persons particularly interested in a community's education ("ED"), and figure 3 describes rural and urban communities in terms of the seven elemental ("E") community factors extracted by factor analysis.

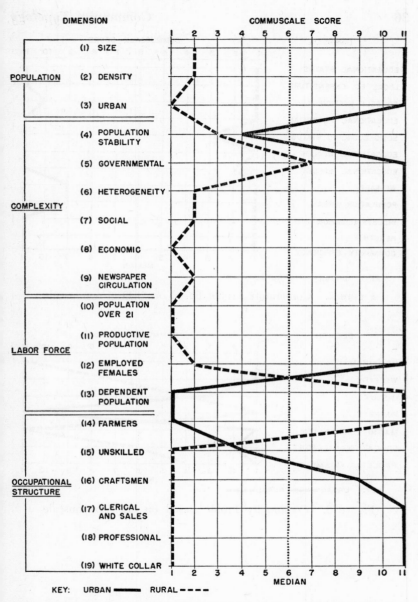

Figure 1. Section of Community Profile Based on "G" Commuscale

35

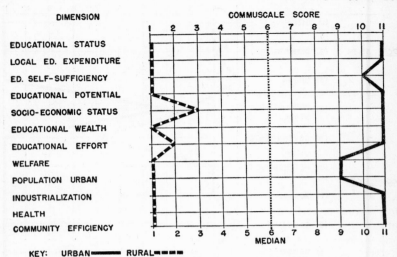

Figure 2.   Community Profile Based on "ED" Commuscale

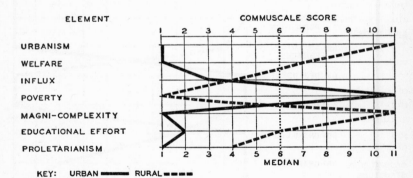

Figure 3.   Community Profile Based on "E" Commuscale

✳ 2. Types of Rural Communities

Allen D. Edwards

Introduction In the preceding chapter on typology, no effort was made to discuss specific types of communities. Rather, the model utilized the county as a unit of analysis, a unit which included both rural and urban areas and characteristics.

Professor Edwards, a rural sociologist, views rural communities in a different way from Professor Jonassen. He is concerned about the five types of rural communities and their multiple subtypes. To the casual traveler on our cross-country roads rural communities look pretty much alike. Unwittingly we distinguish between the rural and urban society and assign to each a specific set of social and cultural characteristics. The rural-urban dichotomy so prevalent in our thinking is of dubious value for understanding the varied complexities of community structure.

It is important to understand Dr. Edwards' descriptive classifying of rural communities because each category possesses a social structure different from the others. The type of structure is related to the spatial arrangement of houses, services, and sources of livelihood. Equally important in determining a particular community structure is the history of initial settlement, the type of economic system, religion, and tradition. The author's classification system clearly demonstrates the relationship of ecology to the social structure of a community. As Dr. Edwards suggests, ecology, the interrelations between man and his habitat, influences community life but does not determine the functioning of the community or the development of its structure.

✳ THERE ARE at least five types of rural communities: (1) town-country, (2) open-country, (3) village, (4) line village, and

(5) plantation. This chapter will define each type, describe the spatial configuration of people and institutions, indicate the factors associated with its development, and note the effect of its ecology, or spatial arrangement of the community, upon social organization. But ecology is not the only factor affecting the social structure of the rural community, for there are variations in each ecological type. Village communities, for example, are divided into subtypes on the basis of economic organization or source of livelihood: (a) agricultural village, (b) cooperative village community, (c) fishing village, (d) mining "patch," and (e) mill village.

THE TOWN-COUNTRY COMMUNITY

In the town-country community farm families live on dispersed farmsteads around a hamlet or village which forms the center of their activities. Most of the residents of the village center are not farmers, although they may be retired farmers or engaged in occupations closely related to agriculture.

C. J. Galpin developed a method for delineating this type of community; he showed that its structure included both the village and the surrounding farms, emphasized the interaction and interdependence between farm and village families, and originated the term "rurban" to describe this relationship.[1]

The town-country community developed along with improved means of transportation and the commercialization of agriculture. When farmers operate on a relatively small scale, they need a trade center in which to sell their farm products and from which they can obtain goods and services. A large-scale commercial farm can operate independent of such a trade center, just as the early plantation did.

Town-country communities are usually described as consisting of several neighborhoods. Community studies show that there is great variation in the significance of neighborhoods as units of social structure. The trend has been for neighborhoods to decline in importance as more economic, educational, and recreational activities became centered on the community level.

The trend for activities to be transferred to larger centers did

[1] Galpin, *The Social Anatomy of an Agricultural Community,* Wisconsin Agricultural Experiment Station, Madison, Bulletin 34 (1915).

not stop with the rural community. Many activities were partially or altogether transferred from the small rural community to larger centers outside the community. Bell suggests that this has been carried to an extreme in Sublette, Kansas, when he reports, "People are no longer oriented to a specific (village) center; the individual is now the center and looks about him in all directions." [2] But even here, social, recreational, educational, and religious activities were still centered in the community trade center. This suggests the interdependence of the rural community with urban centers outside of the local area.

There is considerable variation in the cohesion of communities. Strong neighborhoods, which form the most significant groupings in some areas, tend to lessen integration. On the other extreme, high frequency of contacts outside the community also tends to lessen community cohesion. A community which is new and has a high rate of mobility or a high rate of social change usually has less cohesion than old, relatively stable communities with a minimum of mobility.

Relatively great social differentiation appears to be characteristic of town-country communities since both farm dwellers and village residents with their variety of occupations and income levels are included in the communities. The range of income and occupation depends upon the size of the village center, the type of farming, and other factors.

The town-country community is the predominant type of rural community in the United States and is becoming increasingly common in other parts of the world. The conditions which favor this type of community are also becoming increasingly widespread: a dispersed settlement pattern for farmers producing commodities chiefly for sale, good means of transportation, family-sized farms, and a rising standard of living.

THE OPEN-COUNTRY COMMUNITY

The open-country community is one in which the residences, stores, schools, churches, and other agencies are not located in one

[2] Earl H. Bell, *Culture of a Contemporary Rural Community: Sublette, Kansas*, United States Department of Agriculture, Bureau of Agricultural Economics, Washington, D.C., Rural Life Studies 2 (1942), p. 68.

place but are distributed throughout the community. This type of community has frequently developed from the merging of a number of open-country neighborhoods to form a consolidated school district. The loss of a trade center through the transfer of its service functions to larger centers may reduce a town-country community to one of this type.[3] The Amish communities near Lancaster, Pennsylvania, have not developed trade centers because a rigidly enforced church rule prevents members from engaging in any non-agricultural occupations.[4] Rockville, Virginia, appears to have a common cultural tradition which unified the community and set it off from surrounding communities. Neither the churches, the consolidated school, nor a trading area serve to delineate the community.[5]

Scattered evidence suggests that this is a widely distributed and not unusual type of community, although it is probably much less numerous in the United States than the town-country community. Sanderson quotes studies which suggest that such communities are common throughout the South and even in South Dakota.[6] Holt maintains that in Lee County, Alabama, the trade area does not seem coincident with the community but that a common consolidated school was the basis for community feeling.[7] A study of four scattered Virginia counties reported forty-two communities in the counties but only twenty-three hamlet, village, or town centers of one hundred or more inhabitants. There was a considerable range from all village-centered communities in one county

[3] Waller Wynne, *Culture of a Contemporary Rural Community: Harmony, Georgia,* United States Department of Agriculture, Bureau of Agricultural Economics, Washington, D.C., Rural Life Studies 6 (1934).

[4] Walter M. Kollmorgen, *Culture of a Contemporary Rural Community: The Old Order Amish of Lancaster County, Pennsylvania,* United States Department of Agriculture, Bureau of Agricultural Economics, Washington, D.C., Rural Life Studies 4 (1942).

[5] Dorothy G. Jones, *Youth Adjustments in a Rural Culture, Rockville Community, Hanover County, Virginia,* Virginia Agricultural Experiment Station, Blacksburg, Rural Sociology Report 16 (1941).

[6] Dwight Sanderson, *Rural Sociology and Rural Social Organization* (New York: John Wiley & Sons, Inc., 1942), pp. 285–286.

[7] John B. Holt, *Rural Neighborhoods and Communities of Lee County, Alabama,* United States Department of Agriculture, Bureau of Agricultural Economics, Washington, D.C. (1941), pp. 8–9.

to only one out of eight in another.[8] Bonser and Milk classified seventeen communities in Cumberland County, Tennessee. Three were town-country communities, thirteen were open-country communities consisting of a cluster of neighborhoods, and one was an open-country community consisting of a single neighborhood. There were seven other neighborhoods not a part of any recognizable community within the county, although one of them was a part of an open-country community lying partly outside the county.[9] The authors of a study of Landaff, New Hampshire, insist that it is a community in a psychological sense and is typical of the strictly rural life of New England.[10] Landaff has no trade center. There is only a church and a town building with the dwellings dispersed throughout the community. Trading is done in Lisbon, a village less than four miles away.

The Old Order Amish of Lancaster County constitute an open-country community which shows an almost complete lack of centers of community life. The pattern is described as

. . . amorphous. Churches do not provide focal points for community relations because these people do not have church buildings; schools do not bring about close ties with non-Amish because they are secular institutions and the principle of separation from the world serves to create cleavages in the school districts; villages and towns do not tie trading areas together because of the same principle of separation from the world. Religious, kinship, ethnic, and linguistic ties, on the other hand, serve to make one large sprawling community out of the entire settlement. . . .[11]

Cultural isolation and community feeling are strong in the Rockville, Virginia, community but less so than among the Amish.

[8] W. E. Garnett, *County and Community Standards in Planning*, Virginia Agricultural Experiment Station, Blacksburg, Rural Sociology Report 26, mimeographed (1943).

[9] Howard J. Bonser and R. J. Milk, *Neighborhoods and Communities of Cumberland County, Tennessee*, Tennessee Agricultural Experiment Station, Knoxville, Rural Research Series Monograph 129 (1941).

[10] Kenneth Macleish and Kimball Young, *Culture of a Contemporary Rural Community: Landaff, New Hampshire*, United States Department of Agriculture, Bureau of Agricultural Economics, Washington, D.C., Rural Life Studies 3 (1942), p. 3.

[11] Kollmorgen, *op. cit.*, p. 9.

A common cultural tradition and a strong feeling of identification with the local community help to unify and to set Rockville off from surrounding communities. Formal social and economic agencies do not delineate the community. The people attend five churches, only two of which are located within the community boundary. The consolidated school includes children from outside as well as all of those inside the community. Four general stores are scattered through as many neighborhoods.

The Harmony community includes an elementary school and a church for white people; an all-grade school, a church, and a Masonic Lodge for Negroes. Formerly the community had some trade services of its own, but now it is entirely dependent upon nearby towns, principally upon Eatontown, the county seat which is about eight miles away.[12]

Open-country communities have been exposed to the changes in transportation methods which have been influential in the development of trade center communities. The Pennsylvania Amish, Landaff, and Rockville communities have been successful in resisting or adjusting to these changes. A consolidated school appeared to strengthen the Rockville community, although contacts with the outside were increased. Harmony gradually lost all of its stores in competition with other centers and may eventually lose its separate identity as a community.

No well-defined social classes were found among the Pennsylvania Amish or among the white families of the Rockville community. Definite social classes were reported in Harmony and Landaff, although the range was probably less than if towns had been included.

The open-country communities seem to be less self-sufficient economically than the town-country. Rockville is more self-sufficient than the other open-country communities mentioned above as a result of having several country stores and because of the home-centered economy.

A strong sense of identification may be found in some open-country communities as evidenced by the Pennsylvania Amish and the Rockville community. Some are held together by only the interest of the consolidated school and have only a short history of

[12] Wynne, *op. cit.*, p. 37.

unity with respect to this interest. In general, the relative lack of economic or social self-sufficiency and the distance between the homes tend to lessen cohesion and integration.

THE VILLAGE COMMUNITY

There are several distinct types of village communities: (a) agricultural village, (b) cooperative village community, (c) fishing village, (d) mining "patch," and (e) mill village. The agricultural village and the cooperative village are both agricultural communities but differ in that the land ownership is on an individual basis in the former and on a collective or communal basis in the latter. The distinctiveness of the last three types is found in their dependence upon fishing, mining, or factory work for their livelihood.

AGRICULTURAL VILLAGE

The agricultural village is a rural community in which farm families live in close proximity to each other and to nonfarm families and frequently at some distance from part or all of the land which they cultivate. It is by far the most important type in Europe, Asia, Africa, and much of Latin America. In the United States, the Mormon village is found in Utah and nearby states, and the Spanish American village is found in the Southwest. Estimates are that 30 per cent of the Utah farmers lived in villages in 1930, and of those who lived in the open country, a majority resided in populous sections of the state in a rather compact settlement pattern.[13] Leonard and Loomis mention three types of Spanish-American villages: the scattered village of the mountains, the dry-land farming village, and the more common type located along a river. Although they give no data for the number of people living in villages, it is apparently a common type of rural residence in the Southwestern United States.[14]

Sanderson concludes that, with a few minor exceptions, peo-

[13] Eyler N. Simpson, *The Ejido* (Chapel Hill: University of North Carolina Press, 1937), chap. XVIII.

[14] Olen Leonard and C. P. Loomis, *Culture of a Contemporary Rural Community: El Cerrito, New Mexico*, United States Department of Agriculture, Bureau of Agricultural Economics, Washington, D.C., Rural Life Studies 1 (1941), p. 36.

ple who engaged in permanent agriculture lived in village communities until the Industrial Revolution.[15] He states that village communities become established at different times and places and in different ways: (1) the village may arise from the multiplication of a single family or two or three closely related families when the safety of pioneer settlers is sufficiently assured and where the control of the kindred is strong, *e.g.*, in Germany, in Norway, and among the Punjab in India; (2) the village may grow out of colonization from a parent village or villages when the latter become overcrowded; and (3) it may develop from the settlement of pastoral nomads in villages.[16]

The New England colonists settled in villages which continued to the nineteenth century. The settlements followed, in general, the pattern of the English village. A central square was surrounded by a church, a town hall, a school, and individual homes of the settlers. A mill, blacksmith shop, and other shops were arranged at convenient points. The arable land, divided in narrow strips, the undivided meadow, and the common wasteland and forest surrounded the village proper.[17]

Mormons established the village form in Utah beginning in 1847. In subsequent settlements, it was extended throughout the intermountain area from northern Mexico to southern Canada.[18] This settlement pattern is now found in Utah, Idaho, Arizona, Wyoming, Montana, Colorado, New Mexico, Nevada, and in Alberta, Canada, and Chihuahua, Mexico.[19] It was attempted because it was well adapted to the conditions of living which prevailed at the time.

"The Mormon village," Nelson states, "was definitely planned and established before the farm land was developed. That is to say, the first settlers laid out the village site and apportioned the lots as their first act. They then surveyed the fields and apportioned

---

[15] Dwight Sanderson, *The Rural Community* (Boston: Ginn & Company, 1932), p. 169.

[16] *Ibid.*, pp. 179–187.   [17] *Ibid.*, p. 201.

[18] C. M. Andrews, "The Chronicle of America" in *Colonial Folkways* (New Haven: Yale University Press, 1919), vol. 9, pp. 25–26.

[19] T. Lynn Smith, *The Sociology of Rural Life*, revised edition (New York: Harper & Brothers, 1947), p. 234.

them." [20] The general plan for each settlement followed the "Plot of the City of Zion" designed by Joseph Smith. The fact that many Mormons came from England or New England may have had some indirect effect in the retention of this pattern.

Agricultural villages were also introduced into the Southwest by the penetration of Spanish culture during the first half of the nineteenth century, and in the areas once controlled by Mexico they remain an important factor of rural life.

Classes are not highly stratified in the Mormon villages studied by Nelson or in the Spanish-American village studied by Leonard and Loomis. Relations between farmers and those with nonfarm occupations are closer than in a town-country community where their residence is separate.

The agricultural villages have a highly integrated community life which is ascribed partly to their pattern of settlement. Leonard and Loomis say:

The physical structure of the community is also a significant factor in the integration and stability of the village. The houses are compactly arranged to form the perimeter of a circle, with barns and corrals in the rear. Although such an arrangement interferes with efficient farming, it greatly facilitates living. The house is farther from fields and pastures but is closer to school, church and neighbors. Children are seen playing together, after the chores are done, both night and morning. Childhood associations are almost as close between playmates as between members of the same family. They grow up to know each other almost as well as if they had been reared under the same roof.[21]

Nelson lists as characteristic of the village that it facilitates cooperation, promotes socialization, and gives the farm home inexpensive access to professional and institutional services. Cooperative activities, usually including the maintenance of an irrigation system, were features of both the Mormon and the Spanish-American villages. A common religious background tended further to unify community life in both instances.

[20] Lowry Nelson, *A Social Survey of Escalante, Utah,* Brigham Young University Studies no. 1, Prove, Utah, (1925), p. 3.
[21] *Op. cit.,* p. 8.

COOPERATIVE VILLAGE COMMUNITY

Cooperative communities are those in which land ownership and operation are vested in the group rather than in individuals. Cooperative communities differ from those previously described in that the land is not owned and farmed individually but collectively. This type of community is numerically unimportant in the United States, and efforts to establish communal settlements have usually been brief and unsuccessful unless they were connected with a religious moment. In other countries, there has been a conspicuous development of such communities as evidenced by the ejido of Mexico, the kolkhoz of Russia, and the kvutza of Israel. Common ownership and activities may be limited to production or may be extended to consumption as well. Members may share in what is produced according to need or according to the amount and quality of work performed.

At least 262 cooperative communities are known to have been established in the United States.[22] Lee E. Deets has compiled data on the duration of 130 settlements: 91 lasted less than ten years, 59 less than five years, 50 only two years, and 32 only one year.[23] Of the small number that have persisted over a century, three have disbanded: Ephrata Cloister, Pennsylvania, 1732–1905; the Shaker communities, settled in various parts of the United States, ca. 1778–1940; and the Harmonists, or Rappists, whose settlements in Pennsylvania and Indiana lasted a hundred years, 1805–1905. Three other communities which have existed over a century are still alive: the Amana Community, Iowa, which was founded in Europe in 1714 and moved to the United States in 1842; the Doukhober communities, organized in Russia about the middle of the 18th century, which moved to Canada about 1879 where they are still found; and the Hutterite communities which originated in Moravia in 1528, came to the United States in 1874, and now comprise fifty settlements in South Dakota, Montana, and the Canadian Provinces of Manitoba and Alberta.[24] These early attempts to set up cooperative communities were motivated by religious or social-reform mo-

[22] Henrik F. Infield, *Cooperative Communities at Work* (New York: The Dryden Press, Inc., 1945), p. 13.

[23] *Ibid.*, p. 13.   [24] *Ibid.*, pp. 13–14.

tives. Most of the failures were not a result of economic factors but of quarrels among the members or lack of experience in agriculture.[25]

The modern cooperative community has been a device used by governmental or semi-governmental agencies to improve rural conditions. The aim in Soviet Russia and other Communist countries is the total reorganization of rural society. In the United States and Mexico, the purpose has been the rehabilitation of the low-income farmer. In England, the effort was to settle the unemployed, while in Israel the purpose was to provide an effective organization for colonization and the development of modern scientific farming.[26]

One of the means used by the Farm Security Administration to improve the conditions of low-income farm people in this country was the establishment of cooperative communities. These experiments constituted a relatively small part of the total agency program, but altogether twenty-two such communities were organized between January, 1937, and March, 1942. A total of 407 full-time members joined and the tillable land amounted to 26,829 acres. In July, 1943, the Farm Security Administration announced it planned to sell eleven of the cooperative farms to the groups of participating members; the other ten farms were to be discontinued as cooperatives and the land distributed among individuals.[27]

Infield concludes that these cooperatives made a significant contribution to the rehabilitation of their member families but that they were liquidated too soon to test their effectiveness as a form of rural life that would help the small-scale farmer to use modern methods. Moreover, since their members were recruited largely from relief rolls, there was little indication of how the system would work if a cross-section of capable farm workers had been chosen.[28] The absence of a cooperative spirit was the outstanding weakness. From this, other major difficulties followed, including friction between Farm Security Administration officials and the settlers. Many of the latter withdrew to take up individual farming.[29]

Simpson distinguishes two types of ejidos in modern Mexico

[25] *Ibid.*, pp. 18–19.   [26] *Ibid.*, p. 63.   [27] *Ibid.*, p. 67.
[28] *Ibid.*, p. 83.   [29] *Ibid.*, pp. 83–84.

according to whether the land is farmed individually or collectively.[30] There were in 1944, 696 of the collective ejidos cooperating with the Ejido Bank, probably almost all of the collective type.[31] This represents about 5 per cent of the 14,683 ejidos appearing in the census of 1940. Most of the ejidos then were of the individual type, in which each ejidatario was allotted a plot of farm land which he tilled in his own way with the aid of his family. The minority, the collective ejidos, were at a considerable advantage in making effective use of modern machinery, money credit, scientific agricultural methods, and the various occupational specialties of their members. Problems of the collective farms revolved around lack of effective leadership, insufficient motivation for production, and jealousy.[32]

The principal form of agricultural settlement in Russia is the kolkhoz, of which it is estimated that there were 250,000 in 1940 with an average of 75 families per community.[33] The objectives are to increase agricultural production and to eliminate private ownership of land. The State maintains control of the collective farmer chiefly through the machine and tractor station which furnishes machinery for large-scale farming and advisers on farming practices. Theoretically, membership in the collective farms is voluntary, as it was generally in the ejido of Mexico or the Farm Security Administration in the United States. Actually, the collective communities of Russia were set up by compulsion of the central government. They have been economically successful in that there has been an increase in the farm products which the government has been able to collect even during poor years. Also, some of the collectives have experienced considerable development in education, health, and recreation.[34]

Jewish settlement in Israel was possible only by some such form of collective settlement as the kvutza. It developed through trial and error in relation to the conditions which prevailed during the period of settlement. The first kvutza was organized in 1901 at the point where the River Jordan leaves Lake Tiberias, and it is

---

[30] Eyler N. Simpson, *op. cit.*, chap. XVIII.

[31] Nathan L. Whetten, *Rural Mexico* (Chicago: University of Chicago Press, 1948), pp. 203–204.

[32] *Ibid.*, pp. 211–214.   [33] *Ibid.*, p. 112.   [34] *Ibid.*, pp. 122–130.

still in existence. It practices the highest possible degree of co-operation in both production and consumption.[35] Dunner describes the organization of the pioneer cooperative settlement:

Daganyah, like many other communal settlements that followed its example, resembles a large working family of several hundred members, with an equal standard of living for all. No money whatsoever is used in the internal relations of the settlement. Each works according to his ability and within the framework of a general plan devised by all members in a sort of town-hall meeting.[36]

The number of cooperative communities had reached 79 by 1940 with a membership of more than 20,000 and a cultivated area of 97,500 acres. The Jewish rural population was 142,000 and the number of settlements at the time was 257.[37] The other Jewish communities engaged in many cooperative activities but practiced individual farm operation.

FISHING VILLAGE

Junek has made a thorough study of a fishing village on the coast of Labrador.[38] It is one of 35 settlements which depend chiefly upon fishing and hunting and which vary in size from one family to a population of 1,300.[39]

The community of Blanc Sablon, Labrador, depends upon fishing supplemented by seal hunting and a little trapping. It consists of 13 families comprising 78 persons. The small size of the community and its relative isolation have permitted the retention of the characteristics of a folk society with some elements of the urban culture. The dependence upon primary group controls, the almost complete lack of newspapers, the meager formal education, the lack of modern sanitation and health care, and the emphasis upon family and the church are characteristic of this type of village.[40]

Tangier Island, Virginia, in the center of Chesapeake Bay, is a

[35] *Ibid.*, p. 134.
[36] Joseph Dunner, *The Republic of Israel* (New York: McGraw-Hill Book Co., 1950), p. 142.
[37] Infield, *op. cit.*, pp. 134–135.
[38] Oscar Waldemar Junek, *Isolated Communities: A Study of a Labrador Fishing Village* (New York: American Book Company, 1937).
[39] *Ibid.*, pp. 17–19.   [40] *Ibid.*, pp. 122–123.

fishing village in a climate entirely different from Blanc Sablon. This community has been relatively isolated from the mainland and has retained many of the characteristics of a folk society. The population of 1,120 in 1930 lived on three ridges and comprised one community.[41] The influence of the mainland was sufficient to affect the "folk" culture on the island but not to destroy it. Compulsory education insured a minimum of schooling for youth. Modern medical facilities and the services of a resident doctor were utilized, and extensive use was made of the Sears Roebuck catalog. Attending movies was disapproved by the Methodist Church in the community, but the taboo was not observed strictly. The residents had no folk games and activities such as pool, dancing, card-playing, and mixed bathing were tabooed. The result was a dearth of recreation.[42] Smith Island, not far away, was quite similar to Tangier except the only taboos regarding recreation applied to dancing and card playing.[43]

Fishing villages must have contact with the outside world in order to have markets. Outside contacts facilitate the adoption of inventions most useful in their work. Other inventions tend to be acquired gradually as the people are able to afford them. As contacts increase, cultural uniqueness decreases.

MINING "PATCH"

Mining settlements, or "patches," are frequently located near the mines, and the homes are likely to be company-owned. Living near the mine was essential before the automobile and paved roads made commuting possible. Mines are likely to be located in hilly or mountainous sections with the area available for homes limited by the terrain. Company-furnished houses, utilities, stores, and medical care are characteristic of many mining towns.

Sheppard says of the coke region of Pennsylvania:

The older patches are pretty much alike, springing out of the fields, creeping up to slate dumps, climbing hilltops in rows of identical double houses with narrow frame porches divided in half, fenced back yards, and

[41] Warren S. Hall, III, *Tangier Island: A Study of an Isolated Group* (Philadelphia: University of Pennsylvania Press, 1939), pp. 27–33.
[42] *Ibid.*, pp. 75–76.   [43] *Ibid.*, pp. 105–112.

outdoor toilets. Usually a company store goes with each patch as does a church, a union hall, and a bar; often there is a consolidated school, incongruously large until one discovers how many children there are to use it.

Some of the company towns lately built up the river in Greene County are quite different. Nemacolin, Mather, and the Emerald Mine's housing developments look like pleasant rural villages anywhere.[44]

Before the development of unions, the mining villages tended to be dominated and controlled by the company. The coal and iron police kept the patches closed and an old sign is still frequently found at the place where the village road leaves the highway: "Private Property: All Persons Warned Against Trespassing Under Penalties." [45] Now visiting delivery wagons no longer have to ask permission to enter the company patch, and the company stores compete in an open market.

MILL VILLAGE

Factory towns and villages are widespread although they are especially characteristic of the textile industry. The textile mill village developed because of the necessity for the mill workers to live near the factory. Frequently the factory was built near a river so that both power and water would be readily available. The mill owners built houses, established stores, schools and churches, and generally dominated the mill villages. In many unorganized mill villages, this domination still persists. The pattern of control for Gaston County, North Carolina, is well described by Pope.[46]

In 1939 the five states of Virginia, North Carolina, South Carolina, Georgia, and Alabama had eight hundred textile establishments of the type which usually provide housing for their employees.[47] Of these, 127 had disposed of all or part of their houses by 1948. No data are available to show how many of these mills

[44] Muriel Carley Sheppard, *Cloud by Day* (Chapel Hill: University of North Carolina Press, 1947), p. 5.

[45] *Ibid.*, p. 4.

[46] Liston Pope, *Millhands and Preachers* (New Haven: Yale University Press, 1942).

[47] Harriet L. Herring, *Passing of the Mill Village* (Chapel Hill: University of North Carolina Press, 1949), p. 124.

are located outside of places with a population of 2,500 or more as compared to the number within such places. The textile mills are concentrated in the Piedmont section and they are frequently located near other mills, although they may or may not be within the incorporated limits of a village, town, or city.

The paternalistic pattern of the textile mill village was similar in New England and the South although it has persisted longer in the latter section. Herring says of the Southern cotton mill village that "despite differences in details, in its social and community features it still strongly resembles the rural mills of England and New England a hundred and fifty years ago." [48] Perhaps because textiles are the oldest factory industry, and because early conditions were repeated in each new locale, ways of meeting them have become strongly traditional. The company was forced to furnish housing in the early days in order to obtain workers. Schools and churches were established for the welfare of the workers. Stores were established for the convenience of the workers and were the only non-manufacturing element of the village which made a profit for the mill owner. The paternalistic attitude gradually changed, but the ecological pattern of the mill village persisted. Gradually, workers were secured who lived outside the mill village and, with the sale of houses, many of those living in the mill village worked elsewhere.

Textile mill villages and coal mining patches represent a stage in the development of these two industries. They were built and equipped with services such as schools, churches, and stores, as well as houses to meet the needs of workers and their families. Employers' paternalistic control has been replaced by union control in coal mining sections and in many textile communities. The struggle for control has been bitter and complicated by economic competition and depression. Earlier experiences have left their imprint, but the worker and his employer are less dependent upon each other for survival, and cooperation now is possible and depends upon mutual good will. Welfare activities and recreational facilities are more characteristic of textile mill villages than of other rural industrial communities. In some mill villages, they are highly developed to this day.

[48] *Ibid.,* p. 5.

THE LINE VILLAGE

The line village is a community in which farmers live on the land they operate and dwellings are relatively close together. It differs from the agricultural village in that the dwellings are more scattered and the farmers live on the land they are farming. The farm dwellings are much closer together than in the town-country or open-country types of community. This is achieved through the farms' being rectangular in shape and of relatively narrow width with the homes at the end of the farms and fronting on a highway or other avenue of transportation. A line village gives the appearance of an extended village street with here and there a school, a church, or small trade center where the houses cluster closer together. T. Lynn Smith has called attention to this settlement pattern and has insisted that it constitutes a distinct type of community.[49]

The line village was well established in France by the ninth century. It spread to Holland and Germany and was brought to Canada and Louisiana by French colonists. Line villages or similar patterns have developed independently in many parts of the United States along rivers or along paved highways.[50] It seems to have developed independently in South Brazil and is now to be found throughout Brazil. It is also the type of settlement used in Brazil's extensive private and government colonization programs, so it is spreading rapidly.[51]

The line village combines the advantages of settlement in close proximity with that of residence on the farmstead and avoids the most pronounced disadvantage of agricultural villages (the inhabitants' living at a distance from the land operated) and of open-country or town-country communities (the inhabitants' living at a distance from neighbors, school, church and trade center).[52]

[49] T. Lynn Smith, *The Sociology of Rural Life*, revised edition (New York: Harper & Brothers, 1947), pp. 218–219.

[50] *Ibid.*, pp. 236–239.

[51] T. Lynn Smith, *Brazil: People and Institutions* (Baton Rouge: Louisiana State University Press, 1946), pp. 402–403.

[52] *Ibid.*

There is some evidence that the tendency of farm and rural non-farm families to locate dwellings along improved highways, especially paved roads, is developing a modified line village pattern of settlement in many parts of the United States.

THE PLANTATION

The plantation is a form of social organization in which labor, under unified direction and control, is engaged in the production of an agricultural staple which is usually sold on a world market. It is typically a nucleated community; that is, it contains all of life's activities. The homes of the manager, supervisors, and laborers are located near the center in houses and surroundings suggesting their social rank. On a sugar plantation, the mill is located near the dwellings and chemists and engineers are included in the managerial force.

The plantation is not limited to any one nation or continent. It arises on the agricultural frontier in an area of "open resources" where land is relatively plentiful and labor scarce.[53] Plantations have developed principally in warm temperate or tropical climates because on the agricultural frontiers there a staple crop can be produced for which there is a demand on the world market.

The life cycle of the plantation has been described by Thompson.[54] The plantation represents a transient stage in the development of new lands. When the lands are completely settled and labor is no longer scarce, free labor replaces forced or slave labor. The plantation tends to be displaced by a system of small-scale farming in which dwellings are dispersed and land ownership widespread. Trade towns, greater diversification of agriculture, public schools, and more democratic political life follow.

Although plantations are widely distributed in tropical and semi-tropical climates, they are largely restricted to islands, coastal areas, and river banks. Accessibility to markets is an essential of plantation agriculture, although this may vary with the perishability

[53] H. J. Nieboer, *Slavery on an Industrial System* (The Hague: M. Nijhoff, 1910), pp. 383–387.
[54] Edgar T. Thompson, "Population Expansion and the Plantation System," *American Journal of Sociology,* vol. 41 (November, 1935), pp. 314–326.

and bulk of the product. Sugar, coffee, and rubber are the principal plantation crops. Minor crops include bananas, tea, coconuts, cocoa, pineapples, tapioca, rice, spices, and jute. There are rubber plantations in Malaya, Brazil, and Liberia; tea plantations in Ceylon; sugar plantations in Cuba, Puerto Rico, Hawaii, and the Philippines; banana plantations in Central America and northern South America; and jute and sugar plantations in India.

Tobacco, cotton, and sugar are the principal crops that have been associated with plantations in the southern United States. Plantations with a typical nucleated settlement pattern still exist in the Louisiana sugar growing areas. Cotton plantations more frequently have the dwellings dispersed, so that each cropper or tenant resides on the land that he tills. It has been estimated that in the South in 1935, there were about 30,000 plantations, with five or more tenants each.[55] Charles S. Johnson observed in the early 1930's that that plantation was still "the focus and center of Negro life in the rural community." [56] Morton Rubin's study of a plantation county of Alabama in 1947–1948 reveals that although the plantation is changing in order to adjust to new conditions, it is clearly the dominant social and economic feature of the plantation area.[57]

Extremes of social stratification are found in plantation communities. It is usually a bi-racial community with one race comprising the labor force and the other exercising managerial and supervisory functions. In the southern United States, the white planter had a definitely higher status than the middle- or lower-class supervisors of the same race. The Negro labor force is also divided into social strata with the house servants, skilled workers, and foremen above the field hands. The pattern of social stratification is dramatically illustrated by Vaughan in describing a sugar plantation in the Philippines: the manager of the central had the highest social position, lived in house number one and had tele-

[55] T. J. Woofter, *Landlord and Tenant on the Cotton Plantation,* Works Progress Administration, Division of Social Research, Washington, D.C., Research Monograph V (1936), p. xviii.

[56] Charles S. Johnson, *Shadow of the Plantation* (Chicago: University of Chicago Press, 1934), p. xx.

[57] Morton Rubin, *Plantation County* (Chapel Hill: University of North Carolina Press, 1951), pp. xxiii, 49.

phone number one; in order followed the chief engineer, the sugar engineer, the business manager, the grounds supervisor, the assistant engineer, and the office assistant, all British or Americans; and beginning with house number eight followed the Filipino staff.[58] The Filipino house boy with a daily supply of plantation garden produce visited the houses in that order, even though the houses were arranged in an entirely different order and he found it necessary to retrace his steps several times.

Plantation communities are usually highly integrated; this is usually achieved by the submission of laborers to the will of the planter. Responsibility and control are vested in the planter and his overseers. The present-day cropper on a cotton plantation is not always subject to close supervision and can express his dissatisfaction by moving to another location at the end of the year.

SIGNIFICANCE OF CLASSIFICATION

There are many ways of describing rural communities and of classifying them. The spatial arrangement of houses, stores, schools, and churches in relation to fields or other sources of livelihood is one of the most obvious as well as significant. The ecology is most closely related to the social structure of the community when there is almost complete dependence upon agriculture. Even in agricultural communities, the type of crop grown, the degree of self-sufficiency, the type of religion, and traditional factors influence the social structure over and above any effect the ecology may have.

The influence of ecology upon social structure may be stated somewhat tentatively. The open-country community appears to be the most homogeneous and to foster individualism. The village form of settlement encourages sociability and cooperative activities. The town-country community shows more variation with respect to residence and occupation than either the open-country or village communities. Divisions are more likely to occur, and there is less tendency for inhabitants to cooperate. The line village is more like the village type, although dwellings are not quite so close together and farmers also live on one end of their long rectangular

[58] Elizabeth H. Vaughan, *Community Under Stress* (Princeton: Princeton University Press, 1947), pp. 20–21.

farmsteads. The plantation is a nucleated type of settlement pattern in which the ecological arrangement of dwellings reflects the social-structure of the community. Social status is reflected in the type of house and its location. Although the plantation is highly integrated, its unity is maintained by a stratified system of power arrangements with the planter and his family at its head.

Variation within the different ecological types of communities suggests the importance of other factors upon the social structure. Ecology can be described as a significant facet of community life which influences but does not control the structure and functioning of the community. Although the open-country pattern of settlement tends to encourage individualism, the Amish community of Lancaster County is a very closely knit social group and the Rockville, Virginia, community is also highly integrated. Individualism prevails only within a narrow range of socially approved behavior. Village communities show distinct variation according to the prevailing occupation of agriculture, fishing, mining, or manufacturing. Cooperative communities were more closely knit than those agricultural villages with individual ownership or operation of land.

Circumstances frequently appear to favor the development of a particular ecological type of community. The village is better adapted to defense than the scattered dwellings of the open-country or town-country types. The recent agricultural settlements in what is now Israel were of the village type for the purposes of defense and for making use of diversified skills of settlers who were not always proficient in agriculture. The town-country community has become the predominate type in the United States along with the increasing commercialization of agriculture and the development of trade towns. The line-village type of settlement originated along waterways when that was the prevailing avenue of transportation.

Some writers have evaluated the advantages and disadvantages of the various types of communities. In order to persist, they must be able to adjust reasonably well to changing conditions, although a particular type may persist after altering conditions render it less efficient than some other form of settlement. Traditional factors thus affect the persistence of a given type. The change from the Mormon village to scattered farmsteads in Utah has been gradual and incomplete, and there has been a tendency for these more recently scattered dwellings to group together. The best type of community would vary according to such factors as the need for defense, the method of transportation, the type of agriculture or other means of making a living, the degree of commercialization, the cost of providing essential services, and the desires of the people.

Community Analysis

✳ 3. Social Areas: Typology of Urban Neighborhoods

Wendell Bell

Introduction   A typology gives us a way of classifying and even describing different communities. Dr. Jonassen used the eighty-eight counties in Ohio for his analyses. Professor Edwards described rural communities and their subgroups. Each of these analyses added to our knowledge about the variation between communities and the logic for these variations.

One of the counties Dr. Jonassen studied was Cuyahoga in which the central city, Cleveland, is surrounded by twenty-seven smaller cities, thirty-seven villages, and four townships. At first glance the county may appear to be divided into a crazy-quilt like grandmother's, but perhaps less symmetrical. Moreover, from discussions of such county problems as sewage disposal, transportation, and water supply, one is certain to conclude that the crazy-quilt notion may be plausible. Yet, for the most part, Cuyahoga County divides itself into systematic and orderly subcommunities, each differentiated with respect to many social and economic characteristics. The same would be true for counties and metropolitan areas in Texas or California.

Subcommunities consist of a number of census tracts, each of which is a small geographical area located within a city or large metropolitan area and in which three thousand to six thousand people live. Thus a large city has hundreds, or in some instances, thousands of census tracts. The boundaries of census tracts, initially at least, were established after consideration was given to the homogeneity of social characteristics, types of housing, land use, topography, or a combination of these factors. Every ten years the Bureau of the Census collects data on the population in each census tract. Once they are assembled it becomes possible to do comparative studies of neighborhoods and measure the changes in the social characteristics of communities.

Three sets of general characteristics appear regularly in the census data: economic, family, and ethnic characteristics. "Social area analysis" is a utilization of these three census variables. The following chapter indicates the development, both the theoretical and the empirical, of this analysis. From the work of Shevky, Williams, Tryon, Greer, Kaufman, and Bell (as discussed in the chapter), we now have an empirically tested instrument for determining the small social units of the large urban area. An analysis of the economic, family, and ethnic status of these units, or small social worlds, gives a picture of the orderly structure of the larger area. Change in economic, family, or ethnic status within the larger community is measurable by comparative studies between census years or from utilization of data gathered in field studies. Evaluations of social areas is possible from the scoring system developed by Professor Bell and his colleagues.

This is a most useful research method for studying the metropolitan community. Its use has been widespread and subsequent students of the community have improved upon the original formulation. Because of growing interest and use of social area analysis we can anticipate further refinements of the instrument. The student should read this chapter carefully and explore the computations of the indexes of economic, family, and ethnic status listed at the end of the chapter.

✳ IT IS A MATTER of everyday observation that metropolitan areas are subdivided into different sections, each exhibiting certain distinctive features. There are manufacturing, warehouse, theater, financial, department store, used car lot, residential, and many other districts in most modern American cities. The residential areas themselves are differentiated with respect to many characteristics: some are predominantly inhabited by Negroes, Chinese, Japanese, Puerto Ricans, Italians, Germans, Poles, Swedes, Mexicans, or some other racial or nationality group; some districts are set apart from others because Jews, Catholics, or the members of a particular Protestant denomination live there in relatively large numbers; other districts are characterized by old, dilapidated dwellings, others by large apartment houses, others by access to such desirable places as lake fronts, beaches, or river views, and still others are characterized by prominence of concrete, steel, asphalt, and general neglect. All urban areas have places where the "rich people" live, others where the "poor people" live, while most urban subcommunities are composed of the many gradations in amount of wealth or income of their residents between these two extremes. Other neighborhood communities are marked by the presence of older aged persons, renters instead of home owners, more women than men, or certain occupations such as proprietors, professionals, managers, and officials. Others contain unskilled or semi-skilled workers, some contain many unrelated individuals, and still others are marked by many persons living together in family units.

Recognizing this diversity in the social characters of urban subcommunities, Louis Wirth described the city as "a mosaic of social worlds" and emphasized that the different sections of the city can be conceived as separate worlds with the transition between them often being very abrupt and reflecting their different populations, subcultures, ways of life, and social organizations.[1]

The casual observer usually is aware of these neighborhood community differences, yet he may consider them more as a crazy quilt than a neat, orderly, and systematic pattern. Moreover, on a superficial level he is often correct, since the various neighborhoods do have miscellaneous sizes and shapes. However, various economists, geographers, sociologists, and other social scientists in their studies of the city have located and made clear various kinds of orderly patterns underlying the apparent unsystematic nature, growth, and changes of neighborhoods. In sociology, for example, the study of human ecology has resulted in many generalizations concerning the spatial distribution of different kinds of people and various functions and activities, and such works as

---

[1] "Urbanism as a Way of Life," *American Journal of Sociology*, vol. 44 (July, 1938), pp. 1–24.

those of Hawley[2] and Quinn[3] attest to the fact that the body of knowledge created with ecological concepts and techniques of analysis has been productive and fruitful. Generalizations concerning the orderly patterns of city growth and spatial structure such as the concentric zone theory of Burgess,[4] Hoyt's sector theory,[5] and Harris and Ullman's multiple nuclei theory[6] are to be found in most recent textbooks in introductory sociology and urban sociology published in this country.

Recently, new methods for the systematic analysis of the population differences between urban subcommunities have been proposed, and sufficient work has been done with the methods by enough different research workers that a sizeable body of information is beginning to emerge. One of these methods, first presented by Shevky and Williams[7] and later modified by Shevky and Bell,[8] will be discussed in some detail along with the work of other persons who have worked within the Shevky framework. Occasional reference will be made to a similar method constructed by Tryon.[9] In general, these methods can be referred to as *social area analysis,* although the particular techniques by which neighborhoods are combined into social areas differ somewhat in each case.

[2] Amos H. Hawley, *Human Ecology* (New York: The Ronald Press Company, 1950).

[3] James A. Quinn, *Human Ecology* (New York: Prentice-Hall, Inc., 1950).

[4] Ernest W. Burgess, "Urban Areas," *Chicago, An Experiment in Social Science Research,* T. V. Smith and L. D. White, editors (Chicago: University of Chicago Press, 1929).

[5] Homer Hoyt, *The Structure and Growth of Residential Neighborhoods in American Cities* (Federal Housing Administration, Washington, D.C., 1939).

[6] Chauncey D. Harris and Edward U. Ullman, "The Nature of Cities," *Annals of the American Academy of Political and Social Science,* vol. 242 (November, 1945), pp. 7–17.

[7] Eshref Shevky and Marilyn Williams, *The Social Areas of Los Angeles: Analysis and Typology* (Berkeley and Los Angeles: University of California Press, 1949).

[8] Eshref Shevky and Wendell Bell, *Social Area Analysis* (Stanford: Stanford University Press, 1955).

[9] Robert C. Tryon, *Identification of Social Areas by Cluster Analysis* (Berkeley and Los Angeles: University of California Press, 1955).

This paper is devoted to a discussion of social area analysis, what it is, and some of the uses which have been made of it. Since a logical place to begin is with the basic data which the method utilizes, a discussion of the nature of census tract statistics precedes a description of the social area typology.

CENSUS TRACT STATISTICS

The basic unit of analysis used in the construction of social areas is the census tract.[10] Census tracts are relatively small geographical areas into which certain cities and often their adjacent areas have been subdivided. They are larger than blocks and usually contain between 3,000 and 6,000 persons. A metropolitan area the size of Chicago is divided into approximately 1,000 of these small units, the San Francisco–Oakland area about 244, San Jose as few as 59, and smaller areas may be divided into even fewer. Data collected in connection with the regular decennial census of the United States are published in a form that allows study of population and housing characteristics of these tracts or subareas.

The census tract program is a relatively recent development. At the request of Dr. Walter Laidlaw, New York City and seven other cities having populations over 500,000 were divided into census tracts in 1910, and census data were tabulated by tracts within these cities for the first time. The purpose was to obtain detailed population data for sufficiently small areas within the city so that neighborhood communities could be studied. In 1920, tract data were again tabulated for the same eight cities, and in 1930 this number was increased to 18. By 1940 tract data were available for 60 urban places, and by 1950 as many as 69 urban places in the United States and its territories had been divided into census tracts. The Bureau of the Census hoped to have tracted

---

[10] Other units of analysis can be, and to some extent, have been used such as the county, the state, countries as a whole, etc. However, the chief use of the social area typology to date has been in connection with the census tract; thus, this discussion for simplicity will deal only with research related to the use of census tracts.

by 1960 all cities of 50,000 or more and in addition the entire metropolitan area in all cases where the central city has 100,000 or more inhabitants.[11] Once this goal has been achieved, comparative studies of urban neighborhoods having a scope and adequacy never before possible can be made.

Census tract bulletins were published for practically all of the tracted urban areas for 1950. Some of the information contained in the bulletins represented a complete count of all the persons in the census tracts, and additional information was presented which was obtained from a 20 per cent sample of persons in the tracts. The information given for each census tract is briefly listed below: [12]

Total population	Institutional population
Race	Years of school completed
Sex	Residence in 1949
Nativity	Income in 1949
Married couples	Age
Families or unrelated individuals	Marital status
Number of dwelling units	Employment status
Owner or renter occupied dwelling units	Major occupational group
	Women in the labor force
Type of structure	Persons per room
Condition and plumbing facilities	Type of heating fuel
Year structure was built	Refrigeration equipment
Number of all occupied dwelling units	Television
	Contract monthly rent
Number of persons in dwelling unit	Value of one-dwelling-unit structures
Number of households	
Population per household	Spanish surnames (for certain areas only)
Population in households	

[11] For a discussion of the tract program for 1960, see the "Preliminary Statement on Publication of Statistics by Census Tracts from the 1960 Census of Population and Housing," Bureau of the Census, Department of Commerce, Washington, D.C. (1956).

[12] "Census Tract Statistics," *United States Census of Population: 1950,* III, Series P-D bulletins, Bureau of the Census, Department of Commerce, Washington, D.C. For a further discussion of the history and nature of census tract statistics see *Census Tract Manual,* Bureau of the Census, Department of Commerce, Washington, D.C., third edition, 1947.

The above list, of course, greatly underestimates the total number of useful measures contained in the tract bulletins, since many combinations and permutations are possible. For example, an investigator can use data on age and sex to compute a fertility ratio for a tract by taking the number of women from age 15 to age 44, dividing that sum into the number of children under age 5, and then multiplying by 1,000. Thus, tract populations can be compared with respect to their fertility ratios. Many other such permutations of the above variables giving important information about a tract population can be made.

However, if one wishes to get a coherent and easily understandable picture of the character of a tract population, it is cumbersome and inefficient to deal separately with as many different variables (and their permutations) as are contained in the census bulletins. For example, trying to compare and contrast the 244 tracts in the San Francisco Bay area with respect to thirty or more variables simultaneously, each being handled individually, is a task which would be exceedingly tedious and one which would result in complex patterns difficult to comprehend. Thus, some ordering or clustering of the variables needs to be done as a prior step in constructing a composite of a tract's social characteristics.

ORDERING OF CENSUS VARIABLES

Apart from the variables reflecting sheer size of the census tract, there appear to be three sets of general characteristics in the census tract bulletins. These are economic, family, and ethnic characteristics. There are, no doubt, other ways in which the census variables can be ordered. For example, there are variables which refer to housing and other variables which refer to population, but for the purposes of systematically analyzing the social features of urban neighborhood communities the division of the variables into those which are economic or economic-related, those which indicate the presence or lack of families and those which reflect the presence or absence of certain racial and nationality groups seem most revealing. Looking back over the census variables given above, one can easily group most of them into one of these three categories. This has been done below:

ECONOMIC CHARACTERISTICS	FAMILY CHARACTERISTICS	ETHNIC CHARACTERISTICS
Condition and plumbing facilities	Sex	Race
Persons per room	Married couples	Nativity
Years of school completed	Families or unrelated individuals	Spanish surnames
Income in 1949	Owner or renter occupied dwelling	
Employment status	units	
Major occupational group	Type of structure	
Type of heating fuel	Age	
Refrigeration equipment	Marital status	
Contract monthly rent	Women in the labor force	
Value of one-dwelling-unit structures	Lack of institutional population	

The census variables were first grouped this way in the development of social area analysis by Shevky and Williams. The author verified the classification by using 1940 census data for the Los Angeles area and the San Francisco Bay area,[13] and Tryon, working independently, analyzed all the census variables for the San Francisco Bay area as of 1940 and reached practically the same classification. In addition, Walter C. Kaufman has found that this grouping of variables is, in general, valid for the San Francisco Bay and Chicago areas as of 1950 as well.[14]

It is safe to conclude that census tract populations in the Chicago, Los Angeles, and San Francisco Bay areas have been described about as completely as possible with respect to their economic, family, and ethnic characteristics, and that these fairly adequately represent all the common variation among census variables in the three urban areas. Future research will show whether this conclusion can also be applied to other metropolitan areas.[15]

[13] Wendell Bell, "Economic, Family, and Ethnic Status: An Empirical Test," *American Sociological Review*, vol. 20 (February, 1955), pp. 45–52.

[14] Walter C. Kaufman, "A Factor-Analytic Test of Revisions in the Shevky-Bell Typology for Chicago and San Francisco, 1950," unpublished Ph.D. dissertation, Northwestern University, in progress.

[15] This statement of the social area methodology is unencumbered by a

The interesting work of Van Arsdol, Camilleri, and Schmid is important in this connection. Using the statistical technique of factor analysis with selected variables from the 1950 census tract data for ten large American cities—Akron, Ohio, Atlanta, Georgia, Birmingham, Alabama, Kansas City, Missouri, Louisville, Kentucky, Minneapolis, Minnesota, Portland, Oregon, Providence, Rhode Island, Rochester, New York, and Seattle, Washington—they concluded that this grouping of census variables is an adequate measure of economic, family, and ethnic status in eight of these cities.[16]

INDEXES OF ECONOMIC, FAMILY, AND ETHNIC STATUS

With reduction of all the census variables to three more basic factors, it is possible to construct a picture of the smaller social worlds into which an urban area is subdivided in terms of the economic, family, and ethnic characteristics of the tract populations. It is neither necessary nor efficient to include all the possible measures of the three factors in indexes of them. It was found that a few indicators of a factor are sufficient. Also, of course, some of the census variables are better measures of their particular factor

---

discussion of the considerations underlying the use of the terms "economic status" for "social rank," "family status" for "urbanization," and "ethnic status" for "segregation." The writer is convinced that there are sufficient reasons to warrant these changes in name from the original formulation by Shevky and Williams, although significant alteration in conceptual content is suggested only in the case of the change from urbanization to family status. No thorough discussion of these suggested changes appears in print as yet, but the interested reader is referred for a brief statement to Shevky and Bell, *op. cit.*, p. 68.

[16] Maurice D. Van Arsdol, Jr., Santo F. Camilleri, and Calvin F. Schmid, "An Investigation into the Generality of the Shevky Social Area Indexes," *American Sociological Review*, vol. 23 (June 1958), pp. 277–284. Also see Van Arsdol, Camilleri, and Schmid, "A Deviant Case of Shevky's Dimensions of Urban Structure," Proceedings of the Pacific Sociological Society in *Research Studies of the State College of Washington*, vol. 25 (June, 1957), pp. 171–177. From their analyses in ten cities these writers conclude that the index construction as described in this paper is validated in eight of the cities. It is from studies such as these, however, that the typology can be adequately tested and, if necessary, elaborated or otherwise revised.

than are others. Thus, some census variables were selected to be averaged together as an index of the economic characteristics of a census tract, and the index was named the *index of economic status*. Other variables were selected to be averaged together as an index of the family characteristics of a tract population, and this index was named the *index of family status*. Finally, the average of still other variables was made an index of the racial and nationality characteristics of a tract population and was named the *index of ethnic status*. The variables selected to measure the three factors were as follows:

INDEX OF ECONOMIC STATUS	INDEX OF FAMILY	INDEX OF ETHNIC STATUS
Rent	Fertility ratio	Race
Education	Women not in the labor	Nativity
Occupation	force	Spanish surnames
	Single-family detached	(when available)
	dwellings	

The specific procedures for the computation of the indexes are given in the attached appendix, but it suffices to say here that each census tract can be given three scores—one each for the indexes of economic, family, and ethnic status. These scores have been standardized to range from zero to 100 in the Los Angeles area as of 1940. Therefore, it is possible for tracts to receive scores less than zero or somewhat greater than 100 in other urban areas or in the Los Angeles area at periods other than 1940.

In tracts with high scores on the index of economic status there are many persons having white-collar occupations such as professionals, proprietors, managers, officials, salesmen, clerks; many persons with higher education; and high rents. In tracts with low scores there are many persons with blue-collar occupations such as craftsmen, foremen, operatives, and laborers; many persons with no more than a grade school education; and low rents.

It is possible for tracts to vary greatly in amount of family life regardless of their scores on the index of economic status. Tracts having high scores on the index of family status contain populations which have high fertility ratios, that is, many children under age 5 in relation to the number of women between the ages of 15 and 44; many women not in the labor force, but at home in the roles of housewives and mothers; and many single-family detached dwellings. Tracts with low fertility ratios, many women in the labor force, and many multiple dwellings achieve low scores on the index of family status.

Tracts which contain many Negroes, other nonwhite races, persons with Spanish surnames and foreign-born whites from certain countries receive high scores, and tracts which contain mostly native-born whites receive low scores on the index of ethnic status. This index, of course, is negatively related to the index of economic status, since Negroes and many other American minority groups are most often located in urban neighborhoods of low economic status. However, it is still possible to find some neighborhood communities in which minority groups have high economic status and to find other neighborhoods inhabited by native-born whites of low economic status. Combined with this is the fact that economic status is not the same thing as race and nationality; that is, the social significance of these two types of variables is different, though they have often been confused. Consequently, in spite of the empirical relationship between the indexes of economic and ethnic status, they need to be kept conceptually distinct in any analysis of urban neighborhood communities.

Construction of the Social Area Typology. Since the three indexes are to be utilized as distinct properties of urban subcommunities, they cannot be simply added together; yet some method must be devised to use them simultaneously in the analysis. To do this, types or a typology must be constructed. The use of the concept of type here follows Lazarsfeld who says:

One is safe in saying that the concept of type is always used in referring to special compounds of attributes. In speaking of the Middle-western type of American, one may have in mind certain physical features, certain attitudes and habits, certain affiliations and talents attributed to the inhabitants of this region. In speaking of types of books or of types of governments, a special combination of attributes is thrown into relief.[17]

The special "compound of attributes" used in social area analysis is that composed of economic, family, and ethnic status, and instead of a "Middle-western type of American," "types of books,"

[17] Paul F. Lazarsfeld, "Some Remarks on the Typological Procedures in Social Research," *Zeitschrift fur Sozialforschung*, vol. 6 (1937), pp. 119–139.

or "types of governments," the types are composed of urban neighborhoods. As shown in figure 4, a social attribute is constructed which is bounded by the indexes of economic and family status. Census tract populations near to each other in the social area diagram would necessarily have similar configurations of scores on the indexes of economic and family status. Such tracts are grouped together by the divisions which are made in the indexes segmenting each into four parts. The social space has been segmented by divisions passing through economic status scores of 25, 50, and 75 and through family status scores also of 25, 50, and 75. Thus, potentially sixteen groupings of census tract populations are made, and these are different social types of tract populations. These types are also called social areas. Social areas, so far, are composed of a tract or tracts having particular patterns of scores on the indexes of economic and family status. They are called "social" in that the properties of neighborhood communities dealt with are social properties, and the term "area" is employed in that a geometric space frame is utilized. By similar reasoning the diagram shown in figures 4 and 5 can be referred to as the "social space diagram."

High	1A	2A	3A	4A
FAMILY STATUS	1B	2B	3B	4B
	1C	2C	3C	4C
Low	1D	2D	3D	4D
	Low	ECONOMIC STATUS		High

Figure 4.   Social Area Key Based on Economic Status and
Family Status
From Wendell Bell, "The Utility of the Shevky Typology for the Design of Urban Subarea Field Studies," *The Journal of Social Psychology* vol. 47 (February, 1958), pp. 71–83.

A number and letter designator are given to each of the types as shown in figure 4. Social area 1D, for example, contains tract populations having low economic and low family status. Tract populations contained in social area 1A would have the same economic status as those contained in 1D, but the family status of tracts in 1A would be high instead of low. Likewise, social area 4D varies systematically from 1D, but in this case the family status of the two groups of census tracts is the same while the economic status differs, social area 4D containing tract populations low on family status but high on economic status. Thus, each type of social area delimits census tracts which have a particular configuration of scores with respect to economic and family characteristics (see figure 4 for positions and designators of other social areas).

The third factor, ethnic status, adds to the typology so far constructed by distinguishing those census tracts which contain relatively many members of American racial and nationality minority groups; that is, those tracts which have high indexes of ethnic status are distinguished from those which have low indexes of ethnic status. Tract populations having high indexes of ethnic status are given an "S" along with their social area designators as determined from figure 4, and tracts which have low indexes of ethnic status remain with only the designator as shown in figure 4. Thus, there are thirty-two possible social areas or types of urban subcommunities: 1A, 1B . . . 4D and 1AS, 1BS . . . 4DS.[18]

Some Illustrations of the Use of Social Area Analysis. There is not sufficient space here to discuss completely all the work done using social area analysis. However, a selection of research executed in this framework will illustrate some of the uses and the nature of the findings. The census tracts of the San Francisco Bay area are plotted in the social space diagram in figure 5 according to their scores on the three indexes for 1950. Two hundred and forty-four tracts are included, and the total population of the tracted area is 1,509,678. The social position of each tract population can be seen in relation to all other tracts in the Bay area.

Notice that there is little relationship between the indexes of

[18] Tryon's method of constructing social areas differs somewhat from the Shevky method which is discussed here. However, the results are much the same as is shown by the fact that the social areas of the San Francisco Bay area as of 1940 and as established by the Tryon method are for all practical purposes the same as those achieved by the Shevky method. (Eta = .82)

family and economic status, the correlation being —.13 between them. The correlation between the indexes of economic and ethnic status is —.50, reflecting the fact that Negroes, Orientals, other non-whites, Mexican-Americans, and the members of certain foreign-born groups are most likely to live in neighborhoods characterized by low economic status. These groups are also somewhat more likely to live in areas having little family life than they are to live in areas having a great deal of family life ($r = -.16$ between the indexes of ethnic and family status). This relationship, as can be noted from figure 5, is more marked at the higher levels of economic status.

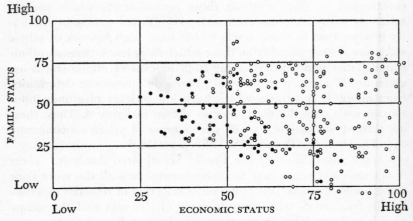

○ Census tracts with low indexes of ethnic status.
• Census tracts with high indexes of ethnic status.

Figure 5.   Distribution of the Census Tracts in the Social Areas of the San Francisco Bay Region, 1950. (From Bell, *op. cit.*)

Similar patterns of relationships have been noted for Los Angeles [19] and Chicago.[20] Whether the relations between the factors will vary markedly for other cities, or whether the stability of these patterns represent a generalization about the social structure of American cities for 1940 and 1950 is a matter for future research. The Van Arsdol, Camilleri, and Schmid research on the ten cities,

[19] Bell (February, 1955), *op. cit.*   [20] Kaufman, *op. cit.*

which was mentioned earlier, suggests that this pattern of inter-correlations may be fairly general, but variation was reported for some of the cities.

Orderly patterns have been found in the relationship between the sex ratio and the social areas in both Los Angeles and San Francisco. The sex ratio varies inversely with family status at low levels of economic status, varies directly with family status at high levels of economic status, and varies inversely with economic status at all levels of family status. Thus, relatively more women than men are located in higher economic status neighborhoods, the greatest concentration of women in relation to men occurring in expensive apartment house areas and the greatest concentration of men in relation to women occurring in the cheap rooming-house areas.[21]

The age distributions of the social areas also show systematic differences. The percentage of older aged persons increases with the economic status and decreases with the family status of a tract, while the percentage of persons under fifteen years of age de-creases with economic status and increases with family status, so-cial area 4D containing the largest percentage of older aged and the smallest percentage of younger aged persons. Although the pat-tern is less clear, the social area distribution of the middle-aged group tends to follow that of the older age group.[22]

Once the census tracts of a metropolitan area have been given scores on the indexes of economic, family, and ethnic status, it be-comes possible to execute systematically a variety of investigations into the nature of different urban subcommunities within the social area framework. For example, an examination of neighborhood place names used by the residents of a city allows a study of the relationship of the subjective evaluations of urban neighborhoods to the social characteristics of the neighborhoods as determined by an analysis of census variables. Below some named places in San Francisco are given with their scores on the three indexes for 1950:[23]

[21] Bell, "The Social Areas of the San Francisco Bay Region," *American Sociological Review*, vol. 18 (February, 1953), pp. 39–47; Shevky and Bell, *op. cit.*; and Shevky and Williams, *op. cit.*

[22] Bell, *ibid.*; Shevky and Bell, *ibid.*; and Shevky and Williams, *ibid.*

[23] Shevky and Bell, *ibid.*, pp. 61–63.

IDENTIFYING PLACE NAME	INDEX OF ECONOMIC STATUS	INDEX OF FAMILY STATUS	INDEX OF ETHNIC STATUS	SOCIAL AREA
Nob Hill (A-12)	91	−4	9	4D
Chinatown (A-15)	46	37	92	2CS
Sea Cliff (E-1)	93	58	10	4B
Potrero (L-1)	38	52	29	2BS
Diamond Heights (N-13)	52	71	11	3B

Studies could be designed to determine subjective evaluations of the social images of the named places such as those given above, and these evaluations could be analyzed not only with respect to the social characteristics of the named places but also with respect to the social characteristics of the persons doing the evaluating.

Land use and topography, as might be expected, are related to the social areas. Generally, in the San Francisco Bay area neighborhoods of low economic status are located adjacent to the industrially occupied, low elevation inner Bay areas, while neighborhoods of high economic status are usually located in areas of high elevation, more distant from industrially occupied land. Neighborhoods of low family status are near commercial areas, especially near the downtown business district, while neighborhoods of high family status are located farther from the downtown commercial area nearer to parks, lakes, or ocean beaches. The census tracts composing a social area, however, are not necessarily contiguous and continuous.

More enlightening with regard to the nature of the people who live in the different social areas are studies such as those done by the author [24] in San Francisco and by Greer [25] in Los Angeles. In the San Francisco study the Shevky social space diagram (see figure 4) was examined, and four census tracts were selected hav-

[24] Bell, with the collaboration of Marion D. Boat and Maryanne T. Force, *People of the City,* Stanford University, mimeographed report (1954).

[25] Scott Greer, "Urbanism Reconsidered: A Comparative Study of Local Areas in a Metropolis," *American Sociological Review,* vol. 21 (February, 1956), 19–25; and Scott Greer and Ella Kube, *Urban Worlds,* Laboratory in Urban Culture, Occidental College, mimeographed report (1955).

ing low scores on the index of ethnic status but having widely different scores in the indexes of economic and family status. In these tracts, an investigation was made of the social isolation and participation of urbanites. The social space positions of the four areas are shown in figure 6 along with their census tract designations and their identifying neighborhood community names. From figure 6 it can be noted that Mission, a low-rent rooming-house area, is characterized by low economic and low family status; Pacific Heights, a high-rent apartment-house area, is high on economic, but low on family status; Outer Mission, characterized by small single-family detached houses and residents of modest means, is low on economic and low on family status; and St. Francis Wood, being a large single-family detached house area with residents who are fairly well off financially, is high on economic and family status.

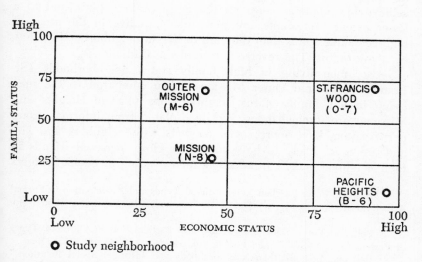

Figure 6.   The Four San Francisco Study Tracts Located in the Social Space Diagram, 1950. (From Bell, *op. cit.*)

After the selection of the study tracts, as described above, probability samples were drawn from a complete list of all the dwelling units within each tract. A total of 701 interviews were obtained with a response rate in excess of 85 per cent, one male over age 21 in each sample dwelling being interviewed.

The results of this study show different patterns of social participation in the different neighborhoods. Men living in high economic status neighborhoods (Pacific Heights and St. Francis Wood) when compared to those living in low economic status neighborhoods (Mission and Outer Mission) belong to a greater number of formal associations, attend formal association meetings more frequently, are more likely to hold offices in formal associations,[26] have a greater percentage of their memberships in general interest types of associations,[27] interact with their co-workers outside of their work association more frequently, have more informal contacts with friends who are not neighbors or relatives, rely more on their co-workers, are less likely to be calculating in their relationships with their neighbors,[28] and are much more likely to achieve low anomie scores on the Srole Scale.[29] Jews, and to a lesser extent Protestants, are more likely to live in the areas of high economic status than they are to live in neighborhoods of low economic status. The reverse is true of the Catholics.[30]

Also, men living in high family status neighborhoods (St. Francis Wood and Outer Mission) when compared to the men living in low family status neighborhoods (Pacific Heights and Mission) are somewhat less socially isolated from informal group participation, have more social contacts with neighbors and kin, and are more likely to have met their close, personal friends in their neighborhoods.[31] In addition, men residing in Pacific Heights

[26] Bell and Force, "Urban Neighborhood Types and Participation in Formal Associations," *American Sociological Review,* vol. 21 (February, 1956), pp. 25–34.

[27] Bell and Force, "Social Structure and Participation in Different Types of Formal Associations," *Social Forces,* vol. 34 (May, 1956), pp. 345–350.

[28] Bell and Boat, "Urban Neighborhoods and Informal Social Relations," *American Journal of Sociology,* vol. 62 (January, 1957), pp. 391–398.

[29] Bell, "Anomie, Social Isolation, and the Class Structure," *Sociometry,* vol. 20 (June, 1957), pp. 105–116.

[30] Bell and Force, "Religious Preference, Familism, and the Class Structure," *The Midwest Sociologist,* vol. 19 (May, 1957), pp. 79–86.

[31] Bell and Boat, *op. cit.*

belong to fewer formal associations, attend meetings less often, are less likely to hold offices,[32] and are more likely to belong to special individual-interest types of formal associations [33] than are men living in St. Francis Wood. With respect to religious preference, Catholics are relatively more numerous in neighborhoods of high family status than they are in neighborhoods of low family status. "Independents," "Agnostics," and "Atheists" are most likely to live in areas of low status.[34]

Using the social areas of Los Angeles, Greer also selected four local areas in which to conduct his study of social participation in urban neighborhoods. His strategy, however, was to hold economic as well as ethnic characteristics constant in his study tracts and to vary family characteristics widely. For 1950 Temple City had a score on the index of family status of 74, Eagle Rock, 64, Silver Lake, 45, and Central Hollywood, 20; each of these subcommunities had scores on the index of economic status of about 70 and scores of 6 or less on the index of ethnic status. From his interviews with persons in these four neighborhood communities, Greer concludes that the greater the amount of family life in a neighborhood, the more neighboring; the more persons who have friends in their neighborhood, the more likely a person is to attend a cultural event in his neighborhood; the larger the percentage of persons who belong to formal organizations whose memberships are drawn from the local area, the more husbands who belong to organizations which hold their meetings in the local area, and the more persons who could name at least one local leader.

Greer also found that persons living in his high family status neighborhoods when compared with residents of low family status neighborhoods are more likely to think of their local area as a "little community," like a "small town," where "people are friendly and neighborly"; they are less likely to mention the convenience of their location in terms of its nearness to "downtown and everything." They are less likely to speak of their neighbors as the "nice people" who "leave you alone and mind their own business," more

---

[32] Bell and Force (February, 1956), *op. cit.*
[33] Bell and Force (May, 1956), *op. cit.*
[34] Bell and Force (May, 1957), *op. cit.*

committed to remaining in their neighborhoods, and more apt to have their friends (other than friends who are neighbors) from other high family status tracts.[35]

These two studies, taken together, offer convincing evidence that the social character of local areas within a city as defined by economic, family, and ethnic characteristics is an important predictor of individual attitudes and behaviors, subcultural patterns, and the social organization. It is crucial in determining the extent to which a local area in a city can even be considered a community in the sense of having flows of communication, interaction, community identification, and social integration among its residents.

McElrath[36] and Williamson[37] also have used social area analysis in the design and analysis of sample surveys. They selected samples using the typology, and they reported that the social areas were predictive of the prestige and esteem ratings for individuals and the degree of their marital adjustment. Curtis[38] has used the method as a sampling device in his study of the employability of aging workers in Buffalo, New York.

There are many other uses to which social area analysis has been put. Studying 1,107 petitioners for change of name in Los Angeles County, Broom, Beem, and Harris[39] find, when compared with the general population, that name changers were more likely

[35] Greer, *op. cit.*; Greer and Kube, *op. cit.* Greer uses the alternative names for the three indexes as do some of the other writers cited, but for the sake of consistency of presentation, economic, family, and ethnic status are used throughout this chapter.

[36] Dennis C. McElrath, "Prestige and Esteem Identification in Selected Urban Areas," Proceedings of the Pacific Sociological Society in *Research Studies of the State College of Washington,* vol. 23 (June, 1955), pp. 130–137.

[37] Robert C. Williamson, "Selected Urban Factors in Marital Adjustment," Proceedings of the Pacific Sociological Society in *Research Studies of the State College of Washington,* vol. 21 (September, 1953), pp. 237–241; and "Socio-Economic Factors and Marital Adjustment in an Urban Setting," *American Sociological Review,* vol. 19 (April, 1954), pp. 213–216.

[38] Jack H. Curtis, "The Employability of Aging Workers in Social Areas of High Urbanization and Low Social Rank," unpublished paper read at the annual meeting of the American Sociological Society, Washington, D.C. (1957).

[39] Leonard Broom, Helen P. Beem, and Virginia Harris, "Characteristics of 1,107 Petitioners for Change of Name," *American Sociological Review,* vol. 20 (February, 1955), pp. 33–39.

to live in areas rated high in economic, low in family, and low in ethnic status. This suggests that name changers may be upwardly mobile persons, who have broken away from family ties, and who have been or are being assimilated into the larger society from membership in and identification with some particular ethnic group.

In another study Broom and Shevky [40] demonstrate the utility of the typological framework for the differentiation of an ethnic group. They find Jewish neighborhoods in Los Angeles in the lower ranges of family status and in the full range of economic status. Tracts lacking Russian-born persons tend to fall in the high ranges of family status, with a noticeable cluster at the lowest levels of economic status.[41] Taking the members of four Jewish fraternities on the Los Angeles campus of the University of California, they find the two rated by campus consensus as having high prestige had members from tract locations having significantly higher economic status than the two fraternities rated by campus consensus as having lower prestige.

Studies of the incidence of suicide and juvenile delinquency have been made by Wendling [42] and Polk.[43] Polk, for example, in his study of San Diego finds juvenile delinquency rates highest in those areas in which minority group members live and lowest in areas inhabited by native whites. Smaller correlations are reported for the other two indexes, but juvenile delinquency is negatively related to economic and family status. The highest rates of juvenile delinquency occur in neighborhoods with high indexes of ethnic status, with low income, occupational, and educational levels, and with little family life. The only significant correlation between suicide and any of the three indexes in Polk's study is a negative correlation between family status and suicide.

[40] Leonard Broom and Eshref Shevky, "The Differentiation of an Ethnic Group," *American Sociological Review*, vol. 14 (August, 1949), pp. 476–481.

[41] Broom and Shevky took the Russian-born persons as an indicator of one segment of the Jewish population in Los Angeles.

[42] Aubrey Wendling, "Suicide in the San Francisco Bay Region 1938–1942 and 1948–1952," unpublished Ph.D. dissertation, University of Washington (1954).

[43] Kenneth Polk, "The Social Areas of San Diego," unpublished M.A. thesis, Northwestern University (1957).

One of the most interesting uses of the typology to date is an attempt to facilitate adequate social welfare planning for local areas in the San Francisco Bay area.[44] The hypothesis is that each of the social areas has certain distinctive social welfare problems related to their differences in economic, family, and ethnic characteristics. This work does a great deal in suggesting one of the many possible practical applications of the social area typology.

Robert L. Wilson of the Bureau of Social and Religious Research, Northwestern University, has used the social area typology for a comparative study of Episcopal, Methodist, Presbyterian, and United Lutheran churches in selected cities throughout the United States. He indicates that generalizations can be made regarding the relation of churches to social areas.

Tryon and those working with him have related social areas to additional variables such as political preference, voting participation, psychiatric hospitalization, and the probability of an individual's attending a university, but there is insufficient space to elaborate with a detailed consideration of these findings.[45] However, his findings and interpretations on the stability of social areas deserve further comment. Tryon argues that:

It is difficult to believe that a social area, including a number of tracts of people having the same configuration of demographic and correlated psychosocial ways, would change much in a decade, or perhaps many decades. A change would be gradual. Individual persons may be born into the area, move out or die, but it should retain its subcultural homogeneity with considerable constancy, short of socially catastrophic events. Even those areas that undergo rapid growth through construction of new homes are likely to incorporate new groups of persons homogeneous with those already there.[46]

Tryon concludes from his analysis of the homogeneity of his 1940 San Francisco social areas with respect to 1950 median rent

[44] Elizabeth Bange *et al.*, *A Study of Selected Population Changes and Characteristics with Special Reference to Implications for Social Welfare*, a group research project submitted in partial fulfillment of requirements for the Master of Social Welfare Degree, University of California, Berkeley, mimeographed (1955). See the chapter on "Social Area Analysis in Social Welfare," pp. 265–329.

[45] Tryon, *op. cit.*   [46] Tryon, *ibid.*, p. 31.

that ". . . little change in homogeneity of the tracts composing the various areas has occurred in 10 years." [47] He also reports a comparison between the 1940 vote for Roosevelt with the 1947 vote for the Democratic candidate for Congress, Havenner, a man identified with the Roosevelt-Truman program. The census tracts show practically the same rank order for Roosevelt as for Havenner, the correlation coefficient being .94.

Other evidence that the social areas remain relatively constant is found in McElrath's study. He reports that thirteen years after the collection of the data on which the social area scores were based, he achieved the anticipated results in his sample survey with respect to differences in economic, family, and ethnic characteristics in his study areas.[48]

This is not to say that tracts do not change their social area positions, but rather that most of them can be expected to maintain consistent social patterns for relatively long periods of time. However, the social area approach is most useful for analysis of current conditions when census data are up to date, close to census years; there is a need for techniques to keep area analysis current in view of the high rates of change in certain parts of most American cities.

Also, Tryon's comments are not to be construed to mean that the *census tract populations* need be homogeneous for the method to be valid. It is not inconsistent with the typology to find some urban neighborhoods which are typically characterized by heterogeneity with respect to certain variables. Census tracts classified together in a social area, however, should have *about the same degree of heterogeneity* with respect to *the same set of variables*.

Another way in which social area analysis can be utilized in connection with urban subcommunity field studies, and one which has not yet been discussed, is in the analysis of the combined or independent effect of personal and unit characteristics on variables dependent on them. Lazarsfeld and Barton have discussed the difference between personal characteristics and unit characteristics:

Personal data characterize individuals . . . Unit data characterize some aggregation of people . . . Of course, people can be aggregated in many

[47] Tryon, *ibid.*, p. 32.   [48] McElrath, *op. cit.*

different ways, some of which imply social interaction and others only categorization by the observer. A "unit" in our sense will be any aggregation—an Army company, a neighborhood, an occupational category, a political party.[49]

In the San Francisco study two subcommunities having high economic status and two having low were selected as study areas. In general, the men living in the high economic status neighborhoods, as expected, have higher educational levels than those living in the low economic status neighborhoods, the median educational level for Pacific Heights and St. Francis Wood combined being "some college or more," and the median educational level for men in Mission and Outer Mission being in the "some high school or less" category. This is a neighborhood or, as defined above, a unit characteristic and can be assigned to all the men living in a particular neighborhood community as an attribute of their residence area. However, there are men living in Pacific Heights and St. Francis Wood who can be classified on the basis of their own educational level, a personal characteristic, as having only a grade school or less education (10.9 per cent so report). Likewise, some men in Mission and Outer Mission, 9.6 per cent, report having some college or more. This raises an interesting question. Does the educational level of the neighborhood in which a person lives affect his attitudes and behaviors even when his individual educational level is controlled? The answer seems to be "yes" in many of the cases so far tested!

Table 2, for example, shows the percentage of men who attend formal association meetings frequently by the average educational level of the neighborhood and by the respondent's own education. Comparing the percentages *within each neighborhood*, the general tendency is for the more frequent attenders to have completed more years of schooling. Of particular interest here, however, is the comparison of amount of formal association participation between neighborhoods, personal education being held constant. In each of the individual education categories the men living in the neighbor-

[49] Paul F. Lazarsfeld and Allen H. Barton, "Qualitative Measurement in the Social Sciences: Classification, Typologies, and Indexes." In the *Policy Sciences*, Daniel Lerner and Harold D. Lasswell, editors (Stanford: Stanford University Press, 1951).

hoods having the higher educational levels are more likely to be frequent attenders than are the men living in the neighborhoods of lower educational levels. Considering that similar differences are found when personal measures of occupation and income are controlled for, it is suggested that the economic characteristics of a neighborhood population as a unit may be important indicators of

Table 2. *Percentage of Men Who Attend Formal Association Meetings Frequently by Neighborhood and Individual Educational Levels* *

	NEIGHBORHOOD EDUCATION	
INDIVIDUAL EDUCATION	LOW (MISSION AND OUTER MISSION) PERCENTAGE	HIGH (PACIFIC HEIGHTS AND ST. FRANCIS WOOD) PERCENTAGE
Some college or more	27.3 (33)	46.4 (181)
Completed high school only	14.5 (83)	28.3 (92)
Some high school	17.3 (81)	30.4 (46)
Grade school or less	7.6 (144)	23.1 (39)

* Men were classified frequent attenders if they attended meetings 37 or more times per year. The total number of cases on which the percentage is based is given in parentheses in each case. Adapted from Bell and Force, (February, 1956), *op. cit.*, p. 31.

the economic reference group of those living in the neighborhood and may provide a set of expectations with respect to the residents' associational behavior.[50]

SUMMARY AND CONCLUSION

In this brief discussion of the nature of social area analysis and some of its uses, it has been impossible to discuss all the studies which have used this method of analysis. For example, in addition

[50] Bell and Force (February, 1956), *op. cit.*, pp. 30–32.

to the studies in Los Angeles, San Francisco–Oakland, Chicago, San Diego, and the other cities mentioned, social areas have been constructed or are being constructed in Dayton,[51] Duluth,[52] Miami,[53] New Orleans,[54] and St. Louis.[55] The St. Louis study is noteworthy because it not only uses the basic census analysis to compare the social areas of St. Louis with those of Los Angeles and San Francisco but also uses the typology to examine political preferences, voting behavior, local governments, and metropolitan problems.

It has also been impossible to discuss here the difficulties of procedure encountered in social area analysis and to present the differing evaluations of its contribution to urban studies.[56] There are those who have concluded that social area analysis represents no advance whatever in urban studies,[57] but this seems a hasty judgment. There have been relatively few uses made of the typology, and there are potentially fruitful results promised by the Metropolitan St. Louis Survey and the study of Dayton undertaken by the Metropolitan Community Studies, Inc.[58]

Some of the difficulties of procedure in a comparative study of American cities will have been solved simply when the tracting of cities for the 1960 census has been completed. There are other difficulties stemming from the nature of census data, and still others

[51] Metropolitan Community Studies, Inc., John C. Bollens, Director. Study is in progress at time of writing.

[52] John H. Mabry, "The Social Areas of Duluth," unpublished manuscript, (1953).

[53] Dean G. Epley, "The Social Areas of Miami, Florida," study in progress.

[54] Olive Reeks, "The Social Areas of New Orleans," unpublished M.A. thesis, University of California, Los Angeles (1953).

[55] Walter C. Kaufman *et al.*, "The People of St. Louis," Metropolitan St. Louis Survey, mimeographed report, (1956).

[56] See the reviews of *Social Area Analysis* by Robert W. Buechley, *Journal of the American Statistical Association*, vol. 51 (March, 1956), pp. 195–197; David B. Carpenter, *American Sociological Review*, vol. 20 (August, 1955) pp. 497–498; and Otis Dudley Duncan, *American Journal of Sociology*, vol. 61 (July, 1955), pp. 84–85.

[57] See Duncan's review, *ibid.*, and the interchange between Bell and Duncan, *American Journal of Sociology*, vol. 61 (November, 1955), pp. 260–262.

[58] It is beyond the scope of this paper to discuss the theoretical framework underlying social area analysis or to comment on the issues recently raised by Amos H. Hawley and Otis Dudley Duncan, "Social Area Analysis: A Critical Appraisal," *Land Economics*, vol. 33 (November, 1957), pp. 337–345.

from the specific techniques employed in the method. In the latter case, for example, Kaufman is presently testing alternative indexes to measure the basic factors of economic, family, and ethnic status.[59] Also, the recent work of Buechley appears promising in simplifying the measures of the three factors.[60] Although minor revisions in the procedures now employed in social area analysis may result from the work of Buechley, Kaufman and others, as presently constructed, the typology has proved useful as an approach to the systematic study of the smaller social worlds which a city's neighborhood communities comprise.

In sum, the various uses to which social area analysis has been put are as follows:

1. *The delineation of subareas.* Through the application of these methods to data available for American cities, it is possible to delineate systematically urban neighborhood communities having different social characteristics. Such a delineation, with the precision with which it can be accomplished, has descriptive value to the social scientist and city planner alike.

2. *Comparative studies at one point in time.* Comparative studies of the social areas of different cities at one point in time can be made. The social areas of Los Angeles can be compared with the social areas of New York, Chicago, Philadelphia, San Francisco, Dallas, St. Louis, Miami, or other urban areas. Social area distribution of the neighborhoods in different cities can be compared to determine patterns differentiated by the regions in which the cities are located, the sizes of the cities, their chief economic functions, their relative ages, their topographies, their ethnic compositions, and their transportation bases.

3. *Comparative studies at two points in time.* Within a given urban area some neighborhood communities are constantly undergoing change. New neighborhoods appear, they grow and develop, they become old, and sometimes they change completely with respect to the condition of the buildings, the type of building struc-

[59] Kaufman, "A Factor-Analytic Test of Revisions in the Shevky-Bell Typology for Chicago and San Francisco, 1950," *op. cit.*

[60] Robert W. Buechley, "On Simple Measures of Social Variables from United States Census Tract Statistics," California State Department of Public Health, unpublished paper (1957).

tures, and the kinds of people. Other neighborhood communitie,
may maintain the same social character for generations like Beaco*
Hill in Boston.[61] The application of the social area typology ca*
result in a systematic description and analysis of social changes in *
neighborhood.

4. *A framework for the execution of other types of research*
In addition to the above uses of the social area method, it can als*
be utilized as a framework for the analysis of attitudes and behavio*
of individuals. As indicated above, neighborhood populations diffe*
not only in demographic features but in values and social struc
ture. It is unnecessary to add that variations between neighbor
hoods have important implications for variations in individual at
titudes and behavior. Even from present formulations in sociologi*
cal theory, it is possible to hypothesize many relationships betwee*
neighborhood differences and the attitudes and behavior of indi
viduals ranging from suicide, voting behavior, religious preference
mental disorder, personal morale, and type of crimes to such thing
as frequency and nature of participation in formal organizations
amount of close contact with neighbors, local community identifica
tion, extent of kinship ties, child-rearing practices, and patterns o*
courtship.

As a tool for urban subarea field studies, the typology serve*
a number of functions:

a. The typology can be used in the selection of neighborhood
for intensive study. In the examples given, census tracts were se
lected that had particular economic, family, and ethnic characteris
tics. As an aid to sampling, the typology allows the research worke*
to select urban subcommunities for intensive study on the basi*
of informed judgment concerning the social positions of the subcom*
munities in the larger urban area.

b. The typology provides an integrative frame for urban sub
community field studies by codifying a large mass of ordered dat*
In the Bell and Greer studies, the relationships are indicated be
tween particular census tracts and all other tracts of the sam*
city with respect to economic, family, and ethnic status. In addi
tion, the analysis of social participation and isolation betwee*

[61] Walter Firey, "Sentiment and Symbolism as Ecological Variables," *Ame*
ican Sociological Review, vol. 10 (April, 1945), pp. 140–148.

neighborhoods becomes possible in terms of economic and family status when ethnic status is held constant in Bell's study and in terms of family status when economic and ethnic status is held constant in Greer's study. This procedure of controlling variables permits studies of the importance of a given characteristic.

c. The typology permits the investigation of the combined or independent effect of personal and unit characteristics on dependent variables. The characteristics of a neighborhood may be related to the behavior or the attitudes of individuals. In the example given, men living in high economic status neighborhoods were more frequent attenders of formal association meetings than men living in low economic status neighborhoods, even though their personal economic characteristics varied. It was suggested that the economic character of a neighborhood population as a unit may be an important indicator of the economic group to which those living in the neighborhood identify themselves, and this may provide a set of expectations with regard to associational behavior for the residents. The relationships between neighborhood characteristics and individual behaviors and attitudes will be an important subject for future research.[62]

Finally, much more empirical work and additional thinking will undoubtedly result in refinements or elaborations of the method, but an appraisal of the work accomplished to date and the uses so far made of the social area method permit the tentative substantiation of claims made for it:

1. It is simple in statement.
2. It serves as an organizing principle.
3. It is theory-linked; it permits the derivation of testable propositions.
4. It is precise in its specifications; it permits observer agreement.
5. It represents a continuity with similar formulations which it aims to replace.[63]

[62] For an elaboration of these methodological features see Wendell Bell, "The Utility of the Shevky Typology for the Design of Urban Subarea Field Studies," *Journal of Social Psychology*, vol. 47 (February, 1958), pp. 71–83.

[63] Shevky and Bell, *op. cit.*, p. 59.

COMPUTATION OF THE INDEXES OF ECONOMIC,
FAMILY, AND ETHNIC STATUS

The procedures for the computation of the indexes of economic, family
and ethnic status are given in this section. The ratios for each variable
are computed directly from census tract statistics, and the standard scores
for the variables from the formulas given. All of the variables composing
the indexes of economic and family status have been standardized to
their respective ranges in Los Angeles as of 1940. A single scale is thus
established for the direct comparison of census tract scores on the re
spective indexes for different cities at the same time or the same city a
different times. The range, lower limit, and conversion factor are given
for each variable for Los Angeles, 1940. The index of ethnic status, o
course, is comparable from place to place and time to time since it is a
simple percentage.

A. The formula for standardization:

$$s = x(r - o)$$

where

    s = standardized score for a particular variable

    o = lower limit of the census tract ratio for a particular
         variable

    r = census tract ratio for a particular variable

    $x = \dfrac{100}{\text{range of the ratio for a particular variable}}$

B. For those variables (occupation, education, and women in the
labor force) which have an inverse relation to the basic indexe
for which they are computed, the formula is adjusted to read a
as follows:

$$s = 100 - [x(r - o)]$$

C. Index of Economic Status

    1. Compute the following ratios:

        a. Occupation ratio—the total number of craftsmen . . .
            operatives . . . , and laborers . . . per 1,000 employe
            persons.

        b. Education ratio—the number of persons who have com
            pleted no more than grade school per 1,000 persons 2
            years old and over.

    2. Compute occupation and education standard scores using th
         formula given in B above and the conversion factors (x) give
         in F below.

    3. Compute a simple average of the occupation and education standard scores. The average is the index of economic status for a census tract.

D. Index of Family Status

    1. Compute the following ratios:

      a. Fertility ratio—the number of children under 5 years per 1,000 females age 15 through 44.

      b. Women in the labor force ratio—the number of females in the labor force per 1,000 females 14 years old and over.

      c. Single-family detached dwelling units ratio—the number of single-family dwelling units per 1,000 dwelling units of all types.

    2. Compute the fertility and single-family dwelling unit standard scores from the formula given in A above and the conversion factors (x) given in F below.

    3. Compute the women in the labor force standard score using formula given in B above and conversion factor (x) given in F below.

    4. Compute a simple average of the fertility, women in the labor force, and single-family dwelling units standard scores. The average is the Index of Family Status for a census tract.

E. Index of Ethnic Status [a]

    1. Add the number of persons designated Negro; Other Races; and foreign-born white from Poland, Czechoslovakia, Hungary, Yugoslavia, U.S.S.R., Lithuania, Finland, Rumania, Greece, Italy, Other Europe,[b] Asia, French Canada, Mexico, and Other America.[c]

    2. Divide the above sum by the total population in each tract.

[a] Categories are for 1950 only, see Eshref Shevky and Wendell Bell, *Social Area Analysis* (Stanford: Stanford University Press, 1955), p. 57 for 1940 categories.

[b] Include foreign-born white from Other Europe only if the category contains mostly foreign-born white from southern and eastern Europe.

[c] For urban areas in Arizona, California, Colorado, New Mexico, and Texas the number of white persons with Spanish surnames can be used instead of the number of foreign-born white from Mexico and Other America. A special tabulation must be requested to obtain Spanish surname data for each census tract. For these states the figures given for native whites should be adjusted by subtracting the number of native whites with Spanish surnames from the total number of native whites in each tract.

3. Multiply the above quotient by 100 to obtain the Index of Ethnic Status for each census tract.[d]

F. The range, the lower limit of the range, and the conversion factor (x) for each of the ratios for the Los Angeles area, 1940, are as follows:

RATIO	RANGE	LOWER LIMIT (o)	CONVERSION FACTOR (x)
Occupation	748	0	.1336898
Education	770	130	.1298701
Fertility	602	9	.1661130
Women in the labor force	458	86	.2183406
Single-family dwelling units	994	6	.1006441

[d] Separate the census tracts into two groups on the basis of their scores on the index of ethnic status. Select as the cutting point the per cent of the total population of the urban area represented by the combined racial and nationality groups listed. Those tracts having more than the average proportion of the combined racial and nationality groups designate as having "high" ethnic status; those tracts having less than the average proportion of the combined racial and nationality groups designate as having "low" ethnic status.

✳ 4. Urbanism and Social Structure: A Los Angeles Study

Scott Greer and Ella Kube

Introduction In the previous chapter the theory and method of classifying urban subpopulations was discussed. In this chapter Professors Greer and Kube investigate the implications of the urbanization index, one of three developed by Professors Bell and Shevky, in a study of social participation in four neighborhoods of Los Angeles. (They use the other indices to "control" variations in the socio-economic rank and ethnicity of the neighborhoods.)

An index is actually a scale, and various positions along it suggest different ways of life. Professors Greer and Kube examine four areas which are similar in socio-economic status and in the absence of large ethnic populations, but vary in "urbanization," that is, the proportion of wives who have outside jobs, the proportion of population living in single family dwellings, and the fertility ratio. The greater the proportion of working wives, the fewer the one-family residences, and the lower the fertility rate, the higher the urbanization score. These three determining factors imply differing "life styles."

Once having determined the variation in urbanization what would you expect to find concerning the social participation of members in each area? As urbanization increases, does isolation and anomie of the individual increase, or does social participation decrease?

This chapter examines the classic theory concerning the relationship

93

between urbanization and the loss of community identity, dependence upon secondary relationships, and the eventual isolation and anomic state for urban residents. However, the quantity of social participation does not vary in a spectacular manner between the four urbanization areas; what is different is the use of different types of social groups and institutional structures for participation. Residents of "high" urbanized areas rely more upon informal groups, kin, and friends and less on institutions, such as the church and fraternal orders, for social participation. Primary relationships according to Greer and Kube are not lost in the large urban society. Have they been "rediscovered," or perhaps were they never lost in the first place, having always existed?

Re-examination of urban theory and family structure in urban society by a growing program of empirical research, of which one illustration is this chapter, suggests revision of old theoretical formulations. The important role of the kin group, friends, and neighbors in the life of the urban dweller is being established. These supportive relationships provide the urban dwellers with the necessary psychological, social, and even economic assistance for sustaining life in our mass society. Professors Greer and Kube demonstrate in a practical manner the utility of the social area analysis in testing basic assumptions concerning social participation in the larger community.

✳ THE HISTORICAL GROWTH of sociology has correlated closely with urban growth, and many of the theoretical and practical problems with which sociologists are concerned result from the force which create great cities. In fields as diverse as demography, social psychology, and industrial sociology, the concepts of the "urban industrial society" and "urbanism as a way of life" are basic to much reasoning and research.

But while interest in urbanism is widespread, there is no general agreement on how it may be studied most profitably. It sometimes is treated as a dependent variable, a result of those vast transformations in the socio-economic system which Wilson and Wilson have termed "increase in scale."[1] It may also be treated as a set of conditions which alter the very nature of man's psychic existence and his self-image—as Simmel and Toennies have done

[1] *The Analysis of Social Change,* G. and M. Wilson (London: Cambridge University Press, 1944).

Or, following Wirth, certain features of large cities may be taken as given—size, density, and heterogeneity—and one may attempt to deduce from them the conditions of social interaction among urban dwellers.[2] It is apparent that the method of study is not dictated by the subject matter (whose nature is largely unknown) but by the particular interests of the investigator.

In this study the writers have been particularly concerned with urbanism as a process which greatly increases variations in social behavior. However, the authors have been less concerned with extreme cases (such as "the gold coast and the slum") than with those variations in way of life which characterize the great middle range of the population. Forgetting, for the moment, the dramatic extremes of urban living, we wish to consider the important differences among the nonethnic population of middle income, occupation, and education.

Such differences are difficult to isolate from the mass data made available by the Bureau of the Census unless one has a clearly defined criterion for selection. One such criterion is that developed by Shevky and Bell (see chapter 3); their work has produced a method of classifying urban subpopulations on three scales, those of social rank (or economic level), segregation (or ethnicity), and urbanization (or familism).[3] The first allows us to place a given neighborhood at one level of socio-economic status according to the occupation and education of the residents; the second allows us to measure the concentration of ethnic populations in the area; the third tells us something about the other variations in "life-style" independent of social rank and segregation.

The urbanization index grew out of various observations of the effects of urbanism upon social structure. As societies become more urban in nature, there is an increase in the individual's dependence upon large formal structures such as the corporation, the state, and other bureaucracies. As this occurs, the family ceases to be a major structure for carrying on productive activity, and its members find employment outside the home. At the same time the absolute values

[2] Louis Wirth, "Urbanism as a Way of Life," *The American Journal of Sociology,* vol. 44 (July, 1938), pp. 1–24.

[3] Eshref Shevky and Wendell Bell, *Social Area Analysis* (Stanford: Stanford University Press, 1955).

of "familism" decline; the procreation of children is no longer considered necessary for every family, but now becomes a matter of personal choice. And, as family values decline and women become employees, the type of dwelling changes; the apartment may better serve the needs of the highly urban family than the detached, single-family dwelling.

Thus the urbanization index is based upon the proportion of women working outside the home, the proportion of the population living in single family dwelling units, and the fertility ratio. The urbanization score is directly proportional to the first and inversely proportional to the latter two components. The index is a rough measure of these three aspects of a population; however, *as an index,* it points toward broader areas of differentiation. Thus, it indicates relative commitment to family and also to neighborhood, local area, and kinship ties. Or, conversely, it points toward the greater involvement of highly urban populations in the larger metropolitan world and lesser dependence upon the neighborhood and other vestiges of primary community.

Historically there has been a strong association between urban growth and decreasing fertility; however, it is doubtful if such an association will continue indefinitely in highly urban societies. Like most projections from past correlations, it is vulnerable to any change in the structure which produced those regularities. And the structure of modern American society is changing basically, producing a world which has never existed before—one in which a surplus of time, energy, and economic value is available to the population as a whole and not to just a small leisure class. It is the authors' belief that this increase in surplus allows an increasing freedom to choose—to vary one's way of life—and that the urbanization index measures an increasingly important dimension of urban society.

Empirically, the index may be thought of as identifying a continuum of life styles in which the relative importance of home, family, and children is one key factor. (The importance of this factor has led Bell to prefer the term "family status" for the index.) At one extreme we may speak of the "urbanism" of the densely inhabited apartment district and, at the other, of the "familism" of the suburbs. The aim of the present study has been to explore the meaning of differences on the urbanization index for social participation.

THE SETTING OF THE STUDY AND
THE STUDY DESIGN

Los Angeles is one of the most telling examples of change in total society and in the nature of cities. A product of twentieth-century technology, it arose in a most unlikely place, violating the rules which have generally governed the location of great cities. On a semi-arid coastal plain, without natural resources other than petroleum and without a harbor, it grew from a city of 200,000 in 1900 to become the nation's third metropolis, an urban complex of some 5,000,000 people, by 1956.

Wealthy, expanding, riding the crest of technological change, it capitalized on such developments as the invention of the movies, television, and radio, the increasing importance of petroleum, the growth of the electronics and aircraft industries, and the demand for consumer goods. At the same time the metropolis experienced a corollary increase in the white-collar occupations. Increase in the professional, semi-professional, and clerical workers necessary to order large-scale enterprise, as well as the sales and service workers for the market, made the work force especially representative of a large-scale and still expanding society. Here, if anywhere, is a modern American city, a place to study the growth of American society and its culture. The meaning of urbanism should become apparent here in the variations of life-styles its residents choose.

With these research objectives in mind, it was necessary to select a number of neighborhoods with varying social characteristics, as measured by the Shevky-Bell indexes. Four were chosen, all within the legal "city" of Los Angeles, all named places, and all at least thirty years old as settled areas. They were chosen so as to have approximately the same socio-economic level, in order that the effects of variation on "urbanization index" scores might be clear. At the same time, they were tracts without large ethnic populations. Approximately a third of the Los Angeles area population is within ten percentile points above or below these sample census tracts in occupational and educational level. This is the great middle range of urban society—neither poor nor rich, a modal population with a modest prosperity. The most highly urban tract is one in central Hollywood, a neighborhood of apartment houses inhabited, not by "stars," but by ordinary working people. The tract more urban than average is called Silver Lake, the tract slightly below average, Eagle Rock, while the tract lowest in urbanism is in Temple City, a suburban settlement in the San Gabriel valley.

In each of the sample tracts an area random sample of dwelling units was selected, and the wife of the head of the house, the female head, or (where there was no family) a randomly chosen female, was interviewed. The total number of interviews was 150 in each tract except Eagle Rock; there it was 162. Eighty-four per cent of the eligible respondents were interviewed, and these interviews are the basis for the data to be reported.

The four areas had similar social rank scores: Temple City and Hollywood had scores of 72, Eagle Rock had a score of 68, and Silver Lake scored 66.[4] Thus there was a variation of only 6 points in social rank among the four areas. They differed sharply, however, on the urbanization index; scores ranged from 26 in Temple City to 36 in Eagle Rock, 55 in Silver Lake, and a high of 80 in Hollywood. None had a concentration of ethnic population above average for the Los Angeles area. They represent the range from the most "familistic" to the most "urban" nonethnic population at middle social rank.

The socio-economic level of the four tracts is about the same, as measured by the Shevky-Bell index. The four samples are also similar, as indicated by the descriptive statistics in table 3. The variation in household income would indicate less wealth in Hollywood, but the average size of household is also smaller there, so that per capita income is similar for the four samples. Temple City and Hollywood, the two extreme tracts on the urbanization index, are slightly higher in social rank than are the middle tracts; the general similarity in socio-economic level is, however, great.

As similar as these samples are in their socio-economic characteristics, they vary widely in the social attributes usually associated with "urbanism as a way of life." In house type, percentage

[4] "Social Area Scores for Los Angeles," Laboratory in Urban Culture, Occidental College, (1954).

Table 3. Selected Characteristics of Four Urban Samples

	HOLLY-WOOD	SILVER LAKE	EAGLE ROCK	TEMPLE CITY
A. Socio-Economic Characteristics				
Occupation: percentage employed residents and husbands in white collar jobs	61.0	56.0	57.5	66.0
Education: percentage residents with some high school	77.6	80.7	86.4	81.3
Household income: percentage under $3,000	25.8	20.7	19.8	21.3
B. Social-Demographic Characteristics				
House type: percentage single family	38.4	51.3	82.7	96.0
Women working: percentage residents employed	51.0	42.0	39.8	26.7
Marital status: percentage single, widowed, or divorced	36.0	25.3	24.7	14.7
Family roles: percentage mother and wife	24.7	38.6	43.8	48.0
Family isolation: percentage single and living without kin	24.0	15.3	12.3	6.7
C. Background Characteristics				
Mobility: percentage living in Los Angeles for 2 years or less	13.2	7.3	8.7	3.3
Regional Origin: percentage whose place of longest residence is the Far-Western states	21.8	32.0	42.2	40.0
Original nationality: percentage whose family was originally from North Europe	68.9	74.7	90.2	90.7

of women working, marital status, and family roles, they differ widely. They differ also, though not so sharply, in mobility—the length of time they have lived in the city—and in their regional origin. Heterogeneity is indicated by the percentage of variation of families whose original nationality was North European. (This is not a direct measure of ethnicity, as this origin may have been many generations in the past.) By these attributes, urbanism increases consistently from Temple City to Eagle Rock to Silver Lake and is most clear-cut in the Hollywood sample. Thus the Shevky-Bell index does isolate populations which vary according to the general notions of increasing urbanism. Once differing population types are isolated, other aspects of social behavior must be investigated—aspects which cannot be derived from mass data.

One approach to social behavior is through the study of interaction, or social participation. The writers chose this approach because, whatever its psychological meaning, participation is a fact of importance in itself, because reported participation may be quantified in a relatively unambiguous manner, and because, no matter how interpreted, participation is factual and unlike attitudes it cannot easily be explained away. The major part of the scheduled interview was devoted to an inventory of the individual's social life; we were interested in where he interacted, with whom, and how often. We measured neighboring, domestic participation, kinship relations, friendship visiting patterns, church participation, and formal organizational participation. We gathered, in fact, a short case history of social involvement. These data were supplemented by items on the respondent's definition of his neighborhood, social class and political behavior, and certain attitude scales.

THE RESEARCH FINDINGS: URBANISM
AND SOCIAL PARTICIPATION

The results will be presented in three contexts: (1) the general frequency of participation in different social relationships among the respondents in each of the four areas, (2) the relative importance of the local area as a social fact in each of the samples, and (3) variations among the four area samples on attributes other than participation.

FREQUENCY OF PARTICIPATION

There was considerable variation among the four areas with respect to participation in both formal and informal social relationships. We shall first consider informal relationships—those existing outside the formal organizational structures. In domestic participation, neighboring, and kinship relations, there were consistent differences between the familistic and the highly urban neighborhoods (See table 4). Eighty-three per cent of the Temple City sample spent three or more evenings a week at home with family members, but only two-thirds of the Hollywood sample did so. Neighboring varied even more; as measured by Wallin's "Neighborliness Scale" only 37 per cent in Hollywood had moderate or high scores, against 62 per cent in Temple City. Kinship participation varied from 64 per cent in Hollywood who visit kin once a month or more to 83 per cent in Temple City. The variation in amount of kin visiting results from the fact that residents of the less urban neighborhoods are more apt to have relations in the metropolitan area. This does not, however, reduce the importance of this variation. The family in-laws and relatives outside the home are less important in the highly urban neighborhoods, while neighboring declines sharply.

There are less striking differences in visits with work associates and other friends. One features of interest, not reported in table 4, is the variation in the proportion of respondents who visit with work associates once a week or more. This increases with urbanization, from 7 per cent in Temple City to 16 per cent in Hollywood. This is partly due to the large number of employed respondents in Hollywood, but when only employed respondents are considered, those who visit with work associates this frequently are 25 per cent of the Hollywood sample and 10 per cent of those in Temple City. One-fourth of the employed Hollywood respondents visit with work associates very frequently.

The amount of visiting with friends who are neither neighbors, relatives, nor work associates is high in all areas; from 70 to 82 per cent visit with such friends at least once a month. Thus in each area a very large majority has close relationships with relatives and with friends, while neighboring, kinship, and domestic participation decrease with urbanism. It is important to note, however, that the percentage of persons totally isolated from informal relationships was almost nonexistent.

Turning now to participation in formal organizations, we find the same tendencies toward increasing participation in the less highly urban neighborhoods. Church participation increases from 36 per cent to just over one half, and participation in other formal organizations increases from 40 per cent in Hollywood to 60 per cent in Temple City. Thus a slight majority in Temple City participates in formal organizations, as against a substantial minority in Hollywood.

Many of these respondents only belong to one organization in which they actively participate. It is important, then, to consider the "joiners" who participate in two or more organizations other than church. This class increases from 13 per cent in the Hollywood sample to 35 per cent in Temple City, with Silver Lake and Eagle Rock falling between.

Some data are available on the formal participation of the respondents' husbands. In general, the difference between areas is consistent with the findings for the respondents; however, the husbands belong less frequently to churches and participate less in churches, while they are more apt to belong to other formal organizations in all areas excepting Temple City. In this area husbands and wives have similar participation rates in clubs and other organizations.

THE LOCAL AREA AS A "SOCIAL FACT"

An important notion in the study of urban society is that the local area is becoming less important. Briefly stated, the hypothesis is that as functions become organized as segments in large formal structures, the local area in the metropolis ceases to be the basis for meaningful interaction among its residents and becomes instead a mere spatial location. Residential areas become dormitory districts and not in any sense communities. Yet many observers have noted the existence within large urban complexes of highly individual "named places." These may be survivals of earlier conditions, or they may have a contemporary reason for existence. In order to test the present importance of the four named places studied here the authors have relied upon several measures: the location of important groups in the local area, informal interaction in the area, access to communications and information concerning the area, and the residents' definitions of the area.

Table 4.   The Social Participation of Four Urban Samples

	HOLLY-WOOD	SILVER LAKE	EAGLE ROCK	TEMPLE CITY
A. Informal Participation				
Domestic: percentage spending three or more evening a week at home with others	67.0	72.0	77.0	83.0
Neighboring: percentage with moderate to high neighborliness scores	37.4	40.0	50.0	62.0
Kinship: percentage visiting relatives once a month or more	64.6	73.3	72.3	83.3
Work associates: percentage visiting once a month or more	28.0	37.3	28.9	32.0
Other friends: percentage visiting once a month or more	74.7	70.6	76.6	82.0
B. Formal Participation				
Church: percentage attending once a month or more	35.9	34.6	40.4	50.6
Clubs and organizations: percentage who belong and attend	40.0	40.0	51.0	60.0

The location of groups in the area.   There is a consistent tendency for the proportion of respondents participating in local groups to decline as urbanism increases. This is accompanied by a decreasing participation in groups whose members are chiefly local residents. At the same time, the proportion attending local churches declines while the proportion of respondents attending churches where they see neither friends, relatives, nor neighbors increases. One-fourth of the Hollywood church-goers attend churches where they have no other social relationship with any of those present.

The importance of local organizations in some urban areas is clear when it is noted that the 150 Temple City respondents belong to and participate in 111 organizations besides church which meet in Temple City. In contrast, the Hollywood respondents belong to 53 local organizations (still a surprisingly large number, until it is remembered that Hollywood is many times as large as any

Community Analysis

of the other "named places"; this inflates the importance of the immediate locale for these respondents' answers).

Table 5. Measures of Community in Four Urban Area Samples

	HOLLY-WOOD	SILVER LAKE	EAGLE ROCK	TEMPLE CITY
A. Social Relationships				
Local groups: percentage who belong to any meeting locally	18.0	19.0	36.0	46.0
Local groups: percentage who belong to any with all local members	16.0	10.0	32.0	42.0
Local churches: percentage who attend	21.0	17.0	29.0	39.0
Local friends: percentage who visit once a month or more with at least one local friend	46.0	29.0	51.0	46.0
B. Information about the area				
Community press: percentage of readers	60.0	66.7	78.9	78.0
Local leaders: percentage naming one or more	14.0	21.3	31.7	26.7
C. Definition of the area				
Preference: percentage preferring other areas for residence	54.0	51.0	37.0	25.0
Felt permanence: percentage expecting to live there "more than ten years" or "all my life"	48.7	62.7	70.8	70.0
Satisfaction: percentage who like living in the area	85.0	87.0	84.0	97.0

Informal interaction in the area. The clear and consistent decrease in neighboring as the neighborhood becomes more urban has already been noted. About one-third of the Hollywood respondents are "neighbors" in a meaningful sense, as against some two-thirds of those in Temple City. Close friendship, however, does not follow this pattern. There is very little difference between Hollywood and Temple City in the proportion having friends in the area. (A check of the friends' addresses indicates that the size of the Hollywood area does not determine this.) Thus close friendship does not follow the pattern of neighboring; it is freer of spatial limitations and allows greater choice.

ACCESS TO COMMUNICATION CHANNELS IN THE AREA

One important communications channel is formal organizations, and we have indicated that participation in local organizations varies consistently with type of neighborhood. Another important channel is neighboring. However, a third channel of considerable importance is the local community press; Janowitz has made clear the power it has in creating social bonds in local areas.[5] In Hollywood 60 per cent read the community paper, two-thirds of the Silver Lake sample did so, whereas just under 80 per cent were readers in Eagle Rock and Temple City.

One measure of effective communications is the ability to name "local leaders." This varied considerably; fourteen per cent in Hollywood could name at least one leader, as against 32 per cent in Eagle Rock and 27 per cent in Temple City. (When controlled for length of residence, the percentage naming leaders was about the same for the two latter areas.) Few women in any area could name local leaders, but the percentage who could was twice as high in Temple City as in Hollywood. The ability to name two or more leaders declines consistently, from 17 per cent in Temple City to less than 5 per cent in Hollywood. In contrast there was no significant difference in ability to name leaders of the metropolitan area as a whole. Roughly 40 per cent in each area could name such men.

THE RESPONDENT'S DEFINITION OF THE LOCAL AREA

Here the respondent made evaluative judgments of the area. When asked if "there is any neighborhood in which you would rather live than here," 54 per cent of the Hollywood sample said "Yes," as against one-fourth of the Temple City respondents. (See table 4) Preference for other areas is related to length of residence, for the area tends to keep as long-time residents those who like it;

[5] Morris Janowitz, *The Community Press in an Urban Setting* (Glencoe, Ill.: The Free Press, 1952).

still, when length of residence in the area is controlled, the residents of highly urban neighborhoods consistently prefer other areas more frequently than do those of the familistic neighborhoods.

When the respondents were asked how long they expected to live in the area, those who expected to stay less than one year increased from 9 per cent in Temple City to 23 per cent in Hollywood. Those who expected to stay more than ten years or all their lives decreased from 70 per cent in the suburban areas to 48 per cent in Hollywood.

While these samples show great variation in their degree of "felt permanence" in the local area, there is little difference in the percentage saying that, in general, they like living where they are. Eighty-four per cent or more agreed in all areas.

In summary, these sharp variations in localism indicate that the disappearance of the "local community" and neighborhood in the city is far from complete. It is most nearly true in the highly urban area, but in those neighborhoods characterized by familism there is considerable vitality in local associations. This is evident in neighboring, local organization and church participation, readership of the local community press, and ability to name local leaders. It is accompanied by an attitude of commitment to the area as "home"—a place from which one does not want or expect to move. In participation and in felt permanence, the highly urban areas had a much weaker hold on their residents.

URBANISM AND ANOMIE

It is often assumed of urban man that he is "anomic," that as he loses his primary group ties in the neighborhood, the extended family, the local community, and other structures characteristic of rural society, he ceases to be identified with the social whole and is, at the same time, less controlled by the norms of his society. Such theorists as Durkheim, Ortega, and Sorokin have emphasized the isolation and malaise of modern urban life; they have been echoed in general sociological thinking, particularly in the field of social organization.

If it has been demonstrated that the four neighborhoods studied do include representative urban social types, of which the Hollywood sample is the most characteristically "urban," then a test of these hypotheses is possible. The authors have used Srole's anomie scale to make such a test. The scale includes five questions measuring such things as confidence in the future and in one's fellow man.[6] We have grouped the respondents into three types on the basis of total scores; these are the "anomics," the "semi-anomics," and the "nonanomics." The distribution of each type in the four areas is shown in table 6.

Though the differences in the percentage of "anomics" are not significant, there are important variations in the percentage of the "nonanomics." However, there is no consistent trend apparent; while Temple City has the highest percentage of nonanomic respondents and Hollywood the lowest, Eagle Rock is nearly as low as Hollywood and Silver Lake almost as high as Temple City. The percentage of "anomics" is very low in each area.

Certain alternative hypotheses were tested, for it is possible that there is sufficient variation in the samples on other grounds to explain differences in anomie scores. The distributions of anomie scores were examined, with nationality background, occupational status, educational level and income being held constant. There was no significant difference between respondents with North European and non-North European background. When respondents were divided into those who are employed and those not employed, there was no difference in anomic responses in any area excepting in Hollywood; in that area, where half the women are employed, those who are working are significantly less likely to be anomic. This would suggest that the neighborhood is much better adapted to the needs of the employed woman than to the housewife; the latter does not participate in the larger world of occupations, and she cannot participate in the smaller world of the neighborhood.

When the sample was divided by the occupational class of the head of the household (using the respondent's own occupation when she had no husband) consistent differences occurred between the "white-collar" and the "blue-collar" households. For each urban area the percentage giving nonanomic responses is higher

[6] We are indebted to Leo Srole for an early opportunity to use the scale, (letter, Srole, 1953). See Srole, "Social Dysfunction, Personality, and Social Distance Attitudes," paper read before the American Sociological Society, Chicago (1951).

in the white-collar group. There is also a consistent association between education and anomie scores. In each area, anomie decreases as educational level goes up. And for the combined sample, one-fifth of those with grammar school education are anomic; ten per cent of those with some high school are anomic; only 4 per cent of those with some college are anomic. The percentage *nonanomic* increases from 35 per cent to 63 per cent to 79 per cent for the same educational classes. The trend indicated for occupational and educational level is equally clear with respect to household income level. When the sample is divided into income groups of under $3,000, $3,000 to $4,999, and $5,000 or over per annum, the percentage giving nonanomic responses increases by striking and statistically significant degrees at each higher level.

Table 6.   Anomie in Four Urban Samples

	HOLLY-WOOD	SILVER LAKE	EAGLE ROCK	TEMPLE CITY
A. Distribution of Anomie Scores				
Percentage anomic	12.5	12.0	8.6	8.7
Percentage semi-anomic	30.5	22.0	31.7	23.0
Percentage nonanomic	57.0	66.0	59.0	67.0
B. Socio-Economic Status and Anomie				
Low occupation: percentage non-anomic in blue-collar households	50.0	61.0	53.0	59.0
Low education: percentage non-anomic with less than H.S. education	27.0	45.0	32.0	36.0
Low income: percentage nonanomic with income under $3,000	41.0	39.0	37.0	50.0

In summary anomic or nonanomic attitudes do not seem to vary consistently with the character of the urban neighborhood as measured by the Shevky-Bell index of urbanization. Nor do they vary with nationality background. However, they do vary consistently and significantly with each of the conventional measures of socio-economic status, for the sample combined and for each area separately. The anomic respondents are those with low occupational and educational levels and low family incomes; this indicates that for this kind of a population anomie is chiefly the result of social class and perhaps economic frustration.

While anomie does have meaning in relation to these measures of socio-economic status, it must be noted that the proportion of extremely anomic respondents is quite low in each area and for the entire sample is only slightly above 10 per cent. The highest proportion is in Hollywood (one-eighth), and the lowest, in Eagle Rock, is one-twelfth of the total.

SUMMARY AND INTERPRETATION

At many levels of social participation there are striking differences in the ways of life found in the familistic suburban areas and the highly urban apartment house district. As urbanism increases, neighboring declines, as does domestic social participation. There is a similar decrease in church participation, membership, and attendance at the meetings of formal organizations and in multiple membership in formal organizations.

Yet certain types of interaction, while decreasing as the area becomes more typically urban, have a considerable stability at the middle social rank. These include the extreme importance of kinship and friendship in all areas. And, as participation in voluntary formal organizations is lowest in the highly urban area, such organizations are also much less important as frameworks within which friendship develops. Almost half of the friends in the Hollywood sample were met outside of organizations, work, the neighborhood, churches, or clubs. Forty-seven per cent of all friends were met in this way, compared to 32 per cent in Silver Lake, 25 per cent in Eagle Rock, and only 21 per cent in Temple City. It is in small, intimate circles, through relatives, other friends, or childhood friends, that the highly urban sample meets half of its friends.

Much of urban sociology theory has postulated an increasing importance for formal, voluntary organizations with increasing urbanism, and a decrease in intimate, primary relationships. Our data indicate the exact opposite occurs within the metropolitan area; as the neighborhood grows more characteristically urban,

friendship and kinship become a larger proportion of *all* social interaction. This is, perhaps, largely by default; organizations and
churches have a shrinking active membership as populations become more typically urban. At any rate, the association of individuals is more predominantly informal and moves more often
through personal channels. The formal structure of society affects
such populations chiefly through work, the market, and commercialized play. Yet they are isolated, not from other people, but from
groups larger and more formal than "social circles."

It is our present hypothesis that the more "urban" an area the
less important are formal voluntary organizations and the more
important are informal, face-to-face primary relations. Such primary
relations are less often created through residential contacts or formal organizations and are more apt to be the result of choice.
Such relationships may be more truly "primary" in nature than
are those which result from the ascribed ties of kinship, neighborliness, or peer group membership.

There is slight variation in anomic respondents among the four
urban areas, and it is not consistently related to urbanism. In general, the anomie scores were remarkably similar and low in all
areas. (Only among respondents with low education, occupation
and income levels was anomie high.) It is possible that primary
relations compensate for whatever loss of "community" occurs in
the highly urban neighborhoods. If Srole's scale is a valid measure,
the inhabitants of Central Hollywood are not unusually disor-
ganized or demoralized personally; nor are they socially disor-
ganized. They are merely organized in different ways.

Another focus in this study was upon the local areas as communities. In general, the findings indicate that the more familistic
areas tend to recreate a meaningful local community in the midst
of the great urban complex. Such a community is a product of
various factors. Individuals are originally attracted to an area by
a wide range of considerations, yet an area selected tends to result
in a relatively homogeneous population. The residents may share
common interests and commitments (home ownership, with all that
it entails, children and all they entail) and just from living closely
together people may form associations which bind them together
socially. These associations limit and control the individual, and

to the outsider searching for a home they seem to affect the character of the neighborhood.

The highly urban apartment house area attracts other types of people—on other grounds. Such individuals lack common interests and commitments and, particularly, any commitment to the local area as "home." Though all of the population in Hollywood did not fit this pattern, a sufficiently large proportion who do so may prevent the "good neighbors" from interacting. This may be illustrated by an interesting finding on "neighborliness."

Less neighboring would be expected for employed respondents than for those who were housewives and mothers and, in general, the employed respondents had low neighboring scores (a majority in all areas, from 55 per cent in Temple City to 71 per cent in Silver Lake). Perhaps more important, however, is the variation in the neighborliness of those who did not work. The percentage with low scores increased spectacularly, from 32 per cent in Temple City to 41 per cent in Eagle Rock, 52 per cent in Silver Lake and 63 per cent in Hollywood. In Hollywood the employed respondents neighbored as much as those who stayed at home.

Our interpretation is as follows: as employed women become a larger proportion of the total female population the opportunities for neighboring decline. Since they typically neighbor less than those not employed, the woman who wishes to neighbor in a highly urban area simply has no opportunities to do so. Thus the particular distribution and location of given population types in an area also set limits on the kinds of interaction possible in the area.[7]

In conclusion we may ask why, in view of the data reported, so many writers have emphasized the isolation and anomie of the urban individual, his reliance upon secondary relationships, and his loss of community. Why has the urbanite been pictured as a lost individual, a particle in a social "dust heap"?

One answer might be based on time lag; much of the theory of urban society derives from work done around the turn of the century by Toennies, Durkheim, and Simmel. Perhaps things were

[7] Similar limits result for the play of children; over twice as many of the women with children in Hollywood as in Temple City say their children do not play with any children in the neighborhood. The opportunities (i.e., presence of other children) do not exist.

different then, and the urban individual was an isolate. Sociology, like the French generals, typically fights the last war and describes a world that existed thirty or forty years ago.

However, we doubt that such conditions ever prevailed for the great bulk of urban dwellers. We suggest that the traditional picture of urban life, glamorous and dramatic as it has been, has been based upon small and highly biased samples. Those who studied "urbanism" in the past looked, usually, for the striking example, "the gold coast and the slum," the "ghetto" and the "hobohemia." Such areas and their populations constitute a very small portion of the people in a great urban center; Zorbaugh's study area was considerably less than one-twentieth of the Chicago area at the time and very unrepresentative of the rest. Furthermore, such studies have generally confused "urbanism as a way of life" with "poverty as a way of life," "wealth as a way of life," or "ethnic identity" as a way of life.

When one separates these dimensions, as Shevky and Bell have done, into socio-economic rank, ethnicity, *and* other variations in a way of life, it becomes apparent that our notions of urbanism have rested upon an unanalyzed abstraction. In general, we suspect that the "anomie" of the urban dweller is the complaint of the poor and ethnic urban dweller; individualism, a luxury of the wealthy and of students not in the labor force. The mosaic of worlds which "touch but do not interpenetrate" is probably a much more complex fabric than has been thought. The evidence from this study of four middle rank, nonethnic areas in Los Angeles indicates that "style of life" varies widely even at the same social, economic, and family levels. Furthermore, the populations we have studied, while duller, are more recognizably human than the denizens of the urban world as they appeared to earlier scholars.[8]

[8] The study was carried out through the Laboratory in Urban Culture, a research facility of Occidental College, with the support of the John Randolph Haynes and Dora Haynes Foundation. A fuller report of the findings is presented in *Urban Worlds: A Comparative Study of Four Los Angeles Areas,* Occidental College (1955).

Community Development

* 5. The Developmental Concept

William W. Biddle

Introduction The majority of studies you have read in this volume whether concerned with community typologies, methods of study, change, or case histories are descriptive of what are or were the conditions of community life at a given point in time or over a long time period. Writers of these chapters have attempted to present factual analyses of community structures and processes. Once this objective has been achieved, the question is then raised: how are the research findings to be used and by whom? The researcher is often off working on another project; the use of his research findings as an action program is ancillary to his principal objectives of descriptive or experimental research. Moreover, for this type of community expert, objectives implying action or improvement of community life are contrary to the standards he and his colleagues have created for promoting and guiding their work.

In recent years a new type of community expert has appeared on the scene. He is less concerned about definitions or orthodoxies and more concerned about human problems. His principal objective is to facilitate the growth and maturity of the individual within the setting of the community. Individual autonomy and creativity are to be developed because the basis of a free democratic society lies in the actions of independent thinking citizens.

Dr. William W. Biddle, the author of the next chapter, is one of the major proponents of the community development approach. He argues that the purposes of community study are for the ultimate goal of stimulating improvement in people by bringing improvement in community life. Improvements result when individuals can "grow" to their problems and

115·

eventually solve them with the advice, enthusiasm, and help of the community expert. Since the development expert is concerned about change, he can avoid the debates on terms or concepts and utilize the approaches or techniques from many disciplines which are best suited to his objective of community betterment.

Dr. Biddle elaborates the developmental concept both in its theoretical and applied aspects. He gives us a vivid description of how Laurel, a small "bedroom" community, "lifted itself by its bootstraps" and developed from a listless and decaying community to an energetic, optimistic, responsible one. In the creation of this new community "look" the expert consulted, sometimes cajoled, but never led. He was a stimulator of change. In time members of the community grew to the responsibility of freedom and helped themselves.

One important observation Dr. Biddle makes is that the developmental approach is not only for "sick" communities, those with severe problems, but it is also useful for "well" or "just normal" communities with less severe or fewer problems. Community development as practiced by Dr. Biddle and others at the present time is essentially a happy marriage between members of a community who have problems and a *desire* to solve them but little "know-how" and the expert who has a desire to be of service and has the know-how and functions in the role of a "community psychiatrist." It will be interesting to learn as the number of community development projects are completed, whether the community-development expert relationship can be severed, and at what point in the cooperative process, without resulting in community regression to old ways or a leveling off in community improvement.

✳ COMMUNITY EXPERTS frequently disagree with each other about the nature of their work. Their differences grow, in part, out of the different communities with which each deals. Even more they grow out of discrepancy in purpose, avowed or tacit.

If the major purpose is descriptive, the end product sought is a monograph, a report, a scientific theory, an analysis of facts and relationships. If the major purpose is developmental, the end desired is an improvement in physical facilities, in human relationships, in people themselves. The first is essentially static, the second essentially dynamic. The two purposes are not mutually exclusive; they are the extremes in the range of objectives common to most students of the community. Ideally the two objectives support each other, but any expert will tend to stress one more than the other.

The static descriptive approach fits more readily into the impersonal objectivity of traditional science. By this approach the social scientist is content to analyze that which exists, and he takes no responsibility for present conditions or future possibilities. The developmental approach is normative; that is, it advances certain values. According to this position the social scientist accepts responsibility to encourage adoption of values he prefers (and the people involved prefer). Part of his objectivity consists in making clear to all concerned the values he pursues and the methods he uses.

The first approach, applied to community phenomena, places much stress upon definition and examination of the characteristics of current organized social life. The second places stress upon change and growth toward or away from chosen objectives. It is possible to work within the first concept without reference to the second, and there are many social scientists who do so. However, those interested in community development cannot make use of the second concept without reference to the first.

Otto G. Hoiberg, in the next chapter, makes clear the function of the social scientist who is interested in community development. In addition to being an observer and collector and supplier of useful information, he must be an educator. That is, he must accept a responsibility for guiding growth.

THE UNIT OF OPERATION

General acceptance of the developmental approach would provide a basis for settling a number of the wrangles that have prevented cooperation among community experts. Among these is the dispute over the size and kind of accumulation of people which can be accepted as *a* or *the* characteristic community. As soon as community experts realize that in the matter of abstract definition the differences of opinion can be endless and the experts set forth as a major objective the growth of people in self-directing responsibility, the local unit of operation can be chosen in practical situations. The theoretical definition then can follow, as it should, upon the field practice.

The question of numbers can turn then from the problem of whether *the* community is represented by a rural hamlet of hundreds or a metropolis of millions to the search for an actual unit of operation that is small enough to allow concentration upon development of individuals. Such smaller aggregations can become a base. They may be pyramided up to any huge numbers as long as their special identity is maintained. Similarly, the geographic size of a unit and the social distance of citizens from each other must enter into the choice of a basic operating unit. Citizens themselves by their actions (spontaneous or encouraged) help to choose those associations through which they can grow.

The developmental concept also tends to keep the operator or theorist from preoccupation with one particular kind of community. American experts, for example, are prone to base their conclusions upon examination of towns or cities in a highly industrialized society, dominated by a middle class.[1] In the total of historical or contemporary times, such a limitation excludes the major portion of men's experience with local collective life. If every community be looked upon as a social atmosphere contributing to individual growth of some sort, no aggregation of humanity is excluded. Every place of human residence comes under scrutiny of the social scientist bent upon improvement.

If the complete gamut of local experience be accepted as opportunity for action, community development becomes a new discipline or skill available to social scientists. It is an active more than a purely investigative discipline, an illustrative example of "action-research." It seeks to form conclusions about human beings by observing their growth as they attempt to accomplish things. It seeks improvement of living conditions, not merely for the material benefit which higher standards will allow but even more for the strengthening of personalities which improvement will induce.

A community is looked upon not just as "something there" to be described, but as an instrument for encouraging the growth

[1] The Subcommittee on Community Development and Research of the Society for the Study of Social Problems makes "a small, homogeneous, stable community, with a large proportion of middle- and upper-class inhabitants" optimal for its research.

of citizens. The objective of individual growth is an increasingly competent, freely chosen responsibility. This value is obviously applicable to every economic and social level. In fact, some critics would insist that the need for personal growth is as great in privileged America as in the clearly underprivileged lands.

Why the emphasis upon increase of individual autonomy? Because the experience of community can be, and has at times, been used to enforce a slavish conformity. Community can become the local instrument of dictatorship. Individual growth can be either toward enslavement or toward greater freedom. An exclusive emphasis upon physical improvements, higher standards of living, even upon improved social relations, if imposed by authority, can result in increased regimentation of the individual. The new discipline of community development, in a free society, must point toward greater self-directing autonomy for the individual citizen.

Various practitioners of the new discipline are developing techniques which are applicable to a wide variety of local situations. Some methods are suitable for tribal communities and villages which are just entering into literacy and the first feeble beginnings of modern thinking.[2] Some others are suitable for agricultural settlements or open rural situations in the United States or other countries.[3] Some are adapted to the smaller urban centers of a decentralized industrial America,[4] while others are best suited for the neighborhoods and suburbs of cities.[5] Still others are appropriate for the complicated problems of a great metropolis.[6]

[2] See the publications of the International Cooperation Administration, Washington 25, D.C. Especially *Community Development Programs*, Team I, II and III (1955).

[3] Baker Brownell, *The Human Community* (New York: Harper & Brothers, 1951). Otto Hoiberg, *Exploring the Small Community* (Lincoln, Neb.: University of Nebraska Press, 1955). Richard Poston, *Small Town Renaissance* (New York: Harper & Brothers, 1950).

[4] H. Clay Tate, *Building a Better Home Town* (New York: Harper & Brothers, 1953). William W. Biddle, *The Cultivation of Community Leaders* (New York: Harper & Brothers, 1953). Jean and Jesse Ogden, *Small Communities in Action* (New York: Harper & Brothers, 1956).

[5] Clyde E. Murray, *Group Work in Community Life* (New York: Association Press, 1954). Clyde E. and Janet Murray, *Guide Lines for Group Leaders* (New York: Whiteside, Inc., 1954).

[6] See publications of American Society of Planning Officials, 1313 E. 16th St., Chicago 37, Ill.; Arthur Hillman, *Community Organization and Planning*

Are there common factors of human development to be found in many or most local situations? Possibly there are, but more action-research experience must accumulate before generalization can be made with assurance. Certainly no formula-like approach is possible for the enormous variety to be found in communities even those within a single culture. But fundamental principles o growth may be found applicable for all human beings in loca action.

AN EDUCATIVE COMMUNITY

When a social scientist thinks of himself as an educator, a Hoiberg says, he finds that communities can be used as educative instruments. Such communities can seldom be assumed to exis ready for the expert to utilize. Rather a geographic accumulation of people must be rendered educative; steps must be taken to create an atmosphere congenial to the type of individual growth sought. The teacher must help to create and maintain his "school." The analogy with a classroom ends here, however, for the problem is to create an atmosphere of growth without dominating it.

An educative community is not one filled with instruction. I is one that is in development, in action, that is achieving its goals Citizens grow as they contribute to improvement of their life to gether. They are not just recipient beneficiaries of learning passed on to them. They are rather participating contributors to their own growth.

The following example will serve as an illustration of a com munity that achieved an atmosphere of growth.

Laurel, Indiana, is a small town which with aid from a neigh boring college moved in three years from discouragement and economic depression to the vigor of democratically planned achieve ment.

It once represented a very common type of community, a settle ment with inadequate economic support. The town was established almost a century and a quarter ago as a way station upon a canal that was meant to be a main artery of commerce. At one time it was

---

(New York: The Macmillan Co., 1950). For a social work approach see, Mur ray Ross, *Community Organization Theory and Principles* (New York: Harper & Brothers, 1955).

thriving and vigorous, receiving income from stone quarries and
breweries as well as from hotels and other facilities dependent on
the canal. But agricultural production fell off when the original
forest cover was cut and when the thin topsoil on the surrounding
hills eroded away. As railroads superseded transportation by water
and the stone quarries were abandoned in favor of concrete, population and industries departed.

Having few sources of income, the town became a characteristic
"bedroom" community. More and more citizens drove to nearby
cities for paid employment. The distances covered daily ranged
from thirty to eighty miles, round trip. There was no passenger
railroad service, no bus line, no bank, no motion picture theatre,
no doctor, no dentist, no hospital, no drug store, no modern
market. Most serious shopping was done in the cities of employment, the purchases brought home over a narrow and twisting
low-speed road.

When the college became interested, there were no telephones
in the town, no sewage disposal system, no rubbish collection. The
municipally owned water system was in a perilous financial condition due to lack of water meters; a flat rate was charged to all customers, irrespective of amount used.

There were seven churches for a village population of approximately eight hundred. The school building was about forty
years old, much too small for the present population of children
and out of date in many ways; for example, it never possessed inside flush toilets or showers. The overcrowded single building
housed both an elementary and a high school. Both churches and
school served families of the surrounding countryside as well as
townspeople.

For twenty-five years, no town board election had been held.
Vacancies on the self-perpetuating board were filled by appointment, leaving some question as to the legality of the actions taken.
A general atmosphere of discouragement was exaggerated by the
misunderstanding between old families and newcomers locally con-
demned as "Kentuckians." These less popular families from south
of the Ohio River began to come in during the year of the Second
World War. They have continued to come, seeking better economic
opportunity.

The first move toward community awakening was inspired, not

by social scientists, but by a lawyer resident in the nearby count
seat. He had been employed as town attorney for a small retainin
fee. Fearful that the board's actions could be held invalid by court
he urged the holding of a proper election. After some effort he suc
ceeded in persuading the existing board to make the necessary ar
rangements. A new board was finally chosen by electors and in
stalled. The new members, aware of problems, determined to pus
toward improvement.

THE RESPONSIBILITY OF THE EDUCATOR

The college took the initiative to assume some responsibilit
for improvement. It sought the opportunity to work with and inspir
developing citizens, but it did not come upon the scene until in
vited. And it continues to operate only so long as citizens we
come the cooperation of students and professors.

The manner of entry of the social scientist to the local scen
is extremely important. The reason for his being on hand and th
attitudes that develop toward him determine whether or not th
community becomes educative. The educator who arrives to lec
ture or otherwise parade his wisdom will not inspire the necessar
local initiative. The one who comes to encourage search for ar
swers to problems can contribute to citizen self-directed growt
He can make his wisdom and experiences available when neede
to expedite the educative process.

In conversation with the lawyer, college representatives learne
that the village seemed ready to start upon a career of vigorou
change. He encouraged college people to become active. His sug
gestion accorded well with college purposes; there was desire t
find a community in which developmental processes could k
stimulated and studied intensively over a period of several year
The lawyer offered to suggest to the new town board that hel
might be obtained from the college's Program of Community D\
namics upon request. The board welcomed the idea and sent a
invitation to attend an official meeting. College representative
agreed to come to talk things over.

The first meeting attended by students and faculty membe
probably proved disappointing to board members. They listed the

problems in great number. They needed to organize a volunteer fire department and obtain fire-fighting equipment, to set up a new bookkeeping system for the town's finances, to obtain telephone service, and so on. The college people replied by asking for more problems, many beyond the normal interest of a political board. What about the school? What about young people? What were the needs of the churches? They gave no solution to any problem. Instead they insisted that solutions would be found when all citizens began thinking and studying and working together. If the board was willing, the college would undertake to stay with the community for several years, meeting with groups of citizens, contributing information when needed, and offering the muscular enthusiasm of students and the wisdom of faculty when either would prove appropriate. The board agreed to such an arrangement in the name of the community as a whole.

Some information was obtained for the new board on municipal financing, taxation rate, water, and equipment for fire-fighting. But in pursuit of broader problems, college people early recommended formation of committees that would call for participation of citizens beyond the town board. The college hoped for an active project involving many people, one that would introduce personnel from the college favorably to the town as a whole. After weeks of considering suitable projects, the board members decided to rehabilitate two parks. A committee structure was set up. College people met with these committees while continuing to attend board meetings. In discussion, the strategy for the park cleanup was laid out.

On several weekends, citizens of all ages, students, and faculty members came together to work. Local people supplied tools, seeds, plants, lumber, paint, and food and hospitality. College people supplied muscle, ideas, enthusiasm, and confidence. Together, each group stimulated the other. The parks were mowed, replanted, made into pleasant picnic spots. Their upkeep has become a permanent town board responsibility. Money is appropriated for maintenance and the junior class of the high school is employed each year to keep the public property in order.

Residents discovered there was satisfaction in achievement for the common good. Even more, they discovered that they could accomplish beyond their timid fears when they cooperated. With one

solid achievement in memory, they began to look about for som«
larger task. The self-educative process of growth was moving to·
ward the next stage.

THE FIRST MAJOR PROJECT

The first triumph of cooperation was followed by five or si·
months of relative quiet. The town board met in routine fashion·
the recently active committees met hardly at all, but the searcl
for ideas and courage went on in individual conversations. (Suc**
a period of seeming slump often appears in the developmenta·
progress of an educative community.)

Eventually, the big and important project came to the fore·
front of public discussion, the construction of an adequate schoo·
plant. A hope of acquiring decent educational facilities for childre·
had lain dormant in people's minds for years. It was the experienc«
of successful cooperation for the common good that made such a·
ambitious undertaking finally seem feasible. Committee member·
who had been active on the park rehabilitation enterprise now
called for meetings to discuss ways to acquire a better school.

One other event added to an emerging awareness of commo·
loyalty and cooperative progress. This was the acquisition of ·
local telephone system. The lack of telephone service had been ·
matter of concern and worry for many months. It had been dis·
cussed often in town meetings. Eventually a small company sough·
to locate headquarters in the community and operate a new syste·
there. The owners were able to reach citizens rapidly and to ob·
tain subscribers through the instrumentality of the general tow·
meeting which had now become a monthly habit. The telephon«
problem was solved, not as direct result of educative activity in th«
community, but because citizens were already in the process of de·
velopment. (Problems are often solved indirectly when a progres·
sive and problem-solving atmosphere invites positive action.)

The months that followed saw the gradual evolution of an or·
ganization to obtain a new school. The chief difficulty was eco·
nomic. The property value and taxing power of the school distric·
were too small to allow financing by normal methods. Yet citizen·

were determined to work on the problem themselves and refused to seek a gift from state or national treasuries.

The details of organization and reorganization, of collective search for answers, of ultimate solution of apparently insurmountable difficulties, need not be recounted, except as these add to understanding of human development. A widely representative committee was formed for discussion of the problem, and it conducted an open meeting at least once a month. Later this committee set up a citizens' foundation to raise money. The foundation was organized as a legal nonprofit entity to purchase property and to erect a building which could be leased to the school district. Increased taxes, supplemented by state payments for rental of the contemplated adequate facilities, offered one means of liquidating the debt to be incurred. Money raised from gifts and from a multitude of community enterprises was another potential means to reduce the debt and provide funds to purchase furniture and other needed equipment.

No neat formula for progress was available to citizens. Certainly the college people offered no blueprint for solution of problems. The foundation, in numerous town meetings, in many committee sessions, in consultation with lawyers, state authorities, school administrators, citizens from other towns, and builders, worried over problems. In trips to consult those who could help, in study, in discussion, and experiment, they discovered certain ways of progressing toward their goal. Theirs was educational growth through concerned participation.

The social scientists from the college offered suggestions and encouragement; along with citizens, they suffered through the process of learning by seeking a solution to a problem. Yet their quiet confidence in citizens and their persistence offered the necessary impetus to keep the process going.

Plans were drawn up by an architect. They were worked out in consultation with citizens' committees and approved by county and state authorities. As was inevitable, the cost of construction proved to be larger than anticipated. Methods of matching hopes to economic realities had to be explored. Among these was the elimination of some desired facilities. But more important was the reliance upon volunteer work. It was decided that some pre-preparation of the site, inside finishing and painting, furniture making, and landscaping could be carried on by citizens, aided by teams of students from the college. Confidence to entrust such responsibilities to unpaid, though competent, volunteers grew out of the successful experience of cooperation. The reliance upon future continued activity to complete the school made likely the continuation of educative cooperation among citizens.

Still it was necessary to have capital on hand to pay for the minimum contract with a builder. The necessary funds could be obtained by the sale of bonds issued by the foundation. The repayment and interest were assured by income from taxes and state payments. So well planned were the financial arrangements that the bonds were quickly purchased by investors who had confidence in citizens who could grow in responsibility.

The money the foundation collected from first pledges was spent for purchase of land and other early expenditures. It was apparent that money-raising was a problem to be faced month after month for a long period of time. Citizen committees were forced to devise a wide variety of events that would bring in revenue from local people and from outsiders who could be enticed to visit a town-on-the-march. Among the events promoted were community fairs, homecomings, fish fries, and dramatic and musical programs from the school. Some programs proved unsuccessful and were abandoned. Others were successful both in raising finances and in promoting the growth of a town atmosphere of active goodwill and organized purpose.

After many experiences of both frustration and triumph, the building work was begun. Citizens could look forward to completion and to the further work they must carry on in order to realize their plans.

With construction on the new school as a visible achievement certain evidences of citizen progress can be described. First, there was a change in atmosphere from calm acceptance of slow deterioration to determined purpose and expectation of growth. Outsiders visiting the town remarked upon the awakened citizenry as well as upon the physical construction. Second, there was a new oneness of purpose. Factionalism had been replaced with a voluntary unity. Earlier there was opposition, some based upon fear of increased taxation, some upon jealousy of the active leadership. With actual construction under way, opposition had all but disappeared. Difference of opinion remained, but almost all people favored community progress.

Finally, with most of the construction details settled, attention gradually turning toward other problems of general improvement. The citizens were now confident about solving other problems, and thereby further continuation of the educative process was promised. Already proposals have been advanced for a village system of sewage disposal. (A modern school with toilet and shower demands some such installation.) Thought was being given to obtaining a doctor to serve the town and surrounding territory and to the establishment of a drug store. There was also a proposal for securing a bank, possibly a branch of one in a neighboring city.

The change that has occurred in the town atmosphere is obvious enough. The changes to be found in individual citizens are more subtle but more important. In many there is a new maturity, an awareness of collective ability to accomplish tasks formerly regarded as impossible. Citizens have accepted responsibility for problems of increasing complexity. They have found their own unique solution for the most difficult of all, a solution better than either educators or county or state authorities could propose. Because that satisfactory solution was worked out by their own thinking, its achievement contributed to the growth of citizens toward the responsibility of freedom.

The change in citizens is evidence that a community has become educative. Work upon a school building provided the means for development, but not because this great project dealt with an educational matter. Any important task which absorbed the interest and stimulated the energy of citizens could have served the same purpose.

AN EXAMPLE FOR RESEARCH

When a social scientist becomes an educator, he can use a community as the setting for adult development. He becomes less an instructor and more a stimulator of an atmosphere of vigor. His function is not so much to carry information or culture to citizens. It is rather to awaken creativity in them, to stimulate the growth processes which are unique to each location and person. When citizens develop themselves in the process of working toward a common goal, they frequently seek the help which educators can offer. The skillful teacher is the one that stimulates the request and offers aid in response to the felt need.

Such an active stimulative role on the part of the social scientist is necessary if he is to understand and describe human behavior adequately. A static description of homo sapiens as he is misses the most important fact about man under the impact of modern conditions, his dynamic flexibility. His potentialities for growth in desired directions can be discovered only by placing him experimentally within situations that encourage growth to occur. When the changes sought move toward greater individual and collective autonomy, the person must also be a participant director of his own growth. A community is one important social instrument for such experimentation. But it cannot be so used unless the developmental concept becomes more common.

The description given of Laurel's development can be considered an example for research purposes. Many descriptions of a great variety of local experience of development will be necessary. Out of an accumulation of such studies can come a classification of community types and ultimately an analysis of methods for stimulating growth.

* 6. Contributions of the Social Scientist to Community Development

Otto G. Hoiberg

Introduction The age of specialization has meant not only complex communities and occupations but also complex problems. Community problems arose with the growth of urban settlements. In time their complexity necessitated the training of experts to assist in their solution. The solving of problems is not the only function of these experts. Since communities are in need of improvement, these specialists of social science have become concerned with community development. Hence solving problems and improving life within a community go hand in hand.

The expert Professor Hoiberg describes in the next chapter is the social scientist, a person who has knowledge about human behavior and about the structure and organization of society. The social scientist of today is also trained as a researcher, so that he can now gather data for the analysis and solution of problems. Frequently he can determine if a problem exists and if answers to important questions can be obtained by scientific study.

Research is not the only function of the social scientist in community analysis and development. He serves as a consultant, assisting communities in working out their own problems. His fund of experience enables him to diagnose and prescribe treatment for "sick communities." While his percentage of successes may not be equal to that of the medical physician, it is on the increase. Success will depend upon improved understanding of human behavior in all its complexities and varieties. This will come about by more vigorous research.

The social scientist also serves as an educator. This is supplementary to the roles of researcher and consultant. To "sell" his ideas and to help others help themselves he conducts workshops, institutes, conferences, gives short courses in programs designed for the continuing education of adults, and even has entered the media of radio and TV.

Professor Hoiberg amplifies the varied contributions of the specialist social scientist to community development. The tasks the social scientist faces in this area are formidable, but a body of knowledge and experience is being gradually acquired which makes this venturesome occupational role less difficult. Dr. Hoiberg concludes his presentation with an excellent bibliography of materials in the field of community development, a list every student should carefully scrutinize.

✳ COMMUNITY LIFE in early America was characterized by a high degree of self-sufficiency. Problems of group living were numerous and pressing, but most of them were handled locally with a minimum of assistance from outside specialized sources. This self-sufficiency can be explained partly in terms of necessity, for local groups often had nowhere to turn for assistance even when it was needed. The agencies were nonexistent that are now available to help community groups with problems ranging from slum clearance to the planning of neighborhood play areas. More important, perhaps, was the relative simplicity of life itself. Much of the work considered essential was within the competence of local citizens themselves.

As the generations have passed, new needs have arisen and social life has become more complex. The specialist can often help the contemporary community, urban or rural, when it finds itself in difficult situations. One facet of it, traffic congestion, has been called "probably the most serious single problem affecting the future development of cities." [1] It is a problem with many ramifications, and progress toward its solution depends upon contributions

[1] Miles L. Colean, *Renewing Our Cities* (New York: The Twentieth Century Fund, 1953), p. 158.

from sociologists, economists, statisticians, demographers, and political scientists, among others.

The small town likewise finds itself confronted with issues which often require the attention of social scientists. In many such municipalities the merchants have become seriously concerned about the loss of business to larger adjoining trade centers. Why are farmers by-passing their traditional trade centers and now going in considerable numbers to neighboring towns to make purchases? What kinds of goods and services do they buy there? What, if anything, can be done to remedy the situation? Questions such as these are debated perenially by small-town chambers of commerce the nation over, but definitive answers rarely can be reached in the discussion process. Research is needed, and it is the social scientist who is called upon for help.[2]

The open country of rural United States also places increasing reliance upon social scientists in its community improvement efforts. The historic report of Theodore Roosevelt's Commission on Country Life early in the twentieth century pointed up a number of ways in which life on the farm fell short of urban standards. The Commission's findings provided stimulus to rural social research and gave strong impetus to the development of rural sociology as a new discipline. Forward-looking people of rural areas have sensed the relevance of this new body of research data to the problems confronting them. Accentuating their interest in such data have been certain social trends whose impact upon rural social institutions has been felt. To illustrate, one might note how the decline in farm population and the growing tendency of farm people to go to the village for their social, cultural, and religious activities have placed the open-country church in a difficult position. The population base upon which this church can draw for members has dwindled, and even those who have remained on the farms have tended to drop their allegiance to the open-country church in favor of sister institutions in the village. The author was recently approached by a country pastor whose church building would soon have to undergo substantial repairs or be replaced altogether.

[2] See, for example, Edgar Z. Palmer, *Some Economic Problems of Clay Center, Nebraska*, College of Business Administration, The University of Nebraska, Business Research Bulletin No. 54 (1950).

In deciding whether to repair or rebuild, one question was paramount in the pastor's mind: "What is the future of our church?" A rural sociologist can be of immeasurable benefit to a congregation in its effort to find a realistic answer to such a question.

Let us examine a few of the more common activities through which the social scientist makes his professional talents directly or indirectly available to community groups. Initially, it must be emphasized that his fundamental and distinctive function in relation to community improvement lies in his search for truth, as exemplified in the *research* process.

Joseph S. Himes has stated that research can serve five important functions in social planning.[3] In the first place, "research provides the basis for precise and accurate definition of the social problem and the occasion of collective action." This may involve quantitative measurement and objective description, as well as the delineation of social issues and value conflicts and, in general, "gives the instigators of planning a measure of the task at hand . . . and enables the leaders to focus their efforts and gear them to the realities of the problem." Second, research serves "to indicate what can and cannot be done." Many action groups have learned to their dismay that the hunch-method for determining feasibility of community projects leaves something to be desired. Where construction of a new school building is being considered, for instance, an intelligent decision requires objective data regarding population trends in the area. A third service of research is "to indicate the experiences of others in similar situations," and here the case study has proved particularly helpful. Fourth, the researcher can help the social planner by assessing "the resources that may be utilized in carrying out the plan." This has reference not only to physical resources but also to personal and social resources of various kinds which are sometimes difficult for the community leader to identify. Finally, it is a function of research "to define the social unit and geographic area of planning." The social planner must know "the nature, size, and limits of the group or area" involved in any given project if effective implementation is desired.

A description of relevant research activity in the various social

[3] Joseph S. Himes, *Social Planning in America* (Garden City, N.Y.: Doubleday & Company, Inc., 1954), pp. 28–31.

sciences is beyond the scope of this chapter. A brief reference to the general types of community research, however, may be in order.

Four Southern social scientists [4] conceive of the community as having the following principal components—the ecological, the structural, and the action-interactional—and they conclude that these represent an appropriate basis for classification of research in this field. Among classic examples of research in the first (ecological) category, one might mention the development of the "delinquency area" concept by Clifford Shaw and associates in Chicago. In relation to the second (structural) approach, extensive research has been conducted on major institutions such as the family, church, education, government, and a variety of other social groupings, both formal and informal. The third (action-interactional) approach is of relatively recent origin and holds much promise, both from the theoretical and practical viewpoints. It provides for the study of the community as a social system comprising a network of interacting elements.

It is of interest to community leaders that the research work of the social scientist often relates directly to problem areas in which they are interested from the standpoint of community betterment. The findings of researchers in the field of group dynamics, for example, have been put to good use by people seeking to function more effectively and efficiently as groups. Agricultural Extension agents welcome bulletins like "How Farm People Accept New Ideas" [5] which summarizes pertinent research findings from the fields of psychology, sociology, and social psychology. It points out that people go through the following stages in learning about and adopting new ideas: awareness, interest, evaluation, trial, and adoption; and it then goes on to describe the media of communication which are particularly effective at each stage.

Communities contemplating hospital construction projects have found a volume by Professor Paul A. Miller and associates in

[4] Harold F. Kaufman, Willis A. Sutton, Jr., Frank D. Alexander, Allen D. Edwards, *Toward a Delineation of Community Research*, Social Science Research Center, Mississippi State College, Social Science Studies, Community Series No. 4 (1954), p. 3.

[5] Agricultural Extension Service, Iowa State College, North Central Regional Publication No. 1 of the Agricultural Extension Services, Special Report No. 15 (1955).

Michigan helpful.[6] This publication presents the findings of a research project covering 218 successful hospital construction projects supported by the government under the Hill-Burton Act, and it throws much light upon methods of project initiation, difficulties encountered, publicity and educational questions, the use of consultants, fund raising, leadership, and a number of other problems which are characteristic of this type of endeavor. By way of further illustration, reference might be made to a bulletin by Professors King, Pedersen, and Burrus at the University of Mississippi which summarizes and interprets Mississippi population statistics for the benefit of the interested layman. In their introductory statement they "point out a few ways in which population facts have been or could be used in Mississippi to help us understand and solve our problems." [7] They show how such data have been vital to the operation of the Mississippi Commission on Hospital Care, to the completion of studies of the state's highway and school systems, and to the work of the Agricultural and Industrial Board in its efforts to encourage and plan for industrial development in the state.

Noteworthy also is a recent pamphlet describing research on the impact of new industry moving into a rural community.[8] What problems are likely to confront a small town when an industry suddenly appears? Is there apt to be an integration problem between the old residents and the newcomers who arrive with the industry? What are the major sociological factors to be considered in working out an action program to meet new needs? These are typical questions being asked by citizens in numerous communities. This study by Hoffer and Freeman throws substantial light upon such problems, and while it deals with only a single Michigan community Charles P. Loomis points out in the foreword that the "needs for action and the elements of the action which are de-

[6] *Community Health Action* (East Lansing: Michigan State University Press, 1953).

[7] Morton B. King, Jr., Harold A. Pedersen, John N. Burrus, *Mississippi's People, 1950,* Bureau of Public Administration, University of Mississippi, Sociological Study Series, No. 5 (1955), p. 5.

[8] Charles R. Hoffer and Walter Freeman, *Social Action Resulting from Industrial Development,* Department of Anthropology and Sociology, Agricultural Experiment Station, Michigan State University, Special Bulletin 401 (1955).

scribed are typical and tend to occur repeatedly in communities that are adjusting to population growth."

It seems true, as Hertzler states, that the "social sciences, with their data regarding factors, processes, and structures have developed to the point where they can be of considerable assistance" in social planning; but it must also be admitted that they are "still in a relatively nascent stage" and that there remain "serious deficiencies in contemporary social-science research" which must be overcome.[9]

One of the challenging roads ahead lies in interdisciplinary cooperation. The team approach has been tried at Cornell University where specialists from the fields of psychology, sociology, anthropology, psychiatry, and social work have worked together in a joint research operation.[10] A somewhat less formally structured program has been in existence at the University of Nebraska for a number of years. Through the interdisciplinary Council for Community Study, ten departments of the University have coordinated a number of their research activities, concentrating the efforts of both faculty members and graduate students upon selected communities from time to time.[11]

A second major activity through which social scientists are making their influence felt on community improvement efforts is *consultation*. This type of endeavor has shown considerable growth in the extension programs of American universities during recent years.

In 1955 a new Division of Community Development was created within the National University Extension Association, having equal status with Audio-Visual Aids, Correspondence Study, and other programs of long standing. The Division of Community Development was an outgrowth of a former Committee on Community Organization through which interested NUEA member institutions for some years had shared ideas and engaged in

[9] Joyce O. Hertzler, *Society in Action* (New York: The Dryden Press, Inc., 1954), pp. 387–388.

[10] Urie Bronfenbrenner and Edward C. Devereux, "Interdisciplinary Planning for Team Research on Constructive Community Behavior," *Human Relations,* vol. 5 (May, 1952), pp. 187–203.

[11] See W. K. Beggs, *Community Study as a Vehicle for Interdisciplinary Research in the Social Sciences,* Council for Community Study, University of Nebraska, Community Study No. 1 (September, 1953).

joint projects. This structural reorganization was indicative of a growing emphasis upon community development activities within the NUEA. In a recent study which provided data from forty-five member-institutions of the NUEA, thirty-four institutions stated that they carried on "activities in the area of community development." Of these, eleven indicated that their community development activities were "primarily conducted by a separate bureau of community development set up for this purpose." [12]

Some representative examples of community consultation programs are as follows:

Earlham College, Richmond, Ind.: *Program of Community Dynamics*, William W. Biddle, Director. In a unique manner, this college conducts a community service program which simultaneously serves as a training opportunity for students in the field of community development.

University of Kentucky, Lexington: *The Bureau of Community Service*, Howard W. Beers, Director. With a small staff and limited budget, the Bureau "seeks to carry into the communities of Kentucky the know-how of specialists in the social sciences. The know-how mingles with the goodwill and determination of the dwellers in a community, and constructive developments follow." [13]

University of Michigan, Ann Arbor: *Community Adult Education*, Howard Y. McClusky, in charge. Through its Extension Service and School of Education the University presents a comprehensive program of services to communities, including consultation in program planning, leadership training, organizational problems, and community self-surveys.

Purdue-Indiana Universities, Bloomington: *Community Services in Adult Education*, Paul Bergevin, Director. One of the major emphases has been upon leadership training, the most recent development providing for research and education designed to improve adult religious education in churches throughout the state.

[12] "Community Development in University Extension," a report by the Administrative Committee, Community Development Division, Norris A. Hiett, Chairman, National University Extension Association, General Extension Division, University of Minnesota (1956), p. 2.

[13] See "Community Service in Kentucky," First Biennial Report of The Bureau of Community Service, Sociology Department, College of Arts and Sciences, University of Kentucky (1950).

Southern Illinois University, Carbondale: *Department of Community Development*, Richard W. Poston, Director. This is one of the most intensive programs in the nation in terms of time spent in communities by consultants. It stresses community self-analysis through voluntary study groups as a basis for community development.

University of Tennessee, Knoxville: *Municipal Technical Advisory Service*, Victor C. Hobday, Executive Director. In cooperation with the Tennessee Municipal League, the M.T.A.S. serves as a fact-finding agency of the University established to provide technical advisory assistance, upon request, to city officials in Tennessee.

University of Virginia, Charlottesville: *Community Services*, Jess S. Ogden, Director. This is one of the oldest and best known programs in the United States. A long record of achievement has been described by the Extension Division in its "New Dominion Series" pamphlets.

University of Wisconsin, Madison: *Bureau of Community Development*, R. J. Colbert, Director. Half a century ago the "Wisconsin Idea" was introduced which began the task of converting an entire state into a university "campus." Among the important phases of the program is one which provides for consultation between university personnel and community leaders concerning problems of community betterment.

In view of the growing interest along this line among colleges and universities, it is only natural that critical attention should be given to the question of *role*. What are the essential functions of a social science professor who is asked to serve as consultant in a community? What type of relationship should exist between him and the group with which he is to work? Questions such as these have by no means been fully resolved, but efforts at clarification are being made.[14] In general, it would seem that his tasks are those of helping people (a) to think intelligently and analytically

[14] See the special issue on "The Role of the Community Consultant," *Journal of Educational Sociology* (December, 1955). Murray G. Ross, *Community Organization: Theory and Principles* (New York: Harper & Brothers, 1955), chap. 8. Blaine E. Mercer, *The American Community* (New York: Random House, 1956), pp. 280–281.

about their community problems, (b) to discover the sources of socially useful knowledge which are at their disposal, and (c) to employ such knowledge effectively in the solution of their problems. Manipulation of people's minds has no more place in a community setting than it does in the university classroom. This, however, does not prevent the consultant from taking a definite stand on local issues or favoring particular types of action programs, but the net effect should be to stimulate action groups to a more careful examination of the problems at hand. If his comments or recommendations tend instead to promote mental laziness and to shift the function of decision-making from the community to himself as an "outside expert," he has forsaken the role of consultant. Care must be exercised not to encourage a feeling of undue dependence upon the consultant which will undermine local initiative and resourcefulness.

Among other problems of consultation programs are those of structure, financial support, and evaluation. As to structure, there seems to be little uniformity. Certain programs are centralized, with most of the community consultation work being channelled through some type of extension office, while others are carried on by academic departments acting independently of each other. Again, some have a minimal superstructure, while others have rather elaborate arrangements with substantial staffs employed specifically to perform this kind of service. Experimentation is continually practiced, and it would be hazardous to characterize any particular form of organization as best.

The financing of community consultation programs reveals a similar lack of uniformity. Funds are variously derived from taxes, subsidies from other extension programs, grants from private benefactors, and fees from the community groups served. In small communities, at least, there is a tendency for universities to provide consultation services free of charge.

The problem of evaluation is difficult indeed because the contribution of the consultant in any given community development project is normally only one of several factors which together determine success or failure. A project may well succeed *despite* the work of a consultant, where the common sense and balanced judgment of local citizens outweigh hasty or ill-considered guidance by the visiting "expert." On the other hand, a project may fail because of schisms, apathy, lack of imagination, poor leadership, or nonsupport, even though the consultant performs in a thoroughly competent professional manner. In other words, a university's community consultation program cannot readily be evaluated by tabulating successes and failures among projects on which help has been given. It is even more difficult to attempt an evaluation on the basis of volume of correspondence, number of telephone calls, frequency of field trips, or number of people contacted. Items like these are of interest, to be sure, but they fail to provide data upon which any type of fundamental evaluation can be based. Careful thought should be given to the development of dependable evaluation techniques in the future. Without them the place of community consultation work in the program of the university will certainly be subject to question.

Closely related to community consultation as a channel of communication between social scientist and community is the broad area of *conferences, short courses, institutes,* and *workshops.* Here is perhaps the most vigorous "growing edge" of the modern university program. Nearly two decades ago the University of Minnesota established its Center for Continuation Study, the first building on any university campus designed specifically for work with adult groups. This has been followed by the Kellogg Center at Michigan State University and a similar center at the University of Georgia and by a considerable number of other institutions of higher learning. Even where no special facilities for continuing education exist there are frequently broad programs housed on a catch-as-catch-can basis in classrooms, auditoriums, and dining halls primarily designed for use by the regular student body.

The extensive scope of this type of activity is reflected in the large output of mailed announcements concerning short-term educational programs for business, industry, labor, the professions, and for adults in general who are interested in self-improvement or community betterment.

Speakers, discussion leaders, and consultants who are capable of carrying on a continuing education program are drawn from a wide variety of fields and sources. Wherever any phase of community improvement is involved, the social scientist ordinarily plays a prominent educational role. Through personal give-and-take around the conference table and through lectures, the expert shares his specialized knowledge with adults who have come to learn. Among numerous examples that could be cited are the Second Mid-winter Forum on Community Development held at Texas Techno-logical College [15] and the Community Leadership Conference con-ducted in Wausau, Wisconsin, under the sponsorship of the Bureau of Community Development of the University of Wisconsin.[16] Rol-land D. Berger of the latter institution clarified the relation of this type of educational endeavor to community improvement in the following statement about the Wausau meeting:

Out of this conference there have already grown many specific programs of community improvement—a city planning and zoning program for two cities; a community self-study program for two more; a trade area analy-sis in another; school district readjustment in another; closer under-standing between resort operators and businessmen in another; a new industry program for another; and so on.[17]

In the realm of *radio* and *television* there are also encouraging developments serving to establish communication between social scientists, on the one hand, and citizens engaged in community improvement, on the other. For example, an arrangement was made between Indiana University and the Educational Television and Radio Center at Ann Arbor, Michigan, by which a wide variety of half-hour educational television programs was to be distributed on a rental or purchase basis through the National Educational Tele-vision Film Service of the Audio-Visual Center at Indiana. Since many of the topics were in the social sciences, they provided a link between research and social action.

An interesting problem-solving approach in educational tele-vision has been developed at station WOI-TV, Iowa State College. In a series of programs entitled *The Whole Town's Talking*, tele-

[15] Proceedings available from Department of Education, Adult Education Program, Texas Technological College (1955).

[16] For a conference summary see the July–August 1949 issue of *Community Development Service*, University Extension Division, University of Wisconsin.

[17] *Ibid.*, iii.

vision viewers saw actual community groups in the process of solving difficult community problems. Community specialists of various kinds were involved in the production of these programs which proved to have considerable significance in stimulating viewers to undertake action programs in their own localities.

The Family Life Institute of the University of Oklahoma has produced successfully a Family Life Radio Forum, a series of radio broadcasts presenting to the general public the latest scientific information on family relationships and child development. Listening and discussion groups are encouraged as part of the program, and pertinent literature is available in advance of each broadcast. Among other endeavors of this type is the Canadian Farm Radio Forum, a radio broadcast providing for the discussion of rural problems.

An effort to encourage and facilitate community improvement through the use of a *film* has been made at the University of Michigan. In 1952 a 16 mm. sound film entitled *Tale of Two Towns* was produced, which told the story of how two Michigan communities solved their problems. The film was specifically designed as a springboard for the discussion of community development problems in localities throughout the state, and to assure maximum effectiveness a manual for discussion leaders was drawn up for use with the film. The manual gives detailed suggestions as to how the film may be most advantageously used and emphasizes that the primary purpose of the program is to stimulate as many people as possible to future action.

Social scientists also put out valuable *publications* to meet the needs for "some material." It is recognized that costly errors can frequently be avoided, with substantial savings in time, energy, and money, where an examination of relevant literature can precede the initiation of an action program. Many of the publications of the social scientists are in technical language; others are popularly written. Some deal with conceptual framework and theory, and others with methods and practice. But whatever their nature and scope, they constitute a medium through which the social scientist can exert a positive influence upon community life.

The following list of organizations and agencies which put out printed materials on community development will be useful to the student.[18]

Adult Education Association of the U.S.A., 743 N. Wabash Ave., Chicago, Ill.

American Council to Improve Our Neighborhoods, Box 462, Radio City Station, New York 20, N.Y.

American Country Life Association, 1201 Sixteenth St., N.W., Washington 6, D.C.

American Municipal Association, 1625 H St., N.W., Washington 6, D.C.

American Planning and Civic Association, 901 Union Trust Bldg., Washington 5, D.C.

American Public Health Association, 1790 Broadway, New York 19, N.Y.

American Public Welfare Association, 1313 East 60th St., Chicago 37, Ill.

American Society of Planning Officials, 1313 East 60th St., Chicago 37, Ill.

Association for the Study of Community Organization, Room 810, One Park Avenue, New York 16, N.Y.

Bureau of Applied Social Research, Columbia University, New York, N.Y.

Canadian Association for Adult Education, 143 Bloor Street West, Toronto, Ontario, Canada.

Chamber of Commerce of the United States of America, 1615 H St. N.W., Washington 6, D.C.

Child Welfare League of America, 345 E. 46th St., New York 17, N.Y.

Community Service, Inc., Box 243, Yellow Springs, Ohio

Family Service Association of America, 192 Lexington Ave., New York 16, N.Y.

International City Managers' Association, 1313 East 60th St., Chicago 37 Ill.

National Association of Social Workers, One Park Ave., New York, N.Y.

National Catholic Welfare Conference, 1312 Massachusetts Ave., N.W. Washington 5, D.C.

National Clean Up—Paint Up—Fix Up Bureau, 1500 Rhode Island Ave. N.W., Washington 5, D.C.

National Conference of Christians and Jews, 43 West 57th St., New York 19, N.Y.

[18] For a more comprehensive listing see Roland L. Warren, *Studying Your Community*, Russell Sage Foundation, 505 Park Avenue, New York 22, N.Y. (1955), pp. 363–369.

National Conference of Jewish Communal Service, 1841 Broadway, New York 23, N.Y.

National Council of the Churches of Christ in the U.S.A., 297 Fourth Ave., New York 10, N.Y.

The National Council for Community Improvement, 818 Olive St., St. Louis 1, Mo.

National Education Association of the United States, 1201 Sixteenth St., N.W., Washington 6, D.C.

National Municipal League, 542 Fifth Avenue, New York 36, N.Y.

National Planning Association, 1606 New Hampshire Ave., N.W., Washington 9, D.C.

National Probation and Parole Association, 1790 Broadway, New York 19, N.Y.

National Recreation Association, 8 West Eighth St., New York 11, N.Y.

National Safety Council, 425 No. Michigan Ave., Chicago 11, Ill.

National University Extension Association, General Extension Division, University of Minnesota, Minneapolis, Minn.

National Urban League, 1133 Broadway, New York 10, N.Y.

Public Administration Clearing House, 1313 East 60th St., Chicago 37, Ill.

Rural Church Center, American Baptist Assembly, Green Lake, Wis.

Russell Sage Foundation, 505 Park Avenue, New York 22, N.Y.

Superintendent of Documents, Government Printing Office, Washington 25, D.C.

The Twentieth Century Fund, 330 West 42nd St., New York 36, N.Y.

United Community Funds and Councils of America, Inc., 345 E. 46th St., New York 17, N.Y.

United Nations Department of Public Information, United Nations, New York, N.Y.

* 7. The Value Element in Community Planning

Arthur Hillman

Introduction Throughout the nation vast and expensive programs of urban rehabilitation are underway. These programs have developed because existing conditions of physical and social life in some parts of our urban centers are unbearable. Obvious blight and deterioration as seen by the naked eye is a good enough reason for making a change. Most of us, too, share the belief that human beings deserve a satisfactory life. This belief can be called a "value," and values like this underlie and support community planning and change. They give the rationale to these two processes. The chapter which follows by Professor Arthur Hillman describes the values which dominate community planning.

Survival is a primary value of community planning. How to prevent physical deterioration, traffic congestion, epidemics, smoke and water pollution, to name but a few, are major concerns of planners and practitioners alike. *Conservation* is another value. Programs are initiated to preserve and rehabilitate older middle-class communities because these represent the stable areas of our communities. Slum clearance in lower-class sections close to the center of a city is valuable for creating buffers for middle-class areas against the encroachment of blight. *"City Liveable"* is a third value. Community planners have long recognized that it is almost impossible totally to revamp an already organized community into a "community beautiful." At best they can preserve what already exists and create aesthetic landmarks when less desirable and less beautiful areas are being cleared and redeveloped.

144

Values, those described above and many others, are not shared equally by those engaged in community planning or even by all members of the society. Value conflicts are often evidenced between parochial and broader community groups. Since self-interest is basic in motivational structure, the question most frequently asked is "What is there in it for me?" or "What about me?" Local storekeepers in the slum redevelopment project who are asked to vacate for the construction of the new shopping center or housing project may have values of self-concern which conflict with others calling for largesse; or their values may conflict with others concerned with improvement of shopping or housing facilities for the whole community.

The community planner must be aware of the role of power in determining desirable and achievable community goals. Somehow he must coordinate values as expressed through self-economic interest with social concern for the welfare of the larger community.

Too often value analysis, as developed by Professor Hillman, is ignored or glossed over in the study of the "whys" and "wherefores" of community planning. Failures or even successes in planning and subsequent change are explained or rationalized without awareness of the latent functions of values. For this reason this selection needs careful reading and study.

✳ THE STATEMENT is sometimes heard in large cities with reference to complex and vexing problems that "things have to get worse before they can get better." The expectation of collective action out of a sense of desperation is a recognition of civic apathy and of the difficulty of organization in massive communities. It also points to the desire for survival as a compelling factor in community action. Much of contemporary city planning is at this level. The question raised by J. L. Sert, *Can Our Cities Survive?* [1] is a real one, even if it is taken as referring to fairly specific things, such as physical deterioration at the centers of cities or the choking congestion of traffic arteries. Besides these observable symptoms there are the more subtle effects of noise and crowding and of the confusing rapid-fire of stimuli which beset persons in cities, all of which indicate some good reasons to plan with sheer survival as sufficient motivation.

[1] Cambridge: Harvard University Press, 1942.

VALUE CONSIDERATIONS

A more positive and less defensive note that enters into community planning is the American culture theme of "keeping up"—or of avoiding obsolescence.[2] The pride in progress, which may indeed equate newness with progress, is stimulated by comparisons between cities. One technique of staff representatives of national organizations is to tell local leaders that a comparable city has just expanded its playground or library facilities or that there is a new trend in some type of agency program. In larger matters, such as the building of superhighways and the redevelopment of close-in downtown areas, action gets spurred by observations and interchange of experience on the part of influential persons. Power figures in the community ask themselves "Why can't we do as well as they did in Pittsburgh" or elsewhere, and they may act as a result in a way that combines concern with survival and progress.

Planning is aimed at achieving a degree of balance and of orderliness in the process of community development. It is a matter of making the various decisions of individuals and of public bodies add up to some order, often identified with health and safety or other generalized values. In the process, there is evident at times a tension between the private rights of individuals as property owners, or of citizens exercising their liberties, as opposed to a regard for the general welfare. The zoning laws, which date from around 1920, were a major extension of the powers of government over the free use of private property and were upheld by the courts with some reservations.[3] The same ordinances can, of

[2] Cf. Nelson Foote's discussion of obsolescence as a factor in personal adjustment in a changing, mass society: paper presented at Detroit meeting of American Sociological Society, Sept., 1956.

[3] Zoning is a major tool for preventing inharmonious mixtures of land uses and for guarding against overdensity, but the purposes served are more varied. Protection against air pollution and other nuisances, traffic hazards, and aesthetically offensive structures are among other value elements involved in zoning and land-use controls. See Norman Williams, Jr., "Planning Law and Democratic Living," *Law and Contemporary Problems,* vol. 20 (Spring, 1955), pp. 331–334. On the constitutional points see in the same issue Corwin W. Johnson, "Constitutional Laws and Zoning," pp. 199–217.

course, be justified as a means of greater protection for individual property rights in that they safeguard the stability of property values. Actually, zoning can help to freeze present land use arrangements and thus be a tool for preventing orderly change.

Zoning laws often represent an encroachment on the freedom of people who might wish to do something other than what is prescribed in the code, and the actual experience of pressure toward amendments of the law and of variations which may be granted by administrative tribunals indicates the resistance of property owners. In recent years there has been a marked extension of public powers particularly in the right of condemnation for such purposes as public housing and urban redevelopment.[4] This is another legally sanctioned way in which the general welfare takes precedence over individual property rights; the courts have held that the land assembly for slum clearance, whether through public housing or through private redevelopment, is essentially a public purpose for which adequate government powers must be available.

Opposition of private rights and public welfare occurs also over urban transportation. The clogging of streets by automobiles, many of which are occupied by only one person, is a concession to the comfort and convenience of the driver, or to what he regards as his best interest before he gets caught in a traffic jam. On the other hand, forms of transportation which serve large numbers and take up less space need to be utilized more fully according to city planners, who are concerned about survival of cities and a rational development of public facilities. Extreme measures such as barring cars from certain streets clearly involve the restriction of the rights of a car driver. In a larger sense debates over expenditures for super highways versus mass transportation are other examples of conflict of values.

Early in the century the city planning movement had as a slogan "the city beautiful" and there is no doubt that this was an oversimplification because consideration for health and welfare, as well as a concern for aesthetic values, entered into large-scale plans. However, in recent decades there has been more emphasis on the

[4] Coleman Woodbury, ed., *Urban Redevelopment: Problems and Practices* (Chicago: University of Chicago Press, 1953), pp. 478–493. See also Johnson, *op. cit.*, p. 207.

city liveable, or the city efficient, with due regard to residences, house locations, density, and transportation.[5]

Perhaps this change reflects a trend toward more considera- tion for the accepted values of equality or freedom.[6] These are some of the broadest kinds of value considerations or themes that may dominate city planning. The difficulty of summing up goals of community planning in a slogan, or in any few words, suggests the problem of grasping the "idea of the city" which Horace Kallen has pointed out.[7] Most of the goals sought are partial and segmental and represent choices between lesser goods rather than being com- prehensive visions, expressing some organic conception of an ideal community.

VALUE CHOICES AND CONFLICTS

One of the most obvious value considerations has to do with the huge economic investment, especially in real estate, near the center of large cities. Land values have often been inflated, and one effect of the federal housing and redevelopment act of 1949 was to provide a subsidy for the writing down of land values to make possible rebuilding of such areas for residential purposes. Part of a motivation for such rebuilding is the concern about clearing out shabby and indecent housing, and thus the health and welfare ob- jectives of "social-minded" people are served at the same time as tax delinquent property is put into shape for more productive use. Moreover, the rebuilding may result in the kind of apartments which would be inhabited by middle- and upper-income people, and thus downtown store owners find it to their advantage to sup- port such redevelopment in order to bring good customers closer to the center of the city. There has been enough slum clearance near city centers to justify the predictions that the long-run effect might well be the replacement of marginal income people with

[5] Christopher Tunnard and Henry Hope Reed, *American Skyline* (Boston: Houghton Mifflin Co., 1955). Paperback edition published by New American Library, New York.

[6] Cf. Williams, *op. cit.*, p. 319.

[7] "City Planning and the Idea of the City," *Social Research*, vol. 23 (Sum- ner, 1956), pp. 186–198.

those of more substantial income. Incidentally, since this is done through planning, however piecemeal, it is an example of a deliberate upsetting of what were considered to be natural ecological processes of competition for space and of selection of area residents.

Farther removed and sometimes encircling the city's central areas are the middle-aged communities which are ripe for conservation programs. Beginnings of deterioration are evident, so that the emphasis is directed toward slum prevention, perhaps by selected demolitions, but generally by improving municipal services and giving attention to traffic and other problems in ways which will insure the stability of the area. Law enforcement and the quality of schools and other community services are recognized as having a relationship to property values. Implied in such conservation programs are obvious middle-class values such as the care of property and also certain habits of living. Thus those newcomers to the city who may not be ready for urban life or who may be more rowdy and irresponsible are regarded as threats to the more conventional values and the way of life within a community.

Conservation programs therefore often involve the conflict between middle- and lower-class people. It might be noted that this is more than a matter of income because stability of employment and even a level of income equal to that of the so-called middle class may only enable lower-class individuals to live their way of life more fully.[8] Social mobility, or movement to another class, is not something automatically to be expected with a rise in income, and many gross and subtle differences in values are inherent in community standards for conservation programs.

In the rebuilding of areas of the city, either by private investors or through public projects, there is often attempted what used to be called the neighborhood unit idea. This represented in part a romantic attempt to recreate small-town values. In recent years rebuilding has become more associated with the idea of a super-block or of a physical unit within a city of such size as to insure against encroachment of blight from nearby areas. Thus what was proposed as a planning area from consideration of the

[8] Rose Hum Lee, Arthur Hillman and St. Clair Drake, "A Resurvey of a Chicago Community in Transition," paper presented at 1956 meeting of American Sociological Society.

social values to be enhanced by greater neighborliness has been supplanted by more concern for having a healthy physical cell within the city. In such areas there tends to be a concentration of people of the same income whether in public housing or in rental apartments, and therefore the building of such neighborhood units is open to the serious objection of segregating people of one economic level. This objection is valid, however, only if one assumes that somehow it is democratic for people of all levels to come into contact with each other. To some extent this economic grouping revives the earlier neighborhood unit philosophy that those who live near each other should be encouraged to be associates.

In the planning of schools some value choices are overt, while others are not so obvious. The kind of facilities decided upon presuppose decisions on general educational policies, such as the years of schooling to be provided, the kinds of vocational emphasis, and the extent of recreation and of special services to be offered under school auspices. To a lessening extent in Northern communities, there are problems of locations with respect to prevailing patterns of racial segregation. In general, the quality of schools —buildings and programs—is a major factor in community attractiveness and hence related to conservation efforts.

City planners dealing with problems of urban renewal, as well as social workers and adult educators, are interested in promoting citizen participation. While this concept is not always clearly defined, it is part of a general emphasis on democratic self-determination, an extension in social work from the principle as it is applied in case work or in group work. The support which physical and social planners are increasingly giving democratic values is both idealistic—squaring practices with the democratic ideology of our society—and pragmatic: plans need substantial and voluntary consent.[9]

However, getting local people to express their own concern and to defend what they conceive to be their own interests may immediately result in conflict with larger considerations in planning. The inconvenience to people in a local area has to be balanced off with consideration of the greater good for the economy and the orderly growth of a metropolitan area to be achieved pos-

[9] Arthur Hillman, *Community Organization and Planning* (New York: The Macmillan Co., 1950), pp. 192 ff.

sibly through such projects as the building of a highway or the development of an area for a different kind of industrial or residential purpose. But the local people are bound to ask, "Why can't we stay here?" and a real problem for community organization workers is to help people reconcile their immediate personal interests with those of the larger city or region. An example of this was evident in the state of Illinois where a bill was introduced in more than one session of the state legislature to require a referendum on public housing projects. That is, a housing project could not be located in an area unless the people within a half mile or a mile radius approved by majority vote. This was ostensibly to give a great weight to the value of local self-determination, but this would be at the expense of such values as the improvement of housing of low income groups regardless of race. Actually the attempted legislation was designed to allow areas to block the entrance of Negroes who would come with public housing. (The same purpose was achieved through the power of aldermen in the principal city who have a virtual veto power of what happens in their wards.)

VALUE GUIDANCE

The examples cited have served not merely to indicate some of the current conflicts that concern persons actively involved in community planning but also to show that considerations of power —politics in a broad sense—are inevitably a part of the process of determining goals and ways of reaching them in communities. Thus, it is possible to steer away from the naive assumption frequently associated with planning that "facts speak for themselves."

Norman Williams develops this point:

The way cities develop, it is not the case that a thorough planning analysis will always reveal a single solution which will best satisfy the needs of everyone involved. In fact, one is sometimes tempted to say that such situations are rare. In many, if not most, instances, there are likely to be opposing forces at work. These opposing forces may involve quite different desires or implications for the future environment; or the problem may be one of distributing insufficient public services to the areas of greatest need. It is remarkable how often, in a highly technical planning discussion, differing uses of various planning devices can be most realistically viewed as rather sophisticated expressions of different social forces—between which a balance must be struck, or a decision made. The fact that these conflicting social forces may not be immediately apparent in connection with planning decisions, or that only one side may be vocal or vociferous, does not mean that the conflicts are not there. Nothing is more important than to be clear-headed about this. When one of these situations arises, normally there is no such thing as avoiding the issue, or making a decision on the "technical" and "non-controversial" problems only, or finding a safe and dignified refuge in accumulating endless piles of unassimilated information and hoping that somehow it will speak for itself. In brief, in these situations there is no such thing as neutrality. There is, however, plenty of opportunity for being so muddle-headed as not to realize what is going on, and what issues are actually being decided.[10]

Professional planners, particularly those working with the physical aspects of community development, do well to recognize their peculiar roles as arbiters and as trustees, if not promoters, of social values. They are in a strategic position to express intangible notions of welfare in visible forms. Often they hold the key to broader value considerations because their concern with land use and physical facilities is understandable and acceptable to conservative interests. It is well to acknowledge that economic self-interest is a key value in the rebuilding of cities, and in its more enlightened forms, it may become merged with welfare considerations, but it may simply be a concern with land values and profits from construction contracts.

Often the city planner is the only important person with any broad interests as the sociologist David Riesman has pointed out in *The Lonely Crowd.*

[City planners] comprise perhaps the most important professional group to become reasonably weary of the cultural definitions that are systematically trotted out to rationalize the inadequacies of city life today, for the well-to-do as well as for the poor. With their imagination and bounteous approach they have become, to some extent, the guardians of our liberal and progressive political tradition, as this is increasingly displaced from state and national politics.[11]

[10] Williams, *op. cit.,* pp. 319–320.
[11] *The Lonely Crowd* (New York: Doubleday & Company, Inc., 1953, p 348).

This reference to city planners who are concerned with the physical development of communities indicates the difficulties and the opportunities associated with their tasks. On the other hand, community organization workers—social planners or "enablers"— play a new role in many American communities, in the conservation programs or in urban renewal generally, working more closely than before with associates who have their backgrounds primarily in architecture and engineering. This helps make up for deficiencies in the professional education of the latter, whose need for background in ethics and the social sciences is obvious, if they are to approach their actual responsibilities with greater awareness of the factors involved in the decisions they help make.

Social planners have new opportunities to make known values which are part of their professional interest, which can now be shown to have a bearing on a well-rounded program for conservation of a community or to be part of what makes a community desirable, and hence also a sound economic investment. An example of the combination of concerns about physical and social aspects of a community is found in a bulletin of a citizen action organization which speaks of "deterioration" in referring simultaneously to run-down property and to the intrusion of organized vice as threats to the quality of community life which must be met in organized fashion. Perhaps a new and vigorous conservatism is emerging, at least a meeting on common ground of groups and interests which formerly were regarded as detached from each other.

The tendency toward a coalition of conservation in property and human values is observable in some large cities, but it is by no means a general trend. Not only may planners with differing concerns be unwilling or unable to work together, but there may also be a gap between professionals and the public in value definitions. Wherever the latter is true, and it is inevitably so to some extent in all communities, the lag in sensitivity to values and to means of implementing them emphasizes the leadership role of planners in helping people define goals for a community and to raise their sights for its future.[12]

[12] Hillman, *op. cit.*, pp. 99–100.

Community Action

* 8. A Study of a Natural Experiment in Community Action

Robert W. Janes

Introduction It is not often that a community or some of the problems or conditions of a community are studied over a fifteen-year period, even intermittently. Most research on the community or, for that matter, research in other social science fields is for much shorter periods of time; in many instances a "snapshot" view is attained—perhaps in a limited interview, and the investigation is completed. Professor Robert W. Janes' chapter on Riverville, its flood, and its efforts at relocation is a longitudinal study of social action and change.

In 1937 a flood nearly wiped out the town of Riverville. The people, at least their leaders, decided to move inland to a safer location. During the following fifteen-year period Dr. Janes lived in or visited Riverville and observed how members of the community were reacting to the relocation of the town. He conducted a series of informal interviews in an effort to discover the members of the community who "got things done." He would permit those he interviewed to express themselves freely about individuals and problems in the community. He discovered that certain individuals were prime movers and were giving leadership to the relocation problem.

Persons of the five key statuses of the Riverville social system reacted differently to the relocation plan. The five Professor Janes discovered and classified are (1) community and associational leader, (2) business and

157

professional, (3) white-collar, artisan, (4) unskilled worker, reliefer, (5) Negro. This status system differs from the social class groupings of W. L. Warner and A. B. Hollingshead with which many students are probably familiar. Status 1 includes the opinion-leaders regardless of occupational affiliation, statuses 2, 3, and 4 are occupational, while 5 is racial.

Members classified in the highest three statuses, those who had the highest income, prestige, and influence, were more favorable to relocation than the unskilled worker, reliefer, and Negro groups. At first glance it would seem that the factors of income, influence, and prestige alone predisposed persons so endowed to favor relocation. Actually it was varied reasons associated with the norms of each status position.

Persons of high key status were directly involved in the issue, were expected to give leadership in dealings with the government concerning relocation, and were expected to be sensitive to the community feelings and attitudes concerning the plan. The higher status occupational groups reacted in terms of economic self-interest. Business men wanted to go back into business and the white-collar home owner thought of a debt-free home untouched by repeated flooding. These individuals supported the move. Members of the unskilled and reliefer groups or the Negro sub-community were indifferent or opposed the relocation. The unskilled whites resented the intrusion upon their independence by being told what to do, and many moved to the new site only when housing was unavailable at the old. The Negroes resented the enforced segregation policy put into practice at the new site and resisted movement.

Factionalism developed from the conflict over key status norms. To-day there are not one but two communities! The chapter is an absorbing study of long-term community change, the variables which affected attitudes and subsequent behavior of a community's members towards relocation of a flood-stricken community. It has important and fascinating theoretical and empirical findings.

✳ WHAT HAPPENS after the members of a community decide to move their town to a new site? How do the consequences and conditions of such a self-imposed community action program contribute to or exemplify the sociological theory of community structure and community action? This chapter describes and analyzes the case of a small town which undertook to move its population and buildings to a new location. Such an unusual effort of local collective action can be regarded as a "natural experiment" containing social variables important in a community action program. The goal of this study is to draw from this case hypotheses concerning the influence of social variables on the outcome of community action programs.

The events of this relocation program occurred over a period of almost twenty years from its inception in 1937. Observations on the project were made at various points in its development during these years. Data were secured through participant-observation, informal interviews where questions did not require specific answers and a variety of documentary materials, and the files of the local newspaper. The first field observations were made in the fall of 1939, reconnaissance visits to the community in 1948 and 1950, and final observations during a seven month period of local residence in 1953–54.

The general orientation of the researcher to the community was that defined by Arensberg as "the community-study method." [1] The author conceived of the community as a social system moving from disequilibrium to equilibrium.[2] The relocation can, in these terms, be conceived as a self-imposed state of disequilibrium. The analysis attempted to define the sources of disequilibrium and to discover how a state of equilibrium was restored as a result of the working out of the relocation program. This problem was made all the more interesting because the new equilibrium was in opposition to the original goals of community action.

BACKGROUND OF THE COMMUNITY
ACTION PROGRAM

In 1937, Riverville (a fictitious name) was a town of about 1,500 people situated on the bank of a large Midwestern river. A great flood in the winter of that year inundated the town compelling the inhabitants to abandon their homes and places of business to the river waters for a period of eight weeks. During these weeks the

---

[1] Conrad M. Arensberg, "The Community-Study Method," *American Journal of Sociology* (September, 1954), pp. 109–124.

[2] Cf., Marion J. Levy, Jr., *The Structure of Society* (Princeton: Princeton University Press, 1952), chap. II, for a definition of equilibrium and disequilibrium.

idea of relocating the community on higher ground about three miles inland from the river gained favor among the groups of refugees. After the townspeople had returned to the community, sentiment in favor of resettling was so general that community representatives contacted a number of state and federal agencies to ascertain if support could be secured for such an effort. Some degree of official encouragement was forthcoming, and the River-ville County Public Housing Authority was licensed by the State Housing Authority to sponsor and direct some kind of relocation project. The commissioners of the Authority, appointed by the Riverville County Board of Supervisors, consisted of the mayor and four leading business men who had been among the original group favoring the move to a new site. The commissioners continued conversations with various governmental agencies, and in late 1937 they prepared a relocation plan which was then presented to the people of the community.

The principle of the proposal was that property owners would turn over their lots and buildings, both residential and business, to the Authority for a credit on a lot and construction at the new site. Persons without property but living in Riverville could contract for property and construction at the new site. The Authority also under-took responsibility for the town planning and construction of necessary facilities, such as roads, sidewalks, public buildings, and utilities. All buildings and utilities which were moveable would be physically transported to the new site, others would be salvaged for their materials. The goal of the original plan was to set up the whole community on the new site with all its facilities and services in operation. The old site with only a few buildings of historical interest left standing would revert to the State as a recreation area. The plan called for total community relocation because the planners felt that if the new community were to function successfully all services and facilities would have to be operating at the new site.

After the provisions of the plan were announced, about three-quarters of the families entered into contracts with the Authority, and the preparation of the new townsite was begun. The pace of actual relocation was comparatively slow at the beginning, largely because of administrative delays in the cooperating federal agencies. Not until 1940 and early 1941 were houses and places of business being completed and ready for occupancy. Then, in 1942, building and transporting came to a halt because of the World War II ban on construction. However, by that date almost all the larger commercial establishments, government buildings, associational structures, and public utilities and facilities had been relocated. After the War when building materials became available, construction began again, and the persons who still intended to relocate did. By 1952 movement to the new site had dwindled, and relative stability in population and functions between the old and new sites was achieved. Approximately 1,350 persons lived in the new section, and between five hundred and six hundred in the original Riverville. The two sections were still one town linked by a one-foot strip of land running along the highway connecting the two sites. The services remaining at the old site were either dependent upon the river, such as fish markets or the ferry, or were consumer services provided by grocery stores, service stations, cafes, and taverns. By 1954 the county housing authority was no longer promoting relocation activities.

Soon after the original relocation plan had been presented, attitudes of opposition had been voiced. Those in opposition remained at the old site, those favoring relocated. The opposition had in time developed into a faction which undertook an active program to disrupt the relocation. The plan of the opposition faction was to challenge the legality of the plan and to secure injunctions against actions of the Authority or to embarrass the Authority in any way which might jeopardize the success of the relocation. These efforts failed, but in 1956 the people of old Riverville, under the leadership of the faction, were able to withdraw from the town of Riverville and to establish themselves as a separate village. With this act the cycle of disequilibrium of the original Riverville social system ended, and there was a new equilibrium of two relatively independent community social systems.

ANALYTIC CONCEPTS: KEY STATUS AND NORMS

Two elements seem of major importance for the analysis of the dynamics of the relocation process—first, the norms of certain key statuses of the community social system, and second, the factionalism which grew out of the conflict of these norms with the provision of the relocation plan. "Key status" refers to a person's most distinctive social relationship as it is defined by the members of his group according to the group standards.[3] It is the relationship by which a person is most widely judged within his community. For most males it is occupational participation in the community division of labor. Each key status carries an appropriate set of norms —the kinds of behavior expected of the occupant of a status—and insofar as a person conducts himself in accordance with his key status, he has a tendency to act in conformity with its norms.

In Riverville there were five such key statuses which seemed significantly related to approval or disapproval of the provisions of the relocation plan. These five were classified as:

1. Community and associational leader
2. Business and professional
3. White-collar, artisan
4. Unskilled worker, reliefer
5. Negro

Statuses 2, 3, and 4 are occupational. Status 1 includes persons regarded by Rivervillers as their opinion-leaders: mayors, ex-mayors, ministers, and individuals whose long local residence had made them informal arbiters in community issues. Status 5 refers to a racial group, the Negro, whose subordinate social position in River-ville is typical of the Border States.

THE RESEARCH TECHNIQUES

The principal techniques of research, as noted above, were participant observation and unstructured interview. The determina-tion of five key statuses and of the norms associated with each status was based on data derived through these two methods. The field-procedures were as follows: in the course of participant-observer conversations or of unstructured interviews, the names of one or more of 118 persons, heads of Riverville families or households, were introduced into the discussion with the phrase, "Who is so-

[3] E. T. Hiller, *Social Relations and Structures* (New York: Harper & Brothers, 1947), pp. 339–342.

and-so?" This question was put to forty-one different respondents in the course of 160 separate interviews. The various respondents described from five to fourteen persons in answer to this question, and 80 per cent of the family heads were classified by the answers of two or more respondents. The content of the answers to this question as it described the heads of families was similar to that which Warner defines as "status reputation." [4] The main content of the statements indicated the way various members of the community considered a person in their relations to him. These statements seemed to be a primary clue to the key statuses of the community. For example, in the case of a man who owned one of the larger stores in Riverville, when the question "Who is so-and-so?" was asked about him, five respondents all answered in approximately similar statements: "He's a town leader. He has to have his say about anything that comes up. He'll try to be in on it." References to business and other activities of this man always succeeded remarks on his community role. This man, therefore, was classified in the key status of community leader. However, when the same question was asked in regard to another owner of a very similar business establishment the consensus of answers was, "He's one of the older businessmen. He and his family have been in business here for years." In this case, references to other activities came after statements about business activity, and this man was classified as possessing the key status of businessman. In the cases where the person of whom the question was asked was well-known in the town, there was a high agreement in the responses in the order in which attributes of a person were mentioned. Therefore, it seemed feasible to establish the key statuses of Rivervillers from recorded field-notes of the responses.

Determination of the relation of norms of each key status to the provisions of the relocation plan was based on answers to the question "Why do people like so-and-so favor (oppose) relocation?" This question was posed after the "Who is so-and-so?" question. Analysis of the responses to this question showed that Rivervillers tended to offer a different set of explanations for the point of view of each key status toward the relocation project. Each set

[4] W. L. Warner, M. Meeker and K. Eells, *Social Class in America* (Chicago: Science Research Associates, 1949), pp. 73–78.

of explanations was an estimate of the possibility of satisfying the expectations of a key status through the provisions of the relocation project. For example, when the question "Why do people like so-and-so favor relocation?" was posed of a man who had been categorized as white-collar the response was "Of course he would favor it. Why he had bought his wife a new living-room suite and just finished the payments on it two weeks before the flood. It was completely ruined in the high water. They can't afford to take chances like that." In this case the respondent defined the favorable point of view toward relocation according to the norms of a key status as these norms related to the plan for relocation. The analysis of the responses to this question was aimed at discovering the typical explanation offered by Rivervillers for the point of view of each key status toward the relocation.

In relating key status to attitude toward relocation, investigators divided the sample of 118 heads of households in each key status into two groups, one favoring, the other opposing relocation. The choice of household as the unit was made on the ground that Rivervillers did not relocate as individuals, but rather as households. It was rare that individuals in the same household took sharply contrasting views by the time that some decision was made in the household about moving to the new site. The final estimate of households which relocated or remained on the old site was made in 1954. The results of these classifications and calculations are shown in table 7.

Table 7. Ratio of Relocating to Non-relocating Households in Riverville, 1941–1954, By Key Social Status of Head of Household

KEY STATUS	RATIO OF MOVING TO NON-MOVING HOUSEHOLDS	NUMBER OF HOUSEHOLDS IN SAMPLE
Community and associational leader	8:1	20
Business and Professional	7:1	31
White collar, artisan	8:1	19
Unskilled worker, reliefer	2:1	27
Negro	3:1	21

The ratios shown in table 7 are measures of the response to the relocation plan by the various key statuses of the community. It would appear that members of the community who had more income, influence, and prestige were the ones who were more favorable to relocation. Further analysis makes it clear that it is not these factors in themselves which predispose persons to favor relocation. Rather the people who favored it did so for reasons associated with their key status norms.

COMMUNITY STRUCTURE: KEY STATUS
AS RELATED TO RELOCATION PROGRAM

This conclusion can be illustrated by an analysis of how closely the relocation plan agreed with and supported the norms and expectations of each key status group.

COMMUNITY LEADERS

First, community and associational leaders became involved in the issue of moving to the new site as soon as the plan was announced. As opinion leaders they had to know the provisions of the plan or as officers of associations such as churches, lodges, or veterans' groups they had to make decisions concerning the relocation of associational property. These persons very soon began to communicate a great deal with the Housing Authority commissioners and sought information about relocation terms and Authority policies. As a group they served as the principal channel of communication to the rest of the community on the technical and policy aspects of relocation. This activity maintained their leadership position in the community. At the same time their relationship to the commissioners was a mutually advantageous interaction in that the commissioners needed persons who would encourage support for the project and the leaders themselves needed the "inside" information to maintain themselves as opinion molders. Several persons in this category became the original leaders of the anti-relocation faction, and when they did they were cut off from the informal flow of policy information. It would appear then that the norms or expectations for this key status called for a high rate of interaction with the commissioners and that the nature of this interaction encouraged a favorable view of relocation by the community and associational leaders.

BUSINESS-PROFESSIONAL KEY STATUS

The norms of the business and professional key status were in agreement with the provisions of the relocation plan for somewhat different reasons. This status was an element in another system of interaction, the competitive offering of consumer goods and services within the Riverville trade area. A favorable position by a businessman or professional person was to a large degree dependent on his capital investment in the establishment where his goods or services were sold and on his investment in inventory. In the decades prior to the 1937 flood there had been a long-run decline in such investment. This trend was partially a consequence of the agricultural depression which began in the 1920's and of the changing regional purchasing patterns resulting from the use of the automobile. Yet, in the case of Riverville, it seemed to be the ever-present threat of floods (there were three major ones from 1898 to 1937), which inhibited investment. The relocation plan offered businessmen a chance to convert their existing plant, in most cases quite obsolescent, for new facilities on a site which would be free of floods. The competitive position of the community business system in the regional trade area would be enhanced. By the provisions of the relocation plan the norms of the business and professional status would be most adequately satisfied.

Why then, did at least fifteen per cent of the business establishments choose not to relocate? The answer does not lie in the plan itself, but rather in the nature of conditions which developed as part of the project. First, all of the old site population did not move as envisaged by the plan. Since some consumers remained, some merchants chose to remain to supply them. However, the businessmen who stayed behind had small establishments; all those with a large investment relocated. Insofar as the population remaining on the old site was economically marginal, so were the businesses which chose not to relocate. A second consideration, important also because it involved the factional development, led businessmen to oppose relocating their establishments. This point concerned the manner of allocating business sites at the new town. Some sites obviously were more favorably located than others. The Housing Authority, operating as a public corporation, did not sell any sites on a competitive open-market basis; rather a standard price was established for all similar lots. Therefore, when two businessmen wanted the same lot, it was the decision of the commissioners, not the price the businessmen were willing to pay, which determined the distribution of the lot. The majority of businessmen seemed to be satisfied with this method. However, there were several cases where two or more parties wanted the same lot, and those persons whose bids were rejected became very dissatisfied and charged that the relocation was being run for the benefit of an "inside" clique. Several businessmen who expressed this view refused to relocate and eventually sold their establishments in the old town. In general, however, it would appear that the expectations of the key status business and professional were met by the plan and procedures of relocation.

WHITE-COLLAR, ARTISAN KEY STATUS

The expectations of the white collar and artisan key status were also, in the main, satisfied by the plan of resettlement. The norms of this status stressed individual effort and productive work which could be symbolized by some material reward. For the older members of this group a debt-free house with a well-kept interior and neat yard was a more important goal than a new automobile. Relocation promised freedom from the destruction of residential property and home furnishings by floods. It would appear that the values of this key status were linked to consumer property and that the plan satisfied these values by offering more security to this property.

UNSKILLED WORKERS, RELIEFERS KEY STATUS

While a large majority of persons in the unskilled labor and reliefer status relocated, they did so in the smallest proportion of any category. The norms of these persons were at marked variance with those of the groups already discussed. Persons in this category showed a devotion to a frontier-type tradition, one that emphasized rights and feelings of the individual including freedom from many conventional restraints and standards. There was less of a work orientation, greater stress on expressive physical behavior such as hunting and fishing, drinking and fighting. Persons rarely were members of associations, and materialistic goals were less evident. The automobile, which could be a truck as well as a passenger car, was the primary household possession, but it was regarded in terms of utility rather than as a symbol of effort. There was an attitude of opposition to personal authority which would have direct control over the individual.

Such values, obviously, would be contradicted by many of the provisions and procedures of the relocation plan. It was often stated by such individuals, "Nobody is going to tell me where I have to live." Yet, about two-thirds of these households relocated. How is this explained by the analysis? It should be noted that these persons had a limited sense of involvement in the community as a social system. For many of them the place of residence, both its location and condition, was a matter of indifference, a view found in the common expression, "What's the difference, the same people will run the town if it's here or there." In the early phase of the project it appeared that the larger proportion of this category would not relocate. The attitude of opposition seemed to center in the building requirement, originally established by the Authority, for indoor toilets which made the price higher for a house, either to buy or rent. This requirement was dropped, and the owners of many of the smaller houses moved them to the new site for renting purposes. As the supply of housing available to the unskilled and reliefers declined at the old site and increased at the new, these persons relocated. Indifference to location of residence led members of this key status to the new site in search of the most available housing despite the fact that certain of their norms opposed the general procedure of the project.

NEGRO KEY STATUS

The key status, Negro, contained certain similarities in norms both to white-collar, artisan, and unskilled labor, and reliefer. There expectations of expressive behavior such as hunting, fishing, fighting, and drinking, but at the same time almost all Negro families owned their own homes. Although opportunities were limited for

Negroes in the Riverville economic system, some worked at trucking and farming to improve their economic position. The stress on security of property would certainly have been in agreement with the relocation plan. However, Negroes were permitted to purchase lots only in one segregated area in the new section. This invidious symbolization of subordinate social position opposed the norms of the status. Negroes said of the relocation program, "It's as Jim Crow as you can get." This conflict was to a considerable extent resolved in terms of economic norms since most Negro employment consisted of domestic service in well-to-do white families or odd jobs for larger business establishments. Since few Negroes owned automobiles, it was necessary to relocate within walking distance of employment.

The analysis of these five key statuses reveals the kinds of considerations which entered into decisions on whether or not to relocate. It would appear that to the extent that the program was successful in reconstituting Riverville at a new location, its provisions met the requirements of the major key statuses in the town. However, the goal of removing the whole population to the new site was not achieved. In fact, in this respect, the consequences of the program were just the opposite of the plan—a new political corporation emerged among the population remaining at the old site. The new equilibrium was that of two community social systems rather than of one. This unplanned consequence was attributable to the operation of factional opposition which, had it been successful, might have jeopardized the relocation program. As it was, this factionalism established the pattern of group interaction that resulted in the new political community on the old site. The analysis of this factionalism leads to certain significant hypotheses concerning the variables which may influence community action programs.

CAUSES AND CONSEQUENCES OF FACTIONALISM

Faction and factionalism are a form of conflict interaction in which one group attempts to obstruct another without at the same time offering substitute or compromise programs.[5] Faction, by this

[5] Cf., Georg Simmel, *Conflict* (Glencoe, Ill.: The Free Press, 1955).

definition, is negative and disruptive, since it does not lead to any accommodation in the conflict of interests. In the Riverville community action program such a conflict existed where the norms of a key status were not in agreement with the relocation plan or the procedures by which the plan was carried out. Such conditions included the segregation of Negroes, the manner of allocating desirable business sites, the requirements of inside plumbing, the maintenance of utilities and facilities on the old site during the course of moving, and the question of whether the Authority could use its power to make relocation compulsory. However, factionalism does not arise necessarily from a conflict of key status norms with the provisions of a plan for community action. It is the manner in which this conflict is handled that determines whether or not factions appear. The issues of conflict can be dealt with through a compromise satisfactory to both parties. Factionalism emerges when there is no such mutual compromise. This is what happened in Riverville. The conditions of the relocation administration were such that the commissioners of the Authority felt that they were unable to make any compromise on issues other than that of plumbing standards. When the conditions under which the project had to operate, once the program was undertaken, are examined, it is possible to see the grounds for the commissioners' point of view.

First, the choices available to the townspeople were absolute and not amenable to compromise—a family could either move or not move. The plan called for a total community relocation of population and facilities. If an individual did not choose to move and if he wished to maintain membership in his present community, he had no recourse but to frustrate the whole plan. The moving of the water works is a case in point. Once the water works were relocated to the new site, families in old Riverville had no water source except private wells.

Second, the fact that the administrative device selected for accomplishing the program was a public housing authority meant that the commissioners were solely responsible for the project. They were their own policy group; their deliberations and decisions did not require responsible interaction with any other body representing community interests. Likewise, as an executive group carrying out policies they were responsible only to themselves. Their interaction with the community was according to rules they themselves had established. An example of such proceedings was the manner of allocation of desirable business sites. To persons who felt that their interests had been infringed by these procedures there appeared to be no method of bringing pressure to bear on the Housing Authority except by factionalism.

Third, the commissioners themselves were Rivervillers, businessmen of the community. Although as commissioners they acted in an official and necessary role, still many Rivervillers thought of them primarily in their traditional local role as businessmen. Such a perception often led, even on the part of persons favoring relocation, to viewing the commissioners as "insiders" whose actions represented not the administrative necessity of the program, but rather the self-interest of businessmen. Such a conception of the commissioners as a favored faction implied that they could be dealt with only through counter-factionalism.

It was these conditions which militated against the possibility of compromise and which seemed to channel the conflict into factionalism. The development of factions led to new patterns of interaction between the population remaining on the old site. The faction leaders became community leaders and a new community system emerged. The cycle from community disequilibrium to equilibrium was now complete; its conclusion was signalized by the establishment of the new political structure on the old site.

CONCLUSIONS: GENERALIZATIONS FOR COMMUNITY ACTION PROGRAMS

The generalizations which are to be derived from the Riverville study can be stated in the form of hypotheses concerning community action programs. The Riverville experience consists of only one case, but since the observations describe the completed cycle of a community action program, these inferences can be of particular interest to students of community action. The conclusions as hypotheses are:

1. Local support for a community action program is directly proportional to the degree to which the provisions of the program satisfy the norms of key statuses in the community.

2. The plan for any community action program will contain provisions which conflict with the norms of one or more key statuses in a community containing a variety of key statuses.

3. Active opposition to a community action program is indirectly proportional to the degree of compromise by the program administrators on issues created when the norms of key status groups conflict with the provisions of the action program.

4. The development of a community action program will create unanticipated conditions which will be in conflict with the norms of key statuses with which there was no conflict at the beginning of the program.

5. Involvement in an action program, either pro or con, is more likely on the part of opinion leaders, business and professional persons, and white collar workers than on the part of unskilled laborers or persons on relief.

6. When persons who are community leaders also operate as leaders of a community action program, there will be a tendency toward local factionalism unless the influence which these persons obtain from their role in the program is to some degree controlled by other members of the community.

7. The greater the number of key statuses which come to participate in the program, the less the likelihood of factionalism.

8. The greater the range of choices provided by the action plan so as to satisfy the norms of key statuses, the less the likelihood of faction.

9. The greater the factional activity associated with an action program, the more the consequences of the program will deviate from the goals stated in the original action plan.

10. The greater the factional opposition created by a program, the greater the tendency for the leadership of the program to operate as its own faction.

*9. Preparing Neighborhoods for Change

Mel J. Ravitz

Introduction In the previous chapter by Dr. Janes a community was faced with a flood which nearly swept it out of existence. Residents had to take immediate action if the community was to survive. The crisis-producing event, the flood, in startling fashion, upset normal social relationships and the functioning of existing community structures and institutions. Dr. Janes' chapter vividly illustrates one type of change, raw, dramatic, perceptible, which requires immediate attention and which usually results in effective cooperation of those involved.

Another type of community change, perhaps less dramatic and perceptible, although keenly discernible to the careful observer, is the change in neighborhood populations. Persons of different backgrounds are constantly moving into neighborhoods where there is already an identifiable population. The process of neighborhood change has been described by the urban sociologist as invasion, concentration, and succession. This process is found in all communities, although the rate of change may vary dependent upon the degree of heterogeneity of people and factors affecting mobility, such as available housing for minority groups and the location of industry in fringe areas.

Since World War II Northern cities like Chicago, Philadelphia, Detroit, and Cleveland have experienced large in-migrations of rural Southern Negroes and mountain whites from such states as Alabama, Tennessee, West Virginia, Georgia, North Carolina, and Pennsylvania. For the most part there is no welcome wagon to greet these newcomers, and they find their way into the slums or transitional areas where housing

173

for a transient population is available. In time, the pressure of over-crowding in the ghetto-like neighborhood and the improved economic conditions of many newcomers push many of them into better neighbor-hoods of the city. The invasion process begins; the invaded neighborhood may erupt in racial, ethnic, or class conflict unless preparatory measures are taken.

What preparations should be made to reduce potential conflict be-tween neighborhood residents of different backgrounds? In the following selection Dr. Mel J. Ravitz, a student of the city who has had extensive experience with these problems in Detroit, describes a series of steps necessary for preparing neighborhoods for such population change.

By his definition a neighborhood is smaller than a community, is approximately one mile square, and is characterized by social interaction and identification among its residents. People are prepared for change in two ways: informed as to the expected changes and taught to understand and live with these changes. Current types of populations involved in neighborhood changes include particularly the lower social class, Negro lower class, middle- or upper-class white, and middle- or upper-class Negro. The different population types usually live in different kinds of physical and social neighborhoods. The Negro and white lower classes inhabit the old, rotten, rat-infested buildings of the slums; the lower middle classes are in the conservative areas just outside the core, usually in twenty-five to thirty-five-year-old "middle-aged" housing; and the mid-dle and upper classes live in the newer homes in the fringe and suburban areas. The potential in-migrants may vary from established populations in at least three characteristics: race, class, race and class. Thus since there are three types of populations and three types of neighborhoods, the possible combinations are nine. While the probabilities are low than an upper-class white population might move into a lower-class Negro neigh-borhood, the combinations of lower-class Negroes moving into a middle-class Negro or white neighborhood or middle- or upper-class Negroes moving into middle- and upper-class suburban communities are probable. Each of these or other possibilities of neighborhood change requires a particular set of neighborhood preparations.

The policies and practices of local government, social and welfare agencies, and churches influence the direction of neighborhood change and integration. Suppose you were given the responsibility of preparing a neighborhood of your community for the integration of newcomers. What things would you do to accomplish this task? In his paper Pro-fessor Ravitz gives ten suggestions for preparing neighborhoods for change. Before you read his list write your own on a sheet of paper and then see how close your procedures are to his. Preparing people for population change is no easy task, and Dr. Ravitz' thoughtful and much-needed analysis merits careful reading by the student of the community.

* As EVERY STUDENT of the city knows, two of its chief characteristics are hetereogeneity and mobility. Our cities are composed of many different ethnic, religious, economic, and racial types. These people tend to move within the city itself and also to and from any particular city. These twin factors of heterogeneity and mobility are the bases from which the concepts of invasion and succession have been developed. In every city there is evidence of the process of invasion and succession wherein one identifiable population begins to move into a neighborhood already occupied by another identifiable population and gradually becomes the majority population of that area.

SOURCES AND TYPES OF CHANGE

The process of invasion and succession is not new to the city; it has occurred any number of times before, especially with ethnic and religious types. There have also been invasions of neighborhoods by Negroes and the gradual succession of an area by them. However, it is only within the past ten years—roughly since the end of World War II—that Northern industrial centers have again been faced with some of the problems brought about by both rapid and widespread invasion and succession.

Into these cities in the early forties and the fifties, years of war and war preparation, flowed an invasion of Southerners— mostly rural in background with a heavy concentration of Negroes and poor whites. When the largest wave of these families came, in the early forties, they were crowded into the core areas of these Northern cities, into the so-called "black belts" and poor white areas, which were already overcrowded and where the housing quality was the very worst. The situation was worse for Negroes than for the whites, inasmuch as they were compelled by a tight ring of formal and informal restrictive agreements to move into and stay in the overcrowded Negro slums.

After the war, many of these Southerners, both Negro and
white, stayed in these Northern cities to make them their home.
Seniority security, brought about by the labor unions, plus a rising
real wage made it possible for many of these families seriously
to contemplate the American dream of self-improvement and to
move out of the slums to a better neighborhood—perhaps even to
buy their own home.

In 1948 by United States Supreme Court decision, the effective
legal barrier to Negro movement was eliminated; restrictive cove-
nents were ruled legally unenforceable. With this court decision
and the greatly improved economic condition of Negroes, the expected bursting out began. Negroes too began to move from their
overcrowded, dilapidated houses and neighborhoods into the physically better houses and neighborhoods nearby. The acute problems
of the changing neighborhood came again to the fore. We may accurately note that there is no more basic problem in these large
Northern cities than the problem of intergroup relations, especially
as it occurs in the changing neighborhood. It is a problem that
affects almost every institution and activity: schools, churches,
public and private housing, shopping, and recreation.

Since the problem is a continuing one, and inasmuch as tensions may explode at any time and in many possible areas of these
cities, it has seemed reasonable to inquire what can be done to
prepare neighborhoods for change of population so that violence
or increasing hatred do not occur. This study does not suggest that
preparing neighborhoods for such population change is an easy
task; it is extremely complex and difficult, not to say delicate. There
are still no simple formulas to distribute to eager and hopeful citizens. We know only a few things that may be helpful.

Before attempting to indicate what some of these are, it will be
useful to define carefully the chief elements of the phrase "preparing neighborhoods for change."

"Change" is defined as the passing from one condition or phase
to another. Thus physical change may mean that one racial group
replaces another in a given area.

By "neighborhood" is meant a geographically identifiable area,
not much larger than a mile square at most, bounded by major
physical features and within which there is a large or small number
of people—men, women, and children—who are in social relation-

ship with each other as they go about their business of making a home, raising and educating children, playing, shopping, worshipping, and working. A neighborhood is people and institutional agencies in social interaction.

One other term needs clarification: the word "preparing." There are at least two ways in which people can be prepared for population change or any other kind of change. They can be informed that it is going to happen and then advised either to accept it or to resist it or to avoid it by running elsewhere. Another way is to teach them to understand the reasons for the change and some of the problems and consequences. This educational approach seeks implicitly to encourage people to accept the change; the other approach seeks implicitly to discourage them.

In line with the democratic ethic, one aspect of which favors free and unrestricted movement of people, it would seem appropriate to encourage people to accept population change of their neighborhood, provided only that this change does not concomitantly bring with it undesirable living conditions. This point should be made perfectly clear; it is not suggested here that every population change or even most changes in and of themselves lower the physical or moral levels of neighborhoods. This is manifestly not true, as evidence of improvement in neighborhood after neighborhood makes clear. On the other hand, some of these population changes can lower living levels, and when this occurs it is difficult to justify encouraging acceptance of the population change. At the very least, people should also be encouraged and aided in maintaining their own neighborhood standards and in assisting the newcomers to understand and meet these standards. This is easier to state than to accomplish because in a neighborhood undergoing change there are basic differences among people in background, in values, and in income. That it can be done or at least effectively begun is evidenced by the fact that as part of the urban renewal program of many cities efforts are underway to develop block and neighborhood organizations dedicated to maintaining physical housekeeping standards. Some of these groups, at least, are not particularly concerned with the racial or religious characteristics of the newcomers; they are very much concerned about their housekeeping habits.

A neighborhood, consisting as it does of families and institutional agencies, is in a condition of constant flux. People are always moving into or out of any urban neighborhood. Neighborhood stability is, at best, only a relative concept. As families grow in size, as incomes vary, and as people marry, age, and die, there are bound to be changed housing needs for the families of a neighborhood. People of all backgrounds in urban neighborhoods move to find new housing better suited to their changed family needs. The rate of such movement may vary with the particular ethnic, religious, social, or class composition of the neighborhood, but all populations change. No problem occurs, unless a new family moving into a neighborhood happens to be either of a different race or class from those already living there. When that happens, and if the usual efforts to resist it fail, a panic may begin and for-sale signs pop up. This occurs especially hurriedly if the new family is Negro of any class. Sometimes this panic selling is deliberately provoked or intensified by unscrupulous real estate brokers, both Negro and white, who deliberately encourage housing sales in order to profit from their resale. Not infrequently this is done by trickery; for example, it is suggested that at times certain real estate firms have hired a Negro salesman to accompany a white salesman to a particular block. Then, while the Negro salesman conspicuously raps on the door of houses on one side of the street, the white salesman carefully points him out to fearful homeowners on the other side and stresses that other neighbors are about to sell to Negroes. Another reported tactic is to have a Negro woman wheel a baby buggy down a block accompanied by one or more small Negro children as evidence to the white homeowners that Negroes have already moved onto the block or at least onto an adjacent one. Under the skillful fear-mongering of adroit real estate salesmen, the woman and her children become the symbol of Negro invasion and home sales increase. One thing, however, should be remembered and repeated: population change of any neighborhood can occur only if, and at the rate, that the original families living there sell or move.

This summary of what happens in neighborhoods as they undergo population change is presented in order to draw some distinctions between the kinds of populations involved in neighborhood changes. One simple distinction, that between race and class, has already been suggested. On the basis of this distinction, we may establish four separate categories of population. These are lower-class white, lower-class Negro, middle- or upper-class white, middle- or upper-class Negro. Add to this list of categories the fact that those neighborhoods that are changing or that soon will change are presently occupied mainly by lower middle- or middle-class whites, and you will see quite clearly the nature of the problem and the several different kinds of education that must be advanced in order to prepare people for orderly population change.

Many large Northern cities consist of three main kinds of housing and population layers: the old city, the inner core, within which is most of the slum housing and within which live a very large proportion of lower-class Negroes and whites. Just outside this central core lies a thick band of conservative neighborhoods with "middle-aged" housing inhabited, until recently, mainly by middle-class and a few upper-class white people, but with Negroes and working-class whites already invading in very large numbers. These are the major changing neighborhoods of our cities, at the present time. Just outside this thick band of neighborhoods are the new growth areas of the city with their new homes inhabited in the main by middle-class and some upper-class families, all white. The movement of population is centrifugal, outward from the core. This direction of movement holds for Negroes as well as whites, for the lower class as well as for middle and upper classes. Examination of an ethnic map of any of the large Northern cities—Detroit, Cleveland, Chicago, Pittsburgh, New York, Philadelphia, Boston—will document this image of the city.

Several distinct kinds of population change must be recognized if we would prepare neighborhoods for them. First, there is the change of population on a sheer racial basis. This occurs when a white middle-class neighborhood is invaded by Negro middle-class families (as we have mentioned, there is usually no problem when the newcomers are of both the same race and class as the present residents). One kind of preparation needs to be accomplished in the instance of pure racial change, which theoretically is no real threat to neighborhood class standards. In line with our democratic ethic, white families now living in these situations ought to be encouraged to remain side by side with their new Negro neighbors at the same class or higher. All residents of such a racially mixed neighborhood ought to organize to conserve and improve their now common neighborhood. In such situations block and neighborhood organization can be emphasized as a major means to maintain neighborhood standards.

Second among the kinds of neighborhood population change is change on a clear class basis. Though this may occur when lower-class Negroes invade a middle- or upper-class Negro neighborhood, it is most apt to occur when lower-class whites infiltrate a neighborhood formerly composed of white middle- or upper-class families. This constitutes another kind of change, involves different problems of preparation, and points again to the problems of potential lowering of neighborhood standards. It may be relevant to hypothesise that lower middle-class homeowners are more apt than upper middle-class or upper-class homeowners to resent and resist any threat to the worth of their most prized possession—their property. Some data available from Detroit seem to support such a generalization, although this point needs to be explored in greater detail.

Still another kind of change is that which encompasses both class and race when, for example, lower-class Negro families move into an all-white, middle-class neighborhood or vice versa. This, too, is happening in some sections of our cities, although it is probably not as widespread as some of us believe. Provided that the property is well maintained and that signs of physical deterioration have not been allowed to creep into a neighborhood, it is likely that the newcomers, whether Negro or white, will be of the class level to afford the property, to maintain it in the style of the area, and, if given the chance, to share many common values with the present residents. If, however, a neighborhood is not well maintained, if it has many obsolete big houses, if traffic is permitted to become overly heavy, if any house is allowed to become so deteriorated that other middle- or upper-class families, Negro or white, are loathe to move in, then that neighborhood will attract a lower-class person, whether white or Negro. There may be a general lowering of condition of a house through no one's deliberate fault but because of a lack of financial means for home maintainance and improvement on the part of the newcomer. In order to meet his rent or monthly payments, he may subdivide and admit other families to property originally intended for only one or two families. Physically, this would contribute to the deterioration of the neighborhood.

We have now indicated four theoretical and three actual types of neighborhood population change that may require preparation. There are other possible kinds of populations too, particularly religious and ethnic, that are often involved in the process of invasion and succession, but we will not deal with these now, although both types present definite problems. As for the types of population change we did mention—different racial, different class, and different class and racial—these three kinds require different preparation or education.

STEPS TO BE TAKEN

In every neighborhood, each new resident should be permitted to move in without question and to have the chance to conduct himself in harmony with the housekeeping habits of the present residents. There ought to be no barrier based on either race or assumed class. If, however, any newcomer or any present resident fails to maintain his property in suitable manner or if he degrades its use by overcrowding, for example, or by an illegal use of the building, then every effort should be made first to encourage and then to compel him to conform to the city's codes and ordinances. As indicated many times before, one of the best ways to maintain high levels of living on a block or in a neighborhood is through sound democratic block and neighborhood organization involving all of the residents. This kind of organization is being encouraged as part of the urban renewal program of such cities as Detroit, Chicago, St. Louis, Philadelphia, and Boston.

To prepare the people of any neighborhood for a change in the homogeneity of population is not an easy task, given the many prejudices and differing values of our people. Nevertheless, there are some things that can be done. If the neighborhood is viewed as a social complex composed of families and institutional agencies within the context of the larger community, then certain focal points for concentrated preparation can be recognized.

As a subgrouping of the city, the neighborhood is influenced

by city-wide factors. For example, the intergroup relation policies
of the city administration, of the board of education, of the police
department, of the library commission affect the people of every
neighborhood; they can be important instruments to help prepare
people of any neighborhood for change. Likewise, the intergroup
relation policies of the semi-public and private city-wide agencies
have an important effect; these bodies include the radio and TV
stations, the religious denominations, the Community Chest member agencies, and the various newspaper organizations. In addition to these city-wide agencies, which usually have local units in
the neighborhood, there are also a few agencies or groups without
any larger affiliation but which exist and draw membership from
the particular neighborhood; civil improvement associations and
block or neighborhood councils are examples. Finally, in any neighborhood, there are some persons who are the opinion makers and to
whom other people listen on matters of importance. In preparing a
neighborhood for change, the greater the number of these agencies,
groups, or individuals that support population integration and the
greater the influence they can muster with which to do so, the
greater the likelihood of accomplishing the change with a minimum
of hostility and a maximum of welcome.

More specifically, we may suggest these things that should be
done to help prepare a neighborhood for population change:

1. Those interested in preparing neighborhoods for change
should strive to secure from the responsible head of local government a clear public statement that the law prohibits any kind of
compulsory housing segregation and that his administration will
strive earnestly to support that policy. The absence of such a
pointed public statement permits the development of an atmosphere
of tension and uncertainty as one group seeks to "push out" and
purchase housing it believes it can afford and another group seeks
to hold it where it is. When a public statement is made, there is
no question in anyone's mind as to the local administration's position and policy; such a firm administrative stand doubtless deters
many people from organizing to resist racial, religious, or economic
invasion. It is the uncertainty of the city administration's policy
or preference that exists in the minds of potential resistors that

induces some of them, at least, to resort to mob action and intimidation.

2. Interested persons should strive to secure this same kind of public statement from the heads of all city-wide agencies—both public and private—to their neighborhood or district chapters. Specifically, such agencies as the local real estate board, the local banking or mortgage lending organization, the local board of education, the local insurance underwriting agent, the local library board should be invited and encouraged to take a public stand. Invariably, this will be easier to achieve once the head of government has made a statement.

3. They should also seek to secure from the head of government and from the police commissioner public assurance that the police of the city will uphold to the limit, if necessary, the right of any family of any race, creed, religion, or nationality to move wherever it chooses to buy or rent.

4. The people working for better relations should seek to have all regular law enforcement officers trained in the handling of intergroup incidents. A special training course could be developed and taught by instructors from the nearest college or university. Every effort should be made to recruit policemen who will uphold the law for all residents to the city and to train these men intelligently so that they will be able to do so adequately. All too often, good intentions are not backed by specific skills to do a job effectively. This is especially true in the delicate sphere of intergroup relations.

5. The responsible heads of the neighborhood churches, schools, libraries should be reached and their support secured in explaining the facts behind the rumors that inevitably crop up when neighborhoods begin to change. Clergymen, principals, librarians, club presidents, and other such formal leaders in a neighborhood can do much to offset the growth of hostility by continually focusing attention on the facts of any given situation.

6. These agencies, as well as such groups as PTA's, neighborhood service clubs, civic associations, neighborhood and community councils, should be encouraged to emphasize in their programs the democratic ethic of equal rights and equal opportunities for all

peoples. They should be encouraged to present through films, discussion, or literature, accurate portrayals of the newcomers as simply people like everyone else, desirous of achieving the same goals as other people of the neighborhood. Such activities as a rumor clinic, films such as *High Wall, Boundary Lines, Picture in Your Mind,* a library exhibit on the races of mankind, visiting speakers on intergroup relations, a conducted tour of various kinds of housing in a city can help in the gradual educational effort to persuade people that race, religion, or nationality are poor indicators of quality of neighbors. In this vein it would be of great interest to develop a theoretically effective sequence of program materials such as those just mentioned and then to test the effectiveness of this sequence in changing peoples' intergroup attitudes. To do this adequately would require selection of two or more matched neighborhoods or groups and the introduction of the particular program sequence into one of the groups only. Attitude testing both before and after the introduction of the program sequence in both neighborhoods or groups would gauge the success of the programs.

7. The informal leaders and opinion molders of the neighborhood should be sought out and efforts made to enlist their help in developing an atmosphere of intergroup understanding and willingness to welcome and work with the newcomers. In this regard it would be important not to overlook such strategically situated persons as the bartenders, the barbers and beauticians, the corner druggist. It might be even desirable to invite these people and other informal leaders to a neighborhood workshop on intergroup relations. Invitations from people of prestige in the overall community would doubtless elicit their interest and support. At such a workshop stress could be placed on the significance of their positions as gate-keepers in the neighborhood and on their civic responsibility to help educate for sound unsegregated neighborhood living.

8. Social workers and visiting teachers assigned to a neighborhood should be able to find many ways of assisting to prepare a neighborhood for change, if they want to. In the first place, they should encourage residents who hold hostile attitudes to review these attitudes. By direct and subtle appeal to established demo-

cratic and religious values of tolerance and brotherhood, they can seek to reveal the inconsistency of such prejudiced attitudes. By attempting to build into the hostile person some increased capacity for seeing what it is like to be a newcomer, it may be possible to lessen the harshness of his hostility; it may even be possible to get some of these persons to admit some doubt about their own knowledge of the newcomers. A second way social workers, whether case workers, group workers, or community organizers, can help prepare a neighborhood for change emerges from a recognition of their position as among the opinion makers of the area. Group workers and community organizers especially can play an influential role by striving to open their various group programs to all residents of the area, regardless of race, religion, nationality, or income. In a dozen different ways they can see to it that no intention or unintential slight is given to any element in the neighborhood but that all are included in the planning of any program. Often this will be most effectively done in committee meetings or in individual conferences. To the extent that the social worker has prestige in the neighborhood, to that extent he or she is a potential agent of improved human relations. Not just on the verbal level either; he has the power often to help structure situations so that people will come together under conditions that encourage sympathetic understanding and friendship.

Finally, it is important for social workers and teachers in the field to strive to build and develop feelings of personal worth and adequacy in neighborhood residents. This is a task that can be attempted on both the individual and group basis. If it is done on a personal basis, as it often can be with some persons, it sometimes occurs more quickly, though fewer people are involved. It would take a long time to affect a neighborhood by working on an individual basis. Perhaps it would be more fruitful if, through the development of block and neighborhood organizations, and in already existing groups of whatever sort, many members could be made to feel that they have a role to play in helping to make meaningful decisions in the neighborhood. One of the chief problems faced is the apathy and indifference on the part of so many citizens; these people do not participate for many reasons, but perhaps two important reasons are that the group to which the worker wants them to come does not interest them and that they feel they cannot derive ego support and prestige from such a group. When people feel a sense of personal importance and confidence resulting from membership in a group, they will return to participate again, even, we may suggest, if the other members of the group were originally considered socially undesirable.

9. Every opportunity should be provided through block and neighborhood organization, through church, school, youth groups, the library, or the PTA, to get old residents and newcomers actually working together at common problems and projects such as the maintenance and improvement of properties in their now common neighborhood. Lawn care, tree trimming, porch repair, rat elimination, projects for alley sanitation and relief of overcrowding—these are specific items that draw together people of different racial, or religious, or even different income-level backgrounds. Experience in Detroit's Neighborhood Conservation Program (as well as the project in Chicago's Hyde Park–Kenwood Area) which sought to develop grass roots organization at the block and neighborhood level, emphasizes this point. This experience provided evidence for the hypothesis that the greater the interest in common problems that can be aroused in Negro and white neighbors on an equal status basis, the less concern there is with issues of racial difference.

10. Finally, people need to do more than desegregate themselves, which is a necessary first step; they need to develop bonds of social integration on the block, the neighborhood, and the community levels—bonds of integration through open communication, shared problems, and shared values. These things often develop as consequences of other factors. The process will occur gradually and slowly as people become aware of their common problems and begin to view each other as able to work cooperatively to resolve them. While it is not true that simply bringing people together automatically eliminates or limits tension and hostility, it does seem to hold true if they are brought together under controlled and favorable circumstances to work at problems common to all of them.

Initially, the aim of preparing a neighborhood for population change may be to prevent any display of anti-social behavior; subsequently, the opportunity will be available to modify attitude of prejudice. The elimination of both anti-social behavior and prejudice is ultimately desirable.

One point must be repeated: change is never absent from any neighborhood; populations are constantly shifting in the modern metropolis. Gradually, as prejudice diminishes, as income levels rise, and as people learn to conserve their homes and neighborhoods, the need to prepare people for population change will disappear. People will be able to move, without fear or suspicion, wherever they wish. All will have been prepared to be good neighbors by the general cultural development of society. That day, however, is still some time off. Its arrival can be hastened by courageous, cooperative action on the part of all who belong to the "fellowship of the concerned." We may hope that social service workers will serve with distinction in that fellowship.

* 10. Organizing Communities for Urban Renewal: A Structural Model and Its Application

Frank L. Sweetser

Introduction Urban redevelopment of American cities begun under the Housing Act of 1949 is a specific effort by local and federal governments to restore the inner life and vitality of the city. Initial programs were devoted to slum clearance and re-use of the land for housing, commercial, business, or industrial development. The programs begun under the 1949 Housing Act were insufficient to prevent the spread of urban decay. In 1954 a new feature to the act enabled communities engaged in redevelopment programs to broaden their activities to include conservation and rehabilitation of partially deteriorated areas. In practice, federal funds were made available for programs aimed at conserving and restoring middle-aged housing in neighborhoods which, though deteriorating, were economically salvageable. Thus, urban renewal was born and its total approach to urban blight was slum clearance (if necessary), rehabilitation programs in neighborhoods which included home renovation, off-street parking, playgrounds, and other facilities, and programs of spot clearance of run-down buildings to prevent incipient slums. Substantial funds were made available to support these objectives, with the Federal Government paying up to two-thirds of the cost of approved programs.

Before a local urban renewal agency can receive federal funds for its program, it has to involve members of the community in its work and give evidence of citizen participation. This provision by the Federal

Government makes sense. For how can the good qualities of a community be preserved without the cooperation of its members? Demonstration projects were begun in selected cities to determine means of securing citizen participation and the type of community structure most suitable for maximum participation.

Boston was chosen as a site for a demonstration project on community organization for urban renewal, and this recently completed project is the basis of Dr. Frank L. Sweetser's report. The first part of his chapter is concerned with the construction of a community organization model to facilitate the maximum of cooperation and communication between individuals in various groups and institutional structures.

The problems of developing an effective model for community organization are many because groupings exist on several participation planes ranging from the citizen with his local neighborhood organization whose immediate concern is what the program is going to do to him, to the community-wide group representing persons of wealth, power, and influence, whose approval is necessary if a project is to succeed and whose concern may envelope the whole of the metropolitan area. Dr. Ravitz in the preceding chapter demonstrated how important government, industrial, civic, business, and welfare associations are as determiners of the direction of social change. These same groups and others representing the economic, domestic, educational, religious, governmental, welfare, and civic elements in a community must be considered in constructing a model of community organization which will produce effective citizen participation in urban renewal.

The second section of Dr. Sweetser's chapter is concerned with the application of the model to two communities involved in urban renewal programs. The structural model was used to assess existing patterns of community organization in these two communities. Also model building in community organization is necessary as a guide for determining the strengths and weaknesses of existing community structures and communication networks. However, as Dr. Sweetser emphasizes, such a model as developed in Boston may not fit the patterns of social structure in Cleveland or Detroit. It cannot be used to evaluate an existing pattern of community organization without a careful study of that community's social structure. No two communities are alike, and minor differences are many. It would be an unfair test of the effectiveness of local community organization if the evaluators were not aware of these variations in structure. If the model is used as a guide or an approximation of what is the "ideal" form of community organization, it then can indicate the strengths and weaknesses of community organizational structure. Even if changes in structure are made, this alone does not insure effective cooperation. The value of the model is in indicating whether structural weaknesses in organization may impede effective community action. We need more model building and application of these models in the community field.

✻ In 1955–1956 the Housing Association of Metropolitan Boston conducted a demonstration project on community organization for urban renewal.[1] This chapter describes a structural model for such community organizations and shows how the model was used by the staff of the Housing Association in its activities.

URBAN RENEWAL AND COMMUNITY ORGANIZATION

A structural model is a simplified and generalized pattern of relationships among the many groupings and associations which together comprise the social structure of a community.[2] Such a model may be described in terms of (a) *dominant elements,* (b) *planes of participation,* and (c) *relationships among groups* of various types on the several planes. *Dominant elements* of community structure are those associations, agencies, and groups which are most pervasively influential in molding people's opinions and attitudes and in determining the course of social change in the community. *Planes of participation* range in geographic scope from community-wide through district to neighborhood and block levels of organiza-

[1] Urban Renewal Demonstration Project # Mass. D-1 was conducted by the Housing Association of Metropolitan Boston under the direction of Dr. William C. Loring, Jr. The author served as Director of Area Research. The project was sponsored jointly by the Demonstration Program Branch of the Urban Renewal Administration, Housing and Home Finance Agency, and by the Massachusetts Department of Commerce. It is described in William C. Loring, Jr., Frank L. Sweetser, and Charles F. Ernst, *Community Organization for Citizen Participation in Urban Renewal* (Cambridge: The Cambridge Press, Inc., 1957).

[2] The present model for renewal-oriented community organization selects and emphasizes those aspects of the whole which are especially relevant to the purposes of urban renewal, but it does not differ in principle from models which might be developed for other community-wide action programs. Thus the present discussion has implications beyond the limited field of urban renewal.

tion. The term *relationships among groups* refers to those links between groups on the same participation plane or on different planes.

DOMINANT ELEMENTS IN COMMUNITY STRUCTURE

People living in urban communities tend to compartmentalize various aspects of their lives, sometimes to an extreme degree, and to affiliate themselves with a wide variety of groupings. These many groupings exist on several participation planes (local, district, or community-wide), and are interconnected by a complex net of group interrelationships. Despite the complexity, however, social scientists have long recognized that human groupings and activities could be classified into a small number of functional categories or types. These categories have been variously described, but consensus on the basic typology is general.[3] For the present purpose, seven categories of dominant elements in community structure are distinguished and are labelled as follows:

1. economic
2. domestic
3. educational
4. religious

5. governmental
6. welfare
7. civic

In American cities today, families, schools, and churches are readily recognized as dominants in the development of individual attitudes, just as the larger corporations or business associations, agencies of government, and larger civic or welfare organizations are recognized as determiners of the direction of social change. These, then, are the types of social groupings which constitute the dominant elements in the social structure of American cities. Each is related in characteristic ways to the problem of community organization for urban renewal, and in the discussion below it will be indicated how each is necessary and useful in a research program.

ECONOMIC ELEMENTS

Urban renewal programs require the coordinated reinvestment of both public and private funds in blighted and partially blighted

[3] Robert S. and Helen M. Lynd, *Middletown* (New York: Harcourt, Brace & Co., 1929). W. Lloyd Warner and Paul S. Lunt, *The Social Life of a Modern Community* (New Haven: Yale University Press, 1941), pp. 28–43.

residential areas. All of the numerous corporations, business associations, and unions with the most direct and the most considerable economic stake in the program can be thought of as potentially active dominant elements.

DOMESTIC ELEMENTS

Families, as the occupants of both standard and substandard dwelling units in an urban renewal area, are among the most important dominant structural elements in a community contemplating an urban renewal program. The attitudes of the heads of families and households toward their homes, the surrounding environment, and improvement of blight may well determine the success of a program of rehabilitation or conservation. If the prevailing attitude is one of indifference to squalor and environmental deficiency or one of despair ("nothing can be done about it"), continuing deterioration is almost certain. Those most interested in improving their own and their family's lot will see no alternative to moving away from the deteriorated area. If these interested families leave, they remove a likely source of local leadership that might otherwise vigorously seek to halt and reverse the spread of blight.

EDUCATIONAL ELEMENTS

Schools themselves—especially elementary schools—comprise a meaningful portion of the environment of the neighborhood. Since Clarence Perry described the neighborhood unit thirty years ago,[4] planners have been in general agreement that city planning for residential land uses was most reasonably conceived in terms of an area populated by the families whose children attend the same elementary school.

The schools and related organizations are linked in many ways to urban renewal activities. City reinvestment in new schools and playgrounds may provide a part of the costs of a renewal project. Elementary schools, as more or less natural neighborhood centers, may provide meeting places for neighborhood groups. School-related organizations such as parent-teacher associations may incorporate urban renewal goals in their programs. Teachers of civics

[4] Clarence A. Perry and associates, *Neighborhood and Community Planning*, The Regional Survey of New York and its Environs, vol. 7 (1929).

or citizenship may organize their teaching and project work around problems of blight and urban renewal. The teachers may offer a source of leadership for citizens' groups, or the school itself may become the structure through which neighborhood stability and continuity of neighborhood interest in conservation is achieved.

RELIGIOUS ELEMENTS

Churches, like schools, are rooted in their neighborhoods. In some denominations with strong parish structures, the neighborhood orientation is clear-cut, and the church's interest in the elimination of environmental blight is plain. Both Catholic priests and Protestant ministers have been active in neighborhood conservation programs in Chicago, Boston, and many other cities.

GOVERNMENTAL ELEMENTS

The agencies of government and their personnel acting in official capacities would not be of direct concern in this analysis of the participation of *private* citizens except for two facts. First, since urban renewal is a governmental program in which the cooperation of participating private citizens is enlisted, the governmental agencies concerned with renewal constitute the central dominant in the total situation. Second, much of the activity of citizens and citizens' groups as they participate in the urban renewal process will naturally be directed toward the official agencies which are administering the program. Thus, while government *as such* is not our subject, the problem of communication between private citizens and citizens' organizations on the one hand and the agencies and officials of government on the other is, in a very real sense, a key problem.

WELFARE ELEMENTS

Most cities likely to engage in urban renewal programs have established some form of centrally federated council of social agencies, like the Somerville Community Council or the Cleveland Welfare Federation. These welfare federations serve to coordinate private welfare agencies of all kinds within the community, to unify fund-raising campaigns in the familiar Red Feather drives, and to provide needed central services, such as research or case referrals. They, together with their constituent agencies, become dominant elements of community structure for purposes of urban renewal in a number of ways. First, as has been repeatedly shown, the incidence of blight and the incidence of many other social problems of concern to welfare agencies correlate very closely in most American cities. This means that the deteriorated areas are likely to be the areas best known to social workers and to contain proportionately more welfare resources than other areas where the need is less. Second, in some cities, the central federations of welfare agencies concern themselves directly with the building up of district and neighborhood organizations, through which citizens may participate.[5] Third, even in the absence of central welfare council concern with district and neighborhood organizations as such, certain types of social agencies usually affiliated with such central councils may well be active in partially blighted areas. Settlement houses are perhaps the most conspicuous example. Not only are the settlements located in blighted or partially blighted areas but their programming often includes a stress on neighborhood or district organization. Fourth, the central welfare federation may include special-purpose agencies directly concerned with renewal problems. The Housing Association of Metropolitan Boston, for example, is a member of the United Community Services. Whether formal affiliation exists or not, citizens' housing or planning associations operating for nonprofit civic purposes are to be found in many American cities. The interest of such associations in urban renewal and their potential importance to the renewal program as channels of citizen participation are obvious.

ELEMENTS IN CIVIC STRUCTURES

By "civic structures" is meant the whole range of organizations and associations devoted primarily to civic improvement and neighborhood or community betterment, aside from those which are more conveniently classified in another category.[6] Leagues of

[5] As Arthur Hillman (author of chapter 7) observes, "In larger cities especially, councils [of social agencies] have encouraged and given staff assistance in the formation of local community or neighborhood councils." *Community Organization and Planning* (New York: The Macmillan Co., 1950), p. 247.

[6] To illustrate: A PTA might be regarded as a civic organization, but its

Women Voters, taxpayers' associations, veterans' organizations, service clubs like Rotary or Kiwanis, civic improvement associations, better government leagues, district or community councils, neighborhood associations, and citizens' councils made up of civic leaders are a few of the many kinds of civic structures which may assume a role in a city's urban renewal program. Some of them, like the neighborhood associations, are probably indispensable as organizations through which citizens may participate in renewal; most of them by virtue of their devotion to civic betterment offer a potential channel for urban renewal participation.

GROUP INTERRELATIONSHIPS AND PLANES OF PARTICIPATION

It is evident from the above review of dominant elements in the community's social structure that the number of private organizations of various types in a modern American city is very large.[7] Fortunately, the requirements of action programs, like urban renewal, usually suggest guides in terms of which the complexity of urban social organization can be unravelled—at least for the purposes of the program. One of these guides is provided by the analysis of dominant elements of community structure. A second guide is found in the conception of planes or levels of citizen participation ranging from blocks or neighborhoods to districts, cities, and even metropolitan communities. Viewing the dominant elements from the viewpoint of the participation planes, it is evident that there are two fundamental sorts of group interrelationships in urban social structure: the *horizontal* links among citizens' groups on one participation plane and the *vertical* links which unite groups on different planes. Essentially, community organization for urban renewal requires that the dominant structural elements in the community be so interrelated horizontally and vertically that (1) there is easy communication in both directions and (2) some measure of coordination is achieved between group

---

direct concern with education leads to its classification as an educational structure; a Chamber of Commerce could similarly be considered a civic organization, and it performs many civic functions, but it seems primarily an economic organization and is so classified.

[7] For a more complete discussion of voluntary organizations see chapter 14.

activities and the progress of the city in the various stages of urban renewal.

A STRUCTURAL MODEL OF HORIZONTAL AND VERTICAL RELATIONSHIPS AMONG CITIZEN'S GROUPS

Figures 7, 8, and 9 show in schematic fashion one of the many ways in which a large urban community might be organized to facilitate the participation of citizens in its urban renewal program. The structural model in these charts describes no actual city and should be applied to a specific city only after careful analysis of its particular social structure. Yet a study of this structural model leads to a statement of criteria which can be used directly in evaluating a city's organization for citizen participation in urban renewal.

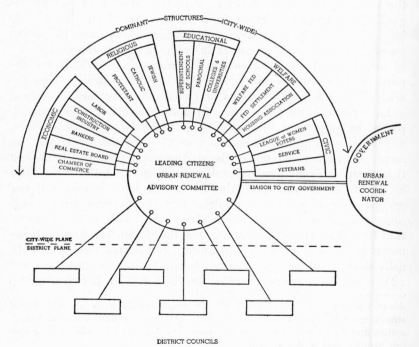

Figure 7.   Leading Citizens' Urban Renewal Advisory Committee

Figure 7 shows a city-wide "Leading Citizens' Urban Renewal Advisory Committee" as the apex of organization. This committee is advisory to the city's Urban Renewal Coordinator and advisory to citizens' groups concerned with urban renewal. The Leading Citizens' Urban Renewal Advisory Committee has the twofold communication function of transmitting to the Urban Renewal Coordinator the attitudes, opinions, and suggestions of citizens and of transmitting information concerning the city's program to citizens and citizens' groups. As figure 7 suggests, these functions require two principal horizontal links—between the Committee and the Urban Renewal Coordinator and between the Committee and other city-wide dominant structural groupings. The horizontal relation with the coordinator may take a number of forms; the important feature is the facility with which information, suggestions, requests, and reports may be passed through it in *both* directions. Similarly, the form of the relationship between the dominant structures and the Leading Citizens' Urban Renewal Advisory Committee matters much less than does its effectiveness in bringing information about the city's urban renewal program to the heads of dominate structures in the community and in turn bringing to the Leading Citizens'

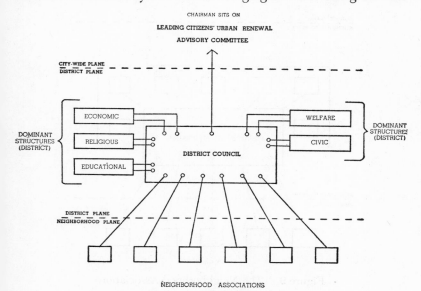

Figure 8.   The District Council

Urban Renewal Advisory Committee and to the Urban Renewal Coordinator the ideas of bankers, churchmen, and other leaders in dominate structures.

The vertical relationships of the Leading Citizens' Urban Renewal Advisory Committee to the District Councils is shown in the lower part of figure 7. Seven District Councils are shown, with liaison provided by the chairmen of the District Councils serving as members of the Leading Citizens' Urban Renewal Advisory Committee (see figure 8). This arrangement provides the necessary channels of vertical communication to bring the Committee the special points of view which characterize various districts of the city, and at the same time, it provides for direct communication vertically from the Committee to the District Councils.

Figure 8 diagrams a model District Council, composed of representatives of district dominants and of delegates from neighborhood associations within the district. The absence of a horizontal link to the city's urban renewal administration should be noted. None is shown because communication with district-level officials is assumed

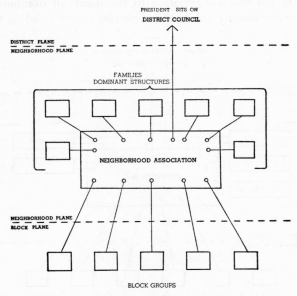

Figure 9.   The Neighborhood Association

to proceed first through the vertical channel to the Leading Citizens' Urban Renewal Advisory Committee, then to the Urban Renewal Coordinator, and finally along the administrative chain of the appropriate city department. Once protocol is thus satisfied, direct horizontal communication facilitates routine business.

The family does not appear as a dominant structure contributing to the membership of citizens' groups on either the city-wide or the district participation planes. When we turn to the neighborhood association, however, as suggested in figure 9, the family is the only type of dominant structure contributing to membership. The very character of neighborhood associations as civic groups oriented generally to neighborhood improvement requires that membership be open to all residents of the neighborhood area who share a common interest in the improvement of the area as a place to live. Horizontal relations of neighborhood associations with dominant structures are built up, characteristically, through the inclusion of family heads who are also identifiable as members of a given church, profession, or occupation group, in addition to being residents and (often) parents. Horizontal relations among neighborhood associations are formally provided for through the joint participation of their delegates to the District Council, as shown in figure 9.

The only vertical relation to higher planes of participation in figure 9 is the link to the District Council through the association president. Once the requirements of protocol are met, direct working relations are established between neighborhood associations and city departments working for renewal.

Block groups, essentially, are small neighborhood associations, and the vertical relations linking these two participation planes serve primarily to coordinate similar kinds of activity in the various geographic subdivisions of the neighborhood. Block chairmen, providing vertical liaison, are also members of the neighborhood association, as shown in figure 9.

THE BALANCE OF ELEMENTS AND PLANES

Study of the proposed structural model for community organization as described above shows that it is characterized by

(a) the *balanced* inclusion of citizens' groups representing relevant dominant elements on all participation planes and (b) the integration of these groups through appropriate vertical and horizontal relationships. These characteristics of the model suggest five criteria which the community organizer can apply in evaluating the structural soundness of a particular city's organization for urban renewal.

1. Relevant dominant elements should be included.[8]
2. Necessary citizens' groups should be present on each plane of participation.
3. Adequate horizontal relations should link groups on each participation plane.
4. Adequate vertical relations should link citizens' groups on different participation planes.
5. Satisfactory liaison should exist between citizens' groups and the city's urban renewal officials.

When, on applying these criteria, the community organizer finds serious weaknesses in an existing urban renewal structure, he can begin an organizing effort, designed to bring into being a sound structure of intergroup relationships through which citizen participation in an urban renewal program can be realized. Structural soundness alone cannot guarantee that a pattern of community organization will work effectively, but since its absence is certain to frustrate many programs and activities, the development of a sound and properly balanced structure of dominant elements and participation planes, adequately interrelated, should be the basic goal of community renewal organizations.

APPLICATION OF THE MODEL TO URBAN RENEWAL ORGANIZATION IN TWO CITIES

Somerville and Cambridge, Massachusetts, provide clear-cut illustrations of the way in which the structural model of community organization may be used in assessing existing organizations and in planning organizing procedures designed to remedy observed structural weaknesses.

---

[8] Relevant to urban renewal that is; community organization for other purposes would emphasize other dominant elements.

SOMERVILLE'S COMMITTEE ON NEIGHBORHOOD IMPROVEMENT

In 1954 leading citizens in Somerville, representing the Somerville Community Council, the chamber of commerce, and the city government, considered the problem of providing an organizational structure through which citizen participation in the city's urban renewal program could be channeled. A special committee of the Somerville Community Council was created, called the Committee on Neighborhood Improvement, to serve as a city-wide coordinating group. The committee was composed of representatives of municipal departments and of a variety of economic, educational, religious, and welfare groups. Indeed, it was drawn together with a very clear realization of the need for involving relevant dominant elements in the urban renewal program.

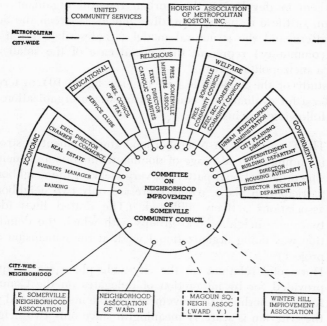

Figure 10.   Committee on Neighborhood Improvement, Somerville Community Council, May, 1956.

Figure 10 shows the organization of the Committee on Neighborhood Improvement as it existed in May, 1956, when the demonstration project drew to a close. A study of figure 10 will show that participation planes in Somerville differ in two respects from the structural model presented above (figures 7, 8, and 9). First, a metropolitan plane of participation is included, and second, there is no district plane, the neighborhood associations being related directly to the Committee on Neighborhood Improvement, which corresponds to the Leading Citizens' Urban Renewal Advisory Committee of the model. These differences arise from the fact that Somerville is a relatively small city (population 102,351 in 1950) situated near the heart of a large metropolitan community. Smaller cities, generally, can be effectively organized with no district structure intervening between local neighborhood groups and the city-wide citizens committee. And cities lying within metropolitan areas may find that metropolitan organizations are able and willing to assist them in developing their urban renewal organization and program. In these respects, then, divergencies between the Somerville pattern and the structural model (as described for a large urban community) represent the special case of the smaller city within a metropolitan area.

A study of the Somerville pattern (see figure 10) in terms of the criteria for evaluating a community's citizen organization leads to the following conclusions:

1. The Committee on Neighborhood Improvement is strong in including a broad range of dominant functional elements.
2. The organizational pattern is very weak in the neighborhood participation plane, where there are only two neighborhood associations actively affiliated. (The dotted lines identify two more neighborhood groups with which the demonstration was doing organizational work at the conclusion of the project).
3. Horizontal relations on the city-wide plane are adequately provided for by interaction of delegates on the Committee for Neighborhood Improvement. On the neighborhood plane, the criterion is scarcely meaningful since only two neighborhood associations are involved.

4. Vertical relations are adequately provided in the inclusion of neighborhood association delegates on the Committee for Neighborhood Improvement.

5. The structure of the Committee for Neighborhood Improvement provides for satisfactory liaison with the city's urban renewal administration by the inclusion of the administrative officers of five city departments or agencies as Committee members.[9]

It is apparent, then, that the Somerville organizational pattern is sound in most respects, but that it is seriously deficient in the second criterion. Indeed figure 10, representing the situation in May, 1956, shows appreciable improvement over an earlier pattern, when only a single neighborhood association, the East Somerville Neighborhood Association, was linked to the Committee. This neighborhood association had been organized by the Committee in the area of the city originally selected as a possible site for a rehabilitation project, expressly to meet the citizen participation requirement of the Federal Housing Act of 1954. For a year and a half, until the winter of 1955–1956, it was the only neighborhood group participating in renewal activities in Somerville. Then, since it had become evident that the absence of neighborhood groups in other parts of the city was seriously impeding effective action toward renewal on the part of the Committee and its related groups, the demonstration field staff undertook to organize additional neighborhood associations. The Neighborhood Association of Ward III was organized in February, 1956, and was a going concern in May when field work terminated. Field organizing work was being initiated in two other areas of Somerville at the end of the demonstration in a further effort to round out the organizational pattern of the city.

CAMBRIDGE'S COUNCIL OF NEIGHBORHOOD ASSOCIATIONS

Just as the Somerville case shows the importance of including local neighborhood groups as part of a city's community organization

[9] Actually, during the Demonstration, the city government was internally divided on the issue of urban renewal, so that in some respects little progress was made: nevertheless, the formal structural criterion is met, so far as the citizen organization is concerned. Loring, op. cit., chap. 4.

for urban renewal, the Cambridge case demonstrates the insufficiency of strong neighborhood organization in the absence of the dominant functional elements. Figure 11 charts the relationship of the Cambridge Council of Neighborhood Associations to other groups on three participation planes as of May, 1956. Like Somerville, Cambridge is a relatively small city (population 120,740 in 1950) near the center of a large metropolitan area, so that the metropolitan participation plane is included and the district plane omitted. It is at once evident from the chart that the Cambridge Council of Neighborhood Associations is a very different organization from Somerville's Committee on Neighborhood Improvement. Consisting in May, 1956, of delegates from eight neighborhood associations, it is altogether lacking in *formal* liaison with either the city government or with other city-wide dominant elements.

1. The Cambridge Council of Neighborhood Associations is weak in possessing no formal liaison with other city-wide

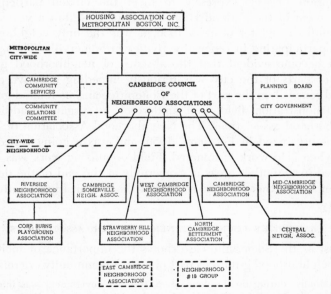

Figure 11.   Cambridge Council of Neighborhood Associations, May, 1956.

dominant elements. Only weak, informal links to two other private groups exist on the city-wide participation plane.

2. The Council is strong in linking eight neighborhood associations, representing eight of the thirteen neighborhoods into which the Planning Board has divided the city.

3. Horizontal relations on the city-wide plane are not adequately provided for, since a formal liaison structure is entirely lacking between the Council and other citizens' groups. On the neighborhood plane, the Council itself serves as the liaison group among the neighborhood associations, and communication channels are adequately built into the organizational structure.

4. Vertical relations from neighborhood to city-wide planes are adequate, although limited to a degree by the inadequate (rather, nonexistent) horizontal relations of the Council to other dominant elements.

5. No formal liaison to city government at all is provided by the organizational structure.

The Cambridge organizational pattern is weaker than the Somerville pattern, since it shows strength only on the second and the fourth criteria in having adequate citizens' groups and vertical relations linking citizens' groups on different participation planes. During the demonstration project the Cambridge Council of Neighborhood Associations was entirely limited to a single type of dominant element: the local civic group. While the Cambridge neighborhood associations were effectively interrelated through the Council, the overall pattern still represented a more serious lack of structural balance than is seen in the Somerville Committee on Neighborhood Improvement.

It should not be supposed from this analysis that the Cambridge Council has been ineffective. On the contrary, the group was exceedingly active and repeatedly succeeded in bringing together city officials and citizens, especially in a series of semi-annual conferences at which various renewal topics were discussed. Nevertheless, it is clear from the above comparison of the Council with the proposed structural model that the Council of Neighborhood Associations was intrinsically ill-adapted to serve as a Leading Citizens'

Urban Renewal Advisory Committee. What was needed in Cambridge at the close of the demonstration was a city-wide committee of leading citizens representing the dominant elements on that participation plane. Demonstration field efforts to bring such a group into being did not succeed directly, although several approaches were explored. But the pioneering educational work of the Council of Neighborhood Associations and the demonstration staff certainly contributed to the appointment, later in 1956, of just such a committee of leading citizens to advise on urban renewal in Cambridge.[10]

FURTHER APPLICATION OF THE MODEL

This chapter has described a structural model of community organization for citizen participation in urban renewal and has explained the manner in which the model emerged from the direct field experience of a demonstration project on citizen participation in urban renewal. In addition, the utility of the model and derived criteria in assessing existing patterns of organization for this purpose has been illustrated by applying it to two concrete cases in Somerville and Cambridge, Massachusetts. It is the hope of the writer that others will make additional applications to problems of organizing citizen participation in urban renewal in other cities and also (with appropriate modifications in the details of the structural model) to other community organization problems which require the coordination of geographic groupings with dominant functional elements on two or more participation planes.

From what has been said it should be evident that the model has severe limitations, being, really, only a first approximation of the refined conceptual structure one would like to offer for such purposes. Two of these limitations are so critical that they require special emphasis. First, the model can be applied in evaluating a concrete pattern of organization only when a thorough study of existing social structure has been made, and then only with the utmost care. This limitation arises from the fact that many variations of form may occur which are of minor importance. Only with

[10] Loring, *op. cit.*, chap. 4. For a diagram showing Cambridge organization for urban renewal after the activation of this committee, see Loring, p. 151.

full knowledge of existing structure, and a sensitive awareness that different forms of relationship may be equivalent in essence, can one reach valid judgments of the structural strengths and weaknesses of the concrete organization as compared to the model. Second, the model can aid in evaluating *structural* strengths and weaknesses in patterns of community organization. But it can tell us nothing of the way in which the groups involved function, or of the actual effectiveness of the formal channels of communication. In this whole broad area where the community organizer does most of his work, other criteria and other bases of judgment must be applied. All that is claimed for the present approach is that sound structural organization very greatly facilitates effective group action and that unsound structure greatly impedes it and may sometimes altogether frustrate the groups' purposes. The present structural model can help achieve effective community organization for urban renewal, or for other purposes, by helping community organizers and social scientists evaluate existing patterns of organization and determine structural needs toward which organizing programs should be directed.

* 11. Resident Responses to Planned Neighborhood Redevelopment

Morton Rubin, Louis H. Orzack, and Ralph Thomlinson

Introduction   The two preceding chapters focused on community redevelopment and renewal. Dr. Ravitz emphasized the need to prepare residents in urban renewal areas for impending change. He suggested that this be accomplished by programs of education and demonstration and networks of communication. Professor Sweetser indicated that the goals of urban renewal can best be achieved by organizing and using community structure models which carefully define and integrate the roles of participants on all levels. While people are being prepared and systematically organized in social structures by professionals for impending neighborhood change several questions require answers, such as, What do the people being affected by this change feel about it? How do they perceive and evaluate the prospect of their community being disrupted and then rebuilt? What action for or against proposed urban renewal can be expected by community residents? Under what conditions will such action occur? Individuals of what social characteristics will support or reject programs of community development?

In this chapter by Professors Morton Rubin, Louis H. Orzack, and Ralph Thomlinson you will find answers to many of these questions. They studied a small neighborhood in Madison, Wisconsin, interviewed 54

of the 58 occupied dwelling units on the 5.1 acres of a
site. Their data include indications of how the social
neighborhood is related to the attitudes and responses c
dents to imminent neighborhood change. Variations in pe
tion, and action in regard to the intended redevelopmei
by interviews with residents covering such areas as the r
about the neighborhood, his "investment," both socially and psycholog-
ically in the area, his contacts with community betterment groups and
other sources of communication which would furnish information on the
impending change, and his background, particularly data on age, sex,
association membership, education, length of residence in area, ethnicity,
and owner-tenant status.

As you might anticipate, a series of factors affect perception, evaluation, and action on proposed community change and create a vast array
of responses. Are the old or the young respondents in the community
most likely to perceive redevelopment clearly? Which age group is most
likely to be satisfied with the area and which one will be least inconvenienced by moving? How does length of residence in the area affect
perception of the problem? Are there differences in perception, evaluation, and action between owners and renters, the old ethnic and new
ethnic group, the educated and the uneducated?

Would persons satisfied with the place of residence evaluate redevelopment differently for themselves than for their neighborhood? Which
aspects of evaluation will be most positive and which least positive? Will
old-time satisfied residents anticipate inconvenience at moving to a new
site? What factors account for resistance to redevelopment or its absence?

This paper asks and answers some basic questions vital to the success
or failure of community development programs. It seeks the feelings,
concerns, and interests of those most involved and affected by the urban
renewal program—the block residents. All too many betterment programs
overlook grass root sentiment. This may be one reason for so many failures.

The authors' detailed empirical study, while microscopic in scope,
is a model for others to follow. The hypotheses which emerge regarding
residents' perceptions, evaluations, and action in response to planned
community change need to be tested by further empirical study within
the same community and by comparative study in other communities.

✳ IN ORDER TO INDICATE the contribution of sociological research
to urban neighborhood planning, this chapter presents the findings

survey of the attitudes of householders on a city block in downtown Madison, Wisconsin, toward a proposed redevelopment of the
block. This block had been singled out by the Madison City Planning Commission and the United States Urban Renewal Administration for a demonstration redevelopment of blighted areas in middle-
sized cities.

One of the problems of such government-sponsored planning
is the reconciliation of the interests of the public at large and those of
the locality directly affected by such change. As sociologists, the
authors attempted to ascertain the variety of factors accounting for
both resistance to and support of proposed change. Knowledge of
these becomes important for the planner.

AREA SELECTED FOR THE REDEVELOPMENT PROJECT

Madison Block 275, the selected area, is a level rectilinear plot
of 5.1 acres located in the Brittingham Park district, known also as
the Greenbush Addition and popularly as "The Bush." The area is
within short walking distance of the State Capitol, the central business district, schools, hospitals, and lake shore recreation facilities.
These advantages are offset by the proximity of railroad loading
areas and by the generally poor reputation of "The Bush."

The Brittingham Park neighborhood is delimited by three main
traffic arteries that transect the area. Businesses serving both local
and city-wide needs cluster along these arteries.

The Brittingham Park area was originally marshy land where
Italian and Jewish immigrants settled before the first World War.
During the depression years, the neighborhood was a focal point
for bootlegging and other illicit activities. It is still noted for its
taverns. The ethnic population and its way of life are undergoing
great change. As the first settlers have become Americanized, have
prospered, and have moved westward in the city, their original
houses have been divided into small apartments, now rented to
rural Wisconsin whites and Southern Negroes. While vestiges of
Italian and Orthodox Jewish institutions and locality sentiments
are still to be found here, only the aging among the original ethnic
population continue to live in the area. The incoming Negro group
has developed some religious and fraternal organizations, but the

rural whites have not, perhaps because they are more transient.[1]

In summary, the neighborhood is changing. An American-born population is displacing the original foreign-born settlers. Although American by birth, this new population encounters for the first time the pervasive problems inherent in urban living. This difficulty is accentuated by the presence of ethnic groups strange to them.

A survey of substandard housing by the Madison Housing Authority in 1949 revealed more specific violations of building codes than could be corrected by legal action alone. In 1950, of the 69 residential units in the block, 54 were rental units and 36 units had no private bath. Average rental was $34.90 per month. A constant decline in residential property values since 1920 has been accompanied by pressure to rezone the property for commercial purposes.

THE REDEVELOPMENT PLANS

In 1954 the Madison City Planning Commission proposed and the Common Council approved a plan to develop Block 275 for *residential* use. Under the plan, present residents and businesses were to be forced to move. With the use of city and federal appropriations, the property was to be appraised, purchased, and cleared of existing structures. It was then to be sold to a private developer for middle-income apartment house construction and rental.

THE BRITTINGHAM PARK CIVIC COUNCIL

Local persons interested in keeping the area for residential use and in raising its status had been organized for a long time as the Brittingham Park Civic Council. The Council promoted its aims through meetings and rallies at City Hall and used the facilities of Neighborhood House, a local community welfare center. While the Council's core membership was drawn from the older ethnic groups that were served by the center's Americanization program of a gen-

[1] Cf., Harvey W. Zorbaugh, "The Natural Areas of the City," in Ernest W. Burgess, ed., *The Urban Community* (Chicago: The University of Chicago Press, 1926), pp. 219–229.

eration ago, newer neighborhood groups were participating increasingly. Both the Civic Council and Neighborhood House favored redevelopment, and they utilized their resources to communicate information to residential and business people in the area.

PURPOSE OF THE RESEARCH

The proposal by city planning officials to redevelop this area of transition led to consultations and to the formulation of questions important for planners and yet amenable to sociological research. Generally, these questions concerned the social organization of the neighborhood and the attitudes and responses by individual residents to planned change.

The items investigated were (1) the residents' perceptions of the change, (2) their evaluation of the change, and (3) the actions they took in response to the change.

1. *Perception of change.* Prior research in sociology indicates the existence of significant variations in individuals' perceptions of their personal roles in the community. It follows that perceptions of a community project may vary in intensity and accuracy and in the degree to which community residents view such change as having personal significance.[2]

2. *Evaluation of change.* Planned change in community institutions may be evaluated in terms of the consequences for the individual, himself, or in terms of the consequences for others (*e.g.*, the community). It follows that the subjects may evaluate change as beneficial or harmful to themselves, as persons, or to others (*e.g.*, the locality).

3. *Action in response to change.* Action may be seen either as urgently and imminently required or as unimportant and distant in time. While neighborhood redevelopment requires moving and decisions on moving, there may be variations in individuals' views of the stages of redevelopment and in decisions of when and how they will move.

[2] Cf., Anselm Strauss and Leonard Schatzman, "Social Class and Modes of Communication," *American Journal of Sociology*, vol. 60 (1955), pp. 329–338. This study describes how persons of varying socio-economic backgrounds perceive catastrophic change as affecting themselves.

While the existence of differences in perception, evaluation, and action is obvious both to the planner and to the sociologist, a mere statement of the differences is insufficient to explain variation in individual behavior. Systematic research in the community yields the most useful data for the analysis of individual reactions to planned change.

Repeated sociological findings indicate that views concerning any impending change are not simply idiosyncratic. As is so often the case with social attitudes and actions, apparent lack of consistent explanations disappears upon serious inspection. Images of a neighborhood and of the character and consequences of proposed changes clearly exhibit a pattern. Residents' perceptions are affected by a variety of social and psychological variables. A major purpose of this study is to determine what specific sociological considerations affect the perception, evaluation, and action responses to redevelopment by the various groups within the community and to determine their attitudes toward planned community change. A product of this research may be an identification of the types of people likely to accept or to reject redevelopment. Such information should be of great value to the planner.

RESEARCH PROCEDURES

After discussion with Madison city planning officials and civic council leaders, the authors designed an interview schedule to focus on perception, evaluation, and action. Interviews were conducted in fifty-four of fifty-eight occupied dwelling units during three weeks in April, 1956. While the interviewer preferred to speak with the head of a household, if after three calls back he was unable to find him at home, he interviewed the wife.

Nine households were vacant, two families were unavailable because of hospital confinement, one family refused interview, and another family was never found at home. The last two were Negro, and thus there was some underenumeration.

The respondents cooperated well. They were personally interested in redevelopment and were sympathetic toward the interviewers. The success of earlier pretest interviews generated interest later on. In only a few instances did outright hostility or evasion occur. The completed data were tabulated on I.B.M. equipment through the cooperation of the University of Wisconsin's Numerical Analysis Laboratory.

SOCIOLOGICAL MEASURES

The following sociological factors were used to explain the variation in perception, evaluation, and action in response to planned change: (a) residents' orientation toward and integration in locality of residence, (b) residents' derivation of personal satisfactions from living in their locality, (c) residents' utilization of different sources of communication about community issues, (d) variation in such personal background factors as age, length of residence, owner-renter tenure, ethnicity, level of education, and participation in voluntary organizations.

In line with the above, certain measures were constructed, as follows: [3]

1. *Perception.* Respondents were asked, "Just where do you believe the redevelopment will take place?" They were also asked a series of questions to ascertain their perception of attained and anticipated stages of redevelopment. Answers were classified as (a) clear and accurate, or (b) vague or inaccurate.

2. *Evaluation.* Respondents were asked the following questions: "Do you think the redevelopment project is a good or a bad thing for you?" "What do you think about the redevelopment project for this neighborhood?" "If you were on the Executive Committee of the Brittingham Park Civic Council, how would you feel about this redevelopment project?" Responses were classified as (a) positive reaction to the project, (b) mixed or neutral reaction, and (c) negative reaction.

3. *Action.* A variety of questions dealt with plans for moving. This will be discussed below.

[3] Some measures were initially constructed using additional variables Correlations between these and the simpler measures derived from only one or two items were almost perfect. Following the principle of parsimony, we used the simpler procedures.

Complete tables in mimeographed form are available upon request from the authors.

4. *Locality Orientation.* Persons were classified as "local" if most of their very close friends lived on the redevelopment block. "Nonlocal" persons were those whose very close friends lived mainly in places other than this block. The very close friends of "mixed" persons lived both on and off the redevelopment block.

5. *Locality satisfaction.* "Satisfied" persons were those who preferred to remain in the neighborhood when they moved and also had not planned to move but for redevelopment. "Nonsatisfied" persons preferred to move outside the neighborhood, and their plans to move were independent of redevelopment. "Mixed" persons gave mixed responses to the above.

6. *Communication sources.* The question was asked, "With whom have you talked during the past month about the redevelopment project?" Responses were classified as follows: (a) family only;[4] (b) neighbor (either in addition to or without family); (c) formal sources (in addition to or without family or neighbors).

7. *Personal background factors.* Among characteristics that describe redevelopment block residents, the following are discussed in the chapter: date of birth, length of residence on the redevelopment block, owner-renter tenure, race or ethnic background, level of education, membership in civic and social organizations.

PERCEPTION OF REDEVELOPMENT

When the respondent's knowledge and understanding of the proposed redevelopment project are compared with other variables, a number of interesting relationships appear. From a comparison of such variables as education, age, length of residence in the neighborhood, and ownership or rental of property with the perception of redevelopment, the following patterns emerge.

More highly educated respondents tended to have a more accurate knowledge of redevelopment than less well-educated persons. Age, on the other hand, was not consistently related to perception. Both the youngest and the oldest age groups perceived

---

[4] This includes "none," which presumes instances of husband-wife discussions not separately reported. Cf., Paul F. Lazarsfeld, Bernard Berelson, and Hazel Gaudet, *The People's Choice* (New York: Duell, Sloan and Pearce, Inc., 1944), pp. 141–142.

the situation and the project clearly, whereas the middle-age range generally reported vague perception or ignorance. Long-term residents tended to perceive redevelopment more clearly than recent residents. Owners, though few in number, tended to perceive redevelopment more clearly than renters.

Table 8. Perception and Selected Variables

SELECTED VARIABLES	TOTAL	PERCEPTION	
		CLEAR	VAGUE
	(54)	(28)	(26)
Education:			
Elementary	25	9	16
High school	29	19	10
Age: *			
Old (over 45)	20	14	6
Middle (35–45)	14	3	11
Young (under 35)	19	11	8
Neighborhood residence:			
before 1951	21	12	9
1951 to June, 1955	20	10	10
since June, 1955	13	6	7
Tenure on the block:			
Owner	9	7	2
Renter	45	21	24
Communication sources:			
Family	21	7	14
Neighbors	17	9	8
Formal	11	7	4
Mixed	5	5	0
Evaluation:			
Positive	32	21	11
Neutral	13	6	7
Negative	9	1	8
Project for self:			
Good	26	16	10
Neutral	15	9	6
Bad	13	3	10

* Excludes "don't know" responses.

There was no consistant relationship between perception and social participation in formal organizations. However, clear perception was more likely to accompany approval of the Brittingham Park Civic Council; vague perception was overwhelmingly associated with no opinion of the Council.

There was a clear relationship between clarity of perception of redevelopment and the respondents' reliance on different sources of communication about the project. Of 21 persons who had discussed redevelopment within family circles or not at all, 14 were poorly informed about redevelopment. Of 17 persons who discussed redevelopment with neighbors, 9 perceived clearly and 8 were vague. Of the 11 persons who made use of formal organizations, 7 perceived redevelopment clearly. It might be concluded from these results that the more outgoing residents tend to be clearer regarding the details of the proposed changes.

Examination of the extremes, that is, those who relied on family in contrast to those who relied on formal sources of communication, shows that reliance on formal channels of communication tends to be associated with old age, long residence on the block, ownership, and higher education. Persons who relied entirely on their own families as sources of information tended to be young in age, resident since 1951, renters, and persons with elementary school education.

Participants in civic organizations, lodges, and social clubs split evenly between formal and informal sources. In contrast, nearly all the nonparticipants used the family as a source of information. Both nonparticipation in voluntary organizations and reliance on personal sources of communication were associated with vague perception of redevelopment.

Thus we see that there is a definite association between a person's perception of redevelopment and (1) demographical variables, such as education, age, duration of local residence, and owner-renter tenure, and (2) such social psychological variables as sources of information, participation, and evaluation of formal groups including the neighborhood council.

EVALUATION OF REDEVELOPMENT

The relation between clarity of perception of redevelopment and the evaluation made of it is clearly important for an understanding of the response of a community to a proposed change. While it is revealing to note that most respondents generally evaluated the project favorably, it is important for the planner to realize that approval and disapproval are related to a number of variables. However, such evaluation was not consistently related to any of the demographic variables.

In relating evaluation and perception it was found that of 32 respondents who approved of the redevelopment project, 21 perceived it clearly and 11 vaguely. Of 13 neutral persons, 6 perceived redevelopment clearly and 7 vaguely. Of 9 persons who disapproved of the project, 1 perceived it clearly and 8 vaguely. In general terms, then, persons favorably disposed toward the redevelopment project tended to view it clearly; those negatively disposed tended to perceive it vaguely.

The more clearly the project was perceived, the more likely did the respondent feel that redevelopment was good for him personally. If he believed the project was good for himself, then he tended to be clear in his perception of it; conversely, if he believed to be bad, then he tended to be vague about it.

Persons who evaluated the project favorably were equally likely

Table 9. Evaluation and Selected Variables

SELECTED VARIABLES	TOTAL	EVALUATION		
		POSITIVE	NEUTRAL	NEGATIVE
	(54)	(32)	(13)	(9)
Communication sources:				
Family	21	10	5	6
Neighbors	17	7	8	2
Formal	11	10	0	1
Mixed	5	5	0	0
Brittingham Civil Council:				
Approve	17	12	5	0
No approval	37	20	8	9
March 1st council meeting:				
Attended	17	9	6	2
Did not attend	37	23	7	7
Inconvenience feelings: *				
Very much	18	4	7	7
Some	15	11	3	1
None	19	16	2	1

* Excludes "don't know" responses.

to have formal and family sources of communication about the project. On the other hand, persons with unfavorable evaluations of redevelopment tended largely to rely on family sources of information. This relationship between evaluation of the project and communication sources is in general agreement with the relationship reported earlier between clarity of perception and communication sources. Furthermore, none of the negative persons expressed a favorable opinion about the Brittingham Park Civic Council (see table 9).

Evaluation of redevelopment may be related to a respondent's feelings of inconvenience at having to move because of the project. The data support this. Persons reporting only some or no inconvenience at all approved the project overwhelmingly. In contrast, among the 18 respondents who reported very much personal inconvenience, 14 were neutral or negative in their overall evaluation of the project. Some individuals may feel personally threatened even in *anticipation* of broad community changes. This affects their generalized attitudes toward community planning.

The complex relationships between anticipated personal inconvenience at moving and respondents' evaluations of the project are clarified by examination of the data in table 10. Persons who reported no inconvenience at having to move were generally likely to view redevelopment as "good" both for self and for neighborhood. None of this group perceived redevelopment as "bad." However, among those who reported "very much" inconvenience, about as many saw the project as "good" as saw it as "bad" when the *neighborhood* was the reference group. Within this same category of those who reported "very much" inconvenience, when *self* was the reference group, respondents were much more likely to see the project as "bad" than as "good."

It should be noted then that on the whole respondents were much more likely to view redevelopment as "good" than as "bad." This was more pronounced when respondents evaluated redevelopment in terms of the neighborhood than in terms of themselves.

Old persons were more likely to report much inconvenience at having to move than those who were young. Recent arrivals on the block reported less inconvenience than long-term residents. Persons with vague perceptions of the project were somewhat more likely

Table 10. Anticipated Inconvenience at Moving and Selected
Variables

SELECTED VARIABLES	TOTAL	ANTICIPATED IN-CONVENIENCE AT MOVING		
		VERY MUCH	SOME	NONE
	(52)	(18)	(15)	(19)
Project for self:				
Good	24	3	8	13
Neutral	15	3	6	6
Bad	13	12	1	0
Project for neighborhood:				
Good	35	6	12	17
Neutral	11	7	2	2
Bad	6	5	1	0
Age: *				
Old (over 45)	20	10	5	5
Middle (35–45)	13	1	6	6
Young (under 35)	18	6	4	8
Neighborhood residence:				
before 1951	21	8	9	4
1951 to June, 1955	19	8	5	6
since June, 1955	12	2	1	9
Perception:				
Clear	28	8	8	12
Vague	24	10	7	7
Locality satisfaction:				
Satisfied	27	15	8	4
Mixed	6	1	2	3
Nonsatisfied	19	2	5	12
Beneficiaries: **				
Neighborhood people	15	0	5	10
Landlords, business	29	11	10	8
Nobody, don't know	11	6	2 .	3
Losers: **				
Neighborhood people	14	4	8	2
Landlords, business	25	12	4	9
Nobody, don't know	19	5	5	9

* Excludes "don't know" responses.
** Multiple answers permitted.

to report greater personal inconvenience than those with clear perception. While there is a very slight association between locality orientation and feelings of inconvenience at moving, there appears to be a closer association with locality satisfaction. Persons who were dissatisfied with the locality did not tend to feel inconvenienced at moving.

Perceived inconvenience associated with moving was related to attendance at the information meeting of the Brittingham Park Civic Council of March 1, 1956. Of those reporting very much inconvenience, half attended the meeting and half did not. However, for those reporting only some or no inconvenience at all, one-quarter attended and three-quarters did not. It appears that persons feeling a great deal of inconvenience might have attended the meeting as a sort of gripe session.

Although, as reported earlier (see table 10), approval of the activities of the Civic Council without exception was associated with approval of the redevelopment project, approval of the Council seemed to have nothing to do with feelings of inconvenience about moving. Attendance at the special meeting, as noted above, was more likely to be associated with respondents' beliefs about personal inconvenience.

Furthermore, inconvenience was associated with the feeling that persons other than neighborhood people or tenants stood to benefit from redevelopment. Only persons expressing little or no inconvenience thought the tenants would benefit. It is interesting to note ambivalent feelings about landlords and businesses. Inconvenienced persons perceived these groups as both benefiting and losing from redevelopment.

ORIENTATION TOWARD LOCALITY

The relationship of an individual with his community and his neighborhood is complex in our pluralistic, changing urban society. Much has been written which indicates the tenuousness of the bond, particularly between the small, conjugal family and its residential environment.[5] Recent research in neighborhoods suggests that the

[5] Louis Wirth, "Urbanism as a Way of Life," *American Journal of Sociology*, vol. 44 (1938), pp. 1–24.

picture thus presented of the anomic urban dweller, depersonalized to his neighbors, uninterested in local affiliations, and relatively friendless, is overdrawn.[6]

With these considerations in mind, the index of locality orientation was constructed to permit the analysis of relationships that might be expected between a person's orientation toward his locality and his community participation and involvement.

In the neighborhood block studied, more than half the respondents were mainly oriented outside the locality; that is, most of their very close friends lived outside the neighborhood block. While this block, as a whole, therefore, might be characterized as somewhat unattractive in terms of the tendency of its residents not to have close friends within it, somewhat less than half did report at least some local friendships.[7] Within this neighborhood, then, which might have been one characterized by anomic interpersonal relationships, there definitely were persons with ties to the neighborhood through friendships. Furthermore, such persons were likely to have orientations to varied community activities that differ from the orientations of persons without such friendship affiliations. What accounts for this variation and what are the consequences of it for the redevelopment project?

[6] Wendell Bell, Maryanne T. Force, and Marion D. Boat, *People of the City: A Sociological Study of Urban Life in San Francisco* (Stanford: Stanford University Press, 1954). Leon Festinger, Stanley Schachter, and Kurt Back, *Social Processes in Informal Groups* (New York: Harper & Brothers, 1950). Morris Janowitz, *The Community Press in an Urban Setting* (Glencoe, Ill.: The Free Press, 1952). Robert K. Merton, "Patterns of Influence: A Study of Interpersonal Influence and Communication Behavior in a Local Community," in Paul F. Lazarsfeld and Frank Stanton, *Communications Research* (New York: Harper & Brothers, 1949). Gregory P. Stone and William H. Form, "Instabilities in Status: The Problem of Hierarchies in the Community Study of Status Arrangements," *American Sociological Review,* vol. 8 (1953), pp. 149–162.

[7] Indices of locality orientation for other neighborhoods in Madison are not available. Hence, it is not possible to conclude that the neighborhood studied is more or less locally oriented than others. Cf., Peter H. Rossi, *Why Families Move* (Glencoe, Ill.: The Free Press, 1955) for a comparison among four areas of high and low mobility and high and low socio-economic status. According to Rossi, the number of friendships varies more with socio-economic status than with mobility (p. 5).

In comparison with nonlocal persons, local persons participated more in civic and social organizations. They were also more likely to have heard of the Brittingham Park Civic Council, to approve of its activities, and to attend its meetings.

While old persons divided evenly in regard to orientation, the young group was predominately nonlocally oriented. Persons resident for longer periods of time split in regard to such orientation, but recent residents tended to be nonlocally oriented. Owners as well as renters tended to be nonlocal. In terms of ethnicity Italians, who are the oldest residents among all ethnic groups, tended to be locally oriented. However, none of the Negro residents, who were newer to the block than the Italians, were locally oriented. The remaining population was mostly nonlocal. Thus only long-term ethnic solidarity was related to locality orientation.

Various sociological and social psychological factors are related to locality orientation. These include beliefs that personal inconvenience is associated with moving, differences in sources of information about redevelopment and about moving, and the respondents' perception of which segments or groups within the community "stand to benefit" or "to lose" as a result of redevelopment. Such relationships, when clarified, shed light on the complex responses to social change planned from outside the community. To these we now turn in detail.

We have already noted a relationship between locality orientation and perceived personal inconvenience. Locally oriented persons reported "some" or "very much" personal inconvenience four times as often as "no inconvenience." Nonlocally oriented persons were only slightly more often inconvenienced than not. Such a finding is interesting inasmuch as it suggests the rather complicated interrelationship between the location of personal friends and an entirely different aspect of life—that is, moving and the difficulties associated with it.

For information about redevelopment, locally oriented persons infrequently relied on formal sources while nonlocally oriented individuals relied as much on such sources as on their families.

There is a striking difference in regard to the reported presence or absence of any source of information on places to move. Locally oriented persons generally stated they had no sources. None of the mixed oriented had any sources. In contrast, a majority of the nonlocal persons reported having sources of information. For reasons not entirely clear, persons with friends on the neighborhood block were not likely to report "use" of such friends or of other sources to provide information about moving.

Opinions on who gains and who loses from redevelopment are related to locality orientation. Most persons tended to feel that people other than tenant neighbors benefited most from redevelopment. Nonlocally oriented persons, with the bulk of their friendship ties outside the block, were more likely than residents who had most of their friends on the block to view redevelopment as beneficial to tenant neighbors.

Locally oriented persons were split evenly on opinions of who loses in the community from redevelopment. This group felt that neighbors lost about as often as landlords or businesses. On the other hand, nonlocally oriented persons stated that tenants lost only one-fourth as often as they stated that landlords and business groups lost. Twice as many had no opinion about who would lose as felt that tenant neighbors would be the main losers.

Table 11. Locality Orientation and Selected Variables

SELECTED VARIABLES	TOTAL	LOCALITY ORIENTATION		
		LOCAL	MIXED	NONLOCAL
	(54)	(15)	(10)	(29)
Perception:				
Clear	28	8	2	18
Vague	26	7	8	11
Evaluation:				
Positive	32	8	4	20
Neutral	13	6	3	4
Negative	9	1	3	5
Locality satisfaction:				
Satisfied	28	11	7	10
Mixed	7	1	1	5
Nonsatisfied	19	3	2	14

Clarity of perception and evaluation of the project are also related to locality orientation. Nonlocally oriented persons usually perceived redevelopment in a clear fashion, whereas locally oriented persons were as likely to have perceived the project vaguely as clearly. One plausible explanation lies in the tendency of many nonlocal persons to rely on formal channels of communication which itself is associated with a clear understanding of the stages of redevelopment (see table 11).

Both orientation extremes tended to favor the redevelopment project. However, those with friends on the block were more likely to be neutral than were those persons with most friends away from the block.

SATISFACTION WITH LOCALITY

Satisfaction with the community differs from orientation toward it. At the same time that persons may have most of their friends on the block, they may report little satisfaction with it. On this redevelopment block, more people were generally satisfied than were not.

But while locally oriented persons were predominantly satisfied, nonlocally oriented persons were more often nonsatisfied than satisfied. Dissatisfied persons were nonlocally oriented five times as often as they were locally oriented. On the other hand, the satisfied were oriented as often to the locality as not. As noted before, friendships in a residential community, the basis of locality orientation, seem to serve limited and particular functions for the individual. Such friendships were apparently not related to satisfaction with the community.[8]

Old persons were more likely to be satisfied than young persons, early comers more likely than recent comers. Owners may have been more satisfied than renters, but frequencies were too small for any certain conclusions to be made. Italians and Negroes were more likely to be satisfied than other ethnic groups, and those with limited education were more likely to be satisfied than those who had gone to high school. Qualitative interview data suggest that many residents were dissatisfied with the changing character of the neighborhood, especially with the taverns and the

[8] Cf., Paul F. Lazarsfeld and Robert K. Merton, "Friendship as Social Process" in Morroe Berger, et al., Freedom and Control in Modern Society (New York: D. Van Nostrand Co., Inc., 1954). Also Merton, op. cit.

immigration of Negroes. If older residents felt as strongly about this as more recent settlers, they apparently had deeper and more varied roots in the community that were broadly satisfying to them.

Table 12. Locality Satisfaction and Selected Variables

SELECTED VARIABLES	TOTAL (54)	LOCALITY SATISFACTION		
		SATISFIED (28)	MIXED (7)	NONSATISFIED (19)
Age: *				
Old (over 45)	20	14	2	4
Middle (35–45)	14	7	1	6
Young (under 35)	19	6	4	9
Neighborhood residence:				
before 1951	21	15	3	3
1951 to June, 1955	20	8	4	8
since June, 1955	13	5	0	8
Perception:				
Clear	28	12	4	12
Vague	26	16	3	7
Evaluation:				
Positive	32	12	5	15
Neutral	13	8	1	4
Negative	9	8	1	0
Project for self:				
Good	26	9	5	12
Neutral	15	7	1	7
Bad	13	12	1	0

* Excludes "don't know" responses.

Persons satisfied with the locality had vaguer perceptions of redevelopment than nonsatisfied persons. This might be explained by the former group's tendency to rely on family as a source of information about redevelopment, or perhaps the nonsatisfied made more of an effort to learn about impending changes.

While both satisfied and nonsatisfied groups approved redevelopment, only satisfied persons evidenced any negative feelings toward the project. Nonsatisfied persons were more likely than satisfied persons to approve redevelopment. Such a plausible and logical conclusion has consequences for planners.

Nonsatisfied persons either uniformly viewed the project as good for themselves or else were neutral. More of the satisfied viewed the project as bad than as good for themselves. Nonsatisfied persons were more likely than satisfied persons to believe that the project would benefit tenant neighbors, while the satisfied more often felt the project would be of benefit to landlords, businesses, or the city than to tenant neighbors. In contrast, satisfaction does not seem related to the selection of losers from redevelopment. Satisfied and nonsatisfied persons in similar ratios saw landlords and local business losing from redevelopment.

Satisfied persons more than the nonsatisfied relied on family sources of communication about redevelopment. Whereas satisfied persons infrequently reported any information sources for moving, nonsatisfied persons more frequently had such sources than not (see table 12).

While there were generally fewer participants in formal organizations than nonparticipants, satisfied persons were more likely than nonsatisfied persons to participate. Similarly, while a majority of persons failed to attend the Brittingham Park Civic Council's information meeting on redevelopment, satisfied persons were more likely to have attended than nonsatisfied residents. Although a minority of respondents approved the Civic Council's activities, such approvers were about as likely as nonapprovers to be satisfied or dissatisfied with the locality.

VARIABLES ASSOCIATED WITH MOVING PLANS

Every respondent acknowledged that he would ultimately move from the block. Differences began to emerge when persons were asked when they contemplated moving, with whom they had talked about moving, and where they had received information about moving.

Redevelopment may simply contribute to an existing predisposition to move, or it may be a decisive factor itself. When respondents were asked, "Before you ever heard about the redevelopment project had you ever made plans to move from this block?", a majority of 33 replied "No." The remainder replied, "Yes." For the latter segment of the community an apparent predisposition to move, independent and perhaps prior to redevelopment, existed.

Younger persons, especially in the 35 to 45 age bracket, recent residents, renters, persons other than Italians and Negroes, and persons with high school education, were more likely to have made previous plans to move, hence were more predisposed to move than old persons, long-term residents, owners, Italians, and Negroes, and persons with only elementary school education. Locally oriented persons were more likely than the nonlocally oriented not to have made previous plans to move from the block.

Table 13. Previous Plans to Move, Things Liked and Things Not Liked About Living on the Redevelopment Block *

THINGS LIKED OR NOT LIKED ABOUT LIVING ON THE BLOCK	PLANNED TO MOVE (21)			DID NOT PLAN TO MOVE (33)		
	LIKED	DIS-LIKED	NO MENTION	LIKED	DIS-LIKED	NO MENTION
"Nothing at all"	6	6	9	0	17	16
"Everything in general"	0	6	15	12	4	17
Apartment, space	3	5	13	5	5	23
Rent	7	0	14	15	0	18
Neighbors	3	9	9	8	6	19
Location of job	2	0	19	10	2	21
Location of schools, churches, shopping, recreation, etc.	11	3	7	24	0	9

* Volunteered responses with multiple possibilities.

When things liked and things not liked about living on the block are considered, certain variables distinguish persons who had made previous plans to move from those who had not. The two groups disagreed concerning their likes and dislikes about "nothing at all," "everything in general," and people they lived near. People who had planned to move were more likely to prefer "nothing at all" about the block, were less likely to prefer "everything in general," and were more likely to report a dislike of their neighbors. Other aspects of the block, referring to apartment, space, rent, and location, were not evaluated differently by previous planners and non-planners to move. Generally, both viewed rent and location favorably.

Persons who had planned to move, yet had not, gave a variety of reasons. These included financial difficulties, scarcity of housing that would permit children, and most prevalently, inability at the time of interview in April, 1956, to decide on a particular dwelling.

To determine the extent to which redevelopment is related to the timing of moves, respondents were asked when in light of redevelopment they planned to move from the block. Of the 21 persons who had made previous plans to move from the block, 12 said they would move within six months, 9 said they would move later (or else did not know how long before they would move). Among the 33 persons who had not made previous plans to move, only 2 said they would move within six months; 31 said they would move later than six months. Thus there was a tendency for persons who had not planned previous moves to see their moves as occurring in the distant future. There were also persons who had made previous plans to move yet did not see themselves moving within six months.

Young persons, residents since 1951, and renters were somewhat more disposed to move soon than were old persons, long-term residents, and owners. Yet all the above groups, and all persons regardless of ethnic status, were generally more likely to move late than soon.

Persons who planned to move within six months were much more inclined to be nonlocally oriented and locality nonsatisfied than persons planning to move later. Persons planning to move within six months tended to be more clear in their perception of redevelopment, to be more positive toward redevelopment, and not to have felt inconvenienced by having to move, in contrast with those whose moving plans were more distant.

While persons intending to move within six months had generally found some helpful sources of information about moving, the other respondents had not. Helpful information about moving was likely to be reported by persons whose information about redevelopment was received through formal channels. Persons who relied on family and neighbors for information about redevelopment infrequently reported having helpful sources about moving. Persons who did not perceive redevelopment clearly were also more likely not to have sought sources of information about moving. Persons negative to redevelopment were also unlikely to have sought sources of information about moving.

Table 14. Planned Moving Time and Selected Variables

SELECTED VARIABLES	TOTAL	PLANNED MOVING TIME [*]	
		SIX MONTHS OR LESS	MORE THAN SIX MONTHS
	(53)	(14)	(39)
Locality orientation:			
Local	15	1	14
Mixed	9	0	9
Nonlocal	29	13	16
Locality satisfaction:			
Satisfied	28	0	28
Mixed	6	4	2
Nonsatisfied	19	10	9
Perception:			
Clear	28	11	17
Vague	25	3	22
Evaluation:			
Positive	31	11	20
Neutral	13	2	11
Negative	9	1	8
Moving information sources:			
Some	21	10	11
None	32	4	28

[*] Excludes "don't know" responses.

CONCLUSION

The implications of this survey of resident responses can make a contribution of sociological research to urban neighborhood planning. The most important findings are presented below.

1. *Age of respondents.* The old respondents on the redevelopment block were likely to perceive redevelopment clearly. They tended more than other groups to use formal sources of information in learning about redevelopment, to be locally oriented and satis-

fied, and to feel very much inconvenienced at having to move. They were likely to delay consideration of moving.

Young respondents were likely to rely on family sources of communication about redevelopment. They were less oriented toward and less satisfied with the locality than were old respondents. On the other hand, the middle-age range of 35 to 45 years was the group that felt least inconvenienced by moving and had made previous plans to move.[9] This age group also tended to be more vague in its perception than the other two.

2. *Length of residence.* Long-term residents tended to perceive redevelopment clearly and to employ formal sources for learning about it. They tended to be satisfied with their locality and did not plan to move soon.

Short-term residents were likely to depend on family sources for learning about redevelopment. They were neither locally oriented nor satisfied, nor did they feel inconvenienced about moving. They were likely to have made previous plans to move.

3. *Owner-renter tenure.* The owners were likely to perceive redevelopment clearly and to employ formal sources for learning about it. Though not necessarily locally oriented, they were satisfied with the locality, felt very much inconvenienced at having to move, had made no previous plans to move, and were delaying moving.

Renters tended to be nonlocally oriented, but they were likely to be satisfied with the locality. They divided on other characteristics.

4. *Ethnicity.* The Italian ethnic group represented the original ethnic community in this area, and its members were locally oriented and satisfied.

Negro respondents represented the newest identifiable ethnic group in the area. While they were not locally oriented, they were satisfied with the locality. Italians, Negroes, and such other identifiable persons as Scandinavians, Germans, English, and Canadians tended to delay moving.

5. *Education.* More respondents with high school than ele-

---

[9] Cf., Peter H. Rossi, *op. cit.* This age group is most likely to need new housing to meet the needs of a growing family.

mentary education were likely to perceive redevelopment clearly and to employ formal sources to learn about it. They tended to divide in satisfaction with the locality but had generally made previous plans to move away from it, while the elementary group tended to be satisfied with the locality and had not made previous plans to move.

6. *Locality orientation.* Respondents who had most of their friends on the redevelopment block tended to perceive redevelopment vaguely, to be neutral to the project, and to use neighbors as information sources about redevelopment. These respondents were likely to be satisfied with the locality. They felt that tenants as well as landlords and businesses might lose by redevelopment, but only nontenants would benefit. They felt inconvenienced by moving, had made no previous plans to move, and were delaying moving.

Respondents who had most of their friends off the redevelopment block tended to perceive redevelopment clearly. Many of them employed formal sources of information about the project, favored redevelopment overwhelmingly, had sought information about moving, and had made plans to move early.

7. *Locality satisfaction.* Respondents who were satisfied with the locality included both locally and nonlocally oriented groups. However, they tended to perceive redevelopment vaguely, to rely on family sources of communication, and to think of redevelopment as being bad for themselves as well as benefiting groups other than tenants. Satisfied respondents felt very much inconvenienced at having to move and planned to delay moving.

Respondents who were dissatisfied with the locality tended to perceive redevelopment clearly and to approve of it both for themselves and for the neighborhood. They relied on formal sources of information about redevelopment and felt the project would benefit mainly tenant neighbors. This group tended to be nonlocally oriented. These respondents were not likely to believe themselves inconvenienced at having to move and were planning to move soon.

8. *Social participation in civic and social organizations.* Participants tended to be locally oriented and satisfied, nonparticipants nonlocally oriented and dissatisfied.

9. *Attendance at the Brittingham Park Civic Council informa-*

ion meeting on redevelopment. Attenders were likely to be locally oriented and satisfied, whereas nonattenders were nonlocally
oriented and dissatisfied. Attenders reported both inconvenience
and no inconvenience in anticipation of moving. Nonattenders were
mainly not inconvenienced by moving.

10. *Approval of the Brittingham Park Civic Council.* Approvers of the Civic Council tended to perceive redevelopment
clearly and to approve overwhelmingly of redevelopment. They
tended to be locally oriented, but they included persons both satisfied and dissatisfied with the locality. They also included persons
who felt both inconvenience and no inconvenience at having to
move.

Persons who did not approve of the Civic Council tended to
have vague perceptions of redevelopment. This group included the
only persons negative to the redevelopment project. Nonapprovers
were nonlocally oriented, but they included persons who were both
satisfied and dissatisfied with the locality.

11. *Communication sources.* Use of family sources for information about redevelopment tended to be associated with vague
perception and a negative evaluation of the project, as well as with
failure to seek information sources about moving.

Respondents who relied on formal sources of information about
the redevelopment project tended to perceive it clearly, to approve
of it, and to seek out sources of information about moving.

The survey findings suggest combinations of variables that can
be used to account for resident perception, evaluation, and action
associated with planned neighborhood redevelopment. While the
survey involved 54 out of a total of 58 resident families on the redevelopment block, the number of cases is unfortunately too small
to warrant further extended internal analysis. At the same time, the
following hypotheses emerge from this study for the use of the
planner and the sociologist repeating and adding to this research
in other middle-sized cities.

Clarity of perception is strongly related to age, education, positive evaluation of redevelopment, and a planned moving time. It
is less strongly related to length of residence, ownership, reliance
on formal sources of communication, and an absence of locality
orientation and satisfaction.

Residents distinguish between self and neighborhood in evaluating the consequences of a redevelopment project. A relationship exists between dissatisfaction with locality and evaluation of redevelopment as good for self. Vague perception and locality satisfaction seem related to evaluation of redevelopment as bad for self.

Anticipated inconvenience at moving is related to locality satisfaction, length of residence, and feelings that groups other than tenant neighbors benefit from redevelopment. The presence or absence of sources of information concerning moving procedures is related to anticipated immediacy of moving.

If a redevelopment project represents the will of the larger community, it might be argued to what degree these local block sentiments ought to be considered. One answer in a democratic society seems to be the expression of local sentiment through neighborhood associations, such as the Brittingham Park Civic Council. Such associations function as clearing houses both for information and solutions to felt problems. Membership in such associations may modify pre-existing relations between the individual and his community. This may change the pattern of interrelationships among sources of communication, clarity of perception, and evaluation of planned community change, as well as individual feelings of inconvenience associated with such change. Increased community participation may therefore be a precondition for effective social action at the local grass-roots level and thus a test of the possibilities of democratic planning.[10]

[10] Cf., Saul D. Alinsky, *Reveille for Radicals* (Chicago: University of Chicago Press, 1946) and Robert M. MacIver, *The Web of Government* (New York: The Macmillan Co., 1947). The significance of urban redevelopment for the urbanite is reported by William L. Slayton and Richard Dewey in Woodbury Coleman (ed.), *The Future of Cities and Urban Redevelopment* (Chicago: University of Chicago Press, 1953), Part III. Their findings from a survey in Milwaukee parallel ours in many ways. Their focus is more ecological and less social than ours, however.

Community Structure

* 12. The Jewish Community

Fred Massarik

Introduction   The community usually has a limited geographical area (not necessarily clearly defined), social interaction between
its members, and a "we-feeling" among them. This is known as a "vertical
community." There is, however, another type which appears to exist
without a specific geographical base, but which does have heightened
social relationships and in-group feelings among its members. It is called
a "horizontal community," and the Jewish community which Dr. Fred
Massarik describes in the following chapter is in this category.

The Jews in Los Angeles, and this is probably the situation in other
communities, are no longer living in ghetto-like concentrations. While
there are indeed areas of high Jewish population density, substantial
Jewish populations are scattered among the residential areas of our metropolitan communities. Some still live in or near the central city in the
areas of initial urban settlement, but many, especially the newer generations, have migrated to the suburbs and to the far reaches of exurbia.
Still most of them are bound closely together and in the classic definition
of the community are receiving satisfactions for basic needs from this
non-geographically based socio-religious community.

Why is the Jewish community important to its members, often perhaps more so than the local community whose residents may be Jewish
or non-Jewish? Dr. Massarik's incisive analysis is devoted to this question.
Religion with its common belief system, heritage, and lack of dogma is
a strong cohesive bond. Welfare embodying the tradition of "caring for
one's own" is strong among the Jews. To meet this challenge elaborate
social and welfare agencies have been established. This "care" involves
not only physical sustenence but maintenance of the cultural and spiritual

qualities of Jewish life. *Economic links* form the third dimension of the Jewish community. The majority of Jews labor in the higher status and higher paid occupations and professions. Class-wise they are more closely linked than non-Jews sharing more fully the lifeways associated with relatively higher class position. Occupational recruitment and business dealings often, though not exclusively, tend to occur within religious boundaries. Endogenous economic practices bolster the in-group tendencies of the Jewish Community, even though the totality of Jewish economic life is closely interwoven with the general occupational pattern.

Dr. Massarik's elaboration of these themes (many of which were based upon research conducted for the Los Angeles Jewish Community Council) and his empirical verification are a much needed addition to our study of the community.

* KNOWLEDGE CONCERNING the Jew in America largely evolves from a mosaic of discrete community studies. This mosaic is not composed of equally lucid pieces that mesh neatly and meaningfully, even though in recent years an increasing number of well-conceived studies have been reported. So far, no nationally representative study of Jewish population has been conducted, and the individual surveys, often sponsored by private welfare and planning agencies, have utilized a wide variety of questions and classification techniques. Therefore, findings have not always been clearly comparable.

The American Jewish Year Book [1] endeavors annually to compile basic data about American Jewish population. For communities in which no formal surveys are available, population figures are obtained by questioning Jewish community leaders regarding *their* estimates of Jewish community size. The sum total of estimates, as variously derived, suggests that the American Jewish population is somewhere between five and five and one-half million. As even gross population counts are relatively crude, it is no surprise that many further gaps exist in our knowledge concerning

[1] See, for instance, American Jewish Committee and Jewish Publication Society of America, *American Jewish Yearbook*, vol. 58 (1957), pp. 65–82 and most prior volumes.

characteristics of people and communities composing the population.

A "TYPICAL" JEWISH COMMUNITY STUDY

The typical Jewish community study is launched by the leadership of the organized Jewish community when plans are underway for a new building or service. In order to obtain a factual basis for the contemplated action, questions must be answered regarding the number and composition of the Jewish population. Sometimes, the study process itself may have certain open and hidden agendas extending beyond the research itself. For instance, a study may provide an opportunity for opposing forces within the Jewish community's leadership to move toward a resolution of the internal conflict.

Some obstacles confront the design of the study. Census data prove of little direct help to the study staff. However, sometimes relatively substantial lists of Jewish households are available, as compiled for purposes of philanthropic fund-raising. It is the word "relatively," however, that from a scientific standpoint gives much trouble, for these lists cannot be assumed to be either representative or exhaustive. Further, the very definition of "Jewishness" is burdened by ambiguity.

Nonetheless, with the fund-raising files as a potential starting point, the study may proceed. Sometimes the so-called "master list" approach is used, especially in small communities; further attempts are made to find additional names not included in the original list. However, if the community is large and highly urbanized, this method frequently falters. The number of names to be added proves to be overwhelming; to find them might very well necessitate a complete door-to-door canvas of great cost and complexity.

Often, supplementary estimates are used to specify the approximate size and distribution of the Jewish population. The various methods, which will not be considered here in detail, include estimates based upon a ratio of "distinctive" Jewish names to names of other Jewish persons, estimates by means of death records, and estimates utilizing data of absences of Jewish children from public school on Jewish High Holidays. These methods sometimes are used uncritically, other times with some awareness of their limitations and with use of various correction factors.

In order to obtain more detailed information, the typical survey recruits interviewers who are to approach either all households as provided by some basic file or a sample of households. Quite often volunteers are sought for this purpose. With skillful recruitment and supervision, such volunteer interviewers can be utilized effectively. However, in many cases volunteers prove to be inconsistent in the pursuit of their task. It is possible that the use of volunteers in Jewish community research is more feasible in the relatively small community, where the mechanisms of interpersonal social control resulting from high community cohesion, function more adequately The experience with volunteer interviewers in Los Angeles, a large heterogenous urban community, has repeatedly been disappointing

Ultimately, the available data are compiled, often without much sophistication, and some attempt is made to utilize the results All too often, the bridge between research findings and community action is none too firm. Much adequate research lies unused or executives' shelves.

JEWISH COMMUNITY AS AN URBAN PATTERN

It is an open question as to whether the pundit who said that "Jewish people are like everyone else only more so" deserves to be called perceptive. However, if we still view America as an essentially urban country, there is little doubt that the pattern of Jewish community in the United States meets all the requirements of general urbanism "only more so." It is true that Jewish population is scattered far and wide in virtually every part of the country and in virtually every community of any size. Nonetheless, it is the urban pattern that stands out.

Assuming that the Jewish population in the U.S. is about 5,000,000 we find that some 3,700,000 are concentrated in a dozen major metropolitan centers. As is well known, New York takes the major slice, with a Jewish population of approximately 2,300,000, followed by Los Angeles with about 400,000. Thus, while the 12 largest Jewish communities account for almost *three-quarters* of the Jewish

opulation, the 12 largest metropolitan areas in the U.S., according
) the 1950 census, account for only about 28 per cent of the na-
on's people.

Within a metropolitan community itself, as for instance in Los
ngeles, there is evidence that Jewish population is settled in par-
cularly substantial numbers within the more urban parts of the
ommunity. The 1951 Los Angeles Jewish population study [2] (which
1all serve as a frequent source of illustrations), found two social
lanning areas, Beverly-Fairfax and Wilshire-Fairfax, as the areas
f greatest Jewish population density.[3] Here, for each one-hundred
esidents, approximately 63 were Jewish. As measured by an adapta-
on of the Shevky-Williams index typology, modified by the Welfare
ouncil of Metropolitan Los Angeles, with the components (a)
umber of unattached persons, (b) population density per acre,
nd (c) absence of home ownership,—the urbanization of these two
reas is well within the top quartile.[4] The "old" Jewish ghetto-like
reas, such as Boyle Heights, scored even higher in urbanization,
alling within the upper 15 per cent of all Los Angeles planning
reas.

However, much as the urban character has been undergoing
ome transformation in general, so changes are found in the Jewish
ommunity. The much publicized movement to suburbia clearly
as affected the Jewish population, and other internal migrations
ave taken place. The impact of these migratory trends has varied
onsiderably from city to city.[5] In some, as for instance in San
rancisco, the "old" Jewish community, well-integrated within the

[2] Fred Massarik, *A Report on the Jewish Population of Los Angeles,* Los
ngeles Community Council (1953).

[3] Planning areas are units of a city composed of one or more census tracts
nd are delineated by social and welfare community councils for the purpose
f describing the population characteristics of the area and for assigning social
nd welfare services.

[4] For a more complete description of the Shevky-Williams index typology,
ee chapter 3.

[5] For some observations of recent trends incorporated in this article see
1imeographed publication of Jan. 23, 1957 of the Committee on Community
rganization, Council of Jewish Federation and Welfare Funds, Inc., 729
eventh Avenue, New York, N.Y. See also M. M. Cohen and M. G. Lerner,
he Growth of Suburban Communities (New York: Council of Jewish Federa-
ons and Welfare Funds, 1955).

total pattern, has remained stable, and the suburbs have been fed principally by a mild stream of out-of-state in-migrants. Elsewhere, the traditional areas of Jewish concentration, which at one time resembled the pattern of the ghetto so aptly described by Louis Wirth [6] have disappeared. For example, in Buffalo during the middle 1920's, the east side accounted for some 70 per cent of the Jewish population. Today, the movement has been largely away from this section toward the north and toward a general pattern of inter-mingling with the rest of the population. In Minneapolis 80 per cent of the Jewish population once lived on the north side. Recently, the movement has been towards the Park area. Still, in spite of this movement, this section accounts for but 15 per cent of the area's Jewish population.

In Newark, the suburbs have become increasingly significant areas of Jewish population settlement. In Los Angeles, it is the east side once more that has gone by the wayside. Here the Jewish population declined from 35,000 in 1940 to less than 10,000 in 1957. Instead a large Jewish population has settled throughout the western part of the city, and a steady and spectacularly large stream of Jewish residents has moved to the various suburbs, most notably to the San Fernando Valley. The latter area's Jewish population has almost tripled from 1951 to 1957, reaching almost 100,000.

Both conventional urban settlements and the new suburban growth are significant settings for today's American Jewish community. Further, it seems that the days of the classic ghetto are a thing of the past. In many metropolitan centers, Jewish population continues to concentrate in certain major areas, but this concentration is less pronounced and sociologically distinct from the historic ghetto past.

THE DIMENSIONS OF JEWISH COMMUNITY

Geographical propinquity may be a necessary but not a sufficient condition in a sociologically meaningful definition of community. As a matter of fact the words "Jewish community" are used in widely differing contexts and often communicate diverse mean-

[6] Louis Wirth, *The Ghetto* (Chicago: University of Chicago Press, 1928) Soft-bound edition published 1956 by Phoenix Books, University of Chicago.

ngs. It may be worthwhile therefore to consider a number of dimensions which may be utilized in measuring the "communityness" of Jewish community. These dimensions make no claim for mutual exclusiveness or theoretical purity, but they do reflect some of the approaches that may be made to the Jewish community concept.

THE RELIGIOUS DIMENSION

"Jewishness" is often viewed as an ethnic phenomenon. As such, it presumably combines the characteristics of religious and cultural forms of social organization. From a religious standpoint, or indeed from an ethnic standpoint, "Jewishness" can serve only as a generic category. Perhaps most ethnic groups can be differentiated into a number of fairly distinct subcomplexes. However, the more monolithic the pattern of social control, the more homogeneous the resulting cultural complex is likely to be. Many Jewish theologians, philosophers, as well as many Jewish "men of affairs," view the essence Jewishness as a common belief system, rooted in a common heritage, involving a highly flexible but significant "bond of faith" that links Jewish people everywhere. This approach to Jewishness leaves a tremendous amount of room for subcultural variations in ritual, language, and institutions within the Jewish community. There is no official "Jewish dogma" in any way resembling, for instance, a papal encyclical. There is no truly centralized source of religiously derived social control. Indeed, at least three major movements, Reform, Conservative, and Orthodox, coexist on the American Jewish religious scene. In addition, there are specific varieties of religious observances such as those espoused by Sephardic Jewry and the "Reconstructionist" viewpoint that concerns itself with the "organic Jewish community" and the religio-cultural aspects of Jewishness. And many Jewish people identify as "just Jewish," 31.9 per cent according to the 1951 Los Angeles study, while the corresponding percentages for Reform, Conservative, and Orthodox were respectively 29.5 per cent, 20.5 per cent and 17.1 per cent.

The diversity in intra-Jewish religious observance is clearly reflected in the organization of the Jewish community. Individual congregations are essentially autonomous. Coordinating bodies or other confederations tie together internally some of the various movements. There is a bond among Reform congregations through the Union of American Hebrew Congregations, while the Conservative movement is linked through the United Synagogues of America. Less clearly internally related are the Orthodox congregations.

Whatever the state of coordination or confederation, congregation autonomy implies that individual congregations will move in the direction of Jewish population concentration when the local leadership is ready and able to make such a move. Typically, Jewish migration precedes the subsequent shift in organized religious facility. No central power is in a position to dictate where a congregation should locate itself, although persuasion and mild pressure are occasionally applied. Efforts at planning often emerge as by-products of community surveys such as those mentioned previously.

In a community such as Los Angeles tremendous geographic mobility influences the pattern of religious organization. The congregation does not serve as the hub of organized Jewish life as it did years ago. Members often travel great distances and frequently by-pass many nearby congregations for reasons of personal preference linking them to a certain rabbi, or because of a desire to be a member of a high-status congregation.

Economic factors are highly influential in determining congregational membership, but this does not mean that high income and high status congregations are necessarily located directly within the high income and high status ecologic area. For instance, in Los Angeles, two large Reform congregations many of whose members live in Beverly Hills, Bel-Air, and Brentwood are located a considerable distance from these areas, and these congregations in addition, attract other high status membership from elsewhere in the city. Thus, the socio-economic-status nexus replaces the geographic neighborhood—ghetto nexus—as an organizing force in the religious dimension of Jewish community.

Possible exceptions to this trend are the small Orthodox congregations that, because of the prohibition on travel by vehicle or public transportation on holidays, continue to serve a relatively narrowly confined geographic area.

The relative importance of the Reform, Conservative, and Or-
1odox modes of Jewish identification varies significantly in various
.ties. Thus, it becomes difficult to generalize the religious pattern
·ithout a broadly representative community-by-community investi-
ation.

THE COMMUNITY INSTITUTION DIMENSION

Private sectarian philanthropy in the Jewish field has become
1 increasingly important organizing force of Jewish community;
1e ideological concept of "taking care of one's own" is of impor-
ınce historically and currently. The practical outcome of this ideo-
ıgical orientation has been the concentration by significant seg-
ıents of Jewish community life on the development, maintenance,
ıd use of Jewish community welfare agencies. The United Jewish
ppeal, Jewish Welfare Federation campaigns, and the similar
:derated drives and hospital campaigns are manifestations of the
ɔwish concern with organized welfare work. In Los Angeles, the
'nited Jewish Welfare Fund is the second largest philanthropic
fort, exceeded in size only by the Community Chest.

Once more the pattern of growth of Jewish welfare agencies
as not been the same in all Jewish communities. While its begin-
ings were rooted in the satisfaction of highly specialized needs—
urial societies often were the first Jewish community agencies—
ɔday the network of service is comprehensive and complex. The
ıovement of federations and community councils has more recently
:erted some coordinating influence upon this involved conglomer-
te of individual agencies.

The care of the needy and of the ill plays a significant role in
ɔwish philanthropy, although many of the agencies meeting these
ɔeds are also related to the Community Chest movement. The
ɔwish community centers through the National Jewish Welfare
ɔard and through the individual implementation of recreation
rogramming have come to be an important force. Service to youth
ırough the B'nai B'rith Youth Organization, through youth councils,
ıd through child care agencies functions as another significant
ɔhesive force in the Jewish community. Jewish education, some-
mes related to central community bodies but perhaps more fre-

quently tied to the congregations themselves without external influence, provides a long-term guiding influence in perpetuating Jewish observance and ideology.

It is worthy of note, however, that the relative heterogeneity and the lack of tight social control has brought with it some degree of alienation and dissatisfaction. For instance, a study conducted by Salisbury [7] has suggested that the level of satisfaction of Jewish people with their own early religious educational experience typically is considerably below the satisfaction level displayed by Catholic or Protestant church members. The frequency of exposure to religious education and the participation in organized Jewish educational life equally falls below other population segments.

The concept of community council or federation is worthy of attention. While internal diversity is the rule, these bodies often seek to relate informally and by methods of persuasion the various segments of the Jewish community. They provide a meeting ground for some forms of social planning and for the resolution of major conflicts. Various voluntary organizations, including those with national affiliation, such as B'nai B'rith, American Jewish Committee, Hadassah, and the American Jewish Congress, here can find a common meeting ground. Typically, the Community Council and Federation conducts major fund-raising campaigns such as those previously noted. These campaigns often raise money for overseas causes; a single fund-raising campaign sponsored by a single agency accomplishes both purposes and becomes *the* Jewish philanthropic effort. Fund-raising has become a noteworthy device in building Jewish community cohesion. Quite often it manages to substitute concrete communality of action for vague assertions of communal unity.

THE ECONOMIC DIMENSION

The economic life of the Jewish community is an integral part of the community's total economic process. While not self-contained by any means, certain typical patterns of occupational concentration persist. In general, the greatest portion of the Jewish male

[7] W. S. Salisbury, "Some Aspects of the Differential Religious Experience of Catholics, Jews, and Protestants"; paper delivered at the meeting of American Sociological Society, 1956.

labor force is classifiable in the "manager-proprietor" category (36.8 per cent in Los Angeles, according to the 1951 study). In many other Jewish communities, the proprietor-manager segment similarly accounts for one-third or more of the Jewish labor force, often followed in size by the professional-technical group, which usually constitutes 10 to 20 per cent of the total, 17.6 per cent in Los Angeles in 1951. Jewish females in the labor force typically fall within the clerical and sales category, 50.3 per cent being so classified by the Los Angeles study.

The findings suggest that the socio-economic level of the Jewish population is somewhat higher than that found in the community generally. While this differential appears to be a common state of affairs, it tells only a part of the story. The very heterogeneity of the Jewish community itself indicates further internal differentiation. This differentiation undoubtedly is linked to a variety of factors, including religious orientation and age. The Reform group tends to be the most well-to-do (mean household income, Los Angeles, 1951: $7,400), followed by the Conservative group (mean income $6,320), while the Orthodox group is characterized by the relatively lowest economic status (mean income $5,680). Further, the Los Angeles study indicates that the sizeable group of "non-identifying" Jews, Jews who view themselves as "just Jewish" without Reform-Conservative-Orthodox preference, give evidence of an economic level even slightly below that of the Orthodox (mean income $5,560).

Younger people, with an extremely high proportion of college education, tend to move more than ever into the professions, but they extend their scope beyond law and medicine; engineering, accounting, and the sciences seem to be attracting increasing numbers from the youthful Jewish labor force. Also, some "non-traditional" occupations, such as banking and insurance, are beginning to attract a higher proportion of young Jewish workers than was true in the recent past.

In considering the pattern of economic organization within the Jewish community as such, we find that being Jewish often is an asset rather than a handicap. Indeed, anti-Semitism and subtle discrimination in business is not entirely a thing of the past in America. But, the high proportion of proprietorship and managership within the Jewish group offsets internally the external traces of overt and covert discrimination. Sometimes the web of informal social relationships within the Jewish community facilitates the job hunt of the young Jewish entrant into the labor force in such a manner that he can more readily find employment by a Jewish proprietor or manager. In Los Angeles among Jewish young people through age 29, 21.6 per cent indicated that being Jewish helped in finding employment while only 13.5 per cent viewed it as a hindrance. No doubt, individual differences in interest and temperament may distinguish the Jewish job applicant who actually makes use of the perceived "assist" in job hunting provided by "Jewishness" from the one who finds employment within the less restrictive range of job opportunities provided by the economy in general. The Jewish employer rarely engages in outright purposeful discrimination against a non-Jewish applicant, so that the firm owned or managed by a Jewish proprietor-manager typically employs a substantial "mix" of Jewish and non-Jewish workers.

ECOLOGY OF THE JEWISH COMMUNITY

Los Angeles hardly is the "typical" Jewish community in America. Still, in a sense it constitutes a blend of social patterns found elsewhere in the country.

Its growth has been fed by a tremendous stream of in-migration, as well as by a substantial birthrate. The vastness of the in-migration is substantiated by a finding in the 1951 Los Angeles study which showed that 28.3 per cent of all Jewish households resident in Los Angeles in 1951 had first settled in the Los Angeles area some time during the five-year interval 1945–1950. In other words, the postwar westward migration within the span of half a decade brought nearly 30,000 Jewish households to the Los Angeles area. Of these in-migrants, nearly half indicated that their last place of residence had been either New York or Chicago.

Above-average fertility ratios, particularly in the suburban sections, are suggestive of the component of growth due to natural increase. For instance, in 1951 in the suburban San Fernando Valley area, there were 239.8 Jewish children under five per 1,000 Jewish persons, 20 to 54, compared to the city-wide average of 153.9.

Los Angeles provides illustrations of at least three significant ecological constellations found widely in Jewish communities: (a) the Dense Jewish Urban Area, (b) Jewish Suburbia, and (c) Jewish Population Scatter.

The Dense Jewish Urban Area is the contemporary successor of the ghetto. However, as we have mentioned, it clearly is *not* a ghetto in the classical sense. As noted, in Los Angeles, the Beverly-Fairfax and the Wilshire-Fairfax areas are nearly two-thirds Jewish. Some sub-parts are almost entirely inhabited by Jewish residents; others are less densely Jewish. The hub of this high Jewish population concentration accounts for at least 50,000 Jewish persons. It epitomizes the Dense Jewish Urban Area.

The Beverly-Fairfax, Wilshire-Fairfax economic level is essentially near the median for the Los Angeles Jewish population. Here, it is the Conservative religious identification that occurs most frequently (about 30 per cent of Jewish households living in area being Conservative), while in contrast the remnants of the more traditional ghetto life (Boyle Heights) are largely Orthodox (nearly 50 per cent). The Dense Jewish Urban Area's homes are largely stucco multiple dwellings erected during the mid-twenties and thirties.

Fairfax Avenue, a major thoroughfare, reflects the intense interaction between Jewish culture and the general culture. Here, some stores, following the traditional dietary laws of "kashruth," adjoin establishments reaching for inspiration in their wares to "exotic" foreign countries: Spain, Japan, France, Italy. "Kosher-style" restaurants and delicatessens reflect the "compromise" brought about between tradition and contemporary American convenience. Non-Jewish stores intermingle and sell goods intended primarily for the Jewish customer. American urban values, a cosmopolitan orientation, and Jewish tradition give rise to a new form of social and economic neighborhood organization that is a complex but novel non-ghetto blend.

Jewish Suburbia is not so very different from suburbia in general. It does not conform in any traditional sense to the closely patterned, geographically integrated Jewish community of the past. Nor is it very much like the dense Beverly-Fairfax, Wilshire-Fairfax area. The San Fernando Valley, Los Angeles' suburbia *par excel-*

lence, is a sprawling portion to the north of metropolitan Los Angeles. Its principal sociological attribute probably is its home-centered, in contrast to a community-centered or institution-centered, approach to life. The homes themselves have sprung up in fantastic abundance since World War II, but especially during the past few years. The number of dwelling units increased from about 140,000 in 1950 to more than 240,000 in 1957. Whether they are small, boxy tract homes, whether they are the modest "ranch" type, or whether they are elaborate high-prestige dwellings in the Longridge Estates, south of Ventura Blvd., they provide the key focal point of thought and action for their inhabitants. Jewish education for the young children (and they are a large group of the population) becomes an important concern. The development of congregations in Jewish Suburbia often centers about this need, whose roots are in the home, but whose satisfaction requires some reaching out to the sphere of institution and community.

The assumption still is widespread that Jewish Suburbia is a very homogeneous "upward mobile, young couple, tract home" type of community. There are many indications that this assumption is a vast oversimplification. At least San Fernando Valley Suburbia includes within its vast geographic expanse all shadings of the socio-economic spectrum, and it has a wider age diversity than inferred by the usual stereotype of "the Valley." Especially, the impressive Valley-bound immigration of 1950–1956 seems to have expanded the numbers of the upper, more "aged" portions of the area's population.

The Valley's Jewish community, though home-centered, develops its patterns of neighborhood living. There appear to be no highly dense Jewish population clusters of any magnitude. Jewish congregations and other community institutions are fairly well distributed throughout the area, and considerable travel often is necessary to reach them. In contrast, the immediate neighborhood, with its "majority" population of non-Jewish neighbors is the immediate, inescapable locus of activity. Here intergroup relations are developed among Jewish and non-Jewish children; reciprocal baby-sitting patterns emerge and a sense of loose local cohesion grows.

Jewish Population Scatter, a third residential pattern, is a catch-all designation for the many areas of the city whose character is basically urban, and whose Jewish population density is relatively low. Here, the rooming house, the large multiple dwelling, the older single-family dwelling provide the typical types of housing. But, once again, one is impressed by the variety in economic level, that ranges from considerably below average (South Boyle Heights, 1951 median family income $2,000), to the very highest (Beverly Hills-Westwood $10,247). Certain areas that once were the neo-ghettos now are but areas of Jewish Population Scatter. The traditional pattern of ecologic succession, with the replacement of one minority group by another, has been clearly operative on the east side (Boyle Heights) and on the near south side (West Adams) as Mexican, Negro, and Japanese populations have taken the place of the earlier Jewish settlers.

In conclusion, a number of trends might be distinguished, though here, the writer's own observation and conjecture, results of research other than those here noted, and, perchance, sheer speculation intermingle. It would seem that the pattern of Jewish community is one of change: decline in the oldest areas of high density, movement toward newer areas of more lofty economic status, and rapid growth of the suburb. Indeed, fundamental change may be taking place within the field of Jewish culture and ideology itself. Herbert J. Gans recently wrote lucidly about the development of a "symbolic Judaism" in America [8]—an approach to Jewish life that substitutes the external symbols of Jewishness for the inevitable and all-encompassing traditions of the past. Jewish youth in America today, in its process of forming the roots of the future's American Jewish community, may be moving into a state of balance with the surrounding non-Jewish community. Being Jewish often appears as a mildly positive value, though not frequently tinged by varying amounts of ambivalence. Mutual acceptance tends to replace intense in-group feeling, but voluntary self-segregation within the Jewish community seems prevalent. The fundamental beliefs of Jewish culture continue to build a strong bond among Jewish people everywhere. We may expect that the Jewish community some years hence will be increasingly permissive in

[8] See Herbert J. Gans, "American Jewry: Present and Future," *Commentary* vol. 21 (May, 1956), pp. 422–430.

terms of ritual observance, increasingly related to the larger community, but still very much a definable entity with strong religious and welfare institutions. It will be a community with a broad sense of "togetherness" which, paradoxically will continue to stem from a complex, heterogeneous—perhaps even from a chaotic—network of social and institutional relations.

* 13. The Relation of Community Characteristics to Religious Organization and Behavior

Russell R. Dynes

Introduction By accident of birth into an American family in an American community, the individual inherits a religion already organized and functioning. If he is born into a Protestant family he becomes a member of one of the 265 denominations and sects into which the worship of Christ is divided in the United States. Theologically, the Jews are less divided, there being only three major groupings, the Catholics not at all. Each of these divisions, denominations, and sects have their own organization, tradition, personnel, service, and theology. Each feels that its way is *the* way to everlasting life. As a result there is much confusion and ambiguity over the Word. The ethic of the brotherhood of man is established in both the Old and New Testaments, yet competition between the various religious organizations is more rampant than cooperation.

The differences among American religious organizations while appearing to be theological in nature probably reflect more the differences in the social characteristics of the American people. Protestants, for example, generally face less discrimination and have greater prestige and influence than Catholics and Jews in most communities, especially those where they are in the majority. Catholics and Jews, on the other hand, suffer more hostility and discrimination as members of minority and alien religions. Among Protestants and even among Catholics and Jews, social

253

differences among believers are reflected in the organization of the particular Protestant denomination, Catholic parish, and Jewish synagogue.

Professor Russell R. Dynes in the following chapter deals with these social differences among religious groups in America as they are related to selected characteristics of American communities. His first inquiry is, Where will you find Catholics, Jews, and Protestants concentrated? Size of the community is an important factor as well as the settlement pattern of the United States. Race, country of birth, and socio-economic status of members are variables related to growth and location of these religious divisions.

Church size is correlated with community size and socio-economic status. The number of churches depends upon the age of the community, population movement, development of suburbia, and stability of the community. Religious participation varies with such factors as community size, race, and age. These are but a few of the areas covered in this paper. The student should consider that a church functions within a community, often one undergoing rapid change. First the characteristics of a community have to be understood, particularly how these affect the church in its function. Then in light of this knowledge modifications in church activity may be necessary if the church is to survive as an effective organization meeting the religious needs of the people.

❊ A BOOK PUBLISHED by the Institute of Social and Religious Research during the 1930's entitled its first chapter "Like City, Like Church."[1] What was implied in this cryptic notation was that religious organization could only be understood in terms of its social context—the community in which it was located. "Like City, Like Church" implies also that the community places limits upon religious organization in the sense that the community's resources, the people and their characteristics, are the raw materials providing both the potentialities and the limitations for a religious program. While it is often suggested that religion, as an idea system, transcends human limitations, inherent in any religious organization are all of the problems which characterize other types of social organization. These community resources of people and their characteristics have meaning not just for the structure of the religious

[1] Ross W. Sanderson, *The Strategy of Church Planning* (New York: Institute of Social and Religious Research, 1932).

groups but also for their functions, their actions, their beliefs, their program emphases.

The statement "Like City, Like Church," however, is too abstract and ought to be rephrased *how* like city, *how* like church to be of more value. It may be possible to work out some form of community classification and relate it to religious organization and behavior. The author, however, intends to construct no new typology and instead will use rather standard generalizations and classifications. The term "community" in this chapter refers simply to a social life contained in a localized area and can be conceived flexibly as a neighborhood, a town, or a city. The generalizations presented below are in many cases tentative; in some instances contradictory evidence is given and exceptions are noted. Many of the generalizations about church size and location will apply less to Catholicism since parish size and location are determined by more comprehensive church strategy than in Protestantism. Judaism, in this respect, shows more similarity to Protestantism.

RELIGIOUS COMPOSITION

The larger the community, the greater the proportion of non-Protestants. For example, 99 per cent of the Jews and 85 per cent of the Catholics live in communities over 2,500. Seventy-seven per cent of the Jews and 28 per cent of the Catholics live in cities over 500,000. This relationship can be seen in figure 12. Every state that has a Jewish population of 2 per cent or more is at least 50 per cent or more urban, while the vast majority of states with less than 1 per cent of Jews are primarily rural. Figure 13 indicates a similar relationship among the Catholic population. Those states with over 50 per cent of their population in urban areas are generally those with a large Catholic population.

The reasons for these associations go back to the settlement pattern of the United States. Most of the initial colonizers in the United States were Protestants, and most of them were scattered along the expanding frontier and in other rural areas. The United States experienced its greatest percentage population increase between 1840 and 1850, when the total urban population increased 92 per cent. About this same time, Catholics and Jews, the former primarily from Ireland and the latter from Central Europe, were major sources of immigration and of this rapid urban growth. The trend toward urbanism, established in the nineteenth century, was even more accelerated in the early twentieth. From 1910 to 1920, the percentage increase to the urban population was nine times as great as to the rural. About this same time, there were new waves of immigration—Catholics who were Poles, Italians, Czechs, Slovaks, and Croats, and also Jews who were coming this time from Russia and Austria-Hungary. This correspondence between

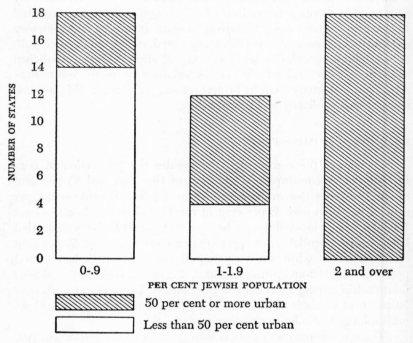

Figure 12. Urbanization and Jewish Population, Forty-Eight States: 1950 (Sources: U.S. Bureau of Census, *U.S. Census of Population, 1950* and National Council of Churches, *Churches and Church Membership in the United States* (1956), table 7. Reported church members of three major faiths is used as a base of 100 per cent for each state.)

urban growth and non-Protestant immigration left the greatest strength of non-Protestants in the largest cities. Generally, as the size of the community increases, the proportion of Protestants to non-Protestants decreases.

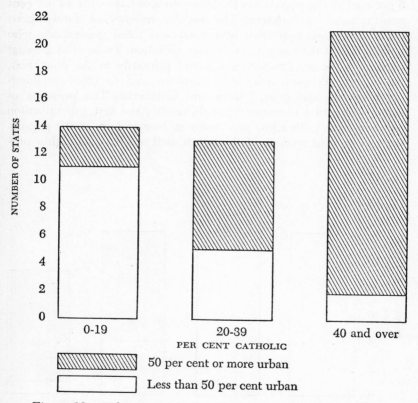

Figure 13.   Urbanization and Catholic Population, Forty-Eight States: 1950 (Sources: as in figure 12)

The greater the proportion of foreign-born in a community, the greater the proportion of non-Protestants. As just indicated, a major source of the non-Protestant groups in the United States has been through immigration, even though both Catholicism and Judaism were "indigenous" religions. While today the rate of immigration has been greatly reduced and the number and the proportion of the foreign-born in the population has decreased, this relationship still holds. Figure 14 indicates that the majority of states with over 5 per cent of the population foreign-born also have over 40 per cent non-Protestant population. The smaller number of foreign-born today are more indicative of second and third generations who have retained their original religious affiliation. Today, the greatest percentage of foreign-born are found primarily in the Northeast, New York, Pennsylvania, Massachusetts, and in other predominately urban states, as Illinois and California. The presence of foreign-born in a community would modify the first generalization —urban areas with a low percentage of foreign-born in the population, as in most sections of the South, will not have as high a pro-

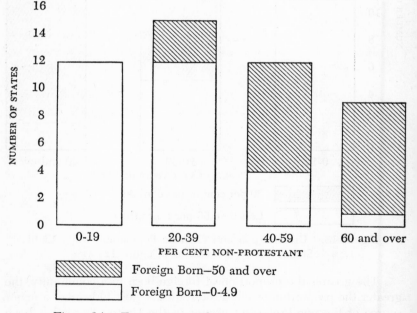

Figure 14. Foreign Born Whites and Non-Protestants, Forty-Eight States: 1950 (Sources: as in figure 13. Non-Protestants include Catholics and Jews.)

portion of non-Protestants as a city of equivalent size in the Northeast or the Middle West.

The larger the community, the greater the proportion of Neo-Protestants. The older established Protestant denominations either have a greater proportion of their members in rural areas or tend to approximate the national distribution of the U.S. population in communities of various sizes—rural areas, small towns, as well as cities. Urban areas, however, have been fruitful sources of religious innovation leading to schisms from these established groups and to the creation of new independent groups. For example, many new religious groups, such as the Christian Science Church, are overly represented in urban areas.[2] Salvation Army Churches are almost entirely urban, and the Church of the Nazarene, some of the Assemblies of God, and other Pentecostal Churches have arisen and flourished in the city. Cities have also been fruitful in the development of cults. These groups often base their separatism upon spiritualistic, "racial," or faith healing emphases. They often mix mystical and esoteric beliefs with certain traditional Judeo-Christian beliefs. Many of these cults depend on the diversity of personality variation within urban areas and draw heavily upon the excess of female population in cities.

The greater the proportion of Negroes in a community, the greater the proportion of Protestants. It is estimated that about 95 per cent of Negro church members belong to Protestant groups.[3] About 90 per cent of these belong to separate Negro denominations. With urban migration, however, Catholicism has made numerical gains among the Negro population due, in part, to welfare activities sponsored by the Church among the Negroes and to Catholic stands against discrimination and segregation in many areas of life.[4]

The greater the proportion of the population of middle and

[2] *Information Service,* Federal Council of Churches, New York, N.Y. (May 15, 1948).

[3] Liston Pope, "Caste in the Church," *Survey Graphic* (January, 1947), p. 59.

[4] Charles Thorne, *The Presbyterian Church U.S.A. in the Inner City of Baltimore, Maryland,* Board of National Missions, Presbyterian Church, U.S.A., New York, N.Y. (1955), table 14 "Total Membership of Inner City Roman Catholic Churches, Baltimore, 1945–1955."

upper socio-economic status in a community, the greater the proportion of members of "traditional" Protestant denominations. Nationally, certain denominations tend to attract individuals from a particular range of the socio-economic hierarchy. For example, one study related church affiliation to socio-economic status on a nation-wide sample.[5] Using the total percentages of the national sample as a basis for comparison, Methodists, Presbyterians, Lutherans, Episcopalians, and Congregationalists exceeded the national percentages in the middle-status category. The Presbyterians, Episcopalians, and Congregationalists also exceeded their upper-status "quota."

In specific communities, individual churches attract individuals from similar socio-economic strata. Generally the ranking within a specific community follows the ranking of the denomination on the national level. In some cases, however, a church which belongs nationally to a predominantly middle-status denomination may function as an upper-status, or perhaps lower-status, church in a specific community. In communities where one denomination has several churches, these may serve somewhat different socio-economic levels. It is rare, however, to find one denomination in a community which encompasses the whole range of socio-economic differences among their various churches. A church becomes identified with a particular socio-economic segment, and other segments do not accept it or are not accepted by it.

The greater the proportion of the population of lower socio-economic status in a community, the greater the proportion of sect members.[6] Most of the "traditional" Protestant denominations are identified with the upper and middle socio-economic strata, and they do not, in most instances, attract a large membership in lower socio-economic groups. Because of this lack of attraction, new sectarian groups arise, gaining their primary support from these "neglected" groups. The sectarian's emphasis on other-worldly goals may offer partial compensation for the lack of status in this world, and his hostility toward traditional churches may allow him satisfaction for his felt rejection.

[5] *Information Service, op. cit.*

[6] Russell R. Dynes, "Church-Sect Typology and Socio-Economic Status," *American Sociological Review,* vol. 20 (1955), pp. 555–560.

CHURCH SIZE

The larger the community, the larger the average size of the church. The 1936 *Census of Religious Bodies* indicated that the size of the church tended to rise with the size of the city. For example, in New York and Chicago the average size of churches was over 1,000 members, while in such cities as Kansas City and Louisville, the average size was over 600 members. Since no comparable religious census has been taken since that time, only partial comparisons can be made with recent data. This same relationship seemed to hold for recent data in Methodism for communities up to 10,000 population.[7]

A more restricted study of Methodism in six states, however, indicated that church size reached its peak in independent cities from 10,000 to 50,000 and dropped somewhat after that.[8] Since Methodism tends to be strongly represented in these smaller cities and underrepresented in large metropolitan areas, whether this decrease would hold for other denominations is not known. Assuming that church size tends to decrease somewhat after cities reach 50,000 population, a partial explanation of this might appear in the decentralization process in urban areas. When city size is 10,000 to 50,000, suburbanization has begun to develop and satellite business areas have started to grow a mile or so from the center of the city. Churches do not move out of the downtown areas as readily as do stores or families. The "first" churches in the downtown area continue to draw their parishioners from a wide area. Their long history, name, tradition, and size of building give them prestige. Since they can draw their members from a wide area, they can raise a large budget, support an active program, hire an outstanding minister, and thereby maintain their prestige. With these resources, church size reaches a peak. Later, when the churches in the suburban areas have become more firmly established, have erected large buildings, and have enlarged their pro-

[7] *Source Book of Methodism in Town and Country*, Board of Missions of the Methodist Church, New York, N.Y. (1955).

[8] *A Fact Book*, Board of Missions of the Methodist Church, New York, N.Y. (1954).

grams, many of the attractive features of the downtown church begin to diminish. The downtown church finds it difficult to hold their old members and have no new population source from which to draw members. The total population resources are then spent several different ways, reducing somewhat the average size of each church. Further research or some future nation-wide religious census can tell if this drop in average church size holds for other religious groups beside Methodism.

The greater the proportion of the population of higher socio-economic status in the community, the larger the average size of the church.[9] One reason why churches which attract members of high socio-economic status tend to be large probably stems from certain attitudes on their part toward religious affiliation and participation. For many participants, religious affiliation is only a segmentalized part of their life. Since other voluntary organizations compete for their time and they often derive more satisfaction for their "secular" affiliations, the large church structure allows them the advantage of selective participation with a minimum of obligation. Since the church becomes only one among many outlets for participation among people in higher socio-economic groups, the church structure, in order to attract a large congregation, becomes more elaborate in appealing to these different segments of interest.

The greater the proportion of population of lower socio-economic status in a community, the smaller the average size of the church.[10] In the smaller sectarian churches, drawing their congregations primarily from lower socio-economic groups, there is more participation in all of the aspects of the relatively undifferentiated church structure. For the sectarian, his religious group is his most meaningful association and source of friendship. His church is more nearly a "fellowship," a community of believers, a primary group relationship. This was shown in one study, which indicated that the sectarian, as compared to those who belonged to large elaborate church institutions, attended church more often, belonged to more activities within his relatively undifferentiated organization, be-

[9] Robert H. Jordan, "Social Functions of the Churches in Oakville," *Sociology and Social Research*, vol. 40 (1955), pp. 107–111.

[10] *Ibid.*

longed to fewer organizations outside the church, and derived most of his close friends from within his religious group.[11] Another way to state these aspects of participation and church size would be that the number of activities varies directly with the size of the church and the extent of participation by members varies inversely with the size of membership.

NUMBER OF CHURCHES

The more recent the settlement of a community, the fewer churches it will have. Since religious organizations are "followers" rather than "leaders" in population shifts, there is always a lag in creating new churches. For example, few churches are found in suburban areas of metropolitan communities as compared with other areas in the city, and there are also fewer churches in the western United States as compared to other areas settled for longer periods of time.[12] It would follow that the more residentially stable a community, the more churches it would have.

The fact that individual churches tend to serve similar population segments leads to other possibilities concerning the number of churches in a community. The more diverse the socio-economic status in a community, the more churches it will have; the more diverse the racial and ethnic groups, the more churches it will have.

PARISH DISPERSION

The fewer the number of churches of a particular denomination in a community, the more residentially dispersed will be their parishioners. People are attracted to religious groups for a variety of reasons. A traditional loyalty may take a person or a family across the city to the church of their choice if another church of the same denomination is not located in their immediate neighborhood.

Traditional loyalties plus the suburbanization process combine

[11] Russell R. Dynes, "The Consequences of Sectarianism for Social Participation," *Social Forces*, vol. 35 (1957), pp. 331–334.

[12] *Churches and Church Membership in the United States*, National Council of Churches, New York, N.Y., series A, no. 4 (1956), table 9.

to create conditions which indicate that the closer a church is to the downtown area, the more residentially dispersed will be their parishioners. Chapin found in one study that churches with scattered parishes are more frequently found in areas of high social deterioration, primarily near the center of the city. His measure of social deterioration was a combined ranking of various sections of the city on various indices of social pathology.[13]

The majority of church members, however, live within a mile of their church. A study of Methodism in thirty selected cities showed that over 60 per cent of church members and church school enrollees reside within a mile of the local church.[14] A study of 1,350 metropolitan Protestant churches indicated that 53 per cent had compact parishes in the sense that two-thirds lived within a mile of the church.[15] If people go to churches in their immediate neighborhood, the chances are that they go with others who are similar to them socio-economically. It would follow that the more homogeneous the socio-economic status within a community, the more residentially compact will be the congregations of the churches in it. For example, one study indicated that, in the suburbs, there are a smaller proportion of residentially dispersed parishes than in other parts of the city.[16] However, if a church is located in a transitional zone, often the congregation sacrifices nearness for similarity of congregation. It would follow that the more heterogeneous the socio-economic status of a community, the more residentially dispersed will be the congregations of churches in it.

A compact parish may indicate other relationships. There is evidence that the ratio of Sunday school enrollment and church membership varies directly with the distance of the church from the center of the city. Chapin has posited that this ratio can be used as an indication of the "youthful vigor" of a church as an institution since a large Sunday school enrollment and a small membership would be indicative of a youthful following. He found

[13] F. Stuart Chapin, *Contemporary American Institutions* (New York: Harper & Brothers, 1935).

[14] *A Fact Book,* Board of Missions of the Methodist Church, New York, N.Y. (1954).

[15] *Information Service,* Federal Council of Churches, New York, N.Y. (January 20, 1950).

[16] *Ibid.*

in a study of Minneapolis churches, that the degree of compactness of the parish of a church varied directly with its index of "youthful vigor" and also directly with its rate of growth.[17] In other words, the suburban churches with their compact parishes are more frequently characterized by growth and "youthful vigor."

RELIGIOUS PARTICIPATION

While data on religious participation are often incomplete and contradictory, certain relationships appear to be rather consistent among various studies. Probably the most certain relationship would be the greater the proportion of women in the population, the greater the religious participation. For example, the 1936 *Census of Religious Bodies* indicated that for every 78.5 men who held membership in a church, there were 100 women. The only religious groups who do not conform to this are those drawing heavily upon male immigrant groups, as the Buddhist or Greek Orthodox. Other corroborating evidence indicates that there is a higher degree of religious interest and higher frequency of church attendance among women.[18]

In addition, the greater the proportion of family units in a community, the greater the religious participation.[19] Parenthood seems to act as a stimulus to participation, probably as a result of the desire on the part of parents to transmit certain religious aspects of the cultural heritage to the children. It might follow that religious interest and participation might be the greatest during the age period of the thirties when children are a more important element in the family cycle. The community study by Bigman and Whitman indicates this. Fichter, however, found among Catholics that religious participation decreased to its lowest peak during the 30 to 40 age category.[20] This may point to interesting differences be-

[17] Chapin, *op. cit.*

[18] Stanley Bigman and L. B. Whitman, "Some Aspects of Religious Behavior in Washington, D.C." Paper presented at meeting of the American Sociological Society, September, 1956. Gerhard E. Lenski, "Social Correlates of Religious Interest," *American Sociological Review*, vol. 18 (1953), pp. 533–543.

[19] *Ibid.*

[20] Joseph Fichter, S. J., *Social Relations in the Urban Parish* (Chicago: University of Chicago Press, 1954).

tween Protestants and Catholics. Perhaps parenthood quickens religious interest and the lack of parenthood has no appreciable effect upon religious participation among Protestants but, for Catholics, the church's stand on birth control may produce guilt on the part of nonparents and also for those parents whose families exceed the limits of the more general cultural definition of an ideal sized family. In turn, these Catholics may withdraw from religious participation during this age period as a means of resolving their ambivalence.

In general, the smaller the community, the greater the religious participation.[21] It is not apparent, however, whether this higher level of religious participation is carried over when people move from a small community to a larger one. Participation in religious activities both requires and, in turn, produces integration in the new community. There is some indication that the greater the proportion of long-term residents in a community, the greater the religious participation.[22] Migrants to metropolitan communities take a relatively long period to approximate the level of participation of the long-term residents, and those who come from smaller communities take a longer time to reach this level than do those who come from areas somewhat equivalent in size.[23]

Negroes had a higher percentage of church membership than did whites in the 1936 *Census of Religious Bodies,* and Negroes have shown a higher rate of church attendance in certain studies.[24] This might be extended to the proposition that the greater the proportion of nonwhites in the population, the greater the religious participation. This proposition probably could be extended to ethnic groups, since churches often function as a major source of identification for these groups. The church among these groups becomes more than a religious outlet and often serves as a haven from discrimination and as a protest device.

Although there is contradictory evidence, several studies in-

[21] H. Paul Douglass and Edmund Brunner, *The Protestant Church as a Social Institution* (New York: Harper & Brothers, 1935).

[22] Bigman and Whitman, *op. cit.*

[23] Basil G. Zimmer, "Participation of Migrants in Urban Structures," *American Sociological Review,* vol. 20 (1955), pp. 218–224.

[24] Bigman and Whitman, *op. cit.*

licate that the greater the proportion of individuals with low income, unskilled occupations, and low levels of educational achievements, the greater the religious participation.[25] In part, this may be due to the fact that among these groups, religious organizations, often sectarian in orientation, tend to be a major outlet for participation. Individuals of higher income, higher skills, and higher education spread social participation over a number of activities extending beyond the church. Since participation in other organizations seemingly acts competitively with religious groups, this would lead to two other possibilities: first, the larger the number of voluntary organizations in a community, the less the religious participation, and second, the greater the proportion of union members in a community, the less the religious participation.

Other factors, of course, have their consequences for religious participation as, for example, parish dispersion. One might hypothesize that the more residentially dispersed a congregation, the less the religious participation, or, conversely, the more residentially compact a congregation, the greater the religious participation. In addition, the generalizations about the religious composition of a community have their consequences for religious participation. It seems generally true that the greater the proportion of Catholics in a community, the greater the religious participation, while the greater the proportion of Jews in a community, the less the religious participation.[26] Although there are, of course, wide variations within Catholicism and Judaism, Protestants occupy somewhat of a middle position in participation. There would be two exceptions within Protestantism—first, the greater the proportion of sect members in the community, the greater the religious participation, and second, the greater the proportion of ethnic Protestants in the community, the greater the religious participation.[27]

Even though the characteristic of the community have meaning for the structure and function of religious organization, there is often a lack of adaptation to them on the part of the church. In many cases, the activities of churches are oriented toward stand-

[25] *Ibid.* Dynes, "The Consequences of Sectarianism for Social Participation."
[26] Louis Bultena, "Church Membership and Church Attendance in Madison, Wisconsin," *American Sociological Review,* vol. 14 (1949), pp. 384–389.
[27] *Ibid.* Lenski, *op. cit.*

ardized denominational patterns of activity and are not adapted to the specific needs of a specific community. Too often it makes little difference to the activities of a church in a specific area whether the people are of one race, one ethnic group, or one occupation; whether there are many children or few; whether there is a surplus of one sex or the other; whether the aged are many or few; or whether the area is growing or declining in population.

Religious institutions are dependent upon the welfare of the community, and if the church seeks to be an adaptive institution, it becomes essential for the church to be aware of new developments in order to seek new directions of adaptation. The church has been one of the last institutions to utilize research as a basis for policy making. Church planning and adjustment require a thorough understanding of the particular social context in which a particular church functions. The community cannot be understood without a knowledge of the age and sex composition, the rates and kinds of mobility, the occupational and racial structure, and the community's unique cultural characteristics. Perhaps as the church begins to utilize research more frequently to broaden its knowledge of the interrelations between church and community, the generalizations presented here will be extended, qualified, or refuted.

14. The Patterns of Women's Organizations: Significance, Types, Social Prestige Rank, and Activities

Mhyra S. Minnis

Introduction The voluntary organization is one of the basic community structures found in modern urban society. Like other structures in an age of specialization, it functions principally to integrate heterogeneous populations around special interests and needs. Thus, organizations give order and continuity to social relationships amid what appears to be the jumbled mass of urban people. As the social scientist probes deeper into the complexities of community structures, he finds very specific rules governing membership in particular organizations, the selection of members, and the conditions and methods of participation. In other words, voluntary organizations are not haphazard groupings of individuals as crowds are. Rather, they follow very specific patterns within a community and are usually arranged in a hierarchial order of status and prestige that represents the social positions of their members.

In one sense, voluntary organizations illustrate cleavage which exists within a community. Persons of similar race, religion, education, income, and ethnic background frequently want to be with their friends and belong to the same organization. Initially, at least, organizations come into being because of this desire, and thus they are replicas of the community social class system.

269

In this chapter, Professor Minnis reports on her study of women's voluntary organizations in New Haven, Connecticut. Her research encompassed several principal techniques: questionnaires to four hundred presidents of women's organizations, participant observation at club meetings and lectures, and interviews with leaders or informants of the several social classes in New Haven. One hundred and seventy-seven organizations were carefully chosen from the pool of four hundred and were rated as to their relative prestige in the community.

Dr. Minnis' study goes beyond demonstrating differentiation, or the groups' reflection of the social structure of a community. She explores the meaning of voluntary organizations in the life of woman today, the multiple services these organizations give to the community including the duplication of their efforts, and the social prestige ranks of these organizations within the community of New Haven, as related to these projects and services.

Social participation as related to social class membership is also described in chapters 4, 9, 16, and 17. Generally, the higher the social class, the greater the participation in community affairs. The modes and types of participation vary within each community and with each situation. Contrary to other studies, Dr. Minnis finds that upper-lower and lower-middle-class members do join organizations, but these are neighborhood rather than community-wide groups. Upper-middle and upper-class persons are more active, especially in all-community organizations.

Four variables—race, religion, ethnic background, and social prestige—are analysed as decisive forces in the differentiation of voluntary organizations. Significantly, the numerous activities of these organizations serve to reinforce the accepted separateness policy and to accentuate the social differences between them. These groups also function to meet the emotional needs of modern women by giving to many a sense of usefulness and belonging. Some who participate seek an alternative to the drabness of matrimony, and others, being college trained, wish to "keep up with things," and need an outlet outside of the home. Women's voluntary organizations centering around humanitarian, cultural, recreational, and social goals serve the needs of its members for expression. As you read Dr. Minnis' comprehensive report you have unveiled before you a prototype of voluntary organizational structure in any community. In other communities, details will differ, of course; there may be fewer or additional organizations, and the names may be different. But the functions are similar, and cleavage exists. Try applying the model to your own community.

$\mathbf{T}$HIS CHAPTER will focus upon: (1) the meaning of voluntary sociations in the life of modern woman; (2) social prestige ranks d characteristics of these organizations; (3) the similarity of rvices rendered by them; and (4) in contrast, the activities ac-ntuating cleavage—racial, religious, and ethnic.[1]

OLUNTARY ASSOCIATIONS IN SOCIETY

The study of associations is of central importance for the field : sociology which deals with the structure and dynamics of group fe. What types of associations people form, who belongs to them, hat functions they perform, and what meaning they have within ie society and in the lives of the individual members thus becomes asic sociological research problems. Furthermore, there is a chal-nging question in what the relation is between associations and ie cultural milieu—i.e., the number and importance of heteroge-eous groups and the diversified and specialized interests of com-unity members in education, occupations, and fine arts.

In this chapter, by an "association" is meant a secondary, or oluntary, organization, or club, in which relationships exist within formal structural framework. Membership participation is seg-ental or tangential in contrast to what Cooley described as the ace-to-face relationship of the primary group. This study is limited ɔ formally organized women's clubs, i.e., those with elected officials, egular meetings, and formal charters of organization. It does not iclude informal or formal cliques or gatherings. This paper also ; limited to organizations located in New Haven proper, i.e., ⱱithin the legal boundaries of the city, although individual members nay reside in Greater New Haven or even contiguous towns. The lubs have an all-woman membership, composed of women eighteen ears of age or over.

Secondary associations represent a selected aspect of the larger ɩeld of group organization. Herbert Goldhamer points out that the

[1] Detailed study made in Mhyra S. Minnis, *The Relationship of Women's Organizations to the Social Structure of a City,* unpublished Ph.D. thesis, Yale University (1951).

voluntary, or secondary, association tends to flourish in a settin in which the community can function as an all-inclusive group In American culture, homogeneity of community composition ha almost disappeared. Especially in urban context, where complexit and heterogeneity have made primary relationships difficult, se ondary associations are fulfilling many basic needs of group livin

The nature of secondary associations has had varied ir terpretations. As early as 1887, Ferdinand Tönnies, spoke (*Gemeinschaft*, or close communal relationship, in contrast to *Gesel schaft*, or organized impersonal relationship.[3] Some material o the associations of Americans in formal organizations from a historic standpoint can be found in the works of Alexis de Tocqu ville [4] as early as 1862, and the later histories of Charles and Mar Beard.[5] The Beards created the impression that Americans wei all a nation of "joiners."

Empirical studies of the last two decades challenge the hi torians' generalizations that all Americans are "joiners." Particip; tion was shown to be related to sex, age, social, and econom status, and educational or family background.

Dr. Mirra Komarovsky,[6] in a study of voluntary associations (2,223 employed adults in New York City found that general they were not affiliated with formal organizations. Participation ; to type of organization varied according to the occupational lev of the worker. In the lower economic class, organized activity largely carried on by men, irrespective of age and marital statu Participation of housewives, even as employed women, goes u with increasing income.

The Lynds [7] came to a similar conclusion regarding particip;

[2] *Some Factors Affecting Participation in Voluntary Associations*, unpul lished Ph.D. thesis, University of Chicago (1943), p. 3.

[3] Ferdinand Tonnies, *Gemeinschaft and Gesellschaft* (1887), Engli: translation by Charles B. Loomis in *Fundamental Concepts of Sociology* (Ne York: The Ronald Press Company, 1940).

[4] Alexis de Tocqueville, *Democracy in America* (1862).

[5] Charles and Mary Beard, *The Rise of American Civilization* (New Yor The Macmillan Co., 1927), pp. 730–731.

[6] Mirra Komarovsky, "The Voluntary Associations of Urban Dwellers *American Sociological Review*, vol. 6 (June, 1941), no. 3, pp. 380–383.

[7] Robert and Helen Lynd, *Middletown* (New York: Harcourt, Brace Co., 1929), chap. 19, "The Organization of Leisure."

on of working-class women. They found that working-class women
ad even business-class women participated much less than working-
ass men.

William Mather,[8] in his study of 708 individuals in Franklin,
adiana, discovered that there is a definite relationship between
come and social participation; the individuals of the upper-
come class not only joined more organizations but more varied
ubs than did those of the lower economic classes. Goldhamer's
udy in Chicago related voluntary associational participation to
lucation, age, and wealth.[9] His study showed the concentration
 memberships in formal organizations to be positively correlated
ith wealth, education, and older age groups.

Dotson,[10] in his study of a sample of fifty working-class families
New Haven, found that formal voluntary associations are un-
aportant in the associational life of most workers. Sixty per cent
 the men and 80 per cent of the women studied had no affiliations
ith formal organizations.

Studies of participation in associations in suburbia have been
ade by Lundberg, and Whetten and Devereaux. Lundberg [11]
 his study of Westchester County found that for the wealthy,
ub activities were the principal leisure pursuit. Less than half
` the adult population, however, belonged to clubs. The findings
` Whetten and Devereaux [12] in the suburb of Windsor, Con-
ecticut, were similar. They found that 62 per cent of the families
udied were without organization affiliation. They feel, however,
aat the economic status of the individual is only one of numerous
cial characteristics affecting participation, others being education,
isure time, and social standing.

On the other hand, some studied indicate that participation
 secondary associations is a deeply-entrenched and major pattern

[8] William Mather, "Income and Social Participation," *American Sociological
-view*, vol. 6 (June, 1941), no. 3, pp. 380–383.

[9] *Op. cit.*

[10] Floyd Dotson, *The Association of Urban Dwellers*, unpublished Ph.D.
esis, Yale University (1950), chap. 6.

[11] George Lundberg, et al., *Leisure: A Suburban Study* (New York: Colum-
a University Press, 1934), chap. 5, "Suburban Organization and Leisure."

[12] N. L. Whetten and C. C. Devereaux, *Studies of Suburbanization in
nnecticut*, Bulletin 212 (Washington, D.C.: Government Printing Office,
36).

of American society. A study by Noel P. Gist, of secret societies in the United States, explains the historical development, ritualistic practices, social structure, and functions of these organizations.[13] He classifies these societies according to sex, age, race, and na tionality. They claim over twenty million members, including women in the many auxiliaries. Charles W. Ferguson, in *Fifty Million Brothers*, also indicates the great numbers belonging to lodges in America whose members make "an effort not so much to escape life as to embellish it . . ."[14] William L. Warner, social class theorist, and associates identified and analyzed 357 associa tions in Yankee City, a small New England community with only 17,000 population, comprising 12,876 members.[15] Similarly, Jones ville, a town of 10,000 population near Chicago, disclosed 13? adult organizations.[16]

In summary, studies which relate associational participation to race, religion, or ethnic factors usually have one of three view points: first, that organizations reflect or help create community cleavage;[17] second, associations are vehicles for the assimilation of diverse groups into the larger community; and, third, organiza tions are instruments both for assimilation and cleavage.[18]

THEORETIC FRAMEWORK IN THE STUDY OF WOMEN'S ORGANIZATIONS

The following study presents data bearing upon the following hypotheses:

Hypothesis I. The type of organization, its activities, and the social characteristics of the members are a function of social prestige rank and may vary with it. Thus membership in a given type of organization is an index to social prestige stratification.

[13] Noel P. Gist, *Secret Societies* (Columbia: University of Missouri Press 1949).

[14] Charles W. Ferguson, *Fifty Million Brothers: A Panorama of American Lodges and Clubs* (New York: Rinehart & Company, Inc., 1937).

[15] W. L. Warner and Paul S. Lunt, *The Social Life of a Modern Commu nity* (New Haven: Yale University Press, 1941), chap. 16.

[16] W. L. Warner et al., *Democracy in Jonesville*, New York: Harper & Brothers, 1949).

[17] Noel P. Gist, *op. cit.*   [18] Warner et al., *Democracy in Jonesville*

Corollary I. Organizational activity is a part of the social 1aracteristics of the members; variation will occur along educa- onal, occupational, recreational, or "cultural" (as fine arts, hobby) 1terests.

Corollary II. If voluntary activity is of a political nature or 1volves a philanthropic service, it will be rendered from the 1gher economic or social level to the lower economic group and 'ill not be reciprocal.

Hypothesis II. Uniformities or similarities, with reference to :tivities of the organization, will reflect (a) the common emotional eeds of human beings (women), and (b) the overall cultural attern of the society.

Hypothesis III. Within the general patterns of the organiza- ons, there will occur variations due to differences of religious, ιcial, or ethnic interests (*i.e.*, due to the basic lines of cleavage r the dominating factors in the social structure). This may be nplied (in contrast to hypothesis II) from the activities of the rganization.

ιETHODOLOGY

The study of women's voluntary organizations in New Haven 'as limited to members, age 18 and over, formally organized and ving within the limits of the city. Four hundred such clubs were sted of which a sample of 177 organizations was chosen. Methods sed to gather material on these organizations included: (1) inter- iews with thirty-five individuals of different socio-economic levels 'ho were familiar with the social structure and services of the rganizations in the community; (2) participant observation and :ctures at women's clubs; (3) correspondence with national and ）cal organizations, study of directories, the *New Haven Register,* terature from the organizations, and newspaper clippings, and 1pplementary interviews with editors of the "society" columns of 1e city's newspapers; (4) a questionnaire to four hundred presi- ents of women's organizations, covering the histories of the clubs, urposes, types, membership, activities, and services; and (5) 1tings by leaders of organizations and public welfare agencies, nd the editors of the "society" columns of the 177 organizations ccording to their relative prestige standing in the community.

SIGNIFICANCE OF VOLUNTARY ORGANIZATIONS
IN THE LIFE OF MODERN WOMEN

In New Haven, there are seven different Junior League clubs. The very names of these clubs—The Junior League of New Haven (Protestant), Catholic Junior League, Junior Community League (Negro), B'nai B'rith Junior League (Jewish), Swedish Junior League, Italian Junior League, and Polish Junior League—reflect the complex, subtle racial, ethnic, religious, and social prestige cleavage of the organizations and membership interests. On the other hand, the similarity of club names further reflects the similarity of club activities and services, within a particular community.

The changing kinds of participation of women in education and social activities can be seen from the past history of club activity. At the turn of the century, women's clubs, with such high sounding names as Clio, Atheneum, Wednesday Culture Club, Elizabeth Browning Circle, and the Literary Society, arose in response to the cultural and limited educational opportunities of upper-class women. This "genteel" class of women would gather on Monday or Wednesday mornings—in contrast to the "Monday Wash Day" working women's world—to present original literary writings and generally to "express themselves." Today, the great variety of women's organizations reflect the greater range and differentiation of women's activities, interests, and services in our changing society. The 379 women's organizations in New Haven alone present a complicated network in response to the great variety of member and community needs. We found that the meaning of clubs in the lives of the members can be summarized as follows: the women wanted a chance for sociability and good fellowship and a chance to work with others; they wanted to receive a feeling of recreation and relaxation either through physical activity or interchange of views; they wanted a chance to develop latent talents in arts, hobbies, and organizational planning; and they wanted mental catharsis and spiritual fellowship, the pride in being part of a special group, and, finally, the "hands across the sea" feeling of communication with other parts and people of the earth.

The following selected quotations from respondents reveal the ·aning organizations have for the members.

A prominent community leader said:

I would say that the club might almost fill a different need in each mber. Some are deeply interested in the kind of work the nursery does, ng particularly interested in children; some find an outlet for their sire to do community work; and some, I think, are just anxious to con- ·ute their time and energy to a worthy cause.

A member of an auxiliary men's fraternal order remarked:

It provides an evening of jollity, conversation on family affairs, chil- ·n, grandchildren, husbands, travel, home decorations, clothing, re- shments—oh yes, all our aches and pains and operations and joys.

more serious note was struck by the president of a Negro religious ;anization:

In our organization we are helping our women by building their ·racter and religious life, but we also enjoy being together. It helps not to be lonely. I've just been sick, and if it had not been for our ·rthy organization, why, I would have been awfully lonely. They ·ught me flowers, and sent me all these "get well" cards, and came to it me. If you don't belong in an organization, why you are all alone this world.

The Lynds,[19] Tomars,[20] and Marcia Meeker [21] call attention the great proliferation of all secondary organizations as a mmunity grows. Women's organizations conform to this growth ttern. Necessary readjustments and reorientation to a dynamic d urban society are basic and fundamental problems for women. ith technological innovations freeing them from previous house- ld tasks and duties, with the developing pattern of a small urban nily, and the decrease in primary contacts, the result is that ne women, especially at middle age, find much time on their nds, and there arises a need for activity and interpersonal relations

[19] *Op. cit.*
[20] Adolph S. Tomars, *Introduction to the Sociology of Art,* Ph.D. thesis ew York: Columbia University Press, 1940), p. 389.
[21] Marcia Meeker, "The Joiners: Male and Female" in Warner, et al., *mocracy in Jonesville.*

outside their homes.[22] One of the answers to such a need may be
participation in a woman's organization. Thus, women's organiza
tions represent a segmental but very essential type of association

On the other hand, the many women who have entered the oc
cupational and business world may wish for greater equalitie
with men and do in fact pursue such goals. In the face of this
the persistence of social inequalities and lack of consensus regard
ing women's role in our society are leading to many contradictions
which modern woman finds difficult to interpret in guiding he
actions.[23] Association with her own sex in a woman's club ma
help to clarify these issues and to establish her role outside th
home.

Another condition which affects the development of associa
tions among women is the changing family situation. A woman'
life falls into discontinuous periods. She may be very absorbed i
her family and children during the early years, but because he
family is small, she may find herself with little to do when he
children have gone off to school or work. Her intense job of chil
rearing ends in her forties, and for some women, this means loneli
ness and frustration. The sense of loss may be a severe shock. A
one of the interviewees, a minister, remarked, "Women in the
forties, in church organizations, seem to have prodigious energ
and they do not know what to do with it." Joining a club ma
tap this energy.

In brief, this study revealed that the need of many women fo
attention, especially during the middle years, a desire to be take
seriously, the use of talents developed in youth and now lyin
fallow, the altruistic intent to help in a world torn by conflict an
hate—all these make participation in a woman's organization
stabilizing or attractive solution. It is easy to belittle—witness th
popularity of Helen Hokinson's cartoons of women's clubs—bu
much more difficult to evaluate the deeper meaning and satisfactio
clubs hold for their members.

[22] Ray E. Barber, *Marriage and the Family* (New York: McGraw-Hill Bo
Co., 1953), chaps. 10–11.

[23] Mirra Komarovsky, "Cultural Contradictions and Sex Roles," *Americ
Journal of Sociology*, vol. III (November, 1946), p. 186.

TYPES AND SOCIAL PRESTIGE RANKS
OF ORGANIZATIONS [24]

The variety of interests and activities of women's clubs are reflected in the numerous types discovered. In New Haven alone, seventeen different types of organizations were classified (see table 15). The largest number of organizations are auxiliaries to churches, 21.5 per cent; second are the service types, 19.8 per cent; and third, the social types, 15.3 per cent. In a large sense, all the clubs are social, since all but two have a "social hour."

Church auxiliary groups are characteristic of the Old American, "American" (those recently Americanized or first generation), and the mixed ethnic groups. The service type is most characteristic of the Jewish, Greek, Irish, Scandinavian, Polish, and German clubs. Lastly, the social type is found mainly among the Italian and mixed ethnic groups.

There is also a significant relationship between type of organization and age of members. While the largest grouping of members in women's organizations is that of women beyond 45, various types appeal to various ages. Social and service types tend to be heavily represented in all age categories; college alumnae, business and professional, Greek letter and educational-service, political, and literary types tend to have a concentration in the age category of 25 to 45; and, lastly, church and labor auxiliaries, religious, and patriotic organizations are predominantly in the category above 45.

A significant relationship was discerned with respect to type and social prestige rank of organization (table 15). Whereas some organizations are found in all social prestige ranks, others are in only one or a few ranks. The relationships are as follows:

[24] For methodology of classification of types, reference is made to the original study, *op. cit.* Space permits only brief mention of methods used. The questionnaire suggested 19 different types of organizations which the respondents could check as characterizing their association. The suggestion was also made to rate their club as first, second, third, etc. The investigator accepted the club's decision and did not superimpose her own ideas. This classification is, therefore, derived from the organizations' own decisions as to type.

1. Literary type of organization appears to be characteristic of the upper social prestige ranks, among both whites and Negroes.
2. Social, service, and recreational clubs are found in social prestige ranks I through V.
3. Educational, college alumnae, and auxiliaries to church types are found in social prestige ranks II and III.
4. Auxiliaries to men's fraternal orders, and to veterans' organizations, Greek letter and religious types are found in the lower three social prestige ranks, III through V.

Table 15. Women's Organizations, Universe and Sample, According to Type, Social Prestige Ranks

TYPE	SAMPLE NUMBER = 177 PERCENTAGE	UNIVERSE NUMBER = 379 PERCENTAGE	SOCIAL PRESTIGE RANK
Literary	1.1	.8	I & III
Social	15.3	15.8	I–V
Educational-civic	5.7	1.9	I–IV
Service	19.8	10.0	I–V
Political	1.7	1.6	III–IV
Hobby	2.3	2.9	III–V
Recreational	1.7	1.3	I–V
Patriotic	3.3	2.1	II–III
Youth-serving	2.3	4.2	II–IV
Religious	6.7	2.9	III–V
Business and professional	1.7	2.9	II–IV
Greek letter	1.7	1.6	III
Alumnae	6.2	6.1	II
Auxiliary to Church or synagogue	21.5	24.6	II–V
Auxiliary to men's fraternal order	2.8	12.1	III–IV
Auxiliary to labor organization	.5	1.6	V
Auxiliary to Veterans' organization	5.7	6.3	IV
Unknown	. .	1.3	. .
Total percentage	100.0	100.0	

Utilizing the criteria of (1) residential area, (2) occupation of usband or, if single, of women members, (3) education, and (4) ocial esteem or reputation of the organization in the community, ie investigator developed a hierarchy of women's organizations ong five social prestige ranks.

The city's largest number of clubs, 66.7 per cent contain the pper-middle and middle social classes, ranks II and III. The very omplexity of the residential distribution of the city's population ppears either to reflect or cause the variety in women's clubs, lub types, and club interests. We must recognize that although an rganization may be within a lower rank, it might at the same me be at the top within its own racial, religious, or ethnic rouping.

In short, women's organizations are not formed according to simple pattern of club differentiation and diversity of member-lip interests, but are arranged in a complex hierarchy of social restige ranks, in which cleavage further occurs in relation to race, eligion, and ethnic origin, reflecting the basic lines of cleavage in community (table 16).

CTIVITIES IN WOMEN'S ORGANIZATIONS

A detailed analysis of activities, services and projects of the rganizations reveal striking similarities which indicate that they nare a common cultural pattern. These similarities appear to mirror raft techniques, recreational interests, along religious, political, ed-cational and social patterns of the larger American society. First, iere appears in these uniformities an assimilation of the common ore of American culture and second, these activities reflect the ocial class prestige ranks of the organization.

A lecturer on the program is a common activity. The upper ocial prestige rank organizations speak of a "lecturer," whereas ie lower prestige ranks refer to a "speaker." Over 53 per cent of ie clubs had a speaker on their programs. Auxiliaries to men's raternal orders and small social clubs do not usually invite speakers. opular topics include current events, book or play reviews, and ctivities relating to education, the psychology of children, diet, ravel, and "the problems of the aging." Specific examples are:

Table 16. Characteristics of Women's Organizations by Social Prestige Rank

PRESTIGE RANK	ORGANIZATIONS		RACE				RELIGION						ETHNIC										
	NO.	PER CENT	WHITE	NEGRO	MIXED	UNSPECIFIED	PROTESTANT	CATHOLIC	JEWISH	GREEK ORTHODOX	MIXED	UNSPECIFIED	IRISH	GREEK	ITALIAN	POLISH	SCANDINAVIAN	GERMAN	OLD AMERICAN	JEWISH	AMERICAN	MIXED	UNSPECIFIED
Rank 1	8	4.5	8				7				1								8				
Rank II	41	23.2	38		3		16	2	2		15	6	1						11	2	15	7	5
Rank III	77	43.5	61	6	7	3	29	8	13	1	19	7		1	7	1	3		9	13	30	7	6
Rank IV	29	16.3	23	6			13	11	2		3		1		6	1		1	1	2	13	2	2
Rank V	22	12.5	15	3	4		9	6	2		5				6					2	9	1	4
Total No.	177		145	15	14	3	74	27	19	1	43	13	2	1	19	2	3	1	29	19	67	17	17
Percentage		100.0	81.9	8.4	7.9	1.8	41.8	15.3	10.8	.6	24.1	7.4	1.1	.6	10.8	1.1	1.6	.6	16.4	10.8	37.8	9.6	9.6

Mexico, the Land of Contrasts," "Bermuda Holiday," "You Are What You Eat," "How Is My Mental Health," "Visual Aid in School," and "Planning for a Fuller Life in Later Maturity." Frequently, the review of books or plays are given by members themselves, especially in the upper-prestige clubs.

Other popular activities include card playing, especially bridge or canasta, "bridge luncheons," or "dessert bridge," crafts, home decorating, sewing for hospitals, and assembling "Care" packages. In addition there are such activities as linoleum block-printing, tile-inlay, and amateur painting. An illustration of a shared American practice is sewing by hand or the folding of gauze which is a popular activity among both social prestige rank I and V clubs. Ranks III and IV organizations are similar concerning their arrangement of benefits and their participation in churches, synagogues, schools, and social service agencies.

Holidays and seasons provide a common program pattern, mainly for ranks II and III. Halloween masquerade balls, New Year's dances and parties, and spring and fall fashion shows are popular. In New Haven, in one year, over one dozen fashion shows were held. There are two ways of giving a fashion show. Either the members themselves dress up and parade as models, while a club member describes each costume in lyric phrases with appropriate background music, or a department store may organize a fashion show for publicity. There was, in fact, so much repetition of activities as to hint at a lack of originality in program planning.

There were, however, a few original programs. Among these were two shows, *St. Raphaels' Revels,* and a comedy, *The Felines.* These shows disprove the common belief that women take their club work "too terribly seriously," for they displayed a great deal of delightful humor and introspective criticism of women's clubs and of women themselves.

The level of activities reflects the social prestige rank of the organization. Thus, upper-prestige clubs have lectures on current events, scientific subjects, and the fine arts, exemplified by "American Measures Up to World Leadership" and "Contemporary World Problems and Their Solution." Large business and professional clubs, with a cross-class membership, have broad departmentalized programs in response to varied interests of the members, such as lectures and demonstrations on "The Art of Rug Making," "The History of Oriental Rugs," "The Formative Period of Utilities," and "The British on the Right Road."

Similarly, in the lower social prestige ranks, as auxiliaries to men's organizations, the activities revolve about men's interest, although the women perform most of the planning and hard work, participating in parades, veterans' parties, and the sale of poppies.

Generally, bazaars and suppers are popular among church or synagogue organizations in social prestige rank II and rank IV, lectures and special movies in rank I and rank II, "silver teas" in rank III, and sewing and devotionals in rank V.

ACTIVITIES AND SERVICES ACCENTUATING
BASIC BELIEFS

Despite the general similarity of activities and projects, the various types of organizations retain a distinctiveness by selection and emphasis of the content of the activities and types of service projects which reflect their basic religious, racial, and ethnic beliefs and traits. Thus each religious, ethnic, occupational, and "feminist" organization chooses books for review, movies, lectures, and social activities that are in harmony with its ethos and which support or highlight the beliefs and purposes distinguishing the organization from any other. These activities re-enforce basic cleavage.

"Christian service" appears to be the dominant emphasis in Protestant organizations. Examples of common lectures are "Missionary Work in Iraq," "Missionary Life in the West Indies," and "Christianity in Japan." Many Protestant clubs partake of devotionals, religious music, and songs before each meeting. The Salvation Army programs are religious in tone and stress "fellowship, service, religion, and education."

Among Catholic organizations, social parties are planned along saints' days as, for example, the popular Saint Patrick's Day bridge party. Movies, *The Perfect Sacrifice* and *Monsieur Vincent*, popularly shown, reflect Catholic faith. Lectures, such as "The Miracle of Blue Country: A Graphic Story of Father Tennien's Missionary Work in China" and "The Catholic and the United Nations," emphasize Catholic interests. In small clubs, such as the Saint Mother Cabrini Society, discussions of the deeds of Mother Cabrini and her miracles are a common and often religiously intense activity. "Communion Breakfast" is another popular activity which strengthens Catholic interest among social club types.

In the Jewish organizations, re-enforcement of basic beliefs are implicit in their activities. Since the creation of the state of Israel, religious and ethnic intensification of original beliefs became more pronounced for some Jewish women's organizations, as revealed in the careful review of activities, collected during 1949–1950, when Israel was in the news. Furthermore, the tragic experiences of the Jews during the Hitler regime and the postwar refugee problems enhanced and challenged the interest of some women's organizations. This interest is exemplified in such lectures, movies, and special programs as "Israel—Its Internal Situation" and "A Program of Jewish and Zionist Education and American Affairs," a refugee film, "A Passport to Freedom," entertainments, represented by "Israel Songs and Dances," and a special three-act play, *And This Is Torah.* Finally, book reviews further intensify basic interests, such as *The Prince of Egypt* and *Shalom Means Peace.* These religious activities were all the more striking since they occurred in clubs that were essentially non-religious and not auxiliaries to synagogues.

The activities of women's clubs point up the concern women have about themselves and their problems. This is reflected in lectures: "Changing Economic Trends as They Affect Women," "1,100 Laws in the United States Discriminating Against Women" by a woman jurist, and "The Country Road," publicized as a lecture by a "woman lecturer-poet-photographer." Such emphasis and reiteration on the accomplishments of famous women reflect strikingly the behavior of women as a minority group.

The hundreds of services, projects, and contributions women's clubs render to their communities and to the members themselves follow in-group loyalty and solidarity. Each group appears to be deeply interested in serving its "own kind," whether they support their church, care for displaced persons, fill baskets for "the needy," serve children's camps, grant scholarships, work in community houses, package food and clothing for overseas, or give parties in institutions for the blind, crippled, aged, orphans, veterans, or those "in great need." Women's organizations render hundreds of services, but usually to their own co-religious or racial group.

On the other hand, we observe a certain amount of cooperation and mutual aid between women's groups. This may operate as an amalgam within the three major religious divisions to bring together some organizations on a common religious basis. Thus, Protestant cooperation is increasing with the creation of the Council of Church Women; Catholics tend to cooperate through the Council of Catholic Women; and all the Jewish associations, excepting a few auxiliaries to small synagogues, now belong to the New Haven Jewish Community Council.

There exists still another type of cooperation. Numerous services and contributions are made to the community, representing cooperation on a large scale. During the time of this study, three inter-club projects were discovered: (1) a cooperative open meeting sponsored by the League of Women Voters and the Junior League of New Haven, entitled "What Is the Community Responsibility to the Schools"; (2) a "Brotherhood Month," sponsored by the Jewish Center in a program titled "This Is America," in which an auxiliary to a Protestant church, a Negro club, a Swedish club, and an Italian club participated; and (3) a polio drive, in which numerous religious and ethnic organizations manned booths together for many hours. These organizations sent workers who gave freely of their time and energies to present a united front in response to the larger needs of the community.

CONCLUSION

While numerous studies have been made of participation in associations, few have focused, as this study does, upon women's organizations in the community as these reflect the social structure of a city. This study reveals that the upper-lower and lower-middle classes do join organizations which are usually small social neighborhood clubs or small auxiliaries to churches. This contradicts the conclusions of other researchers. However, the largest number of women's organizations are found in the upper-middle class.

The study revealed that (1) race is the sharpest line of cleavage,

(2) religion is the most pervasive; (3) ethnic background is contributory within the larger religious divisions, depending upon the denomination; and (4) social prestige acts as a further divisive force within the other three differentiated organizational groups. In brief, cleavage of women's organizations was shown to result in a complex, interweaving pattern in which certain elements of cleavage as, for example, ethnic origin or social prestige, create further subdivisional patterns in the already differentiated religious structure.

This research study also revealed that the functions of women's organizations—their activities, services, and projects—accentuate or re-enforce the basic structural cleavage. However, the similarities of some of these activities and projects point up a process of assimilation into the larger American culture, and the activities are an important means of bringing cultural, social, recreational, and humanitarian satisfactions into the life of modern women and their communities.

✳ 15. The Coordinating Council and Urban Demography in Los Angeles County

J. D. Mezirow

Introduction In large metropolitan areas there exist numerous planning and coordinating councils whose many functions are related to community betterment. The growth of these councils has paralleled the growth of large scale enterprise in an age of specialization. As population in cities increased and spread over wide geographical areas and occupational specialization increased, the city resident lost "control" over his neighborhood and the area around it. Decisions had to be made which affected not only his own neighborhood but those surrounding him. Frequently, decisions were made concerning land use, zoning, placement of utilities, services, and roads which appeared to favor one neighborhood at the expense of another. This imbalance in community planning and functions prompted the organization of area planning councils such as those described by Professor J. D. Mezirow in the following chapter.

In Los Angeles County coordinating councils came into existence in 1931, and today there are over ninety such active neighborhood groups. These councils are concerned with needs and problems of community recreation, health, welfare, education, safety, and rehabilitation. Their activities may broadly range from an educational program aimed at new arrivals and dealing with the existing social and welfare services available in the community to a critical study of current sex offense ordinances and the problems of sex deviation. Councils are made up of laymen and professional persons who represent the active civic organizations, government and private social and welfare agencies of the county.

One important question asked concerning coordinating councils is, Do they do what they are supposed to do? How effective are they, and why does one survive and another die? In this study Dr. Mezirow reports on the success or failure of council programs as related to the size of the community, its social rank, degree of organization, and rate of population mobility. The distribution of communities by population size was based upon 1950 census findings. Social rank and urbanization indexes were based on the Shevky and Bell model.[a] The rate of population mobility was determined by the percentage of persons living in the same household for one year.

After classification of the seventy-six councils on the four population variables an objective evaluation of council effectiveness was made by a nine-point rating instrument. Scope of membership, types and number of committees and projects, and regularity of meetings were the three major categories used by judges in rating effectiveness.

How do you think the four population variables would be related to council effectiveness? Can councils survive and be successful in communities of low urbanization and social rank? Is community size and success of council operation related? Are communities of higher social rank and urbanization most conducive to success? Why? Is the degree of urbanization related to council failure or success? And is the high rate of population mobility in and out of a community related to the effectiveness of council activity?

Dr. Mezirow's careful empirical study provides answers to these questions. From his analysis of population characteristics he identifies those communities which are more or less conducive to council organization and eventual success. He brings us much closer to the creation of a predictive instrument for estimating the probabilities of a council's success when organized under such considerations as degree of urbanization, population size, social rank, and rate of population mobility.

✳ THIS CHAPTER represents an attempt to analyze the relationships between the success of the coordinating councils of Los Angeles County and four major population variables of the com-

[a] For a full description of the theory and application of this model see chapters 3 and 4.

munities in which they function: population size, social rank, urbanization, and population mobility.

Coordinating councils are delegate assemblies of agency and organization representatives and unaffiliated individuals; they are organized for community betterment and youth service in over ninety local neighborhoods and communities in the county. Council policy is formulated by a general assembly and executed by an elected executive board through a committee structure. Executive, membership, recreation, case conference, safety, and health committees are most common. The most common projects are community development, recreation, community events, health, welfare, youth activities, education, safety, and environmental control, the two main ones being community development and environmental control. Typical community development activities are distribution of community calendars and directories, campaigns to acquire community services and facilities, and self-surveys. Representative environmental control projects are sex offense ordinance studies, theatre codes of conduct, narcotics education conferences, and studies of the control over sale of liquor and salacious literature to minors. There is a trend toward direct council sponsorship of projects except in the highly institutionalized areas of education and welfare where preconceived ideas of the proper role of the layman probably have been responsible for a relatively higher incidence of educational and welfare programs. In these areas councils have largely confined their activities to somewhat limited youth service projects.

An average of thirty-four people participate in a council's monthly general assembly meeting. Most delegates come from governmental agencies and civic organizations; private agencies send the third largest group, and religious organizations, the fourth. Proportionately, representation from government agencies increased over the 1940–1950 decade, and civic and religious group representation declined. The proportion of private agency representation increased only slightly. Among governmental agencies, the public schools, recreation, police, and health agencies are best represented. PTA's, Women's Clubs, veteran organizations and their auxiliaries, chambers of commerce, and Lions and Kiwanis clubs have the heaviest representation among civic organizations. Total representation on the councils is down 260 per cent from the high of 1940 when, under WPA sponsorship, about eighty councils were serviced by one hundred workers, one assigned as executive secretary to each council. Until recently, ten professionals and a supervisor devoted their full time to the council movement, working out of the offices of the County Probation Department. This function has now been transferred to a County Department of Community Services, and the professional staff has been increased in number.

Councils are members of a county-wide federation which is organizationally the counterpart of the local council and provides a means for councils to deal with problems of greater than local scope. The movement has been flourishing for some time, and it observed its twenty-fifth anniversary in 1956.

RELATED RESEARCH

There has been a certain amount of research relating to the coordinating councils of Los Angeles County. Six unpublished studies deal directly with this subject. With the exception of a comparative historical investigation by Conliffe [1] which traces the relationship between the Council of Social Agencies of Los Angeles and the coordinating councils over fourteen years of operation, each study attempted to evaluate council success and identify relevant variables either for individual councils or for the movement as a whole. Three of the investigations are case studies of the membership and operation of arbitrarily selected "successful" or "unsuccessful" councils or both.

Ostendorf [2] examined the attitudes of members of two successful councils toward their leadership, factors contributing to council success, and types of programs thought most important. Councils

[1] Archie John Conliffe, *Community Organization Process in the Relationship between the Council of Social Agencies and the Coordinating Council in Los Angeles,* M.S.W. thesis, University of Southern California (1944).

[2] Fred Otto Ostendorf, *A Comparative Study of Personal and Social Factors Contributing to the Success of Two Community Coordinating Councils,* M.S.A. thesis, University of Southern California (1949).

were matched for community population size, membership size, and geographical location. Ostendorf defined a successful council as one

. . . which has consistently sustained interest in the completion of community projects since its formation, has increased and maintained a membership commensurate with the community's population and has acted as a representative body of the community.[3]

Data were gathered and analyzed from 100 respondents to a questionnaire sent to members of the two councils studied. Over 30 per cent of the respondents had been members of other coordinating councils, and 68 and 76 per cent in the two councils had held office or a committee post. Average length of residence in the community was 16 years in one case, 9 years in the other; members had been attending council meetings on the average of 5 years in one community and 11 months in the other.

Projects undertaken and committee work were factors deemed most important to council success by members; personality of leaders, publicity of work accomplished, and professional consultant help were thought important. Most respondents felt their council was of "great" benefit to the community, that attendance at council meetings was time "always" well spent, and that they were afforded opportunities to make suggestions effecting success of their council.

The history, organization, and procedures of the councils and the membership, attendance, and projects of eleven "typical" counties were studied by Marquardt[4] in 1938. He also examined the history of four councils, two "successful" and two "weak." No criteria were presented for the selection of councils studied or for success or typicality, and conclusions were virtually unsubstantiated, *e.g.*, "the original purpose of the councils, that of agency coordination, has been accomplished."

In 1939 Williams[5] utilized case study and interview methods to analyze successful and unsuccessful councils in a large and a

[3] *Ibid.*, p. 10.

[4] John Frederick Dalman Marquardt, *A Study of the Los Angeles County Coordinating Council—Plan, Organization, and Procedure,* M.S.S.W. thesis, University of Southern California (1938).

[5] Adelaide Williams, *The Social Consequences of the Coordinating Council,* M.A. thesis, University of California at Los Angeles (1937).

small community—a total of four councils in all. The study also failed to define "community," council "success," or the basis of selection of "typical" councils for study. Williams suggested that relative population size of a community does not affect success of the council plan which, however, is dependent upon participation of "leading citizens," development of projects rooted in real community problems, leadership that fosters members' cooperation, and representation that is "democratic" and inclusive of all local groups interested in youth.

Bradley [6] evaluated the council movement by observation, interviews, and a questionnaire. Seventy-four councils were contacted to determine their organization, membership, types of meetings, forms of publicity, finance, and relationship to the agency providing consultant service. In her favorable evaluation Bradley reported eight highly generalized achievements of the movement, e.g., "Lay participation has aroused a community sense of social responsibility," and ten weaknesses of the councils, e.g., "Councils have too much faith that mere provision of adequate recreation facilities will solve a delinquency problem." Council weaknesses were "outweighed by the strong features by a considerable margin."

A more comprehensive analysis of the council movement was undertaken by the author in 1955.[7] In addition to providing considerable historical detail, trends in committee structure, projects, and membership of the councils over both a decade and one-year periods were reported. Descriptions of the role of the professional consultant and the federation of councils were included. The data and analysis presented below are based upon findings reported in this study.

DEMOGRAPHIC VARIABLES

The study presented below is designed to ascertain the characteristics of communities in which coordinating councils appear

[6] Esther Reynolds Bradley, *A Study of the Coordinating Council Movement of Los Angeles County, with Particular Emphasis upon Its Sociological and Educational Implications,* M.A. thesis, Claremont College (1941).

[7] Jack David Mezirow, *The Coordinating Council Movement in Los Angeles County and Its Implications for Adult Education,* Ed.D. dissertation, University of California at Los Angeles (1955).

most and least likely to be established, to survive, and to succeed. Communities of Los Angeles County were differentiated in terms of certain key population characteristics. These major variants of urban society are (1) population size, (2) social rank, as measured by a composite index of educational and occupational levels, (3) urbanization, as measured by a composite index of the proportion of children to women of childbearing ages, proportion of women in the working force, and proportion of single family dwelling units, and (4) population mobility, as measured by the percentage of persons living in the same house for one year.

Indexes based upon 1950 census findings, were applied to 123 geographical communities of varying populations as these communities were defined in terms of multiple, contiguous, census tracts by the Division of Community Services of the Los Angeles County Probation Department, the agency which for twenty-four years provided consultant services to the council movement. The distribution of communities by population size is reported in table 17.

Communities with similar indexes of social rank and urbanization were grouped into sixteen "social areas" by plotting them with

Table 17. *The Distribution of Communities in Los Angeles County by Population*

POPULATION	NUMBER OF COMMUNITIES
Over 100,000	4
90,000–99,999	4
80,000–89,999	7
70,000–79,999	3
60,000–69,999	1
50,000–59,999	6
40,000–49,999	8
30,000–39,999	15
20,000–29,999	27
10,000–19,999	20
5,000– 9,999	19
Under 5,000	9
Total	123

the social rank scale as the base line and the urbanization scale for the ordinate as illustrated in figure 15. In this illustration the position of 122 communities has been plotted. (One community has been omitted because of the small size of the population.) The third element, that of population mobility, is taken into account by indicating the communities whose population index scores fell in the highest decile by a triangle and by indicating those falling within the lowest decile by an inverted triangle.

With one exception, communities falling into the highest decile of population mobility appear within the middle ranges of social rank. The largest proportion of communities with the most extreme mobility are found in areas of high-middle social rank. Social Area VIII, of high urbanization and low-middle social rank, has the highest proportion of high mobility communities falling within it. The four communities in this social area have populations of between 28,000 and 82,000. Two of the three are within the highest decile of mobility. One of the three communities in social area XII is also in the highest decile, and adjacent social areas V, VI, and X, those with the largest number of communities in them, each have two high mobility communities. Communities falling within the lowest decile in mobility are broadly distributed throughout the attribute space, with a concentration of four found in social area XII which is composed of a total of seven communities.

The social rank-urbanization-mobility pattern itself indicates the existence of several potential social problems. Congested and underprivileged communities of high urbanization and low social rank with their chronic instability of employment and concentration of vagrants are likely centers of delinquency and crime. These communities have urgent need of new forms of citizen organization for social action to secure special consideration and services for both immediate social remedies and long-range improvement. Environmental and housing deficiencies are apt to be most acute in areas of low social rank and high mobility. As high mobility in Southern California is to a large extent associated with immigrants coming into communities, when this characteristic is coupled with low social rank, the major social problems which arise from old buildings, overcrowding, and lack of integration may be expected.

Communities characterized by high mobility-middle social rank-low urbanization afford a relatively new area for community organization and development. In California's flood tide of new settlements many community planning groups are pioneering in cooperative citizen efforts which can, with assistance, be broadened into hitherto unexpected fields of common endeavor. These communities have a high proportion of children. In them, whole populations are making a new start, building new autonomous groups and values, and learning new skills of cooperative problem-solving in facing community situations without access to needed services and the usual formal service organizations. Child-care programs and the whole constellation of youth services which have often been established in response to council efforts are also much needed in the communities with the highest proportion of women in the working force, particularly when this factor is coupled with relatively low social rank, indicative of low ability of the inhabitants to pay for private care, welfare services, and recreation. Com-

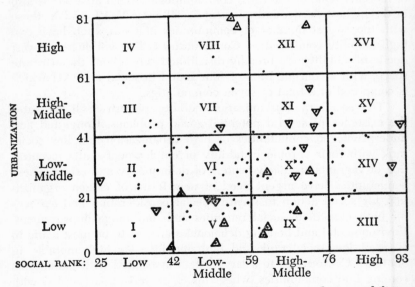

△ Communities with high indexes of population mobility.
▽ Communities with low indexes of population mobility.

Figure 15. Social Areas (Scattergram)

munities of low urbanization and social rank with high proportions of children and teenagers especially need the kinds of youth service programs which have become associated with council activity in Los Angeles County. Vocationally oriented adult education is an urgent need in communities with low levels of schooling and occupation, *i.e.*, social rank. Here public health problems may be anticipated, a concern which will extend into the middle social rank-high urbanization areas. Councils operating in communities of higher social rank should be those best able to turn their attention toward solving social problems of increasing complexity.

DISTRIBUTION OF COUNCILS BY SOCIAL AREA

Figure 16 indicates the number of councils functioning in 1950 in each of the sixteen social areas.

The 85 councils included in this study were found operating

						Per Cent Communities Organized
URBANIZATION	IV Comm.: 1 Councils: 1	VIII Comm.: 3 Councils: 0	XII Comm.: 3 Councils: 3	XVI Comm.: 2 Councils: 1		55.5
	III Comm.: 4 Councils: 3	VII Comm.: 4 Councils: 4	XI Comm.: 7 Councils: 5	XV Comm.: 5 Councils: 3		75.0
	II Comm.: 7 Councils: 5	VI Comm.: 25 Councils: 18	X Comm.: 20 Councils: 13	XIV Comm.: 8 Councils: 7		71.7
	I Comm.: 5 Councils: 3	V Comm.: 14 Councils: 11	IX Comm.: 10 Councils: 6	XIII Comm.: 3 Councils: 2		68.7

SOCIAL RANK: Per Cent Communities Organized

70.6   71.7   65.0   77.7

Figure 16.   Distribution of Communities and Councils by Social Areas

in 15 of the 16 social areas in communities from under 5,000 to over 200,000 in population. Only area VIII, with the largest proportion of high mobility communities in the county, was without council service. No significant relationship could be statistically determined between the frequency with which councils were formed and the comparative social rank and urbanization communities. Councils were found in areas of low social rank and high urbanization, such as III, IV, and VII, areas characterized by two conditions which, in association, usually constitute slums. These three areas, with communities of from 20,000 to 50,000 population, together with council-less area VII, which also possessed slum conditions, had over 66.6 per cent of their 12 communities organized. This percentage compares favorably with those of the other three-quarters of the attribute space. The four areas in the upper right portion of figure 16 had 70.6 per cent of their communities organized, those at the lower left had 72.5 per cent, and those in the lower right quarter, 68.3 per cent. This finding appears to belie any assumption that councils can be organized only in communities of middle social rank.

Between 70 and 80 per cent of the communities in each column and row on the attribute space had councils, with two exceptions. Areas of highest and lowest urbanization respectively had 55.5 per cent and 68.7 per cent of their communities organized, and the areas of high middle social rank, 65 per cent. The sharpest drop in proportion of communities organized is evident in social areas of high urbanization. No comparable dip occurs anywhere in the social rank continuum. As might be expected, areas with a low ratio of children to women of childbearing ages and a high proportion of working women, *i.e.*, areas of high urbanization, are least likely to manifest an interest in organizations concerned with the welfare of youth.

In summary, it should be noted that only thirty-six out of 121 communities, 29 per cent, were found to be without coordinating councils in 1950, and these were widely distributed throughout the attribute space. No significant relationship could be established between social rank and urbanization of communities and the frequency with which councils were found to be operating in them. Eighty-five councils were operating in fifteen of the sixteen social areas in communities with populations from under 5,000 to over 200,000. The single unorganized area had the highest proportion of its communities falling within the highest decile of population mobility. Councils were found in areas having slum characteristics in roughly comparable proportion to other social areas. Communities of high and low social rank compared favorably with those falling in the middle of the social rank scale in the proportion being served by the councils. Between 68.7 and 77.7 per cent of communities in the low, low-middle, high-middle, and high categories on both urbanization and social rank scales were served by councils.

THE MEASUREMENT OF COUNCIL SUCCESS

To permit an objective evaluation of council effectiveness, a nine-point rating instrument was developed which included standardized descriptions of seventy-six councils, all of which had been in existence for at least five years. These one- and two-page case studies, or descriptive profiles, listed without comment ten categories of information pertaining to each council: (1) community population, (2) membership composition by agency and organization, (3) total number of participants and average attendance at monthly meetings, (4) committee structure, (5) projects undertaken, (6) number of federation meetings attended, (7) attendance at federation's annual conference, (8) frequency of council meetings, (9) date of organization and reason given for initial organization by the person consulted, and (10) miscellaneous facts, e.g., number of consultants servicing the council over the period reported. Whenever available, comparative data were included for 1949, 1950, and 1953 to present a picture of five years of council growth. Selection and organization of information included in the profiles followed that made by the Division of Community Services over more than two decades of surveying and studying the council movement. Identity of the councils and communities was withheld. Judges were asked to formulate their own criteria of council effectiveness based upon the data listed in the profiles and to apply them to each council described.

Nine consultants in community organization employed by the Los Angeles County Probation Department to service the councils on a full-time basis served as a panel of judges. With one exception, all had been serving in their present capacity for thirty-five months or longer. All were graduates of four-year colleges, majoring in various social sciences. All had taken some graduate work, and four had recently attended a two-week session at the Western Training Laboratory in Group Development conducted by the University of California. Each of the men had volunteered for the transfer to the Community Organization Section from other units of the Probation Department.

Judges assigned varying importance to the categories of information found in the profiles, some combining data into their own original categories. In general, (1) scope of membership, (2) types and number of committees and projects, and (3) regularity of meetings were items weighted most heavily. One judge devised a criterion of membership of one for each one thousand in the population of the community. Information was grouped into the following original categories by the judges: "Interest Beyond Local Area," "Evidence of Interest Outside Community," "Action Revealing Attempts to Function Better as a Group," "Action Revealing Diversity of Problem Awareness and Involvement in Problem Solving," "Action Revealing Extent to Which Council Relates to Problems and Events Outside Local Community," "Increasing Significance of Committees," "Increasing Significance of Projects," "Participation in Inter-Agency Activity," "Leadership," and others. It is apparent that these criteria constituted an effort by several judges to formulate some yardstick of group growth or council maturity, a qualitative factor of another dimension other than the quantitative organization of data found in the profiles. They are interesting too as reflections of the image of the councils held by those who are in a position to exercise real leadership in shaping the council movement in the county.

The mean council rating was 5.44 on the nine point scale with a range of 1.83 to 8.27. Raters varied in their reactions to the profiles on an average of four scale points. While there was an expected difference of opinion in rating the middle range of councils, the greatest agreement was on two councils falling within the middle of the ranking order, and there was no high degree of agreement given councils of extremely low rank. There was a difference of 2.5 points in rating two councils, 3 points in rating six, 5.5 points in rating four, and 6 points in rating four. Sixty councils were rated with differences of from 3.3 points to 5 points.

One important limitation of the rating system was that councils were compared for their relative success without knowledge by the judges of the varying characteristics of the communities in which they had been operating except for population size. Councils in slum areas could have done a heroic job which would show up modestly in the quantitative data of the profiles, whereas councils in communities of greater advantage would have a much easier time making the same record.

COUNCIL EFFECTIVENESS AND THE NATURE OF THE COMMUNITY

It should be noted that whereas earlier attention was focused upon community characteristics more and less conducive to the organization of councils, the present consideration deals with councils which have been operating for five years or more—a fair measure of survival. Consequently, it is of interest to determine the kinds of communities in which these councils have taken root successfully. Table 18 reports the distribution of the councils by community population.

Table 18. *Distribution of Communities and Councils Operating Five Years and Longer by Community Population*

POPULATION	NUMBER OF COMMUNITIES	NUMBER OF FIVE YEAR COUNCILS	PER CENT ORGANIZED
Over 100,000	4	3	75.0
90,000–99,999	4	4	100.0
80,000–89,999	7	4	57.1
70,000–79,999	3	3	100.0
60,000–69,999	1	. .	. .
50,000–59,999	6	5	83.3
40,000–49,999	8	5	62.5
30,000–39,999	15	9	60.0
20,000–29,999	27	19	70.4
10,000–19,999	20	15	75.0
5,000– 9,999	19	8	42.1
Under 5,000	9	1	1.1
Total	123	76	

It has been contended that the coordinating council is a form of community organization which has grown up to meet small town or rural community needs and is less likely to operate functionally over a sustained period in larger urban communities. This contention is not confirmed by table 18. Quite to the contrary, well-established councils are found in all but 6 of the 25 communities of over 50,000 population (76 per cent), while the poorest showing was in communities under 5,000 (1.1 per cent organized) and from 5,000 to 5,999 (42.1 per cent organized). A significant relationship was identified statistically between community size and the proportion of well-established councils (*i.e.*, those existing for five years or longer) ($X^2 = 5.33$, df $= 2$, $.10 > p > .05$).[8] Whereas the 25 communities of over 50,000 population (20.3 per cent of the 123 communities in the county) had 19 established councils, or 25.0 per cent of the total of 76 councils, the 28 communities of less than 10,000 population (22.8 per cent) had only 9 established councils, or 11.8 per cent of the total. The 70 communities with populations ranging from 10,000 to 49,999 comprised 56.9 per cent of all communities in the county and had 48 established councils (63.2 per cent of the total).

To determine other community characteristics more and less conducive to the council success, the 75 councils were grouped under four headings: "Excellent," "Good," "Fair," and "Poor." These classifications represent the quartile in which councils fall on the basis of their mean ratings: Q4, Q3, Q2, and Q1. Findings are presented in figure 17.

Several features merit comment in this presentation. An examination of the distribution of these well-established councils over the attribute space in figure 16 warrants the conclusion that councils *survive* in communities of almost every degree of urbanization and social rank. An impressive 82.5 per cent of the councils operating in Los Angeles County in 1950 had been in existence for five years and longer. But how well do surviving councils succeed? It may be observed that the proportion of "Excellent" councils and the combined proportion of "Excellent" and "Good" councils increase as the reader moves from the bottom half of figure 16 to the top half and from the left half to the right. Generally, and with some obvious

[8] See chap. 17, p. 339.

exceptions, it may be concluded that councils are more apt to achieve success in communities of high urbanization and social rank.

URBANIZATION

		IV	VIII	XII	XVI
High	Excellent	–	–	1	1
	Good	–	–	1	–
	Fair	–	–	–	–
	Poor	1	–	1	–
		III	VII	XI	XV
High-Middle	Excellent	–	–	3	2
	Good	–	1	1	–
	Fair	1	–	–	–
	Poor	–	1	1	1
		II	VI	X	XIV
Low-Middle	Excellent	1	2	2	2
	Good	–	5	6	1
	Fair	3	4	4	1
	Poor	1	6	–	2
		I	V	IX	XIII
Low	Excellent	1	1	2	–
	Good	–	3	1	1
	Fair	1	5	1	–
	Poor	–	2	1	1
SOCIAL RANK		Low	Low-Middle	High-Middle	High

Figure 17.   Distribution of "Excellent," "Good," "Fair," and "Poor" Councils by Social Area

More specifically, statistical analysis revealed a significant relationship between council rating and community social rank ($X^2 =$ 6.38, df 1, .02 > p > .01).[9] Among the 39 established councils located in communities of low and low-middle social rank, 14 (35.9

[9] Chap. 17, p. 339.

per cent) were rated "High," (*i.e.,* "Excellent" or "Good") in effectiveness, and 25 (64.1 per cent) were rated "Low," (*i.e.,* "Fair" or "Poor"). Of the 37 councils located in communities of high and high-middle social rank, 24 councils (64.9 per cent) were rated "High," and 13 (35.1 per cent) were rated "Low."

While no statistically significant relationship could be determined for the proportion of successful councils established in high social rank communities as distinct from those of high-middle social rank, there is certainly a particularly high frequency of successful and established councils in high-middle social rank communities. Twenty-five councils are located in communities of high-middle social rank in figure 17. Seventeen (68.0 per cent) of these are reported "High" in effectiveness, and eight councils (32.0 per cent) were rated "Low." Of the 12 councils operating in communities of highest social rank in figure 16, 7 (58.3 per cent) were rated "High" in effectiveness and 5 (41.7 per cent) "Low."

The low range of the social rank scale has the lowest proportion of council successes. In social area VI, an area of low-middle social rank and urbanization, falls the largest number of councils of any area on the attribute space, but nearly one-third of the seventeen were rated "Poor" and only two were rated "Excellent." In the low and low-middle range of social rank, councils have little better than a 50 per cent chance of attaining "Good" or "Excellent" status. In cases where low and low-middle social rank was combined with low and low-middle urbanization (this was true for the largest number of communities in the county), 62.8 per cent of the 35 councils were rated "Poor" or "Fair," against 37.2 per cent "Good" and "Excellent." Communities falling in the lower right quarter of figure 17 more nearly approach a normal distribution in rated effectiveness than those found in any other quarter of the attribute space. It is in these communities in which are found the greatest proportion of "Good" councils. For example, social area X includes twelve councils, half of which were "Good" and none of which were rated "Poor." Sixty per cent of the councils in the lower right quarter of the attribute space were rated either "Good" or "Excellent."

While there is about a 10 per cent decrease in "Poor" councils from communities of low and low-middle to those of high and high-middle social rank in figure 17, there is almost an equal *increase* in such councils in communities of high and high-middle urbanization over those of low and low-middle urbanization. No significant relationship is statistically demonstrable, however, between council success and community urbanization comparable to that between council success and community social rank. In the communities falling in the upper left quarter of figure 17, none of the four councils were "Excellent," two were "Poor," and one was "Fair," and only one was "Good." Thus while councils are organized and even survive in slum communities, they find it hard going. Again, it should be remembered that these councils were rated for relative effectiveness against councils in communities much more favorably situated. Consequently, the success of the "Fair" and particularly the "Good" council is particularly noteworthy. The situation is quite dramatically reversed for communities falling in the upper right quarter of the attribute space. Here, of twelve councils, seven, the highest proportion of any quarter of the attribute space, were rated "Excellent," and only three "Poor." Councils stand the best chance for outstanding success in communities of high urbanization and high social rank.

The hardiness of the councils in communities with widely diverse characteristics is attested by the fact that the council rated highest among the seventy-six is located in the social area of lowest urbanization and lowest social rank, while the council rated fourth highest is located in a community of the highest urbanization and highest social rank. Moreover, the community with the highest population mobility in the county had a council rated in the top quartile of effectiveness. No definitive relationships were discovered between the mobility of a community and the effectiveness of the council serving it. Eighteen councils falling in the upper quartile in rated effectiveness were found to have a mean percentage of mobility in their communities of 25.8, only 1.6 points above the mean percentage of the communities with councils falling in the lowest quartile of rated effectiveness.

A statistically significant relationship was established between community size and council rating ($X^2 = 10.94$, df 2, $p < .01$): [10] the larger the community, the larger the proportion of established councils which seem to have succeeded. In communities of over 50,000 population, 15 out of 19 councils were rated "High" in effectiveness, a percentage of 78.9. In communities of less than 10,000

[10] Chap. 17, p. 339.

population only 4 out of 11, or 36.4 per cent were rated "High" in effectiveness.

SUMMARY OF FINDINGS

Only 29 per cent of the communities of Los Angeles County were without coordinating councils in 1950. Over 82 per cent of the councils had survived for five years or more, and many had achieved a relative degree of success in communities of almost every combination of social rank, urbanization, population mobility, and population size. A significant relationship has been found between community size and the operation of councils five years old and older; the larger the community, the more likely are relatively successful councils to be found there. In addition, a statistically significant relationship has been identified between community size and council success, communities over 50,000 population enjoying a relatively greater proportion of effective councils than those under 10,000.

Communities of higher social rank and urbanization are most conducive to council success. Council effectiveness and community social rank have a very significant relationship: the higher the educational and occupational levels of a community, the more successful will the established council be operating there. Communities of lower social rank are the most difficult for councils to succeed in. Councils in communities with slum characteristics generally have difficulties, but half of those organized in 1950 had survived for five years or more. Chances for council success in communities of higher social rank and lower urbanization can be roughly estimated on the basis of a normal distribution. No statistically significant relationships were found between council success and urbanization or population mobility.

INTERPRETATION

The relationship between social class position and social participation has been carefully examined by sociologists.[11] Findings

[11] For a summary of studies and bibliography see Leonard Reissman, "Class, Leisure, and Social Participation," *American Sociological Review*, vol. 19 (February, 1954), pp. 76–84.

generally indicate that those in "higher" (middle) class positions are more active and diverse in their participation than those in "lower" positions. Although class position has been determined by different variables, studies have been largely based upon common categories of analysis. Reissman [12] has enhanced the comparability of these investigations by testing the relationship between class and participation in a single sample alternately with the three most commonly used variables: education, occupation, and income. His study established the existence of a similar pattern regardless of the class variable, and this made possible his conclusion that differences among previous studies are not crucial. Reissman categorized earlier investigations which reported class differentials in organization activity, organization leadership, church attendance, visiting and friendship patterns, and reading of books and magazines. He proceeded to examine variations in these criteria of participation in occupational, income, and educational groups in his sample. In summary,

. . . it was found that regardless of the variable used to measure class position—occupation, income, or education—the higher class shows a higher degree of participation and involvement in the community. That is, individuals in this class read more books and magazines, attend church more frequently, belong to more organizations, and more often hold office in those organizations. The present study thereby lends further support to previous studies on that relationship. Phrased in more general terms, it can be said that the middle class, on the whole, tends to dominate the organizational activity, the intellectual life, and the leadership of the community.[13]

The variables of education and occupation, significantly related to council success and social participation, may well also reflect the receptivity with which individuals and communities will react to the typically middle-class programs sponsored by councils and other formal organizations. Community social rank may constitute a useful rough index of anticipated community support and "readiness" for council type organization and community betterment projects. Practitioners in community development may find this index valuable in formulating norms for anticipating the amount and kind of

[12] *Ibid.*   [13] *Ibid.*, p. 83.

professional help which will be required to deal with community problems of certain types.

In arriving at a pattern of relationship between certain major population factors in the communities of Los Angeles County and the establishment and effectiveness of coordinating councils in these communities, it has been possible to identify communities more and less conducive to council establishment and success. Councils have been located which have been found atypical in their achievement of longevity and success in communities generally not conducive to this achievement. From the point of view of research in council development, the ground work has been laid for investigation of clues which may indicate operational principles in building a more representative and more broadly distributed movement within the county. Even more valuable, research may now be conducted to attempt to identify common interests, needs, leadership patterns, power structures, factors of community readiness, and patterns of participation indigenous to the relatively homogeneous social areas delineated by this study. Organizational and educational efforts, as well as council programs, can be then more realistically keyed to these local considerations. Areas in which many councils have experienced a disproportionately high incidence of marginal operation may well require professional attention and organizational approaches different from those appropriate to communities in which councils have never been able to become firmly established.

Community Problems

16. The Influence of Social Participation on Community Programs and Activities

John M. Foskett

Introduction To paraphrase Shakespeare, the community is
but a stage and we, a selected we, are actors upon it. This is the key to
Professor John M. Foskett's thesis in the following chapter. People who
participate in community affairs affect the life of the whole community.
Social participation, that is, participation in community affairs, is related
to decision making; those who make decisions are leaders and have power
and authority. Consequently, their beliefs and values dominate the course
of action which may be pursued.

What are some of the reasons for high and low participation in community activities and in the solution of community problems? What are
the consequences of differences in participation between social class
groups upon the decisions reached in a community? How can more people
be induced to take an active part in the life of their community so that
the base of social participation can be broadened from a segment of the
population to the population as a whole? To these and many other questions Professor Foskett gives us some answers.

For some time theorizers and researchers have noted that persons
who are active in the community and who usually give leadership to its
social, religious, welfare, educational, and other institutions and to the
solution of community problems are those individuals who are the best
educated, have the highest income, and are in prestige occupations such

311

as management and the professions. In the study which you are about to read these same results were obtained. A "General Community Participation Score" was developed and used to measure formal and informal participation and activity in a variety of community participation areas, such as voting, membership in voluntary associations, and discussion of civic problems. What is more interesting and important is the question of why these three factors, education, occupation, and income, are so importantly related to social participation.

The opportunity and need for contact and communication with others is related to the nature of one's job and the place of work. The ability to communicate, to express oneself, and to be aware of social issues is associated with educational achievement. Time and finance are important factors in social participation. Who in the community can afford the $3.00 luncheon meeting in the downtown hotel which may begin at twelve noon and continue until two thirty in the afternoon? The person with suitable income and the non-punch clock kind of job can participate but a drill press operator cannot afford this kind of meeting, and even if he could, it is doubtful if he would be given the time off from his job.

In any society there develop in time some expectations regarding appropriate behavior for each position. Sometimes these are called role expectations. We "expect" the educated, well-paid, white-collar, managerial, or professional person to participate in community affairs. In fact participation is a "value" of our higher social classes, and this value is so internalized within the psycho-social structure of these classes that non-participation often results in extreme feelings of guilt.

Participation often depends upon the relevancy of a problem. Those problems which affect one most personally, such as the location of a mustard factory on the lot next to a group of mortgaged but privately owned one-family homes, will result in a high degree of social participation. In the illustration, of course, people of the upper classes would be the most likely to own one-family houses and thus to participate.

There are many consequences of differential social participation. One important result is that problems are solved and programs are initiated in consonance with the orientation and values of the participators, usually a segmented group of special interests. While equal full participation by all members of a society would be difficult to realize, broadening the base of participation is certainly in keeping with the concept of democracy. Professor Foskett describes some excellent techniques for increasing social participation.

Professor Foskett conducted his research in a small community. Would you expect to find different results in a larger one? In populated urban areas there are many highly organized social systems such as unions

aternal orders, community councils, and neighborhood associations.
ome of these groups are made up of members of the working class and
present their interests. Is it reasonable to assume that one would find an
creased participation score for working-class members in the larger
mmunity than in the smaller one? Or would what appears to be a high
rticipation level of working-class members in community life be more
dicative of organized union cr brotherhood activity than social participaon of individual members of the working class?

In any community there is a wide range of influences which
perate directly and indirectly to affect community activities and
ograms. Some of the influences, such as physical environment,
tural resources, population size, and relative location to other
mmunities, constitute the basic conditions of community life and
termine in part the kinds of problems or needs with which the
ople of the community must deal. Other influences, such as power
d leadership structures, communication networks, political or-
nization, legal arrangements, and social class composition, have
uch to do with the way people go about solving community prob-
ns and hence the kind of decisions eventually reached. In the
st, community studies have tended to focus attention on the prob-
ns or needs themselves or with the factors creating difficulties.[1]
ore recently, increasing attention has been given to the decision-
aking process itself and the manner in which the people of a com-
unity seek to resolve their problems.[2]

[1] Examples of this earlier literature include M. R. Davie, *Problems of City*
e (New York: John Wiley & Sons, Inc., 1932); Robert S. and Helen M.
nd, *Middletown: A Study of Contemporary American Culture* (New York:
rcourt, Brace & Co., 1929); R. D. McKenzie, *The Metropolitan Community*
ew York: McGraw-Hill Book Co., 1937); Louis Wirth, "Urbanism as a Way
Life," *American Journal of Sociology*, vol. 44 (July, 1938), pp. 1–24; Howard
olston, *Metropolis: A Study of Urban Communities* (New York: Appleton-
ntury-Crofts Company, 1938); C. C. Zimmerman, *The Changing Community*
ew York: Harper & Brothers, 1938); Harvey W. Zorbaugh, *The Gold Coast*
l *the Slum* (Chicago: Chicago University Press, 1929.)
[2] It is not implied that the earlier type of community study is disappearing
is not of value, but rather that a new dimension is being added to commu-
y research. Illustrative of this new interest are Floyd Hunter, *Community*
ver *Structure* (Chapel Hill: University of North Carolina Press, 1953);

One of the most obvious of this second type of influence i. "social participation," that is, participation in matters of communit concern. In general, the kinds of decisions made and the proces by which they are reached will be a consequence of the people wh do and who do not participate in the affairs of the community and of the manner in which the participation is carried on. Communit zoning policies determined primarily by the merchants of Mai Street would undoubtedly be different from those arrived at by group of working-class home-owners. Decisions reached throug "bargaining" would undoubtedly differ materially from decision growing out of an objective analysis of needs and resources. A understanding of the decision-making process should make it poss ble for communities to deal more effectively with their numerou and varied problems. Social participation, as a major dimension of the decision-making process, offers an initial point of departure fo an investigation of the process.[3]

DIFFERENTIAL SOCIAL PARTICIPATION

One of the most basic and significant facts about social par ticipation is that it is not uniformly distributed throughout th population but tends to be concentrated in a minority of the citizen Some people are relatively inactive and only on rare occasior relate themselves to some community activity, while others ar relatively active and identify themselves with a range of communit affairs. Some people are active in one area, while others are activ

---

Elihu Katz and Paul F. Lazarsfeld, *Personal Influence: The Part Played l People in the Flow of Mass Communications* (Glencoe, Ill.: The Free Pres 1955); Robert K. Merton, "Patterns of Interpersonal Influence," in *Communic. tions Research 1948–1949,* edited by Paul F. Lazarsfeld and Frank K. Stantc (New York: Harper & Brothers, 1949); Peter Rossi, "Community Decisic Making," *Administrative Science Quarterly,* vol. 1 (March, 1957), pp. 415–44 Harry M. Scoble, "Yankeetown: Leadership in Three Decision-Making Pro esses," paper presented to American Political Science Association, Washingto D.C. (September, 1956).

[3] For a systematic statement of the several dimensions of the decisio: making process which has served as a guide for the study being reported he see, Vincent Ostrom, "The Political Dimension of Regional Analysis," *Pape and Proceedings of the Regional Science Association,* vol. II (1956), pp. 85–9

another. Some concentrate their participation in one or a few tivities, while others divide their efforts among a host of issues or ograms.

It is this fact of differential social participation that provides e starting point for the analysis that follows. Among the many estions that are suggested, three have been selected for conieration here. First, what are the reasons for high and low social rticipation? This question is primarily theoretical and has faraching implications for the study of social structure and related pects of community organization. Second, what are the conseiences of differential participation in terms of the kinds of decims reached? To the extent some people are more active than hers, certain values or interests may prevail and thereby give a rticular direction to policy determination. Third, by what means n the rate of social participation be modified either for particular gments of the population or the population as a whole? If social rticipation is too limited, many of the resources of the people ill be lost and the democratic process itself may be threatened.

The procedure in this chapter will be to identify some of the ore significant factors associated with high and low participation, interpret these empirical findings in terms of available general eory, to consider the relation between differential social participaon and the nature of policies that are formulated, and to suggest me of the practical implications of the findings for community ograms and activities.

HE NATURE OF SOCIAL PARTICIPATION

In the study of social participation, some means of identifying measuring the extent to which individuals participate in comunity affairs must be established. Immediately, therefore, the queson arises as to what shall be included or excluded under this cateory. In a very broad sense any human interaction is social and can e regarded as participation in the social system. Such a usage of e term, however, is too broad for the purpose here. "Social paricipation" will therefore be limited to those acts of individuals hich more or less directly relate to issues, problems, or proposals aving to do with some phase of community life.

Even this delimitation of social participation does not entirely
resolve the problem of measurement, for there is a great diversity
of behaviors in an equally large variety of decision-making situations. Because it is not possible to include all instances of social
participation in a single measure, some form of sampling is required
Whenever a selected set of acts are used to identify or measure
the presence or extent of social participation, there is bound to be
present a bias which will overrepresent or underrepresent the actual
participation of certain individuals. If a single channel of participation, such as voting, is used those people who do not vote but are
very active otherwise will be excluded. If formal participation, such
as holding memberships in voluntary associations, is used those
people who are not joiners but who have extensive personal relations
with leaders and officials will be excluded.

In the research project of social participation which provide
the data to be used here,[4] an effort was made to avoid the limitations of single channel measures or measures based on formal participation alone. A measure was developed which included both
formal and informal participation and activity in a number of
channels. Known as the Oregon General Community Participation
Score (GCP Score), it is derived from responses to sixteen questions pertaining to frequency of voting; frequency of serious discussion of educational, governmental, and civic affairs with members of one's family, with friends, and with officials; membership
and activity in voluntary associations; involvement in local issues
attendance at meetings where educational and governmental affairs
are a subject of major consideration; and frequency of association
with leaders and officials. The GCP Score for each respondent was
determined by giving one point for each of the sixteen questions
answered affirmatively. All scores of ten or more were consolidated
producing an eleven point scale ranging from zero to ten. This
measure was administered to a randomly selected population of

[4] Unless otherwise indicated, the data used in the following analysis are
derived from an interdisciplinary study of policy formation carried out at the
University of Oregon under the auspices of the Cooperative Program in Educational Administration and supported by a grant from the W. K. Kellogg Foundation.

52 adults of both sexes in Valley City II, a rapidly growing indus-
rial community of 16,000 population.

HE SOCIAL PARTICIPATION PROFILE

As noted above, one of the more significant facts about social
articipation is the wide range of differences between individuals.
asual observation reveals to community leaders, social scientists,
nd to citizens alike that some people approach a zero point as far
s participation in community affairs is concerned, while others
eemingly relate themselves to whatever is happening. It also ap-
ears that the majority of the people in any given community tend
o fall at the inactive end of the participation continuum.

The extent to which this casual observation is valid is revealed
y a number of studies which have sought to work out the distribu-
on of people on a participation scale. In all instances it has been
ound that the distribution takes the form of a J curve with the
najority of the population concentrated at the low end of the scale.
n an early study Komarovsky[5] found that approximately 60 per
ent of the adult populations of two suburban communities did
ot belong to any voluntary associations, about 25 per cent belonged
o one association, 6 per cent to 10 per cent belonged to two
ssociations, another 2 per cent or 3 per cent belonged to three
nd 1 per cent or 2 per cent belonged to four or more associations.
. recent study of a similar type made by Axelrod[6] revealed a dis-
nct but less steep J curve. His findings showed that 37 per cent
elonged to no formal group, 31 per cent belonged to one group,
6 per cent to two groups, 8 per cent to three groups and 8 per
ent to four or more groups. While differences in the communities
udied and in the procedures followed may account for the differ-
nces in the percentages, the important point is that there is a gen-

[5] Mirra Komarovsky, "A Comparative Study of Voluntary Organizations of
wo Suburban Communities," *Publication of the American Sociological Society,*
l. 27 (May, 1933), pp. 83–93.

[6] Morris Axelrod, "Urban Structure and Social Participation," *American
ociological Review,* vol. 21 (February, 1956), pp. 13–18. See also Julian L.
oodward and Elmo Roper, "Political Activity of American Citizens," *Ameri-
n Political Science Review,* vol. 44 (December, 1950), pp. 872–885.

eral pattern of distribution of participation as measured by member
ship in voluntary associations.

In the study of social participation carried out in Valley City II
by the University of Oregon Community Study Project, a similar
distribution was again found as is shown in table 19 below.[7]

Table 19. Distribution of GCP Scores for Valley City II

Score	0	1	2	3	4	5	6	7	8	9	10	Total
Number	144	147	107	98	75	60	30	23	18	24	26	752
Per cent	19.1	19.6	14.2	13.0	10.0	8.0	4.0	3.1	2.4	3.2	3.5	

It is significant that, despite differences in the population
studied and in the measures used, the several studies reported here
and others which have been made are in essential agreement in
regard to the distribution of people on a participation continuum.
The characteristic distribution, usually taking the form of a J curve
suggests that participation may be a situational or cultural phenome
non. In all the studies reported here at least 75 per cent of the
populations observed were found to fall within the lower half of
the participation scale or continuum used. In the Valley City I
study where an 11 point participation scale was developed, 52.5
per cent of the population received GCP Scores of 2 or less while
only 9.1 per cent received scores of 8 or more. As will be shown
below, this marked skewness in the distribution of participation
may be less a matter of "lethargy" and more a matter of social struc
ture.

FACTORS ASSOCIATED WITH
SOCIAL PARTICIPATION

One of the most outstanding features of social science research
during recent decades has been the accumulation of evidence that
the behavior of individuals is closely related to the place they oc
cupy in the social system. For instance, there are a series of be
haviors that are characteristic of college book salesmen and which

[7] A fuller report of the distribution of GCP scores for both Valley City
and Valley City II is given in John M. Foskett, "Social Structure and Social
Participation," *American Sociological Review*, vol. 20 (August, 1955), pp
431–438.

are different from another set of behaviors which are characteristic of commercial fishermen. The same is true for other classes of people be they children or adults, males or females, musicians or miners. While the native equipment and developmental history of individuals are significant, it has become increasingly clear that certain kinds of behavior become attached to certain positions or roles. Much of contemporary social science research is devoted to the nature of this relationship. Sometimes the approach is through an analysis of social class structures; sometimes it is through a social-psychological study of groups; at other times the focus is on institutional patterns and the corresponding role expectations. In any event, increasing recognition is being given to the influence of situation on human social behavior.

When attention was first given to the problem of social participation and particularly to the reasons for the relative inactivity of a large segment of the population, there was a tendency to explain away the lack of social participation in terms of the "lethargy" of people. This widely accepted explanation was essentially circular, for it amounted to little more than saying people were inactive because they were inactive. More recently, researchers have come to recognize the situational nature of social participation, and inquiry has become increasingly productive.

As early as 1933, Komarovsky found evidence of a relationship between membership in voluntary associations and such situational factors as income, occupation, ethnic status, and work place. A series of similar studies that followed added further evidence of the same general kind.[8] In the study being reported here, further data will be brought to bear on this basic question.

[8] Komarovsky, *op. cit.* Subsequent studies include, W. A. Anderson, "Family Social Participation and Social Status Self-Ratings," *American Sociological Review,* vol. 11 (June, 1946), pp. 253–258; Axelrod, *op. cit.;* Floyd Dotson, "Patterns of Voluntary Association Among Urban Working Class Families," *American Sociological Review,* vol. 16 (October, 1951), pp. 687–693; William G. Mather, "Income and Participation," *American Sociological Review,* vol. 6 (June, 1941), pp. 380–383; Leonard Reissman, "Class, Leisure, and Social Participation," *American Sociological Review,* vol. 19 (February, 1954), pp. 76–84; Alvin H. Schaff, "The Effect of Commuting on Participation in Community Organizations," *American Sociological Review,* vol. 17 (April, 1952), pp. 215–220.

EDUCATION AND SOCIAL PARTICIPATION

When people at different educational levels are compared it is found that those with high formal education have very much higher GCP Scores than do those with lower educational attainments. In Valley City II, those whose education did not go beyond the ninth grade had an average GCP Score of 1.9; those whose education stopped at the 10 to 12 grade level had an average score of 3.11; and those who had at least some college had an average score of 5.03, two and a half times that of the lower educational group.

Despite the close relationship between level of formal education and degree of social participation, it cannot be assumed that it is education itself which makes for participation or non-participation. Rather, as will be discussed below, those individuals who have had more formal education may tend to occupy those kinds of positions in the social system where social participation is both possible and functional, while those with less formal education may tend to occupy positions where participation is difficult and not functional or possibly even dysfunctional.

INCOME AND SOCIAL PARTICIPATION

Although not as marked, the relationship between income level and degree of social participation is similar to that for education as reported above. As is shown in table 20, those respondents in Valley City II reporting family incomes below $4,000 had an average score of 2.33; those with incomes of $4,000 to $9,999 had an average score of 3.38; and those with incomes of $10,000 or more had an

Table 20.   Average GCP Score by Income and Educational Levels for Valley City II

INCOME LEVEL	GRADE LEVEL			TOTAL
	1–9	10–12	College	
Below $4,000	1.75	2.61	4.06	2.33
$4,000–9,999	2.36	3.45	5.20	3.38
$10,000	1.88	3.36	8.33	4.57

average score of 4.57. Even when incomes are broken down by smaller intervals, the progression of participation scores remains constant. Because of the positive correlation between education and income, it is to be expected that both would have a similar relation to a third variable such as participation.

Not only are the factors of education and income not completely separate and self-contained but they interact in such a manner that the relation of one to social participation will be affected by the nature of the other. Thus, as shown by the breakdown of both income and education in table 18, the average GCP Score for individuals within any income level rises continuously as the level of formal education rises. For example, the average GCP Scores for those with incomes under $4,000 rises from 1.75 for those at the 1–9 grade level to 2.61 for those at the 10–12 grade level and to 4.06 for the college level group. Similarly, the corresponding scores for those with incomes of $10,000 and above are 1.88, 3.36, and 8.33. It is of interest to note, however, that the opposite relation of income and education does not hold consistently. When education is held constant the GCP Scores do not rise with increase in income in all instances. It is only when education is at the college level that there is a consistent and marked rise of participation with rise of income. Here the increase is from 4.06 when income is under $4,000 to 5.20 when income is $4,000 to $9,999 and to 8.33 when income is $10,000 or more. For those at the 10–12 grade level the relationship is less marked, and at the 1–9 grade level there does not appear to be any definite pattern. It would thus appear that education is a somewhat more significant factor than is income.

OCCUPATION AND SOCIAL PARTICIPATION

As would be expected because of its relation to both education and income, occupation is a third significant factor as shown by the tabulation of average GCP Scores on page 322.

Just as income and education interact to affect the relation of either to social participation, so occupation interacts with both income and education to affect the relation of the former to participation. Thus, for all occupational categories the average GCP Score drops well below the mean for the total group when education is low and rises well above the mean when education is high. The same is true for level of income.

Occupation reflects specific patterns of behavior and might be thought to have a direct effect on participation independent of both education and income. By itself, however, occupation is not related to participation. Being a proprietor or an unskilled worker does not insure a high or a low GCP Score for an individual. A store owner with a low income and low education will in most cases have a much lower score than one with high education and a good income.

Professional and Semi-Professional	5.49
Proprietors, Managers and Officials	3.65
Clerical and Sales	3.90
Craftsmen, Foremen, and Skilled Workers	3.27
Operatives	2.49
Unskilled Workers	2.45
Retired	1.77
Housewives	2.54 *

* The average score for all women is nearly identical to that of all men. Many of the more active women are employed and hence been tabulated under other categories with the result that those shown as housewives only have a somewhat lower average score.

While there are a number of other situational factors such as age, place of residence, length of residence, family status, and the like that affect participation scores in one way or another, the three that have been considered here are sufficient to reveal the relativity of social participation to the circumstances of the individual.[9]

REASONS FOR DIFFERENTIAL SOCIAL PARTICIPATION

In the above analysis of the data on social participation, it was suggested that the three factors considered, education, income, and occupation, do not function automatically and separately to make

[9] For similar discussions of the situational nature of social participation see, Axelrod, "Urban Structure and Social Participation," *op. cit.*; Wendell Bell and Maryanne T. Force, "Urban Neighborhood Types and Participation in Formal Associations," *American Sociological Review*, vol. 21 (February, 1956), pp. 25–34; Bernard Barber, *Participation and Mass Apathy* (New York: Harper & Brothers, 1950), pp. 477–504; Foskett, "Social Structure and Social Participation," *op. cit.* and "Differential Discussion of School Affairs," *Phi Beta Kappan*, vol. 37 (April, 1956), pp. 311–315.

for high or low participation. The reason is that people in different educational, income, and occupational categories occupy different positions in the social system. It remains to explain more fully how these factors operate.

1. *Contacts with others.* An essential condition for social participation is communication contact with others and particularly with other participators. Contact is necessary both to bring about involvement in the first place and as a means for carrying on activities. There are marked differences between individuals as to the place and frequency of communication contacts with others. In general, an unskilled worker in a mill located in an industrial area will have little opportunity to be in contact with anyone but his fellow workers, his family, and neighbors. On only very special occasions will he have an opportunity to associate with leaders and officials or other active citizens. The nature and place of his work tends to isolate him from public affairs. In contrast the merchant on Main Street, the lawyer, and the city official meet a wide range of people in the course of everyday activities. Contacts are made in the store or office, on the sidewalk, at the luncheon club and at a variety of meetings. Indeed, the frequent complaint is that contacts with others interfere with the performing of duties.

2. *Ability to communicate.* Closely related to contact as an essential element in social participation is the ability to communicate in a contact situation. Again, there are very great differences among individuals in this regard. Such differences include vocabulary, verbal skills, awareness of civic events and issues, and a feeling of rapport. It is on this basis that education and occupation become significant. The well-educated lawyer or business executive is accustomed to meeting people, is practiced in the expression of ideas, has continuing acquaintance with community affairs, and feels he is accepted by whomever he meets. If necessary, he can preside at a meeting or even talk to a group. The less well-educated auto mechanic, however, more frequently will be devoid of the communication skills and experience and will be less inclined or able to play an active role in connection with the community's needs or problems. For this same reason, others will be less likely to invite his activity.

3. *Time and financial capacity.* Social participation is expen-

sive for the individual in terms of both time and money. Meeting and talking to people, attending meetings, planning, traveling, and reading can easily consume many hours, even if just a single issue is involved. For the most part, those with lower incomes and routine jobs are not in a position to take time from their workday and are too tired in the evening to attend committee meetings or hold an informal conference. It is very much different for the manager of a department store, who can leave his office at almost any time and whose telephone is within easy reach. Indeed, in many instances such a person is expected by the firm to devote a significant amount of time to civic affairs.

Social participation is also expensive in that it often involves financial costs for transportation, membership fees, meals, dress, and entertainment. A person with a low income may not be able to include such costs in his budget and may not possess the clothes appropriate for many occasions. On the other hand, a professional person will have the necessary means for such activity and may even be able to include them as a business expense.

4. *Expectations of others.* Some of the principal guides for human behavior are the expectations others have of a person; the concept a person has of himself is in part composed of the internalization of these expectations. Once a set of expectations becomes established be it for a child, a delinquent, a marriage partner, or a household servant, they tend to persist and control behavior. In our culture there has developed a differential set of expectations for participation in community affairs, so that there is strong pressure for some people to maintain active roles in the life of the community and little or no pressure for others. Expectations for a person may involve his holding membership in a variety of voluntary associations, running for office, serving on committees, attending meetings, or voting. In general, it appears that individuals at higher educational, income, and occupational levels are expected to participate much more than those at the lower levels. The extent to which this is true is reflected in the frequent complaints by the leading merchants, the executive heads of industries, lawyers, and other leaders concerning the demands on their time and energies.

5. *Functional relevancy.* Clearly one of the most important reasons for the differential social participation of the different socio-

economic segments of the population is the difference in the relevancy of participation to their pattern of living. A large portion of community problems and issues are of such a nature that they touch more obviously the lives of people in business and the professions, people with larger incomes, or people with more education. Such issues as zoning rules, location of public buildings, development of recreational facilities, or traffic control have a very direct bearing on business and investment interests. It is not surprising, then, that members of the city council tend to be composed of people in the commercial and industrial world. Social participation can be relevant in another way. For some people, such as lawyers or insurance agents, it is helpful to be well known and activity in public affairs is an effective way of becoming identified. In contrast, questions involving the opening of an area to light industry, the location of a new city hall, or changes in the routing of traffic do not, at least on the face of it, affect the unskilled worker whose income is spent entirely for current living needs. In addition to differences in the actual effect of policy decisions on the different elements in the population, there is a difference in the perception of the relevance of policy to one's circumstance. The merchant can often recognize immediately the future consequences for his enterprise of a shift in foot traffic in front of his store as a result of moving the city hall to a new location, but the average homeowner may not be aware of the effect the opening of a new street will have on the value of his property.

6. *Value systems.* In a less obvious but possibly even more fundamental manner than in the above cases, differences in the value systems of different components of the population will operate directly and indirectly to facilitate or limit activity. Issues or problems that do not involve one's values can hardly elicit a response. Broadly, those issues that arise in a community tend to involve the values of the middle and upper economic classes more often than the lower. This may be due in part to the fact the upper socioeconomic class is in a better position of power to raise questions or suggest programs, but it may also be a result of the way community life has become structured in the course of the past. In any event, typical questions of public health, educational policy, recreational facilities, civic centers, building codes, and city plan-

ning correspond to middle- and upper-class value and receive their greatest support from them. Even programs designed for under-privileged children, for instance, may be conceived of and intro-duced by those whose children have every advantage. Help for the underprivileged is itself an upper-class value.

By its nature, college attendance modifies the value pattern of people or reinforces certain values that may have been acquired in the home. A liberal college training increases the probability of an interest in such things as community theaters or art centers, the landscaping of public grounds, and the introduction of extra-curricular activities in the public schools. Similarly, people with larger incomes come to demand more social and cultural activities and are willing to lead in an effort to create them. Civic pride often takes the form of seeking to establish the values of the upper educational, economic, and occupational groups.

CONSEQUENCES OF DIFFERENTIAL PARTICIPATION

The consequences of differential participation are undoubtedly diverse and complex. Possibly the most immediate result, however, is that policies and their execution will be biased in the direction of the values and interests of the higher participation portion of the population. In most instances this bias will favor the upper socio-economic segment.

This unequal influence may be expressed through such formal channels as voting or by means of informal discussion with leaders and officials. Using voting in school elections as a measure of formal participation, investigators found in Valley City II that only 32.7 per cent of these at the grades 1–9 educational level were characteristically voters in contrast to 59.6 per cent of the college level residents. The corresponding percentages of those with incomes below $4,000 and those with $10,000 or above were 34.8 and 56.7. This ratio of nearly two to one cannot help but give emphasis to those school policies in accord with the particular orientation of the upper educational and income level group.

Similar results are obtained when a particular form of informal participation is examined. In Valley City II only 20.4 per cent of those at the 1–9 grade level reported they "often seriously discussed" school affairs with other members of their family but 45 per cent of the college group frequently make the schools the subject of serious discussion. Similar results are obtained when the discussion of school affairs is with friends, teachers, or officials.

Caution must be exercised in generalizing as to the degree of bias in any particular community activity. The degree of differential participation will vary from one program or policy issue to another to the extent the factors causing differentiation are present or absent. Opportunity for contact, ability and means to communicate, uniformity of expectations, generality of relevance, and values involved will vary from one case to another. When, in Valley City II, a campaign to establish a community hospital was carried out, there was no significant difference between educational, income, and occupational levels in degree of participation. The drive, which was organized and directed by a professional campaign manager, provided nearly equal contacts for the entire population, communication channels were opened up for nearly everyone, a common set of expectations were created to the extent participation was "fashionable," and by its nature the hospital had much the same relevancy to the life of all persons—the basic value of health is universal.

In addition to the effect of differential social participation on the kind of decisions reached or the particular programs undertaken, there is a corresponding effect on the support given to a decision or a program. All too often communities reach sound decisions or adopt worthwhile programs, but since support is lacking, the final results are poor. If participation at the decision-making or planning level is limited to a few or to particular segments of the population, then it becomes their problem and not the problem of the whole community. Support for a program exists only when the proposal grows out of the thinking of the wider group. The best way to insure support at the solution level is to secure full participation at the problem defining and decision-making level.

IMPLICATIONS FOR ACTION

The practical problem of how to secure wider or more representative participation in community affairs is not a simple or easy one. The fact of limited or unequally distributed social participation is too deeply rooted in the very nature of our culture to be subject to facile manipulation. Indeed, full and equal participation can only be a fascinating utopian idea.

In a small and homogeneous society where there is little division of labor and all persons occupy somewhat similar positions in the social system and hence have much the same opportunity and motivation, there might be little difference among people as to the part played in community affairs. But even here there would be differences. In contemporary Western culture with its highly developed division of labor and differentiation of position in a complex social system, the sources of unequal participation are intensified to the point where large segments of the population have become isolated from the programs and activities of the wider community. The problem is that of finding ways to avoid or overcome the consequences of the division of labor without having to abolish the essential elements of our culture.

If the reasons given above for limited and differential participation have any validity, it would follow that there are a number of strategies or practical procedures for increasing the extent or distribution of community endeavors. No one of the possible strategies would remove all the obstacles. Just as the reasons for non-participation do not operate alone but interact with each other, so opportunity and ability to communicate, time and resources, the expectations of others, relevancy to one's pattern of living, and value systems are all part of a complex whole.

In the first place, leaders and those already active will have to find ways of making community issues and undertakings relevant to a wider range of people. It may be that in the past leaders have discussed and presented community problems and issues in a manner that appealed to those segments of the population that were known to be traditional supporters. If more people are to become involved, community affairs must be made relevant to more people. In part it is a matter of developing programs that have wide relevancy, and in part it is a matter of making the relevancy clear.

In this same connection, people often can best perceive the relevancy of a given program if they have participated in locating and defining the problem. Very frequently a small group decides what is needed and then seeks general support for a proposed solution. In such instances the problem is not internalized by the wider group, and there is little or no motivation to participate. When, in contrast, the membership of such a broad association as the League of Women Voters makes the problem of delinquency in a community the subject of study and gathers data as to the extent of the problem, there is much less difficulty in securing support for a program designed to deal with the problem.

Secondly, and closely related to the strategy of establishing the relevancy of activities, there are possible strategies that will recognize the diversity of value systems. In general, those activities that involve basic values common to many people will elicit wider participation than those involving the particular values of a few. In part this means that programs need to be formulated in a manner that they will involve the values of many people. If such is not the case, there may be some question whether wide participation can legitimately be expected. Undoubtedly the cry of "lethargy" is frequently a selfish one originating from people with a private rather than public interest in mind.

Third, there are strategies that can compensate for or modify abilities to communicate. In addition to continuing education, experience itself is a key means to develop skills and confidence. Possibly the problem of non-participation is just as much a result of people not being given an opportunity as it is a matter of people not taking advantage of opportunity. Particularly within organizations and associations there can be a conscious and deliberate effort to provide experience in communication and thereby build up a broader base of people who are able to express themselves. If the programs of PTA groups are limited primarily to featured speakers, the membership may never extend its capacity to interact. Community leaders, in many instances, are responsible for structuring programs and do so in such a manner that communication is kept to a minimum and participation is thereby restricted.

A fourth type of strategy would involve innovations in the time, place, and circumstance of participation whereby differences between people in regard to free time and resources would be made less important. Leaders and officials might have to seek out

groups of people not normally in contact with or aware of particular
need situations. This seeking out will not be to gain support for
some proposal but to create involvement. Informal neighborhood
gatherings may include many people who are excluded from downtown luncheon meetings. Requests to employers might secure
released time for interested and helpful persons who otherwise
cannot leave their place of work.

Finally, participation needs to be made respectable and a source
of prestige for anyone. This is not to be achieved through preaching
civic responsibility but through a modification of the role expectations people have of themselves and others. This is not easy
and is a long process. Currently, many people have a picture of
themselves such that they regard it as "improper" for them to be
so "presumptuous" as to ask questions, express an idea, or appear
at certain places. It will be only when public officials and leaders
welcome rather than fear inquiry and discussion that this hesitancy
will begin to disappear. Participation must be a rewarding experience rather than a source of censure. Possibly leaders and officials do not really want fuller and broader participation but rather
want support for their particular views or proposals.

Our past history has witnessed a trend by which many problems
and activities that were once regarded as private and personal
have come to be viewed as the concern of the group as a whole.
Mental health is a recent example. This trend will undoubtedly
continue and result in an ever increasing number of "community"
needs and programs. As the responsibilities of the community
increase, there will be an ever greater need for the abilities and
efforts of the citizenry if the tasks are to be carried out successfully.
There is an unlimited number of ways in which social participation
can be increased if one is aware of the basic factors limiting participation. The few suggestions given above are but general illustrations of some of the principles involved. The more specific strategies
will be the result of "inventions" made by leaders who are aware
of both the immediate situation and the basic social processes at
work.

✳ 17. Social Correlates of Adult Leisure-Time Behavior

Saxon Graham

Introduction What do people do with their leisure time? This is a question raised by both reformers and researchers. The work week is growing increasingly shorter, and some prophets of the new leisure age predict a four-day work week of thirty-two hours by 1975. This shift from the long work week to the long leisure period is largely the result of industrialization, principally the process of mechanization of industry. Increasingly more and more goods can be produced both in the factory and on the farm to support more and more people who have to work fewer and fewer hours.

This paper is not concerned with how people *should* spend their leisure time but with how they *actually do* spend their non-working hours. More specifically, Dr. Saxon Graham has intensively studied the activities of two thousand randomly selected adults of Butler County, Pennsylvania, a county with a population of 100,000. This is the first study of American recreational behavior done with a large cross-section of our population.

Traditional views concerning how Americans spend their leisure time are subjected to careful study and analysis by Dr. Graham. Are Americans lovers of sports to the extent that they actively participate in them? Well, some do, but the majority do not. And baseball, the national pastime, according to sportswriters and broadcasters—how many do you think participate in this sport? For that matter how much are the people of Butler County concerned with watching baseball or with any spectator sports? Relatively little, according to Dr. Graham. Nevertheless, other spectator activities of all sorts, especially radio, television, and motion pictures, occupy probably a larger part of the leisure time of the people of Butler County than any other single kind of recreational activity. Their prime interest is in passive, non-creative, commercially-organized activity.

America has long been described as a nation of "joiners," a country where everybody belongs or wishes to belong to an organization, whether it is a society for the protection of ant life or one to save the world from the Martians. Sinclair Lewis in his 1922 novel *Babbitt* epitomizes the "joiner" as a person who is conventional, uncultivated, and conforming. Obviously, the satirical model of Lewis' George Babbitt does not fit all Americans, but the belief that it does persists both here and abroad. In Butler County only about 25 per cent of the population belong to more than one organization, and joiners are found more in the upper than the lower classes. Class differences in membership and participation in recreation including religiously oriented recreation are similar to those discussed by Russell R. Dynes in Chapter 13.

Life in the country has been characterized as warm, intimate, and friendly, affording the ultimate in wholesomeness, joy, and fulfillment. The city, in contrast, is considered an unhealthy place in which to live or to obtain the warm and friendly relationships so necessary for a pleasant existence. Some writers have described this belief as the anti-urban bias, deeply imbedded in the thinking of both urban and rural dwellers, a belief which originated in the preindustrial era. Dr. Graham examines this belief and in light of his data concludes that the reverse is the case. Urbanites of Butler County, more than rural people, engage in recreational and religious activities which are most likely to produce warm and personal relationships and enriching experiences.

This chapter deserves careful reading and study. In a very substantive and empirical manner Dr. Graham explodes some of the myths about the pursuit of leisure time in American society.

✳ IN THE PAST half century, a number of circumstances have combined to effect substantial decreases in the work week for many segments of the American population. This has reached the point where the industrial worker and the city dweller generally have as much effective time away from their economic occupations as at them. In terms of time spent, leisure-time activities have become as important as economic ones. Despite this and other evidence of the impressive role of recreation and of religiously oriented leisure activities in American society, little investigation has been conducted into the nature of leisure-time behavior.

Economists have concerned themselves with the costs of recreation, historians have traced recreational trends, and social workers have written on methods of organizing mass recreation.[1] But aside from the classic study in this area by Lundberg, sociologists have for the most part neglected the analysis of recreational behavior.[2] Lundberg's study, of course, was conducted many years ago in Westchester County, a community that is far from typical of American communities in general. In addition, two recent studies, one by White,[3] and another by Clarke,[4] furnish some more modern data on recreation. While these two investigations make a definite contribution to the literature, the first excludes the upper socioeconomic groups from analysis, and the second bases its data upon questionnaire returns, with all the bias of self-selection which such a method implies. Few, if any, studies of religiously oriented uses of leisure have been reported.

Observers of primitive and contemporary societies, as well as of earlier American culture, have hypothesized a close link between recreational and religious activities.[5] Anthropologists note that religious ceremonials contain many recreational elements such as dancing, music, and the use of graphic arts. Writers on recreation in earlier America emphasized the impact of the austere Puritan

[1] See, for example, J. Frederick Dewhurst and Associates, *America's Needs and Resources*, Twentieth Century Fund, New York, N.Y. (1955), pp. 347 ff.; Foster R. Dulles, *America Learns to Play* (New York: Appleton-Century-Crofts, Inc., 1940; and Elizabeth Halsey, *Development of Public Recreation in Metropolitan Chicago*, Chicago Recreation Commission, 1940).

[2] George A. Lundberg, Mirra Komarovsky, and Mary A. McInerny, *Leisure* (New York: Columbia University Press, 1934). See also, Jesse F. Steiner, "Recreation and Leisure Time Activities," in *Recent Social Trends* (New York: McGraw-Hill Book Co., 1933).

[3] R. Clyde White, "Social Class Difference in the Uses of Leisure," *American Journal of Sociology*, vol. 61 (September, 1955), no. 2, pp. 145 ff.

[4] Alfred C. Clarke, "Leisure and Levels of Occupational Prestige," *American Sociological Review*, vol. 21 (June, 1956), no. 3, pp. 301 ff.

[5] Pitirim Sorokin, Carle Zimmerman, and Charles Galpin, *A Systematic Source Book in Rural Sociology* (Minneapolis: University of Minnesota Press, 1931) vol. 2, p. 445; see also Arthur W. Calhoun, *A Social History of the American Family* (New York: Barnes & Noble, Inc., 1945), pp. 111–114.

religion on recreational patterns, and today it is recognized that some of the activity indulged in during the free time of the population is organized around the religious institution. Investigation of the use of leisure time then must include consideration of religiously oriented behavior as well as more purely recreational forms of behavior, and for this reason, an investigation of religious behavior is reported in this chapter.

Because of the few studies that have been made of leisure, it is not surprising that statements found in sociological literature on the subject are often open to question and, equally often, contradictory. Some authors suggest that leisure is highly dominated by commercial interests in America, that the majority of the American's free time is occupied in recreation which he pays for, such as attendance at motion pictures, spectator sports events, and the like. Similarly, it has been characterized as being a mass recreation, *i.e.*, Americans are said to enjoy their recreation not as individuals or small groups, but as large, mass audiences, and the popularity of television, the motion picture, and other forms of entertainment are cited in support of this statement. Another suggestion is made to the effect that America is a nation of "joiners," that much of their recreation is carried out in organizations, and that there is a passion on the part of each individual for joining ever more organizations. Sports enthusiasts write that American recreation is dominated by outdoor sports. Others contradict the notion and claim that Americans are interested rather in spectator sports and do not participate enough in active sports. Some have noted that the church serves as a focal point for organized recreational activities; others have suggested that Americans are so irreligious that they participate little in activities related to the church.

Moreover, it is implied there are differences between urban and rural recreation. Some sociologists have suggested that urban recreation is characterized by isolation of the individual, that he interacts less with close friends in going to parties, visiting, and entertaining than in the rural areas. The rural area is characterized as a setting for warm interaction among individuals in their recreation, while the urban area is characterized as a setting for mass commercial impersonal recreation. Again, the rural area is characterized as being more concerned with religion and religiously dominated recreation, while the urban area is characterized as being less interested in church-related activity. Finally, some few statements have been made which assert that there is a good deal of difference among social classes in recreational forms. The upper classes have been said to be more interested in creative, expensive, and time-consuming forms of recreation, while the lower classes are characterized as devoting themselves primarily to passive, non-creative forms which are inexpensive in both time and money.

We discover, then, that despite the fact that there have been few well-conducted studies of the leisure-time behavior of individuals in America, there has been no dearth of attempts to describe it.

The statements which have been made are often highly imaginative, despite their frequent contradictions, and they are useful as hypotheses to be tested in future studies of the subject. This chapter reports on a testing of the hypotheses suggested by statements in the above paragraphs as they applied to Butler County, Pennsylvania, in the summer of 1954.

METHODS OF INVESTIGATION

Basically, the method consisted of interviews with a relatively large sample (3 per cent) of the county's population. Basic questions were first asked regarding occupation, education, racial, ethnic, and urban-rural background, spatial mobility, housing characteristics, marital status, sex, and age.

Specifically regarding recreation, respondents were asked to designate three leisure-time activities in which each adult in the household spent most of his free time. Subsequently, the respondent was asked to state whether or not each adult in the household had participated in the week prior to interview in mild exercise activities, such as walking, playing golf, fishing, and the like, in more strenuous exercise activities, such as team sports, tennis, and swimming, in socializing, such as parties, visiting, and dinners, in spectator activities, such as radio, television, and movie-viewing, in spectator sports, in reading and games in the home or in hobbies in the home, and finally in driving in the car for pleasure. Noting that recreation traditionally is thought to be often associated with religion and sometimes oriented around religious institutions, investigators put the question: "To how many religious organizations, including church, does X belong?" and "How many meetings related to religious organizations has X attended in the three months prior to interview?" The final questions were asked about the number of memberships each adult in the household had in clubs or lodges or other voluntary associations and the number of meetings of these organizations he attended in the three months prior to interview.

These questions were asked of the 2,051 adults contained in a probability sample of 3,403 persons drawn at random from the population of Butler County. Of the total sample, there were approximately 990 adult males, and 1,060 adult females. The rest were children, whose responses were not considered in this analysis. The sample combined geographic divisions and proportionate representation of urban, rural-place, and open-country population. Employing aerial photographs of the county made in 1951, the researchers divided the area of the county into segments and chose groups of houses at random from each segment. After a training period, a crew of interviewers were sent to the households which had been designated to them on the aerial photographs.

Several limitations on the interpretations of the results of this study need to be recognized. First of all, it must be emphasized that the interviewing was carried out in the summer months of June and July in 1954, and that information on recreation during this period may not typify information which might be obtained in other times of the year. Some voluntary organizations, for example, curtail activities in the summer months of the year, and persons ordinarily active in them would be engaged in other activities during the three summer months. However, statements on participation were made regarding the three months prior to interview so that some sample of non-summer experience was obtained. Secondly, caution must be observed because researchers had only the respondents' statements as to the kinds of activities in which they indulged. Thus, where we asked the individual to remember the number of meetings he attended in the past three months, the problem of accuracy of his recollection may be serious. Again, only one responsible adult individual in the household was interviewed, and he was asked to make statements regarding other adults in the household. Here is another source of possible error. At the same time, however, analyses of sampling variation indicate a relatively small error in estimation on the rural-urban distributions, total population, and age and sex composition, and the similarity of survey results with those obtained in the 1950 census on these and other variables lends further evidence of their accuracy.

BUTLER COUNTY: THE SETTING FOR THE STUDY

Bulter County consists of slightly over 100,000 persons distributed over rather hilly terrain in an area north of Pittsburgh, Pennsylvania. While the southern border of the county is adjacent to Allegheny County, the area dominated by Pittsburgh, Butler County has no land use which could be called an extension of the Pittsburgh metropolitan area. The major urban aggregation in the county is Butler City, located some forty miles north of Pittsburgh. About half of the county's population lives in the open-country areas, almost 20 per cent are in small towns of less than 2,500 population, and the rest of the population, a little over 30 per cent, lives in urban aggregations. Economically, the population is concerned with mining, industry, and to a small degree, with farming. The population numbers very few Negroes, and a smaller proportion of persons are of recent European background than would be expected on the basis of national population statistics. In educational attainment, the population contains fewer people than Pittsburgh who have very great or very little schooling. Similarly, when the housing characteristics of Butler County are compared with those of other counties in Pennsylvania, Butler appears to contain a smaller proportion of homes of either extremely poor or exceptionally high quality. In regard to religion, Protestants predominate, and what Catholic population there is, is found mainly in Butler City. Politically, the county is primarily Republican, although as in the case in many American cities, there are more Democrats found in Butler City than in other parts of the county.

We have no statistical material with which to compare recreational facilities in Butler with those in other areas. Lacking this, we can briefly describe the facilities available in the county. In regard to commercial recreational facilities, there are two movie theaters in Butler City and four in other parts of the county. Television programs can be received in every part of the county. There are probably fewer government-sponsored facilities than usual either in Pennsylvania or the United States as a whole. There is no overall county recreational program in Butler, although this is not an unusual situation. There are a total of five public parks; in addition, this county has abundant rural, wooded land which probably serves similar functions to those of parks to the population. There are fair library facilities, with the city library and a traveling library plus school libraries to serve the parts of the county outside of Butler City. Programs of recreation for rural people in the county are large in number and very active. Similarly, there is an exceptionally large number of voluntary associations, approximately 180 known to have more than fifty members. This does not include church organizations of which there are many.

THE PATTERN OF RECREATION IN BUTLER COUNTY

It was in this kind of setting, then, that we examined recreation. The survey provided an opportunity for at least a partial testing of the several hypotheses regarding recreation mentioned earlier. To begin, the overall pattern of recreation in the county will be indicated.

Answers to both free response and specific questions, as tables 18 and 19 show, suggest that spectator activities, especially television viewing, make up a large part of leisure-time activity. It is noteworthy, of course, that spectator sports are shown to be relatively unimportant in answers to both of these questions. They are not cited at all among the first fifteen most frequently mentioned activities in table 21, and they rank next to last among the persons who stated that they had participated in various specific activities in the week prior to interview. We must conclude, then, that spectator sports do not loom as large in the recreational picture as some writers have stated; America's "national pastime" baseball, for example, is not as important in total recreation as sports writers assert—at least in Butler County.

Table 21. *Activities Mentioned as Those Most Frequently Indulged in, in Answer to an Open-Ended Question, in Per Cent, in Order of Importance*

ACTIVITY	NUMBER N = 2051	PER CENT
Television	509	24.8
Reading	474	23.1
Gardening, farming	403	19.6
Repairing home equipment	267	13.0
Sewing	231	11.3
Fishing	198	9.7
Rest, sit	151	7.4
Hunting	144	7.0
Radio	111	5.4
Movies	108	5.3
Golf	107	5.2
Swimming	99	4.8
Visiting, parties	99	4.8
Crocheting	99	4.8
Card playing	94	4.6

Table 22. *Proportions Indulging in Various Specific Forms of Recreation in the Week Prior to Interview, in Order of Importance*

	MALE N = 984	FEMALE N = 1048	TOTAL N = 2032	X^2 *	PROBABILITY
Spectator activities	90.8%	91.8%	91.3%	p	$\approx$ .40
Reading, games at home	69.1	72.0	70.6	p	$\approx$ .15
Driving in the car	79.8	57.8	68.5	p	$< .001$
Parties, visiting, get-togethers	38.7	43.7	41.3	p	$< .05$
Mild exercise	41.0	29.0	34.8	p	$< .001$
Spectator sports	23.5	14.3	18.8	p	$< .001$
Strenuous exercise	18.5	13.5	15.9	p	$< .01$

* X^2 (Chi Square) is a statistical test of difference between two quantities for their significance. When p (probability of occurring by chance) is greater > than .05 the differences could occur by chance too often (5 out of 100 times) to be regarded as significant. The smaller the p (.001) the more confident we are that the difference found between two quantities found in the sample represents the total population under study. The symbol $\approx$ means that the difference is not significant at an accepted level of probability.

These findings have some other implications as well. It should be noted that in the answers reported in table 21, few activities involving either mild or strenuous exercise are mentioned, and that in table 22, few people stated that they had indulged in strenuous exercise or even mild exercise in the week prior to interview. Far more important were such spectator activities as motion picture and television viewing, reading at home, and parties, visiting and "get-togethers" with friends. The findings suggest, then, that those persons who accuse America of having what to them is a dread disease, "spectatoritis," are indeed correct in their diagnosis. It would seem that Americans are not predominately interested in sports, either in participating in them themselves or in watching others play. Tremendous interest is evinced in other spectator activities, however, and a large proportion of people also are interested in other activities centered in the home. These, which include reading and participation in hobbies, are not necessarily passive activities.

Another striking implication of the findings, revealed particularly in answers to the open-ended questions, is the importance of unorganized, informal, family recreation as opposed to the more organized forms. Mention of organized forms of recreation, such as that sponsored by professional recreation directors, was excluded from the structured questions, but answers to the unstructured questions indicate few recreational activities which are carried out in an organized setting. Exceptions, of course, might be recorded in the case of gardening associated with participation in garden clubs, sewing in association with sewing circles, and the playing of golf at country clubs.

The findings suggested by table 21 are reflected again in answers to the question regarding memberships in voluntary associations, clubs, lodges, and other such organizations. Table 23 shows that over half of the population said that they belonged to no voluntary association whatever. Another quarter of the population stated that they had a single membership in a voluntary association, and the rest said that they had more than one. It is clear that if the Butler County experience is typical, America is not a nation of "joiners," *i.e.*, not all people join and are active in voluntary organizations. Mirra Komarovsky's findings in New York City, and my own in New Haven are congruent with the situation discovered in Butler County.[6] Certainly the entire population of a city like New Haven or a county like Butler does not participate in voluntary organizations, not more than 25 per cent, and only a small proportion are active in the organizations to which they belong. Only about 30 per cent of the sample had attended meetings of any organization during the three months prior to interview. Of these, only half had attended as often as once a month, although a similar proportion had attended more frequently. Only one in eight persons, in other words, had attended any meetings of any organizations of which they were members more than once a month.

Table 23. Activity in Voluntary Associations, by Sex in Per Cent

	MALE	FEMALE	TOTAL	X^2
Number of memberships				
0	46.2%	60.2%	53.5%	
1	28.6	22.0	25.2	
2	12.9	8.6	10.6	
3 or more	12.3	9.2	10.7	p < .001
N	986	1052	2038	
Number meetings attended 3 months prior to interview				
0	69.1%	72.3%	70.7%	
1–6	22.2	21.2	21.7	
7 and over	8.7	6.5	7.6	
N	981	1051	2023	p $\approx$ .15

In our investigation of religious activity undertaken in leisure time, we first examined membership in religious organizations. We would assume that the proportion of the population which had but one membership would be members of the central church or synagogue alone. Persons having more than one, however, could be considered to have a membership in the central religious organization, which might be designated as purely religious, and

[6] Mirra Komarovsky," The Voluntary Associations of Urban Dwellers," *American Sociological Review*, vol. 11 (December, 1946), pp. 686–698. See also Saxon Graham, "*Selection and Social Stratification*," unpublished Ph.D. dissertation, Yale University Library (1951), pp. 122 ff.

additional memberships in organizations which have a social and
recreational purpose as well as a religious one. It was found that
53 per cent of the population had just a single religious membership.
However, slightly over one-quarter of the population had, in addition, memberships in religious organizations with social and
recreational purposes. Religious interests, it would appear, thus
comprise no small part of the leisure-time activities of a large
proportion of the population of Butler County.

This conclusion is also supported by the findings on the amount
of activity in religious organizations in three months prior to interview. It was found that approximately 18 per cent had attended
thirteen or more meetings related to religious organizations in the
three months prior to interview. This constitutes an attendance at
meetings of once a week or more during that period.

AGE AND SEX DIFFERENCES IN
RECREATIONAL BEHAVIOR

In general, it appears that males engaged significantly more
than females in recreational behavior involving mild or strenuous
physical exercise, such as gardening, tennis, hunting, and golf. Men
also participated more in spectator sports and automobile driving
for pleasure. But table 22 shows that in activities such as television
viewing, listening to the radio, watching the movies, and reading,
the difference between men and women was negligible. Women
were somewhat more active in visiting and having parties.

With regard to participation in voluntary associations, some
other interesting sex differences were revealed (see table 23).
Thus, many more men belonged to such organizations, and a
larger proportion had a variety of memberships than was the case
with women. Only 40 per cent of the women had voluntary association memberships as compared to 53.8 per cent of males. In
actual activity in voluntary associations, however, little sex difference
was revealed.

While proportionately more males than females were members
of voluntary associations, the opposite was true with regard to
religious memberships. About 75 per cent of the males had religious memberships, but this was true of over 83 per cent of the
females. Thirty-three per cent of the females had two or more

such memberships, but only 18 per cent of males had this many.
This difference in memberships in religious organizations is reflected
in the relative amounts of attendance at religious meetings by the
sexes (see table 24).

Table 24. Religious Activity, by Sex in Per Cent

	MALE	FEMALE	TOTAL	X^2
Number of religious memberships				
0	24.9%	16.7%	20.7%	
1	56.6	49.8	53.1	
2	14.4	22.7	18.7	
3 or more	4.1	10.8	7.5	
N	984	1048	2032	p < .001
Number meetings attended 3 months prior to interview				
0	34.0%	24.9%	29.2%	
1–12	52.0	53.8	53.0	
13 and over	14.0	21.3	17.8	
N	980	1044	2024	p < .001

Some differences were also revealed in the recreation pattern
of various age groups: in virtually all the kinds of recreation, the
proportion of persons who stated that they had participated in the
week prior to interview decreased with age. This was particularly
true of such categories of recreation as mild and strenuous exercise.
In the activities which do not involve physical exercise, it would
appear that there is less decline in participation until after the age
of sixty-five. A similar situation was discovered with regard to the
number of religious and voluntary association memberships and
the amount of activity in these organizations.

RURAL URBAN DIFFERENCES AND
RECREATIONAL PATTERNS

Generally speaking, urban adults participated as much or more
in a variety of recreational activities than did rural persons.[7] Thus,

[7] For purposes of this study, urban population was defined as that residing
in aggregations of 2,500 or more, rural place population as that residing in

table 25 shows that in answer to the specific question as to participation in spectator sports events in the week prior to survey, 25 per

Table 25. *Participation in Various Types of Recreational Activity, by Regional Background in Per Cent*

	URBAN	RURAL	OPEN COUNTRY	X^2 PROBABILITY
Proportions participating in specific activities in week prior to interview				
Spectator activities	89.3%	90.6%	92.2%	$p \approx .15$
Reading, games at home	71.3	76.9	67.7	$p < .01$
Driving in car	54.4	39.0	58.0	$p \approx .07$
Parties, visiting, get-togethers	42.2	38.8	41.4	$p \approx .60$
Mild exercise	43.8	35.0	29.2	$p < .01$
Spectator sports	25.2	18.8	14.7	$p < .001$
Strenuous exercise	17.8	15.2	14.9	$p \approx .40$
Number of persons	609	394	1028	
Persons having one or more voluntary association memberships	51.3%	50.0%	42.3%	$p < .001$
Number of persons	315	197	436	
Persons attending one or more meetings of voluntary associations in three months prior to interview	30.8%	34.5%	26.3%	$p < .01$
Number of persons	188	136	271	
Persons having one or more religious memberships	87.2%	77.1%	75.5%	$p < .001$
Number of persons	531	303	778	
Persons attending one or more religious meetings in three months prior to interview	73.5%	72.1%	68.5%	$p < .07$
Number of persons	444	284	703	

incorporated named places up to 2,500 population or in unincorporated named places from 1,000 to 2,500, and the remaining population was designated as residing in the open country.

cent of the urban persons answered affirmatively as opposed to only about 15 per cent of those in the open country. Again 43.8 per cent of urban persons reported that they had indulged in mild exercise in the past week as compared with only 29.2 per cent of open-country persons.

Not only did urban people participate more in spectator sports and mild exercise than rural dwellers, but a larger number of them reported they had indulged in reading, games, and hobbies in their homes in the week prior to interview. The rural-place population, however, had the highest proportion reporting home activities of the three groups. In strenuous exercise, visiting, and indulging in spectator activities, there was practically no rural-urban difference. Critics of American culture often stress as one of the disadvantages of city life the lack of facilities and opportunity to participate in various forms of exercise. In Butler County, however, this did not appear to be the case. Again, critics of urban life emphasize the isolation in social relationships as characteristic of the city. Our statistics on visits and "get-togethers" in the Butler rural and urban population would indicate that there is just as much of such activity in the city as elsewhere.

Furthermore, the findings on numbers of religious and voluntary association memberships and the amount of activity in these kinds of organizations again indicate more activity in the urban population than in the open-country population. Thus, only 42.3 per cent of open-country persons reported that they had a voluntary association membership. This was true of 51.3 per cent of urban persons and exactly half of the rural-place persons. A similar picture was discovered with regard to religious memberships, with three-quarters of the open-country population having religious memberships, and over 87 per cent of urban persons similarly affiliated. Like findings were discovered with regard to participation in religious and voluntary associations. Again the largest percentage of persons reporting no participation resided in open-country areas.

It is interesting that in both religious memberships and activity, urban people participate as much or more than rural individuals. This finding throws into question the traditional conception of the city as being a social aggregation which pays little attention to religion. The so-called sinful city discussed so much in earlier sociological writings apparently is as much or more religious than the open-country areas. This may be partially a result of the activity of the greater Catholic population which is found in the cities. Again, the greater activity in spectator sports, mild exercise, and voluntary associations, as well as in religious organizations, may be a product of the proximity of city-dwellers to the centers of such activities. Nevertheless, the fact remains that the data in Butler County indicate less isolation in the recreation of urban persons than of persons living in open-country areas and more concern with activities related to religion in their leisure hours.

Some writers have suggested that the automobile, by making all kinds of recreational activities accessible to rural dwellers, is fostering the disappearance of rural-urban differences.[8] Our findings indicate that many differences still exist. They are particularly significant because the distance that even the most remote farm family must travel to indulge in these activities is shorter by far in Butler County than in areas in the South, Midwest, and Far West. Regardless, it is obvious that the city, open-country, and rural-place people in Butler County are quite similar in many of their recreational patterns. They have almost identical participation in spectator activities, visiting, and parties, as well as in strenuous exercise, urban, rural-place, and open-country persons. Furthermore, contrary to the statements of some critics of urban culture, city people seem to do their share of participation in face-to-face contacts at parties and get-togethers, and they seem to be even more active than rural persons in indulging in religious activities in their leisure time.

SOCIO-ECONOMIC DIFFERENCES IN
RECREATIONAL BEHAVIOR

It was found that in answer to all queries regarding participation in specific recreational activities in the week prior to interview, the upper classes responded affirmatively in larger proportions

---

[8] Alvin L. Bertrand, "Rural Locality Groups: Changing Patterns, Change Factors, and Implications," *Rural Sociology*, vol. 19 (June, 1954), pp. 174–179.

than did those of low socio-economic status.[9] In all cases, differences were statistically significant. A study by White in Cuyahoga County, Ohio suggests a similar finding.[10] White studied only the upper-middle, lower-middle, upper-lower, and lower-lower classes, defining them through Warner's Index of Status Characteristics. Although he excluded the two upper-class groups, he found that the highest class studied was more active than the lower classes in a number of the recreational activities studied here.

Differences between the upper and lower classes, as shown in table 26, were rather large on participation in mild exercise, strenuous exercise, reading and games in the home, and visiting. Each of these results is congruent with the findings of an earlier investigation carried out on a sample in New Haven.[11] The smaller participation of the lower classes in exercise activities may be a function of the physical effort they expend in their work life. With regard to participation in spectator activities and pleasure driving in automobiles, there was no regular decrease in participation from class I to VI. It is interesting in connection with the latter finding that almost the same percentage of class I as of class V persons reported participation, and the proportion of class I persons reporting this activity was substantially higher than the percentage in class VI. It will be recalled that the Lynds noted the semi-skilled and so-called working classes in general to be highly dependent upon their automobiles for recreation. It is interesting to observe, however, that while this is true in Butler, the upper classes appear to be even more interested in this form of activity than those in the lower socio-economic categories.

It was found that in numbers of voluntary association memberships and in the amount of participation in such organizations in the three-month period prior to interview, the upper classes were again significantly more active than the lower classes. This finding

[9] Socio-economic status was defined according to the system based on occupational groupings suggested by Alba M. Edwards, *Population: Comparative Occupation Statistics for the United States, 1870–1940* (Washington; U.S. Government Printing Office, 1943).

[10] R. Clyde White, *op. cit.*

[11] Saxon Graham, "Class and Conservatism in the Adoption of Innovations," *Human Relations,* vol. 9 (March, 1956), no. 1, pp. 91–100.

Table 26. Participation in Various Recreational Activities by Socio-Economic Background in Per Cent

	I PROFESSIONAL	II MANAGERS	III CLERKS, SALES	IV SKILLED	V SEMI-SKILLED	VI UNSKILLED	FARMERS	X² PROBABILITY	
Proportions participating in specific activities in week prior to interview									
Spectator activities	95.1%	84.4%	91.0%	91.3%	91.2%	93.9%	84.7%	.01	.001 *
Reading, games at home	80.6	76.3	71.7	70.6	68.5	67.6	65.0	.07	.05 *
Driving in car	74.8	70.5	66.9	71.0	73.4	63.6	57.1	.04	.001 *
Parties, visiting, get-togethers	62.1	45.1	48.8	43.1	34.9	38.8	34.4	.001	.001 *
Mild exercises	47.6	29.5	41.6	34.7	38.1	31.9	20.3	.001	.001 *
Spectator sports	25.2	19.7	21.1	23.6	15.2	18.4	8.6	.01	.001 *
Strenuous exercise	21.4	18.5	22.3	18.3	17.6	11.5	6.1	.03	.001 *
Number of persons	103	173	166	504	467	407	163	.02	.001 *
Persons having one or more vol. assn. memberships	71.9%	53.8%	55.5%	41.2%	47.1%	42.5%	46.6%	.001	.001 *
Number of persons	74	98	91	206	220	173	76	.001	.001 *
Persons attending one or more meetings of vol. assn. in three months prior to study	53.1%	33.5%	57.8%	26.6%	28.9%	24.9%	27.6%	.001	.001 *
Number of persons	52	58	62	133	135	101	45	.001	.001 *
Persons having one or more religious membership	81.6%	90.1%	92.6%	77.6%	77.0%	77.0%	75.5%	.001	.001 *
Number of persons	84	155	150	389	358	312	123	.001	.001 *
Persons attending one or more religious meeting in three months prior to interview	83.5%	79.9%	79.0%	65.1%	69.5%	68.9%	73.8%	.001	.001 *
Number of persons	17	34	34	175	142	125	42	.001	.001 *

* This test computed on class I–VI and farmers. Probability figure not designated with asterisk is computed on socio-

is in agreement with the results of previous research in New York and New Haven.[12] Apparently, the majority of "joiners" in each of these communities are found in the upper classes.

Similar results were found with participation in religious organizations. About 84 per cent of class I persons attended one or more meetings of such organizations in the three months prior to interview. This was true of 79 per cent of class III persons and only 69 per cent of those in class VI. Almost 10 per cent of class I persons attended twenty-five or more meetings in the three-month period, as compared with 8.6 per cent in class III and 3.2 per cent in class VI.

This finding duplicates that of Hollingshead in Elmtown.[13]

With respect to memberships held in religious organizations, however, a somewhat different pattern was revealed. A larger proportion of class I than of class VI were members of religious organizations, but classes II and III had an even greater percentage of persons so affiliated. This finding is also roughly similar to that discovered in Elmtown. Hollingshead found that there was a direct relationship between high prestige and activity in religious organizations. Nevertheless, he too found that the middle classes were more active than any of the others. Bultena, in Madison, Wisconsin, and Hadley Cantril, using a national sample, also found a decline in religious memberships with a decline in socioeconomic status. Lenski, studying Indianapolis data, however, found no differences.[14] Nevertheless, his techniques of measurement were

---

[12] *Ibid.;* Mirra Komarovsky, *op. cit.*

[13] August B. Hollingshead, *Elmtown's Youth,* (New York: John Wiley & Sons, Inc., 1949), pp. 459–460.

[14] In interviewing in Indianapolis, respondents were asked to give their opinion as to, How much you have been interested in religion since marriage? and How frequently have you attended church or Sunday school during your married life? Very seldom, seldom or sometimes, or often or regularly? In each case, the respondent is asked to make a judgment, rather than report on specific items of behavior in a well-defined period of time. On this account, the findings may not be an accurate reflection of actual religious behavior. See Gerhard E. Lenski, "Social Correlates of Religious Interest," *American Sociological Review,* vol. 18 (October, 1953), no. 5, pp. 533 ff. See also Louis Bultena, "Church Membership and Church Attendance in Madison, Wisconsin," *American Sociological Review,* vol. 14 (June, 1949), no. 3, pp. 384 ff.

so different as to make it difficult to compare them with the techniques in the other studies.

In the analysis of Butler County, farmers were treated as a separate group, thereby making it possible to compare the other socio-economic strata in the county with those in New York, New Haven, Elmtown, and elsewhere. Little data exists against which findings on the activities of farmers can be compared. Nevertheless, it can be stated that on the several specific activities in which individuals participated in the week prior to interview—spectator activities, home activities, pleasure driving, socializing, exercise, and spectator sports—farmers in each case reported less activity than did any other socio-economic group. It is interesting, however, that in regard to memberships in voluntary associations and in participation in them, farmers appeared to be in the middle range as far as activity was concerned. This is a particularly provocative finding in view of the fact that the meeting places of voluntary associations are often located at some distance from the farmer's home. This finding adds some credence to the thoughts of those who believe that modern methods of transportation and communication are bringing to rural populations the advantages which were formerly exclusively open to urban population.

Other findings supporting this view are related to activity in religious organizations. While a slightly smaller proportion of farmers had memberships in religious organizations, the amount who participated in them was fairly similar to that in classes III or IV. Again, this may be evidence that with automobiles farmers are becoming less isolated from urban association than was formerly the case.

To sum up, we can say that the upper classes were more active in most of the forms of recreation studied here than were the lower classes. There were fairly large differences in the proportions of upper and lower classes participating in mild and strenuous exercise activities, in home activities, and in visiting. Furthermore, more class I than class VI individuals mentioned participation in spectator activities, although the lowest participation recorded was found in the middle classes. A similar situation was discovered with regard to pleasure driving despite contrary earlier findings which suggested that the lower classes were primarily dependent upon this form of recreation. The "joiners" in Butler County apparently are concentrated in the upper classes, and this is true for both voluntary associations and in religious organizations. Reflecting the findings of Hollingshead in Elmtown, the middle classes had the most religious organization memberships of all. Hollingshead remarks that participation in religious activities was a mark of status in Elmtown which set the middle classes apart from the others. Indeed, it was a distinction of which they were proud. Perhaps the same thing is the case in Butler County. Finally, it was discovered that in most individual recreational activities, farmers were less active than any other group. It was interesting, however, that in the case of activities in both voluntary associations and religious organizations, farmers were as active as any other group and indeed were more active than the lower socio-economic groups.

CONCLUSIONS

The Butler study is unique in that it is the first time that broad aspects of the leisure-time behavior of individuals have been studied through the use of a random sample of the entire population of a county. The findings on the approximately two thousand adults in the study can be generalized to all the adults in the county population of over 100,000 with a fair degree of confidence. These can not be legitimately generalized, however, beyond the borders of Butler County. Nevertheless, the findings which have been developed in the course of research are useful in that they allow an examination of traditional concepts and hypotheses on recreational behavior. The findings uphold some earlier conceptions regarding recreational behavior and present several new notions as well.

For example, Americans are frequently characterized as lovers of sports, especially of outdoor sports. The data uncovered in Butler, however, indicate that although many Americans do participate in sports, particularly the young male adults, the activities which bulk largest in the recreational picture are non-sports activities which involve little physical exercise. Again, although baseball is called America's national pastime, we find that at the height of the baseball season, during which interviewing took place in the study, spectator sports, including watching baseball, ranked extremely low in the number of persons who mentioned them as the activities in which they most frequently participate. In addition, only about 19 per cent mentioned that they had witnessed a spectator sports event in the week prior to interview. This is an extremely low figure when compared to the 91 per cent who reported indulging in spectator activities, such as watching television and motion pictures, in the same period.

Another typical allegation about Americans is that they are a nation of "joiners." Studies in New Haven, New York, and now Butler indicate, however, that joiners represent only a very small proportion of the population in these places. In Butler, for example, only about one-quarter of the population belonged to more than one organization. Seventy per cent of the population had attended no meetings of any organizations during the three months prior to interview, and this, of course, would include the active season for most voluntary associations. Data on socio-economic status indicate that the joiners in Butler County are concentrated largely in the upper classes.

The assertion that recreation often is associated with religious organizations appears to be borne out to some degree in Butler County. Eighteen per cent of the population went to meetings of church organizations more often than once a week during the three-month period prior to interview. This, of course, does not make religious leisure activities among the most popular in the country. Nevertheless, more attended church-sponsored meetings than voluntary association meetings in the same period. As we noted earlier, however, Butler County may be slightly aberrant in this respect. The county has an unusually large number of churches and many of these sponsor recreational organizations to a somewhat greater degree than is true elsewhere. The fact remains, however, that roughly a quarter of the population belongs to at least one church-sponsored recreational organization in addition to a formal tie to the sect.

The hypotheses of earlier writers relative to socio-economic differences in recreational behavior are borne out in the study of Butler. The Lynds, Hollingshead, and Warner all indicated that upper-class persons participate in more recreation than lower-class persons. That finding was observed in Butler County. The differences were quite conspicuous in almost every type of participation which we measured. Farmers, however, were fairly different from the rest of the population in having a generally lower rate of participation in all kinds of activities. They were not too aberrant, however, in the spectator activities such as viewing television and motion pictures, or in their activity in voluntary associations and church-related organizations.

This brings us to traditional conceptions regarding urban-rural differences in recreation. Writers in the past have suggested that social isolation is predominant in cities and that the warm personal relationships in recreation and other affairs characteristic of rural areas are not found in the urban milieu. The Butler experience indicates the opposite to be true. As far as the data can reveal, the urbanites in Butler County have more of the warm, intimate association than is true in the country. They participate more in voluntary associations and religious-related organizations, and they also report a greater degree of visiting, getting together with friends, parties, entertaining, and the like. Generally speaking, urban people are more active in all kinds of recreation than the rural people in Butler County.

Finally, the assertion frequently has been made that the rural area is more concerned with religion and religious activities than is the urban population. Again, we found the opposite to be true in Butler County. The urban persons in Butler belong to more religious organizations and are more active in the organizations to which they belong than do the people in the rural parts of the county. This may be partly because of the proximity of the urban dweller to the meeting places of such organizations. Nevertheless, insofar as Butler County is concerned, it would be impossible to agree with earlier statements that the urbanite neglects things of the spirit.

The overall impression to be gained from the analysis of recreational behavior in Butler County is that the population primarily is interested in recreation involving no physical effort and little mental effort. It is the non-creative, passive recreation in which the county population participates most frequently. This was also demonstrated to be true in New Haven. Critics of American culture decry the American's dependence upon commercialized, passive recreation and feel that the prognosis for the disease they call "spectatoritis" bodes ill for everything from mental health to national security. While these findings support their assumption that Americans are prone to "spectatoritis," the data cannot suggest whether the results of this condition are good or bad. It is possible that the American is so active in his work life that in leisure hours he is too drained of creative energy for his recreation to be anything other than passive. Regardless, there is little evidence supporting the critics' notion that creative, active recreation represents the best use of leisure time.

* 18. Ecological and Attitudinal Factors in Church Desegregation

L. K. Northwood

Introduction Two recurrent problems face American churches today. One is the fantastic growth in church membership; the other is racial integration of this membership. Since Professor L. K. Northwood's chapter is concerned with the second of these problems, only a few observations are necessary on the first. The high rate of church growth creates concern about overtaxed church plants, bulging Sunday schools, church additions, new churches, shortage of ministers, and the like. Aside from these problems, many theologians are concerned about the meaning of this growth. Some call it a spiritual awakening; others see it as part of a powerful force to conform. They claim it has become the fashion to belong and that people take up church membership seeking social respectability and not salvation. So great is the impulse to be like others, they say, that the fear of being different or individualistic is of greater concern than the fear of hell.

The problems associated with racial integration are related to the development of urban society, particularly to the large migrations of rural and urban populations. Since World War I, the rural South has exported large numbers of its children. Rural non-whites, in particular, make up the largest group migrating to Northern, Midwestern, and Western cities. Meanwhile old-time residents of these cities have sought to escape the

355

dirt, smells, grime, and people of the central city by moving out into rural-like fringes of the central city, developing there suburban life as we know it today.

Churches are caught in the middle of this process. While they are organized to meet particular needs, and I might add wishes of their members, as institutions with creedal beliefs concerning the brotherhood of man, they face the dilemma sooner or later of taking a stand on church desegregation.

This is especially true of churches in transitional areas of communities where non-whites are moving into what were once all-white sections. Churches in such a situation can decide to open their doors to the non-white newcomers and develop racially integrated church membership; or they can keep to themselves, withhold the invitation to the non-whites, and witness the gradual disappearance of their members who move into the suburbs beyond seeking Caucasian seclusion; or they can attempt to be a "downtown" or city-wide church, still segregated, attempting to serve a congregation from the area beyond the immediate neighborhood; or they can decide to move out into a suburb where some of their members have moved.

The minister's beliefs, the type of church, the denomination, the parishioner sentiment, the centralized or local organizational ties are but a few of the factors affecting desegregation. In Professor Northwood's chapter we have an excellent empirical study of the above factors which affect racial segregation and integration in churches in Des Moines, Iowa. The analysis of the connection between "church type" and policy formation, location of churches, and behavior of ministers on racial matters is a new and incisive approach to the complex factors affecting church desegregation. Policies on desegregation, as Dr. Northwood suggests, often are determined by "ecological determiners" such as the movement of church members from the community and the in-migration of non-church members. These ecological determiners may be in conflict with "social determiners," *e.g.*, negative attitudes towards non-whites. The discussion by Dr. Northwood on the ecological versus social determiners of a church desegregation policy clarifies some of the ambiguities concerning decision-making in church biracial practices.

✻ Findings on church segregation generally have been that "Protestantism, by its policies and practices . . . is actually contributing to the segregation of Negro Americans." [1] While there is general agreement with this, the chapter will attempt to show that the race relations policies of selected Protestant churches in Des Moines, Iowa, seem to be affected by a variety of factors ecological and attitudinal, such as: (a) racial composition of the area in which the church is located, (b) income and occupational composition of the membership, (c) size and stability of church, (d) the church type: sect or denomination, (e) the position on segregation of the national body with which the local church is affiliated, (f) the attitude of the minister and the local congregation toward racial segregation.

Prior studies have been of selected denominations across the nation; this is a case study of a single city. The approach is organic rather than statistical. It attempts to relate a pattern of social activity (race relations) to certain religious institutions prevailing in a particular area of the city.

The data of the research are so organized that the following questions emerge.

1. What are the typical patterns of racial integration in churches?
2. To what extent is church desegregation related to social class and caste patterns?
3. Does the size of the congregation increase or decrease with the advent of minority members?
4. Do churches remain in areas undergoing racial transition?
5. How do sects and denominations differ in race relations policy and practice?

In the first half of the chapter, stress is placed on the ecological concomitants of church segregation: church size, location, stratification, stability. Evidence indicates that genuine racial desegregation seems to be paired with favorable attitudes of minister and congregation and with the general religious philosophy of the church type. Consequently, there is a detailed analysis of social

[1] Dwight Culver, *Negro Segregation in the Methodist Church* (New Haven: Yale University Press, 1953), p. 8.

psychological factors in the race relations of the two church types of sect and denomination. The purpose here is to strike a balance for ecological and social psychological factors.

RESEARCH DESIGN

The sample is of 78 Protestant churches located in three groups of census tracts, contrasted by income and racial composition of the residents.[2] They include (a) seven lowest-income census tracts with less than 1 per cent non-whites; (b) eight lowest-income census tracts containing 8 to 46 per cent non-whites; (c) six highest-income census tracts with less than 1 per cent non-whites. In terms of the Burgess Zonal Hypothesis, these tracts are the central business district, the zone of transition bordering on the central business, and selected best residential areas at the outer limits of the city.[3] It should be noted that churches in (a) and (b) are always near a "Negro neighborhood" and thus have the geographical potential for desegregation.

For the rest of the chapter, the three areas and the churches located in them will be identified as (a) white low-income, (b) mixed low-income, (c) white high-income.

Interviews with the ministers lasted approximately two hours and ranged over a variety of subjects concerning the church organization and the minister's attitudes. The strategy of the questionnaire design was that discussion of the race relations policy of the church and the minister's attitudes be deferred till the latter portion of the interview, after peripheral questions had been asked in advance.

This "funnel technique" operated in the following way.[4] At

[2] Half of the sample are of five Protestant denominations: Lutheran, Baptist, Presbyterian, Methodist, Disciples of Christ. Twenty other Protestant denominations are represented by one to four churches. Eight churches have no national affiliation.

[3] R. E. Park, E. W. Burgess, and R. D. MacKenzie, *The City* (Chicago: University of Chicago Press, 1925.)

[4] An extensive description of the questionnaire technique is included, since it suggests a device that may be especially helpful in race relations surveys. The logic is that if the covert reason for questioning is not known, then the respondent will be less likely to shape (distort) his answers. In the present study it is believed that much information concerning racial bias was secured which might not have been elicited through a more direct form of questioning.

the very beginning, while investigators stated the purpose of the study, they emphasized that:

> We are interested in the church in the modern urban society, and in the attitudes of its ministers. We are interested in the kinds of programs that the church offers for the community and for the people who live in the neighborhood right around the church.

The purposes deliberately were made very general, and the interviewer was instructed to indicate interest in race relations only in reply to a direct question on the subject.

The first sequence of questions dealt with the minister's training, his daily routine, the church affiliation. The purpose was to determine the extent to which the policies of the national were binding on the local church in respect to race relations and to see whether the minister would be likely to visit "people who live right around the church." The key question in the second sequence was:

> Now I'd like to ask you a general question about the neighborhood in which your church is located. Suppose for a moment that a good friend has the opportunity to move into this neighborhood right around the church. Let's suppose also that he doesn't know anything at all about the neighborhood or the people who live there. He is interested in finding out something about the different kinds of people that live here, and how they get along together and how he'll like them. So he visits you and asks, "What are the people in the neighborhood like?" What would you say?

Then followed a series of direct probes about the neighborhood.

A third sequence dealt with such items as the number of members, their age, sex, occupation, income, and changes in membership. A typical question was:

> Do you have any special groups or nationalities attending your church at the present time? What groups are these?

In each open-ended probe, the minister was encouraged to speak fully. At this point, the familiar check-list items on conservatism-radicalism, prejudice, anomie were determined.[5] Next were items

[5] T. W. Adorno, et al., *The Authoritarian Personality* (New York: Harper & Brothers, 1950).

about community and social action of the church; and then a final sequence on race relations starting with

Do you have any members of your congregation that are of another race or color?

Included were queries about experiences of the church with members of another race, attendance at activities, policies on inviting cross-racial membership, officeholding, brotherhood programs and activities of the church, attitudes and policies of the church membership and the minister. The final question dealt with minister attitude to church segregation.

DEFINITION OF SEGREGATION

In this study, segregation is conceived of as "that form of isolation in which social distance is based on physical separation." [6] Churches containing members of one race only are called segregated churches, regardless of the population composition of the area in which the church is located.[7] Non-segregated churches are called "mixed" or "desegregated." A church is called "integrated" when one to five persons attending are not of the same race as the majority of the members. There are marked differences between churches which have more than 1 per cent adult members of another race and those which have one adult member and less than 1 per cent of another race. The former are called "substantially integrated churches," and the latter "partially integrated churches."

In making this classification only official church members were counted as they were identified by the minister, and his estimate of the race of a member was accepted. While there may be some question about the minister's ability to recognize all members of a race by skin color, the number of Negroes "passing" is probably small in this moderate-sized city.

[6] Louis Wirth, "Segregation," in *Encyclopedia of the Social Sciences* (New York: The Macmillan Co. 1934), vol. 13, p. 643.

[7] It should be noted that segregation may be either voluntary or involuntary. It is conceivable that a church may be located in a geographical area where segregation is inevitable because it is inhabited by one race only. However, the description of the population composition of the church is still as a segregated population; that is, there is no value connotation attached to the concept "segregation."

DES MOINES: SETTING OF THE STUDY

Des Moines is a Midwestern city of approximately 175,000 population with the "Northern" traditions concerning race relations. The public facilities are not legally segregated. A state ordinance prohibits discrimination in public accommodations and is enforced. The largest unions are the United Packinghouse Workers, United Automobile Workers, and United Electrical Workers. All have active programs against discrimination.

Approximately 5 per cent of the population are non-white. There are some non-whites residing in 43 of the 44 census tracts into which the city is divided. In no single census tract is the density of non-white population greater than 46 per cent of the population of that tract. However, 85 per cent of Des Moines Negroes reside in one of nine census tracts, forming three separate neighborhoods in the poorer residential sections of the city.

COMPARISON OF PARTIALLY AND SUBSTANTIALLY INTEGRATED CHURCHES

In all, twenty-six churches, one-third of the sample, were found to have at least one member of another race than the majority of the congregation. There are, however, considerable differences in the patterns of integration (see table 27).

PARTIALLY INTEGRATED CHURCHES

The typical racial pattern of partially integrated churches is for them to have a single family of Japanese Americans, a "Spanish" family, or a Puerto Rican family—and very few Negro members. Six churches are known to have one Negro member each.[8] Another enrolled 30 Negro children in Sunday School, but Negro adults "hardly ever" attended regular services, and "none are members." The exception church in this type includes "the only five Episcopal Negroes in town," about .004 of its congregation.

The token integration is accented when it is seen that 18 of these churches have approximately 18,400 members. The median

[8] Two of these six churches did not provide a count of Negro members in their estimates, thus were not totalled in table 24. Their number is less than ten.

Table 27. Selected Characteristics of "Substantially Integrated," "Partially Integrated," and "Segregated" Churches: Race Composition of Members

CHARACTERISTICS OF MEMBERSHIP AND CHURCHES	TYPE OF CHURCH INTEGRATION		
	SUBSTANTIALLY INTEGRATED	PARTLY INTEGRATED	SEGREGATED
Number of Churches in Sample	8	18	52
Size and Stability of Churches —Total Number of members (minister's estimate)	2,700	18,400	17,800
Median Number of members for each church	285	600	105
Median Number of years church has been in existence	34	29	44
Number of Members of Minority race in Congregation of Churches			
Negro adults	68	9	0
Negro children	0	30 °	0
Other non-white adults	27	27	0
White adults (in "Negro" churches)	0	6	0

° In one church.

size of the churches is large, about 600; included are seven of the largest churches in Des Moines, having over 1,000 members each.

Approximately 60 per cent of the partially integrated churches are made up of persons having professional and business occupations and a comfortable income, according to their ministers' estimates. Most of them are located either on high-rent downtown corners or in the exclusive or better residential sections of Des Moines. Approximately half of the churches were established over 80 years ago; most of the others less than five years ago in the new, growing middle- and upper-class residential neighborhoods.

SUBSTANTIALLY INTEGRATED CHURCHES

These contain larger numbers and proportions of non-whites. The cross-racial membership is largely Negro, though not always so. The 35 non-whites in the Watchtower Church make up 27 per cent of its membership; the 2 per cent membership in Disciples of Christ, nevertheless, numbers 30 Negroes and Orientals, some of whom have been members for decades.

The 2,700 members of the substantially integrated churches are found in eight churches, having a median membership of 285 each. Five of these congregations are small enough that they might be considered as "primary groups"; that is, there is a direct face-to-face interaction among all members of the congregation. On the other hand, one of these churches numbers 1,600 members.

All of these churches are classified by their ministers as being comprised of persons with low or moderate incomes and working-class occupations. Two of the churches are located downtown; the other six are in low income areas, four of these situated in census tracts having over 10 per cent non-white residents. Three-quarters of these churches have occupied their present site for twenty years or more. The oldest of the churches traces its interracial membership to the Civil War.

A comparison of the two types of integrated churches with the segregated churches is outlined in table 27. Let us examine some of the implications of the findings.

CHURCH SEGREGATION, CASTE, AND CLASS

Many researchers have pointed to two kinds of barriers that exist between Negro and white in the United States today: caste and class barriers.[9] Class refers to an economic grouping in society with the occupation of or income of the individual being an index to his relative class position. The caste is also largely an economic grouping, but with the further restriction that movement between castes is made difficult by bans on intermarriage, segregation, and other unequally distributed privileges. Moreover, such caste barriers in the United States have followed racial lines with the Negro as the lowest caste, the white as the highest caste, and the Oriental somewhere in between.

Applying this theory to church desegregation, it would seem

[9] Oliver Cox, *Class, Caste and Race* (New York: Doubleday & Company, Inc., 1948).

that the Negro is more likely to break through the caste barriers at his own class level and in white churches having members of similar income and occupations. The finding holds for Japanese-Americans as well. Orientals in the Midwest seem to hold professional and business occupations. In Des Moines, they have been integrated into churches with similar occupational composition.

Furthermore, in almost all cases, the cross-racial membership is upward toward a higher caste or status. Very few whites affiliate with largely Negro churches; no Orientals did so. The patterns in church membership are also paralleled by the residency patterns of Orientals; they seldom live in census tracts having a large proportion of Negroes.

CHURCH STABILITY AND RACIAL INTEGRATION

Two problems often are raised concerning church stability and race relations. First, does the size of the congregation increase or decrease with the advent of minority members? Second, do churches remain in areas undergoing racial transition? A church with "stability" was defined in this chapter as one in which "stability" existed at the time of the interview and which had a presiding minister or officer to provide information about the church. The present sample, drawn from the telephone directory, membership lists of the ministerial association, and newspaper advertisements of Easter services, undoubtedly underrepresents transitory cults and sects. The present sample represents the churches stable enough to be in existence at the time of the interview and where the minister would grant such an interview.

In the interview, the following information was systematically gathered: number of members, size trends, composition of membership, length of time church has been located on present site, reasons for moves in site.

In addition, the following questions were asked in this order: (a) On the average, how many people would you estimate attend Sunday services? (b) How many of these people who attend Sunday services would you say are *not* members of the church? (c) In general, how does it happen that these non-members attend regular Sunday services?

The purpose of this sequence was to distinguish more sharply between members and attenders. It should be noted that the questions on church stability *specifically were not keyed to race relations*. On the contrary, they were introduced prior to any racial reference. In all, adequate information was gathered on church stability for 60 of the 65 predominantly white churches and for none of the Negro churches.

TRENDS IN MEMBERSHIP

The facts about the size of membership and median number of years each type of church has been in existence are shown in table 27. They demonstrate for this sample of churches that there was some degree of stability over time and in membership, regardless of the racial composition of the congregation.

Partially integrated churches, 600 members on the average, had larger memberships than the substantially integrated (average of 285 members) and the segregated churches, which had the smallest average memberships, averaging 105. The median number of years each type of church had been in existence was 29 years for partially integrated, 34 years for substantially integrated, and 44 years for segregated churches.

However, the data on church growth or decline were not so specific.

In general, very few ministers reported that the size of their congregations had become smaller—only three ministers of 68. Two-thirds estimated an increase in size, and the balance stated that there had been neither growth nor decline.

Table 28 relates these estimates to trends enumerated in the 1950 Census. The areas of greatest proportional population growth also contained the greatest proportion of churches reported to have increased in membership.

For example, the high-income white areas relatively had the greatest population growth of the three area-types. Likewise, 83 per cent of the ministers to churches in these areas reported increase in membership. Low-income areas remained relatively stable with the Negro population growing more rapidly than the white. The increase in church membership would necessarily need to come from outside the area unless there had been greater concentration

*Table 28.   Relation of Population Growth in Selected Census
Tracts of Des Moines, 1940–1950 to Estimates of
Growth in Predominantly White Churches*

TYPE OF CENSUS TRACT	PERCENTAGE INCREASE IN WHITE POPULATION 1940–1950	PERCENTAGE INCREASE IN NON-WHITE POPULATION 1940–1950	PERCENTAGE OF CHURCHES REPORTING GROWTH IN MEMBERSHIP
High income, white (less than 1% non-white)	33.8	154.1	83.0
Low income, white (less than 1% non-white)	1.2	41.9	69.0
Low income, mixed (26% non-white)	13.2	30.2	31.0

Source: 1950 U.S. Census.

of church-goers residing in the area. The former premise is more likely, since these churches are right downtown. Their ministers also indicated that the growth was coming from all sections of the city, rather than from within the immediate neighborhood. The large proportional increase in non-white population for both white areas in neither case amounted to more than a few hundred persons, less than 1 per cent of the total population in these census tracts.

Fewer churches in the mixed neighborhoods than in other areas reported increases in membership size. It is noteworthy that three of the four growing churches in mixed areas were partially or substantially integrated, whereas six of the seven segregated churches recorded no increase. From this it would seem that the mixed churches supplemented their memberships from the increased proportion of non-whites who moved into the area. Table 29 gives the proportions of church types reporting growth in their congregations.

These data would seem to show that, at a minimum, partial integration does not inhibit church growth in the predominantly white areas, and that church desegregation may be conducive to growth in some churches in the mixed areas. However, evidence as to the effects of integration on the size of church membership is ot clear-cut. Confusion is reflected in the comments of ministers to partially integrated churches, as reported below:

Table 29. *Per Cent and Number of Churches by Church-Types*

	PERCENTAGE OF ALL SUCH CHURCHES REPORTING INCREASE IN MEMBERS	NUMBER
Substantially integrated churches	50	4
Partially integrated churches	87	14
Segregated churches	62	26

I don't know what would happen if 75 or 100 Negroes moved in. It would depend on how they conducted themselves. They get picked on by their own people for belonging to a white church. It would probably cause some stir. (1135 members in downtown church)

I don't believe that groups of Negro people would be encouraged to attend. I believe that there should be separate churches for Negroes and whites. Both groups find it more helpful to be among their own. This is not because of any deep rooted prejudice on my part. (3000 members in downtown church)

We extend general invitations to join the church to any and all people. Negroes are welcomed and made to feel at home . . . However the Negro children often have a persecution complex . . . I believe colored folks are happier when they are among themselves. Also whites. However, we have no aversion to them. They are welcome in all services. (667 members in church in mixed area)

Our membership has been slowly dwindling and growing smaller. Colored folks have pushed many good folks away. Our congregation has moved away. Probably people feel that there are enough colored churches to take care of the colored people, and they don't need to come to our church. (40 members—2 Japanese-American—in mixed area)

The presence of segregated churches in mixed areas is absolute evidence that there is no automatic inclusion of minorities because of changes in the racial composition of the neighborhood around the church. Rather, the comments of ministers above suggest that desegregation is an evident problem of churches located in areas where there is high potential for admixture.

Perhaps there is more urgency to desegregate where there are growing proportions of minorities around the church site. The critical test would seem to come when increasing numbers of the minority attend a church and apply for membership. Sometime during this process, the congregation will need to decide either (a) to relocate the church where residential segregation would reduce the likelihood that church desegregation would become "a problem," or (b) to admit or exclude the minority.

DECISION TO DESEGREGATE

Three statement best summarize the findings on the decision-making process. The first proposition is:

1. Where there are few members of the minority race living around the church, church desegration is not seen as a crucial problem. Nevertheless, there are crystallized attitudes on race relations policy.

Two-thirds of the ministers to churches located in the high-income, all-white areas stated that no Negroes lived in the immediate neighborhood and that the problem of church membership, therefore, had never arisen. The seven partially integrated churches in this area had in their combined memberships Japanese-Americans, one Puerto Rican, and one Negro. The ministers to the churches which had no Negroes in their congregations indicated that Negroes probably would be received to membership if they applied. However, this possibility was considered as rather remote.

The ministers to the sixteen segregated churches located in the same high-income white areas, as a group, were less favorable to Negro inclusion. About half of these commented:

There aren't any Negroes to call on in this neighborhood. Our members might be upset if they wanted to join.

We have a colored church in Des Moines. We would encourage them to back that church. If there were not a colored church, they would be welcome. We're not prejudiced to any race.

I don't think most people would object, though a small group might.

It'd be kind of half and half. Some have testified they don't like them (Negroes). Others are OK.

Such remarks came in response to the question, "Has any Negro person ever attended any religious service or any other function of your church?" These comments substantially reported the real situation, since the 1950 Census listed only a fraction of 1 per cent Negroes living in the area.

Questions were included in the interview to discover whether formal or informal measures on racial inclusion had been adopted by the local church. A question worded, "Does your local church have a formally stated policy concerning segregation and discrimination?" yielded four affirmative answers among sixty-eight ministers. All of these stated that the local action was in support of a national pronouncement by their parent body in opposition to racial segregation. These were the *only* formal actions by local churches in support of national resolutions that were noted.

In addition, different ministers cited decisions by the local congregations on the racial composition of the church. The significant aspect of this anecdotal evidence is that every instance of group decision concerning racial composition of membership occurred within congregations located in the mixed residential areas, or which had been located in such areas and moved out. There were *no* reports of such group decisions in other churches in the sample.

Four types of decisions are represented in the reports below.

Decision to leave interracial area:

The old neighborhood was becoming predominantly Negro. Our members were moving out here (high-income, all-white area), and it was thought that Des Moines was moving in this direction. We decided to move too. (480 Members).

Decision to move into interracial areas:

Our church located here because of the missionary need in this part of the city. (75 Members) There was a chance to establish better relations between races. (250 Members). It was definitely the lead of God. (50 Members, 75 Members) This was a natural site—my home had formerly been the church. (150 Members).

Decision to remain segregated:

Our church discussed this. A Negro lady sent two children, and there was some objection. The Sunday school teacher and others thought attendance by Negroes steadily would break up the congregation. (70 Members).

Decision to desegregate by two substantially integrated churches:

There were minor difficulties when Mrs. Jones joined (Negro). Parents withdrew their child from the Sunday School. Also there was a little stir in the neighborhood among non-members. One of the Mexican girls and her husband were anti-Negro, but they were reconciled. We took a congregational vote to let Mrs. Jones become a member. It was unanimously in her favor. (84 Members).

We have approximately 30 Negroes in our membership. When I received the last Negro, I lost a family of whites. The family of whites are now seeking a church that will not take Negroes and as yet have not found a church that will promise that. (1,600 Members).

The discussion suggests that attendance of Negroes in any predominantly white church—regardless of size or location—is an event to be noted, discussed, and speculated about.

However, it is not unlikely that the large, easily accessible downtown churches by accident alone might acquire a handful of minority members. The contradictory comments of ministers to the partially integrated downtown churches show that policies on race segregation have not been established and tested in these churches. The most frequent attitude is: "I don't know what would happen if seventy-five or one hundred Negroes moved in."

On the other hand, the issue of desegregation inevitably would seem to evoke a policy decision in small-sized congregations, where the proportions of minorities might increase substantially by the addition of half a dozen members.

The following propositions seem warranted:

2. Where there are growing proportions of a minority race attending a church, there is greater likelihood of church decision on desegregation.

3. The smaller the church the more imminent the decision on desegregation.

DESEGREGATION IN SECTS AND DENOMINATIONS

Thus far we have discussed the interrelation of ecological and attitudinal factors with church segregation practices. Now, what types of churches are likely to desegregate?

For many years the major cleavage in Protestant churches has been among those groups affiliated with the National Council of Churches in Christ and those affiliated with the American Council of Christian Churches. The former are called "modernist" or "liberal," and the latter, "fundamentalist." Braden further equated NCCC affiliates with the church type of "denomination" and the ACCC with the "sect." [10]

Braden's typology, of course, embodies two of the four church-types developed earlier by such men as Troelsch,[11] Becker,[12] and Pope,[13] and which have received more recent treatment by Brewer,[14] Dynes,[15] Pfautz [16] and others.

The four church types are "ecclesia," "sect," "denomination" and "cult." As described by Becker:

The fully developed ecclesia attempts to amalgamate itself with the state and the dominant classes, and strives to exercise control over every person in the population. Members are *born into* the ecclesia; they do not have to *join* it. It is therefore a social structure somewhat, though remotely, akin to the nation or the state.[17]

Obviously, there is no ecclesia in the contemporary U.S. Consequently, we will not be concerned with this church type.

Furthermore, very little emphasis will be placed in this chapter on the cult, which is described as a usually small "very amorphous, loose textured, uncondensed type of social structure" with the goal for its members being "purely personal ecstatic experience,

[10] Charles S. Braden, "The Sects," *Annals of the American Academy of Political and Social Sciences*, vol. 256 (March, 1948), pp. 53–62.

[11] Joachim Wach, *Sociology of Religion* (Chicago: University of Chicago Press, 1943).

[12] Howard Becker, *Through Values to Social Interpretation: Essays on Social Contexts, Actions, Types, and Prospects* (Durham, N.C.: Duke University Press, 1950), chap. 2.

[13] Liston Pope, *Millhands and Preachers: A Study of Gastonia* (New Haven: Yale University Press, 1942).

[14] Earl D. C. Brewer, "Sect and Church in Methodism," *Social Forces*, vol. 30 (May, 1952), pp. 400–408.

[15] Russell R. Dynes, "Church-Sect Typology and Socio-Economic Status," *American Sociological Review*, vol. 20 (October, 1955), pp. 555–560.

[16] Harold W. Pfautz, "The Sociology of Secularization: Religious Groups," *American Journal of Sociology*, vol. 61 (September, 1955), pp. 121–128.

[17] Becker, *op. cit.*, p. 114.

salvation, comfort, and mental or physical healing." [18] There are few, if any, cults represented in the present sample.

The largest proportion of churches in the sample (and the U.S.) are probably denominations and sects. The sect is defined as a smaller religious social structure, often withdrawn or in opposition to the dominant culture patterns of a society, and which enforces strict ethical and personal behavioral norms among its members. Membership is elective and exclusive with religious leadership arising not as a consequence of special training, but open to all those who can obtain a following.

Sects which persist often become denominations. Compromises are made with the secular world; membership requirements eased. Leadership is less frequently charismatic and more often bureaucratic or traditional. A professional clergy emerges. The church membership increases; its functions broaden. The sect is stabilized and becomes a denomination.

Any movement from cult to sect to denomination is not inevitable and can be reversed. The increase in size and stability of the cult or sect, however, would seem to cause specialized division of labor and professionalization. Existence in a secular world has its impact on the more ingrown church types, both through opposition by outside secular forces and through values of society internalized by its own members.

The classification above probably does not cover the full range of possible types. Pfautz and Yinger, for example, would like to add the "institutional sect." [19] This church type usually has more members than the cult or sect. Its social structure is more complex, its leadership "official," if not professionalized.

Pfautz had described the membership characteristics of the institutionalized sect in terms which have meaning for race relations policy. He states:

[The membership] grows increasingly homogeneous, as a result of a more selective basis of recruitment. While it is a growing group, in comparison with the sect, the rate of growth tends to be decreasing. It tends to be

[18] *Ibid.,* p. 117.

[19] Pfautz, *op. cit.* J. Milton Yinger, *Religion in the Struggle for Power* (Durham, N.C.: Duke University Press, 1946).

national (and even international) in distribution, *but it is, at the same time, highly segregated.* [italics added] [20]

Pfautz, of course, is not referring to racial segregation, but rather to the homogeneous beliefs within the institutionalized sect (and the sect), in contrast to a diversity of beliefs within the denomination.

In examining the church types in this study, specific questions were considered: (1) Which type of church, sect, or denomination is most likely to desegregate? (2) Is there greater consistency between the racial prejudices of the sectarian minister and the segregation practices of the sect than between the racial prejudices of the denominational minister and the segregation practices of the denomination?

Churches were classified as sects or denominations by asking each minister questions about the community activities of his church, including the use of church facilities by outside groups, passage of resolutions on current affairs, petitioning, and other social action. The minister was further queried about his personal activity with citizens' groups, whether he or other members had run for public office, and what the social issues were in that campaign. All of these questions provided specifics which were crystallized with the probe:

How important do you think it is for your church to provide non-religious activities or services for people who are *not* members of your church—that is, for the entire community?

In addition, other sections of the interview provided the minister with an opportunity to express his view on secular activities and points of religious emphasis. The total response to these questions was judged, and the church was classified as community-oriented, *i.e.*, denomination, or inner-church oriented, *i.e.*, as a sect. No attempt was made for a refinement of sect types. The dividing line in the operational definition was determined by the community outlook of the church. Unless the evidence was substantial, the church was not classified and thus would not be included in the subsequent analysis. Classification was possible for 59 of the 68

[20] Pfautz, *op. cit.*, p. 126.

predominantly white Protestant churches, 36 as denominations, and 23 as sects. The predominantly Negro churches were not included in this analysis.

CHARACTERISTICS OF SECT AND DENOMINATION

1. *Church size and location.* Of the 23 sects, only 6 exceeded 200 members; the largest was 667. Average membership of all sects was 166 members. There were no sects located in the most wealthy census tracts (5 of the 8 predominantly white, upper income census tracts). Over three-quarters of the sects were in downtown and lowest-income census tracts.

On the other hand, denominations were large, averaging over 850 members each. Only three denominations (8 per cent) had memberships of fewer than 200. The national affiliations of these three smaller denominations suggest their recent sectarian origin: Friends, Evangelical United Brethren, Disciples of Christ. The bulk of denominations located either in the heart of downtown or in the higher-income census tracts. About 30 per cent of the sects locate in mixed residential districts compared with 8 per cent of the denominations.

2. *Occupational class composition.* Considering the foregoing, it is not surprising to find that ministers to 61 per cent of the denominations reported that their congregations were made up of business and professional workers, as shown in table 30, whereas not one sectarian minister reported this. The findings are similar to those of Dynes, Pope and others.[21]

3. *Professional training of ministers.* One of the principal differences between sect and denomination suggested by the writers in this field is that denominations have professionalized leadership, whereas ministers to the sect lack formal training in their calling. In this sample, all denominational ministers were trained in college or theological seminary. Only 55 per cent of the sectarian ministers had received such training. Sectarian ministers reported "mail order courses," "rising through the ranks," and other evidence tending to support the distinction.

4. *Theological beliefs.* Braden has suggested that sects usually

[21] Dynes, *op. cit.* Pope, "Caste in the Church: The Protestant Experience," *Survey Graphic*, vol. 36 (January, 1947), pp. 59–60.

Table 30. *Occupational Composition of Sects and Denominations in 59 White Protestant Churches in Des Moines, 1954*

PREDOMINATE OCCUPATIONAL COMPOSITION OF CHURCHES	PER CENT OF ALL DENOMINATIONS (N = 36)	PER CENT OF ALL SECTS (N = 23)
Manual workers	22	56
Skilled workers	17	44
Business and professional workers, managers	61	0
Total	100	100

emphasize one or more of the following points in their religious beliefs: extreme fidelity to the scriptures, millennial hope or expectation, desire for holiness or entire sanctification, the present experience of Pentecost or possession by the Holy Spirit, and a stress on evangelism.[22]

In the survey, at least three questions tapped such beliefs. They were (a) What do you think is the most important thing in religion? (b) How important do you think religion should be in a person's life? (c) What do you consider to be the most important teachings of the Bible?

The findings strikingly support Braden's contention. With only two exceptions, sectarian ministers (91 per cent) specifically mentioned one or more of the five themes. However, 30 per cent of the denominational ministers also mentioned one or more of these themes.

On the other hand, over 70 per cent of the denominational ministers cited "nonsectarian" themes, as compared with 13 per cent of the sectarian ministers. Such recurrent nonsectarian themes include:

It is very hard to pick out any special teachings of the Bible because they are all important. The main thing is faith in Jesus Christ.

"Sincerity." I just feel that's the basis of religion. Love your neighbor as yourself. When you do that you can solve any problem.

Service to your fellow man—that is the thing.

[22] Braden, *op. cit.*

Living a Christian life is the most important thing.

Religion should offer the resources to help people achieve a satisfactory adjustment to life. The most important thing is the sacredness of human personality.

The essential characteristics of nonsectarian themes are the concern with the human personality and social relations in the world today, with a general acceptance of the philosophy and ethics of the Bible without overemphasis on any single ritual of practice. The church is considered as an instrument of social policy and a source of ethical behavior rather than an end in itself.

5. *National affiliation.* It is noteworthy that all of the churches classified as denominations which have national affiliations belong to the National Council of Churches in Christ, whereas only two churches classified as sects (Lutheran) belong to the organization. The sects have other national affiliations, if any. Such sects are the Nazarene, Lutheran, Open Bible, Baptist, Bethel Mission, Evangelical Mission Covenant, Assembly of God Mission, Church of God, Gospel Assembly, Four Square, Assembly of God, Church of Christ, Samaritan Union, Watchtower, Gospel Light House, and Beams of Grace. Thus Braden's assumption about the denominational character of the National Council was borne out in the sample.

SEGREGATION AND CHURCH-TYPE

What are the racial practices of sect and denomination? These are summarized in table 31 for the 18 sects and 18 denominations located in and around the central business district, *i.e.*, in and near interracial areas. A similar analysis, based on 23 sects and 36 denominations, was also completed, but it will not be summarized here since the findings for the two samples are identical.

In both samples, larger proportions of denominations than sects effected some racial integration. However, the patterns of integration differ sharply. Sects which begin to desegregate are more likely to go the whole way, whereas the typical pattern for denominations is partial integration. The majority of both church types follow the dominant pattern of society in racial segregation. The contrasting patterns of sect and denomination are seen as a consequence of the organizational and doctrinal characteristics noted for each church type.

Table 31. *Segregation Patterns in Sects and Denominations Located in and Nearby Interracial Areas in Des Moines, 1954*

	SECT	DENOMINATION
	NUMBER	NUMBER
Segregated	11	10
Partially integrated	2	6
Substantially integrated	5	2
Total	18	18

Sectarian patterns. In most cases, membership in the sect depends on fundamental belief in the religion of the sect, not on personal characteristics of the applicant, such as race, income, or occupation. This does not mean that anyone who subscribes to the fundamental beliefs automatically and inevitably is acceptable as a member, regardless of race. It means, instead, that rejection of a potential member because of his race might be interpreted as setting aside religious tenet in favor of a secular view on segregation. Thus, there are cross-pressures within the sect which require resolution of the question: Do we admit Negroes? Furthermore, as pointed out earlier, the small size of the sect, its frequent location in mixed residential areas, its aggressive visitation practices could bring the sect into continual contact with Negroes, and thus accent any contradictions.

Consequently, the sect will decide to segregate or not to segregate. There will be few sects where the decision has not been resolved. Under these conditions there are very few partially integrated sects.

The decision on racial inclusion or exclusion is made without guidance from a national body: first, because many sects are without national affiliation; second, because such national ties when they exist are binding only with respect to religious dogma and not for secular beliefs. The author was unable to find statements on race relations by sectarian national bodies.

Denominational patterns. Many factors mitigate the need for group decision on racial inclusion among denominations. The effect of size and location have been noted. Furthermore, the denomination eschews aggressive visitation practices and depends instead on advertisements, a wide range of activities, outstanding musical events, and noted ministers. These are the main appeals for large attendance.

The traditional pattern of the denomination is to tolerate or even encourage a wide range of views in the church.[23] This may extend even to challenges of the central tenets of the church. The denomination is characterized by the antithesis of sectarianism: it is nonsectarian. With the denomination, the range of church beliefs usually is in accord with the range of secular beliefs. Consequently it is seldom faced with the conflicts noted by the sect. It has no inner compulsion to solve the problems of society. It is conservative.[24] Its typical race relations pattern is segregation. However, a greater extent of partial integration is also to be expected since, in general, the presence of a few Negroes is not seen to be a threat requiring immediate resolution. As a matter of fact, the presence of a few minority members permits the denomination to preserve its aura of tolerance. To this extent, partial integration is functional for the denomination.

Denominations usually have a national affiliation, as is the case with all but one church in the present sample. Further, all the national affiliates of the local denominations are officially opposed to church segregation.[25] However, considering the Protestant tradition of representative church government with strong emphasis on control by the local congregation and the minister, it is unlikely that there will be full knowledge by local ministers of their own national policies.[26] Desegregation in the denomination, much as in the sect, depends on the decision of the local congregation. This is not meant to deny that the national bodies of some Protestant

[23] Morris R. Cohen, *American Thought—A Critical Sketch* (Glencoe, Ill.: The Free Press, 1954), chap. 7.

[24] Sidney E. Mead, "American Protestantism since the Civil War: From Denominationalism to Americanism," *Journal of Religion,* vol. 36 (January, 1956), pp. 1–16.

[25] Alfred Kramer, "Protestant Churches: Are They Racially Inclusive?," *The City Church,* vol. 3 (March, 1952), pp. 13–14.

[26] Charles H. Page, "Bureaucracy and the Liberal Church," *Review of Religion,* vol. 16 (March, 1952), pp. 137–150.

churches are without moral or financial power. The Unitarian church will not give money to local affiliates which refuse membership to minorities. Another example was reported by an Episcopalian Minister:

> We had segregation one time here in Des Moines. Many of the elite Negroes wouldn't invite the poor Negroes to the church. When they lost their priest, the bishop refused to get them another. They were integrated into a white church.

The incident was verified by two other ministers.

The lack of congruence between local practice and national policy is shown in table 32.[27] One-third of the ministers did not know of the existence of a national policy opposed to segregation. Of the 11 ministers who did know the national church policy, only 4 served desegregated churches. On the other hand, 4 of the 6 ministers without such knowledge served racially mixed churches.

Table 32. Ministers' Knowledge of National Church Policy on Racial Segregation and the Practice of Selected Denominations in Des Moines, 1954

	LOCAL CHURCH PRACTICE		
MINISTER'S KNOWLEDGE	SEGREGATED	PARTIALLY INTEGRATED	SUBSTANTIALLY INTEGRATED
Knows of national policy against segregation	7	2	2
Doesn't know of national policy against segregation	2	4	0

Data were available on 40 local affiliates of 10 different denominations. Only 2 denominations demonstrated consistent knowledge by all the ministers of national policy: 5 Presbyterian affiliates and 7 affiliates of the Disciples of Christ. Contradictions were noted among ministers to the following church-groups: Episcopalian, Methodist, American Lutheran, United Presbyterian, Baptist, Evangelical United Brethren, and United Lutheran.

[27] The NCCC has a complete file of statements by its affiliates on race relations.

MINISTERS' OWN BELIEFS AND DESEGREGATION

The findings in every section of the chapter point to the local congregation as the group with effective power on the question of desegregation. It is also likely that the minister, as the key leader in the congregation, will be a strong factor in affecting the group decision.

However, it is probable that the sectarian minister will be more influential in this respect than the denominational minister. This is a direct consequence of the primary group character of the sect and the secondary group character of the denomination. For example, the ties between the denominational minister and the majority of his following are formalized, ritualistic, and impersonal. They must be if only because of the size of the group he leads and the large turnover. Furthermore, the denominational minister is often superimposed on the congregation or, at least, is a stranger to the congregation. On the other hand, the sect is small, intimate, with frequent participation and interaction of most members, with strict discipline. Above all, frequently the sectarian minister rose from the congregation he serves or was responsible for drawing together his following into what became a church.

The findings in table 33 for the present sample demonstrate the greater congruence of practice of the sects with their ministers' attitudes than for the denominations with their ministers.

Table 33. Ministers' Beliefs and Segregation Practices in Selected Sects and Denominations in Des Moines, 1954

TYPE OF CHURCH AND RACIAL COMPOSITION OF CONGREGATION	FOR SEGREGATED CHURCH	AGAINST SEGREGATED CHURCH	TOTALS
Sect			
Nonsegregated	2	4	6
Segregated	9	1	10
Denomination			
Nonsegregated	3	5	8
Segregated	4	6	10

A large majority of sectarian ministers favor segregation, and do segregate as a matter of church practice. On the other hand, of the five ministers who oppose segregation, four serve interracial congregations. Moreover, these four sectarian interracial churches have the largest proportions of minority members of any churches in the sample, one including 27 per cent of its congregation as members of minorities.

Eleven of the denominational ministers are opposed to segregated churches. But six have no members of another race than the majority of the congregation. The contradiction is compounded when it is seen that three of the seven integrated denominations are led by ministers opposed to mixed churches. However, it should be noted that wherever ministers are opposed to mixed churches, the racial admixture is token. The minority members are Orientals or Negro children, not Negro adults. The token character of this integration in sect and denomination where the minister favors segregation is shown in the blunt statement of one sectarian minister:

The Filipino and his wife were here when I came. Our church sponsors an African Missionary Association, and the Negro and his wife came to us and wanted to go and work among their own people and preach the word of God. Therefore, they wanted to affiliate and get instructions. Because of our doctrine and our sponsoring the African Missionary Association, we could not turn them away.

The evidence of greater congruence of sectarian minister with his congregation, of course, is not conclusive, even though it may have statistical significance. Nor can the lack of congruence between national church policy and the practice of local denominations be properly assessed in the absence of comparable data for sects.

Nevertheless, the findings are supplementary and help support the conclusion that the two church types have typically different patterns of racial integration when such integration occurs. For the denomination, it is more likely to be partial integration, and for the sect, it is substantial integration. The findings also suggest a close relationship between substantial integration and the favorable attitudes of the minister to that course of action.

APPLICATION AND SIGNIFICANCE OF THE STUDY

STUDIES OF CHURCH DESEGREGATION

On most points, there is accord between this and national studies that segregation is the dominant racial pattern of Protestant churches. However, there are two important differences between this and the national studies.

In the first place, Loescher in a comprehensive survey of denominations affiliated with the National Council of Churches in Christ found:

This survey of almost 18,000 churches in six denominations has failed to discover a single "white" church with an "open" or mixed membership *in an area undergoing transition.* It is only when colored members are in the majority that membership in transition areas is open.[28]

In contrast, the Des Moines sample included 21 "white" churches in the zone of transition. With one exception, the seven churches with the largest proportion of non-whites (5 to 27 per cent) were in this zone; the exception was located across the street from a census tract with 12 per cent Negroes. Furthermore, the transition area also included churches with partial integration.

Loescher's findings were also questioned in a later National Council study by Kramer, of 13,597 local affiliates of the United Lutheran Church in America, the Congregational Christian Churches and the Presbyterian Church in the U.S.A.[29]

A second generalization, subscribed to by two leading researchers in this field, Loescher and Culver, also stands in need of modification. Loescher states:

The Negro-white pattern of church membership and participation is essentially like the larger community pattern.[30]

The findings in this chapter support this statement, but Loescher continues:

If there are very few Negroes in the neighborhood integration may occur. If there are many, segregation usually occurs, both in the neighborhood and the church.

[28] F. S. Loescher, *The Protestant Church and the Negro: A Pattern of Segregation* (New York: Association Press, 1948).

[29] Kramer, *op. cit.*   [30] Loescher, *op. cit.*, p. 68.

Both authors cite minorities in towns and small cities which have been successfully integrated into the "white" churches. This generalization, which may apply in some small towns and cities (in the North), is not true of Des Moines, a city of 175,000. The census tracts containing the largest proportions of non-whites (8 to 46 per cent) include 8 all-Negro churches, 7 all-white churches, 2 predominantly Negro churches with some whites, and 6 predominantly "white" churches with some colored members. This "pattern of church participation and membership is essentially like the larger community pattern." On the other hand, with the 88 Negroes living in the higher-income census tracts, the pattern is non-integration in the church, even though they are less than 1 per cent of the entire population of the area. The contrary holds for the 40 Japanese-Americans living in these tracts; they are usually integrated into the predominantly white churches located there.

From the foregoing, in Des Moines it would seem that Negro desegregation in predominantly white churches has occurred in 99 per cent white residential areas.

The findings of Loescher and Culver largely are the product of a selected sample. If the Des Moines study had been restricted to the 27 local churches of the seven denominations studied by these authors, similar conclusions might have been derived. The conclusion points to the need for caution in generalizing from any study of selected denominations, including the National Council of Churches.

CLASS, CASTE AND CHURCH SEGREGATION

Inasmuch as the present sample included both the middle-class denominations affiliated with the National Council and the sects, drawn primarily from the lower-income and occupational categories, it has been possible to point up some class-oriented patterns of church integration. It was found that the integration of minority races was more likely to occur in churches where the majority of the members were of the same income and occupational class as the minority seeking admission. Further, in almost all cases cross-racial membership represented upward mobility for the minority member, seldom the reverse.

The volume of cross-racial membership in Des Moines, of

course, is very small amounting to a fraction of 1 per cent of the total membership of the churches in the sample. As such, there is very little use by Negro minorities of the predominantly white church as a vehicle for vertical mobility.

These findings are in accord with other research. They again reaffirm the almost universal characterization of the church as a conservative, change-resisting institution. Moreover, studies of religion and class structure have come to similar conclusions. In 1948, Pope examined the occupational composition of selected Protestant, Catholic, and Jewish congregations. He concluded:

There is little evidence that religion will operate in the near future to change American Class structure appreciably. . . Unless a drastic transformation comes about in the churches, they will probably continue for the most part to adapt to class divisions, and even to intensify them, as they have done in the past.[31]

The class differentials in vertical mobility found in this research were also noted by Greenblum and Pearlin in a study of prejudices of white, male non-Jews. In general they discovered that there is a maximum of prejudices among upwardly mobile persons who claim middle-class membership, "the group least secure about its status." [32] People of the middle classes, whether upwardly mobile or in that strata for a long time, were more willing to exclude Jews and Negroes, than upwardly mobile persons with working-class identifications. These findings about the dynamics of prejudice may help to account for the affiliation of Orientals with the middle- and upper-class white churches and never with the Negro. Further, they suggest that the substantial integration of Negroes in churches made up of persons with low-income occupations may be because these churches contain fewer upwardly mobile persons who would resist their entry. By the same logic, greater resistance to Negroes in the upwardly mobile middle-class denominations is expected and found.

[31] Pope, "Religion and Class Stratification," *Annals of the American Academy of Political and Social Sciences,* vol. 256 (March, 1948), p. 91.
[32] Joseph Greenblum and L. I. Perlin, "Vertical Mobility and Prejudice: A Socio-Psychological Analysis," in Reinhard Bendix and Seymour Lipsit, *Class, Status, and Power* (Glencoe, Ill.: The Free Press, 1953), p. 487.

SEGREGATION AS AN ECOLOGICAL-SOCIAL PROCESS

The finding by Loescher and Culver, cited above, of the relationship between the proportion of the minority and the likelihood of their inclusion in the group logically could be interpreted as supporting evidence of the ecological theory that there are impersonal, social, and competive forces that underly the organization of human life and its institutions. Moreover, this ecological-distributive force is, in the long run, a more potent determiner than such social factors as tradition, group decision, and group sentiments.

This view is one of the major themes about which there has been much controversy among human ecologists. The present research should be seen as one of the recent chain of empirical studies relating attitudes to ecological process.

The findings below indicate what some of these interrelations may be. In general, the author holds that the position that church size, location, and stability are external conditions which affect the decision of the congregation on racial segregation.

1. Where there are few members of the minority race living around the church, church desegregation is not seen as a crucial problem. Nevertheless there are crystallized attitudes on race relations policy.

2. Where there are growing proportions of the minority living near the church, there is greater likelihood of church-group decision on desegregation.

3. Where there are greater proportions of minority attending a church, there is greater likelihood of church decision on desegregation.

There is rather extensive evidence in sociological literature demonstrating that prejudiced attitudes have been overcome with more frequent contact among Negroes and whites. The frequency of contact, of course, is not solely the product of increased proportions of the minority. However, some researchers, such as Deutsch and Collins, are emphatic that a mere token representation of Negroes would not provide a sufficient amount of interracial contact necessary for change in attitudes.[33]

[33] M. Deutsch and M. Collins, *Interracial Housing* (Minneapolis: University of Minnesota Press, 1951), p. 55.

This evidence is directly contrary to the views of Loescher and Culver. However, it is fairly clear that desegregation is not unilaterally determined by an ecological force, but that there are many causes and conditions that affect the process.

INCONSISTENCY, GROUP DECISION AND DESEGREGATION

The study explored the relationships between national policy, the attitude of ministers, and local church practice. Incomplete data on the national position of sects prevented comparison with the denominations. Furthermore little recognition was given to difference in the degree of centralized control within the denominations in the sample.

In the available literature there is some evidence, especially in the Catholic Church, that national pronouncements opposing segregation are enforced locally.[34] Thus, the national pronouncement may be more effective in a highly centralized organization than in the church government which is representative or congregational and where the ties between national and local are voluntary and non-binding. This finding is in accord with desegregation in other organizations having a powerful top echelon, such as armed forces, unions, government, and industry.

The lack of congruence of policy between national and local Protestant churches in the present sample is not surprising, considering the relative lack of centralization of authority. Glock and Ringer in a study of 234 Protestant Episcopal congregations and their ministers also found a marked diversity of opinion on social issues within separate parishes and between the parish and the national church.[35] Where the minister was subjected to opposed view of national and local, he tended to support the national, especially where parishioner sentiment was relatively unsettled, as on the issue of desegregation. Glock and Ringer concluded that the national church is more receptive to social change than its parishioners.

[34] G. E. Simpson and J. M. Yinger, *Racial and Cultural Minorities: An Analysis of Prejudice and Discrimination* (New York: Harper & Brothers, 1953).

[35] Charles Y. Glock and Benjamin B. Ringer, "Church Policy and the Attitudes of Ministers and Parishioners on Social Issues," *American Sociological Review*, vol. 21 (April, 1956), pp. 148–156.

If these findings apply to denominations other than the Episcopalians, then it would help to explain the inconsistencies noted for the present sample.

We have seen that both denominations and sects follow the enduring, conservative patterns of segregation in voluntary groups. They are resisting trends that have occurred in many other spheres of life.

The sectarian minister, oriented to his local congregation, consistently follows the norm of this primary group, for segregation or against. The denominational minister may state that he is opposed to segregation and reflect the more progressive position of his parent body. But he may be under crossfire from his own congregation. Under controversy, his response is typical of persons lacking clear-cut norms in a stressful situation—he compromises, or withdraws from activity; *i.e.*, he does not raise the national position favoring desegregation with his local church.

This explanation of the inconsistency of attitude and practice of ministers has inferred that the minister's behavior rationally follows the norms of one reference group or another, his national church, local congregation or community, and that whatever inconsistencies there are flow from divergent group norms. However, it is an often noted characteristic of race relations attitudes that they are not always logical, consistent, and rational. This is an area in which prejudice, stereotyping, and mythology intervene to distort reality. It was beyond the scope of the chapter to investigate fully the relative effect of contradictory group norms as compared with distorted individual perceptions and beliefs. However, in the valid assessment of the relative importance of ecological factors in desegregation, both group norms and individual prejudices will need to be taken into consideration.

✳ 19. Social Stress and Mental Illness in the Community

E. Gartly Jaco

Introduction Increases in the incidence of mental illness have paralleled increases in the complexity and diversity of our communities with their concomitant social problems. Complexity and diversity of community life in turn imply for many individuals an increased potential for frustration in achievement of their desires or goals. Life is full of possibilities for frustration. Desired goals are scarce, and the means for attaining them are not equally present for everyone. Besides, man in the complex community is dependent and not independent. For instance, he may easily lose his job or even his family. No longer his own producer of goods or services, man has to rely upon others for his sustenance, and he works in an economic system where the spectre of unemployment is ever present. The contemporary family, reduced in size when compared to one of 1890, is largely held together by affection between its members and has lost many of its former functions or is sharing them with other institutions in the society. Thus, it is a small and fragile unit easily broken by death, early emancipation of children, separation or divorce of its members.

The social conditions of family disruption, loss of a job, isolation in a neighborhood, to name but a few, may produce, as psychologists suggest, social stress for some individuals. While there is no general agreement on the definition of social stress an individual affected by it is under duress, feels frustrated and blocked in achieving desired ends, and the customary social roles he plays are inadequate in the new and disruptive social situations. It has been hypothesized that social conditions described above may produce stress and trigger the onset of mental illness. This notion concerning social factors in the etiology of mental disease has been frequently suggested, perhaps extensively accepted, but not often tested by empirical research.

Professor E. Gartly Jaco in his chapter studies specifically the relationship of stressful social conditions to high and low rates of psychotic disorders, the more serious forms of mental illness. He does this with an interesting and unusual method. Retrospectively he determines the high- and low-rate areas for psychoses in Austin, Texas, by classifying according to census tract all first admissions of diagnosed functional psychoses to the local state hospital for the years 1940 through 1952. Once the high- and low-rate areas were determined a systematically random sample of residents within each area was chosen for interview. Eight hundred and twenty five interviews were conducted covering interaction patterns and the social conditions within the area. *Social isolation* was an important factor related to the high-rate communities. The amount of home-ownership which is often used as an index of *spatial mobility* was not found to be particularly related to the incidences of high-low functional psychoses found in these communities. *Occupational mobility, economic instability,* and *family dislocation* are other variables presented for discussion by Professor Jaco. The data suggest that these three variables (vertical and not horizontal mobility) were significantly associated with the lifeways of people living in the high-rate psychotic areas in contrast to those residing in low-rate communities.

The finding that more stressful life-conditions are found in high-rate than in low-rate areas strongly suggests that social factors are causally related to the onset as well as incidence of mental disorders. The specific role of stress in the etiology of mental disorder for any given individual case has not been analysed. This is a most difficult task, and another needed step in the study of social stress and mental illness in the community.

✳ Because of its pervasive presence, the community is a major source of mental health and mental illness for its inhabitants. The physical environment, the institutions, the modes of social interaction, and the social adjustment process that comprise the social milieu of the community combine to develop a set of circumstances that affects the risk of becoming mentally ill. That these conditions do not exist similarly in all communities is demonstrated by the differences found in incidence rates of mental disorder between various areas, such as urban and rural communities, and between ecological areas within urban communities.[1] Indeed, such findings were conceivably instrumental in the reconsideration of many biogenetic and psychogenetic theories which had omitted social factors in the etiology, or assignment of causes, of mental disease.

Despite the accumulation of considerable ecological research, the question as to which *social* conditions of communities are conducive to stress and instrumental in the onset of mental disorders is still largely unanswered. If stress is a causal factor in the onset of mental illness, then do communities exhibiting high rates of mental illness have a more stressful social milieu than low-rate areas? Specifically to what stressful social conditions are inhabitants of high-rate communities exposed that persons living in low-rate areas are not? This paper will attempt to supply some empirically determined answers to these questions.

SOCIAL ETIOLOGY OF MENTAL DISORDER

While no general consensus on the causation of mental disease yet exists, three rather nebulous groups of etiological factors have been differentiated: the biological, the psychological, and the social. The interplay of these sets of factors in the onset of mental breakdown is generally recognized.[2] One of the most promising recent developments has been the separation of what are termed "precipitating factors" from so-called "predisposing factors." [3] The former

[1] See Robert E. L. Faris and H. Warren Dunham, *Mental Disorders in Urban Areas* (Chicago: University of Chicago Press, 1939); E. R. Mowrer, *Disorganization: Personal and Social* (Philadelphia: J. B. Lippincott Co., 1942), chap. XV; C. Tietze, P. Lemkau, and M. C. Cooper, "Personality Disorders and Spatial Mobility," *American Journal of Sociology,* vol. XLVIII (July, 1942), pp. 29–39.

[2] For representatives of these three aspects of etiology, see Ernest W. Burgess, "Social Factors in the Etiology and Prevention of Mental Disorders," *Social Problems,* vol. 1 (October, 1953), p. 53; Franz J. Kallman, "The Genetics of Psychoses: An Analysis of 1,232 Twin Index Families," *American Journal of Human Genetics,* vol. 2 (December, 1950), p. 390; A. H. Maslow and B. Mittelmann, *Principles of Abnormal Psychology,* revised edition (New York: Harper & Brothers, 1951), chaps. 10–12.

[3] Such a distinction is used, among others, by Burgess, *op. cit.;* Mabel A.

are regarded as consisting of those factors which accelerate or "trigger-off" the onset of the disorder, while the latter are composed of those factors which present a susceptibility, tendency, or predilection toward acquiring the breakdown.[4] This is an elaboration of the etiological process of stress-induction and reaction to stress by persons incapable of coping therewith.

Social conditions are usually designated as precipitating factors while the biogenetic and psychological aspects of personality makeup may be classified as predisposing factors.[5] However, theoretical difficulties arise when this distinction is pursued to its logical end, and one finds himself involved in the antiquated group-versus-individual dilemma. It is worthwhile at this point to present a brief summary of generally accepted theory on the etiology of mental disorder in terms of these two categories of factors.

Every socialized individual is *potentially* a mental case. As an organism, he has physical limitations to the tensions he can withstand. This limitation applies to human *populations* as well as individuals, and thereby there is a predisposition for group mental breakdown. But the community also contains groups whose systems of values and interaction processes within the ecological setting comprise additional sources of stress and strain that can contribute to mental breakdown of human *collectivities, i.e.,* interacting members of society.[6] Such primary groups within the community as the family, play-groups, and peer-interaction groups can predispose to mental stress of an individual through their contributions to the

---

Elliott and Francis E. Merrill, *Social Disorganization,* third edition (New York: Harper & Brothers, 1950), pp. 281–284; James D. Page, *Abnormal Psychology* (New York: McGraw-Hill Book Co., 1947), pp. 86 ff.

[4] Rennie has defined these factors as follows: *Predisposing factors* refer "to the conditioning factors in the early years of life . . . that comprehensively shape what has been called the individual's basic personality. . . ." *Precipitating factors* refer "to those situational conditions which . . . can operate as sources of strain so severe as to precipitate psychopathological disability." (*Op. cit.,* pp. 213 ff.)

[5] See Burgess, *op. cit.,* p. 54; E. G. Jaco, "The Social Isolation Hypothesis and Schizophrenia," *American Sociological Review,* vol. 19 (October, 1954), p. 568.

[6] For a recent discussion of social stress and illness, see Leo W. Simmons and H. G. Wolff, *Social Science in Medicine* (New York: Russell Sage Foundation, 1954), chaps. 4–5.

socialization process of their younger members as well as through the demands imposed upon the responsible actors who maintain such groups. The community's formal social institutions other than the family, such as the school, church, political, economic, and recreational structures, may provide stress for its inhabitants. The social structure of the community in terms of its roles and statuses supply further potential sources of stress.

Both populations and social structures thus possess elements predisposing its members toward mental illness. Consequently, one's chances of acquiring a mental disorder are significantly affected, depending upon the extent that these conditions predispose toward mental aberration and depending upon one's physical constitution and the extent of his interaction in the social milieu. In this manner, organic capacities and deficiencies along with social circumstances operate simultaneously in developing predilections or tendencies toward mental illness for human populations and for individuals within social systems.

A *predisposing population* contains inherent biogenetic and emergent psychogenic deficiencies that set different internal limits on the development of defenses against stress and tension for its human organisms. A *predisposing social milieu* is that which causes such internal limits of populations to be reached or exceeded more frequently by its incumbents in the process of interacting in or being exposed to that system than would occur in other social systems. A social system can predispose to mental breakdown by putting a high number of traumatic pressures on an individual who interacts in and maintains his identity in that system. In meeting the responsibilities and requirements of a social role, for instance, the role-player may be required frequently to cope with situations that create anxiety, tension, and stress. In performing a role over a long span of his life in a social organization containing excessive stress-elements, by continually being forced to meet these stress-situations, that system may predispose him and others to a mental breakdown. That is, the individual becomes susceptible or "set up" for the eventual "straw that breaks the camel's back," for the final precipitating event that "triggers off" a mental breakdown. A predisposing population and social system, therefore, possess a large quantity of *potential* precipitators, *i.e.*, stress-inducers, for a large portion of its members. It must be emphasized that these stress-inducers are latent in the individual and intrinsic in the social system and *in themselves* may not induce stress.

Social precipitating factors (or "precipitators") are *elements* in social acts of which an individual becomes aware by being required, compelled, or obliged to adapt to. This accelerates a demand on him to adjust or readjust and thereby induces stress. Added to this may be a failure to develop ways for preventing or relieving stress-reactions in a socially acceptable manner. *Personal precipitating factors* involve the perceptive ability and "psychological set" of the personality which affect a person's *reactions* to stress (stress-re-actors). These reactions are in terms of his own defenses.

In terms of social psychology, when predisposing elements of the social system confront a predisposed member of the population with a crisis, threat, or disturbing force to his self or ego which demands simultaneously a reaction from him that he is unable or inept to cope with in terms of his defenses, a stressful reaction is precipitated. These elements may serve as sources of rationalization. He may attempt to suppress them from his conscious thoughts; he may try to avert stress by projecting his problems on to others with hostility or by creating anxiety in his own method of "prevention." This can lead to (1) a *loss* of personal identity ("anomie"), (2) a *confusion* of identity (ambivalence, cultural conflict), or (3) a *distortion* of identity (inappropriate responses, hallucinations, delusions, fantasies, grandiosity).

Another important aspect of this theory is that according to it predisposing factors affect populations and total society without reference to the individual identity of any particular person in that population or social system. Precipitating events apply to specific individuals in the population, who interact in and react to the social system, and both the population and social system contain predisposing elements internal and external to the person. It is when the two conditions are combined in a particular individual that the person acquires the mental disorder. The mental aberration, thus, is the consequence of the person's mode of reaction to social and personal predisposing and precipitating forces. Theoretically, the rate of mental disease can potentially be 100 per cent for a population, but this never occurs because no population is entirely predisposed toward mental breakdown nor no social system entirely predisposed to stress and tension for its members. It is the difference in the frequency of such predisposition and precipitators in populations and social systems that together account for different rates of mental disease between groups, communities, regions, subcultures, and societies. A suggested conceptual outline of the total etiology of mental illness is presented in figure 18.

Predisposing Factors—Intrinsic Stress Processes

SOCIAL:

Precipitating Factors—Stress Elements *(Stressors)*

Precipitating Factors—Perceptual and Attitudinal Elements of Personality *(Reactors)*

PERSONAL:

Predisposing Factors—Bio-Psychogenic Susceptibilities

Figure 18.   Conceptual Outline of the Total Etiology of Mental Illness

The interplay of social and personal predisposing and precipitating factors can be illustrated in the marriage institution. In our contemporary society, marriage conventions allow the individuals involved to choose their marital partners. Such choices often run the risk of error, leading to frequent conflict between spouses who may not have made a happy choice. Disparities in the socio-cultural backgrounds of the marital partners often may, for instance, make a harmonious marital adjustment difficult. Separation or divorce may eventually result. Such action may precipitate a mental depression in one of the marital partners. The marriage system may be viewed as the social predisposing factor, while the divorce or separation can be regarded as the social precipitating event. The conjugal marriage system may thus predispose to a greater frequency of mental illness in the population than another type of marriage institution in that it may contain more elements of stress which contribute to a higher incidence of broken marriages.

On the other hand, not everyone obtaining a divorce becomes mentally ill, in that not every individual reacts to social stress in the same manner or degree. It is at this point that the personal predisposing and precipitating factors become relevant as causes. The varied makeup of individuals may not always adequately prepare every individual similarly to withstand the stresses of the marriage institution or its breakup. An inadequate nervous system of the human organism and an individual's unsuccessful early conditioning in the home in the development of a self-identity are regarded as personal predisposing factors. Certain attitudes toward others, toward marriage and divorce, certain perceptions and evaluations of stressful experiences may precipitate a psychiatric disorder in that individual, a disorder that others would be able to defend their self-identity against.

Consequently, an explanation of social etiology, apart from personal etiology, is sufficient when it has accounted for those factors affecting a significant portion of a population, group, or collectivity. If the sociologist determines that the divorced exhibit a significantly higher rate of mental disorders than the married or other types of marital status, then he has obtained sufficient data for a theory or explanation of social etiology for this segment of society. His analysis is actuarial, concerned primarily with rates, and not in isolating factors that predict the individual case. From the point of view of personal etiology, that is, an explanation is insufficient until it has accounted for the factors affecting a specific individual's mental disorder. Thus, social etiology is necessary but not sufficient to explain how an individual in a population, or group, becomes mentally ill. Conversely, personal etiology is not sufficient to account for those factors comprising the social etiology of mental illness in that the individual has only a limited impact on his social structure and institutions.

The province of sociological inquiry into mental disorders can be feasibly confined to social etiology—the viewing of stress in the actuarial sense with applications to populations or collectivities and predictions in terms of incidence rates for communities, groups, and role-incumbents. Psychiatrists and psychologists, on the other hand, adopting a perspective more closely approximating the clinical approach, engage in studies of personal etiology in attempting to explain how specific individuals acquire mental disorders in terms of their experiences in the social environment, their reactions to their environment, and their abilities to cope with problems of life with which they, as individuals, are confronted. Their joint inquiries into social and personal etiology thus mutually contribute to the total etiology of mental illness.

THE COMMUNITY AND MENTAL DISORDER

The community is viewed as providing a setting in which an array of social forces operate as significant variables in influencing the behavior of its inhabitants which in other communities, or in the same community at a different time, may not exert the same influence. The economic role of a profession, for example, may affect the status of its incumbents differently, say, in a New England community than its incumbents in a Southwestern community. Dwelling in an apartment house may not impose the same social relationships for an occupant of a large metropolis as it would for a resident of a small town. By the particular composition and juxtaposition of social roles, status-relationships, and other components of social organization, the community provides a social milieu peculiar to itself. The community's structure, whether a product of so-called subsocial processes or cultural values, becomes an autonomous social universe, which furnishes a range, depth, and interpretation of human experiences for its occupants which may not exist to the same degree and kind in other communities within the same society. Consequently, social factors found to induce stress in some communities may not do so in other communities.[7]

[7] A major purpose of an earlier inquiry was to test the universality of the ecological pattern of distribution of mental disorders found in cities. Since such studies had been confined to commercial-industrial types of urban communities, a replication was made in a political-type city. The "typical" pattern of the highest rates being in the central business district and decreasing toward the periphery was not found; this suggested that when the ecological base of a

The family and other primary groups in the community may be viewed as mediating influences between its members and the community's social forces. These groups can either soften the frequently harsh impact of the larger community's forces or stand aside and allow their members to feel the full weight of such influences. Secondary groups are also mediating factors in the individual's relationships with the community. The socialization process whereby an individual becomes a social being is also affected by the community environment and the community's mediating groups. The combination of forces involving the ecological base, the mediating social groups, and the socialization process of the community, thus vitally influence personality formation and its healthy or ill functioning.

When the sociologist says that a particular community predisposes toward mental disorder, he is referring to the existence of stress-inducers in that community. By residing in that community, the individual is running the risk of encountering stressful conditions more than if he lived elsewhere. If he is internally predisposed to mental breakdown, then his chances of mental aberration are even greater. Continued interaction in the area may eventually confront this person with a stressful event that upsets him to the extent that his self-defenses are no longer capable of resistance and recovery, and it precipitates a mental breakdown. In this manner the links can be made between social and personal etiology in mental disorder and an attempt made toward explaining the total etiology of mental disorders.

In terms of this conceptualization of etiology, a harmonious interdisciplinary relationship between the social sciences and psychiatry can be achieved, provided that representatives of the different disciplines are content to confine their contribution to a *part* rather than the whole. Sociologists need not feel dissatisfied if their theories do not explain how every individual mental case occurs while psychiatrists and psychologists need not include the social system in their explanations of personal reactions to stress. A

community varied, the distribution of mental disorders also varied. Another implication was that the pattern found by Faris and Dunham is typical of only the commercial-industrial type of city. See Belknap and Jaco, *op. cit.*

sufficient explanation of total etiology of mental disorder must in-corporate as necessary parts the predisposing and precipitating factors of both social and personal etiology.

PURPOSE OF THIS STUDY

Functional psychosis is the major grouping of serious mental disorders whose etiology is generally regarded as involving en-vironmental elements. The purpose of this study is to determine if certain characteristics of the social life of inhabitants of communities exhibiting high rates of functional psychoses (schizophrenia and manic-depressive reactions) differ significantly from those living in communities having low rates of these disorders. Or, are more functionally psychotic individuals exposed to potentially stress-inducing conditions in their community than those in other areas which generate fewer such mental cases? Furthermore, what are some of these stressful community conditions?

If the findings provide some satisfactory answers to the above questions, then the next logical step would be to study patients with a functional psychosis to determine to what extent they were ex-posed to such social stress factors and thus to what degree this affected the onset of their illness. Before such factors, however, can be held as personal causal agents of these disorders, the de-termination must further be made of (1) the differential "exposure" to these conditions of persons with functional psychoses, and (2) the degree of tolerance (immunity) or susceptibility of persons to react stressfully to such conditions. This latter endeavor, however, lies beyond the scope of this chapter.

The study of mental patients' backgrounds *alone* may help to reveal much of the sources of their particular stress-reactions. But at the same time other persons may not react stressfully as these patients to similar conditions, and other patients may react stress-fully to social conditions that other patients do not. Not everyone reacts to stress similarly, even if such conditions are a part of their "definition of the situation." Therefore, to establish *general* social conditions in the community to which all mental patients and non-patients are exposed, potential or actual, is held to be of value in understanding further the social etiology of mental disorder.

THE HYPOTHESES

Stresses engendered in the community by social relationships and conditions to which individuals susceptible to mental breakdown are exposed are involved in many dynamic theories of the functional psychoses. Social conditions that are considered to be potentially stressful, therefore, constitute the types of factors that are sought in communities exhibiting high and low rates of these disorders. These conditions and hypotheses about them are as follows.

1. *Social isolation.* The pathogenic effects of social isolation have long been recognized and described, particularly in connection with the onset of schizophrenia, the major functional psychosis.[8] Isolation, however, might feasibly be involved in the background of other types of functional psychoses, such as the manic-depressive psychoses, since the reactions to reduced social contact might take many aberrant forms.[9] Cameron and Magaret have offered the term "desocialization," which may be regarded as a consequence of social isolation. They define desocialization as being "a reduction in the social articulation of behavior, resulting from the partial or complete detachment of an individual from participation in the activities of the social community."[10] In this anonymous state, the individual is cast adrift in the community without benefit of the stabilizing and socializing forces available to others who are active participants in community life. He may occasionally attempt to restore relations with others in a compulsive manner and, if failing, might become extremely depressed and suicidal. Other reactions to isolation could encompass such mental states as the "paranoid

[8] For some studies discussing the disorganizing influences of social isolation, see E. Durkheim, *Suicide* (Glencoe, Ill.: The Free Press, 1947); Faris, "Cultural Isolation and the Schizophrenic Personality," *American Journal of Sociology*, vol. 39 (September, 1934), pp. 155–169; H. W. Zorbaugh, *The Gold Coast and the Slum* (Chicago: University of Chicago Press, 1927).

[9] A certain amount of isolation was indicated in the adolescent backgrounds of manic-depressive patients in a recent study. See Melvin L. Kohn and John A. Clausen, "Social Isolation and Schizophrenia," *American Sociological Review*, vol. 20 (June, 1955), pp. 268–269. It is also likely that other modes of deviant behavior may be reactions in some degree to social isolation.

[10] Norman A. Cameron and A. Magaret, *Behavior Pathology* (Boston: Houghton Mifflin Co., 1951), p. 481.

pseudo-community," [11] or self-indulgence in autistic daydreams, distrust, aversion, fantasy-thinking, and overt hostility.[12] Isolation, therefore, may render stressful the performance of social roles in the community, make status-relations nebulous and disruptive, and contribute to a possible loss, confusion, or distortion of personal identity.

In defining social isolation as a condition in which contact with others is at a minimum, the question still remains as to what elements in social interaction may be singled out as particularly conducive to isolation. With no ready measurement of social isolation available, the following array of factors, amenable to enumeration, are given as provisional criteria of social isolation.

Anonymity is offered as a plausible element of social isolation. If a person knows none of his neighbors' names and has no friends or acquaintances, he can feasibly be regarded as leading a relatively isolated existence in the community. These conditions are stated in the form of null hypotheses, as follows.

There is no difference between the inhabitants of high- and low-rate functionally psychotic communities in (1) knowledge of the names of their neighbors, (2) estimated number of their personal friends, and (3) estimated number of their acquaintances.

Low frequency of interaction with other communities may reveal a lack of contact with other persons not living in proximity. Some characteristics of such reduction in interaction are contained in the following null propositions.

There is no difference between the occupants of areas of high and low rates of functional psychoses in (4) the number of visits with friends during the past month, (5) number of visits to other areas of the city in the previous month, and (6) number of visits out of town during the past year.

Low frequency of participation in groups and institutions may

[11] Cameron, "The Paranoid Pseudo-Community," *American Journal of Sociology*, vol. 49 (July, 1943), pp. 32–38; reprinted in Arnold M. Rose ed., *Mental Health and Mental Disorder* (New York: W. W. Norton & Company, Inc., 1955), 180–189.

[12] For a recent discussion of some reactions to isolation, see S. Kirson Weinberg, *Society and Personality Disorders* (New York: Prentice-Hall, Inc., 1952), pp. 226–228.

be an indication of social isolation. Failure to participate in an occupational group or to belong to certain voluntary associations, to participate in the larger community by voting, or to belong to a church are encompassed in the following null propositions.

There is no difference between the residents of high- and low-rate functional psychotic communities in (7) membership in professional organizations or labor unions, (8) membership in lodges or fraternal organizations, (9) the amount of voting in national and city elections of a previous year, and (10) active church membership.

In sum, social isolation is postulated as a potentially stressful condition. Indications of the existence of this condition are hypothesized in the form of anonymity, low frequency of interaction with other communities, and low amount of social participation.

2. *High spatial mobility.* A high frequency of shifts in places of residence minimizes opportunities for establishing enduring social contacts and stable relationships with others in the community. Such a condition is postulated as conducive to stress in the form of a rootless, disruptive existence, which may be tested by the following null propositions.

There is no difference between the inhabitants of high- and low-rate areas of functional psychoses in (11) the number of persons renting or owning their places of residence (assuming that renting rather than owning one's abode indicates potentially higher mobility on the part of its occupants), (12) the number of times moved within the city, (13) number of places lived before migrating into the city, and (14) length of residence in present abodes.

3. *Occupational mobility.* Contemporary urban society places a high value upon upward vertical mobility, the achievement of a social position higher than one's status given at birth through the family of orientation.[13] For males, such achievement is accomplished in the urban community primarily through his occupation while for the female the customary channel of upward mobility

[13] Sociological literature abounds with this postulate, with particular reference to the "middle-class ethos." See, for instance, W. Lloyd Warner, *American Life* (Chicago: University of Chicago Press, 1953), chap. 5; and Robert S. and Helen M. Lynd, *Middletown in Transition* (New York: Harcourt, Brace & Co., 1937), chap. 2.

is marriage. Failure to achieve a higher status can be therefore considered as potentially stressful.[14] What Warner has called "blocked mobility," [15] or, more extremely, the occurrence of loss of status through downward mobility, is regarded as another instance of social conditions conducive to stress. Horizontal mobility also may be considered as stress-inducing. The pressures of new demands, responsibilities, norms, and personalities caused by a shift in affiliation that may or may not accompany vertical mobility can feasibly enhance tensions.

A common procedure for analyzing differential mobility is the comparison of occupational levels of father and son. By amplifying this intergenerational method to encompass a contrast of occupational statuses of husband, his father, and his wife's father, the dual effects of vertical mobility upon both the male and female can be studied simultaneously. Occupational mobility will be examined here in two ways: horizontally, by shifts in occupational "situs" [16] and vertically, via changes in occupational prestige scores, by the key members of families of orientation and procreation.

Horizontal mobility will be indicated for high- and low-rate areas by (15) shift in occupational situs of husbands from that of family of orientation, (16) shift in situs of wives from that of family of orientation, (17) shifts to specific situses among those husbands shifting, and (18) shifts to specific situses among those wives shifting. Downward occupational mobility will be indicated by (19) sons now engaged in lower prestige occupations than their fathers, and (20) daughters marrying husbands with lower prestige occupations than their fathers.

4. *Economic instability.* Since economic values are esteemed extremely highly in the urban community, successful performance of economic roles and maintenance of a stable position in the eco-

[14] These implications, among others, are discussed by Talcott Parsons, *Essays in Sociological Theory* (Glencoe, Ill.: The Free Press, 1949), chap. 12, and by A. B. Hollingshead and F. C. Redlich, "Social Stratification and Psychiatric Disorders," *American Sociological Review*, vol. 18 (April, 1953), p. 164.

[15] Warner, *op. cit.*, pp. 117–121.

[16] Situs can be described as a relatively distinct and homogeneous hierarchy of occupational "families." See P. K. Hatt, "Occupation and Social Stratification," *American Journal of Sociology*, vol. 50 (May, 1950), pp. 533–543.

nomic institution are important to self-esteem. Failure to meet these sanctions are viewed as conducive to stress. The degree of economic instability is tested in terms of two propositions: (21) amount of unemployment, and (22) work instability as indicated by the number of jobs husbands have held.

5. *Family dislocation.*   One possible product of stress-situations in families may be reflected in the number of stepbrothers and stepsisters in the family of orientation and of stepchildren in the family of procreation. The presence of offspring of marital partners who are not members of the immediate family may create stress on the part of both siblings and parents who have to care for them. Furthermore, their presence is also an index of broken and "repaired" homes, especially through divorce. The employment of women may also be a source of potential stress for members of the family group. The husband may covertly resent his wife's working as casting reflection upon his status in the family through his inability to provide adequately for their needs. The working wife may frequently find herself in an ambivalent situation induced by the conflicting demands of her economic and family roles. The children may lack adequate parental support and attention due to the absence of their mother during the working day.

Differences in the degree of family dislocation between the high- and low-rate psychotic communities will be determined by the following propositions: (23) number of stepbrothers and stepsisters in family of orientation, (24) number of stepchildren in family of procreation, and (25) number of employed women.

Tested in the form of null hypotheses, the amount of rejection of the above twenty-five propositions at statistically significant levels would indicate the prevalence of the stress conditions engendered by social isolation, high spatial mobility, horizontal and downward vertical occupational mobility, economic instability, and family dislocation in communities with high incidence of the functional psychoses.

PROCEDURE

First admissions to a locally situated state mental hospital who were residents of the city of Austin, Texas, during the period of

1940 through 1952 constituted the basis for determining the high- and low-rate areas of the functional psychoses (schizophrenia, affective, and involutional psychoses). As in the case of typical ecological studies of mental disease, census tracts of the city constituted the areas for which rates of incidence of the three psychoses to be studied were calculated. Austin in 1950 had fifteen census tracts wherein 132,459 people resided. For the thirteen year period, 668 persons were found to have been actual residents of the city of Austin at the time of their commitment for a mental disorder to the local hospital. Of these persons committed, 112 (16.8 per cent) were diagnosed as without psychosis.

Rates of incidence for this period for the functional disorders, standardized for age and sex, were then computed for each of the city's fifteen census tracts. After the determination of the differential rates of functional psychoses by census tracts, the four tracts having the highest and the four with the lowest rates were selected as the communities to be studied. The standardized rate for the high-rate areas was nearly five times greater than for the low-rate areas.

A pretest of a series of questions designed to secure information on interaction patterns of the residents of the high- and low-rate psychotic communities was first accomplished before final interviewing was conducted. A random sample was systematically drawn from every other block in each of the eight census tracts composing the high- and low-rate psychotic communities. Both open-ended questions and a check list of other items were employed in the schedule. A few of the questions which were open-ended in the pretest were later re-ordered into a check list of categories of response. The sequence of many of the questions was altered to present the less intimate and more formal items at the beginning and the more personal and intimate toward the end as the informant "warmed up" in the interview. Each interview averaged from thirty to forty minutes. Chi-square tests of significance were computed to determine the probability of any differences being due to chance, with the customary 5 per cent level of confidence being selected as the basis for rejection of the null hypotheses.[17]

[17] See chap. 17, page 339.

FINDINGS

1. *Social isolation.* All three of the null propositions indicating lack of an anonymous existence for the inhabitants of the high-rate communities were rejected at high probability levels. Residents of these areas showed significantly less knowledge of their neighbors' names and had lower estimates of the numbers of their personal friends and acquaintances than those in the low-rate areas (P = .001).[18]

Occupants of the high-rate areas were also found to have visited their friends less, visited other parts of the city less, and visited out of town less than those residing in the low-rate areas, all of which indicates less social interaction (P = .001). Significantly less social participation in several spheres was also found for the residents of the high-rate over the low-rate areas, as indicated by less membership in occupational groups, lodges, or fraternal organizations, and in voting (P = .001). No difference was found in the amount of church membership.

Consequently, with the rejection of nine out of the ten null hypotheses dealing with social isolation, this factor can be regarded as a significant characteristic of communities exhibiting high rates of the functional psychoses.

2. *Spatial Mobility.* The amount of home-ownership has often been held as an index of stability, and a low degree of spatial mobility by ecologists, while a large proportion of renters would indicate high, potential or actual, spatial movement. This was not found to be the case in this inquiry and thus demonstrates the risk of ecological analysis which omits necessary social correlates. Occupants of the high-rate areas rented their homes significantly more than owning than those in the low-rate areas (P = .001), but the former had moved no more nor less than those in the low-rate communities, had lived in significantly *fewer* places before migrating into the city, and had a significantly *longer* length of residence in present abodes than those living in the low-rate areas (P = .001). Thus, while occupants of the high-rate communities rented their homes more than those in the low-rate areas, such a factor was not

[18] *Ibid.*

related to high spatial mobility in this particular city. Furthermore, inhabitants of the high-rate areas demonstrated an unexpectedly lower degree of spatial mobility than their counterparts in low-rate psychotic areas. Spatial mobility, consequently, cannot be regarded as particularly related to these functional psychotic communities.

3. *Horizontal occupational mobility.* The procedure used in testing this hypothesis was to determine if a significant amount of shifting in occupational situs took place between the present generation of husbands and their fathers, and husbands and their wives' fathers. No significant shifting in occupational situs between either the husbands' or wives' families of orientation and procreation occurred between the present generations living in the high- and low-rate psychotic areas. Hence, hypotheses 15 and 16 cannot be rejected. However, a further analysis was made of those who had shifted their status from the family of orientation to procreation. In the high-rate communities, significantly more husbands shifted to the service and manual work situses and less to the professional and business situses than husbands in the low-rate areas (P = .001). For the wives, no significant shift to the service situs was found, but significantly more shifting to the manual and less to the professional and business situses was found in the high-rate over the low-rate communities (P = .001). Therefore, although the overall frequency of horizontal occupational mobility did not differ significantly between the areas, the direction of such situs changes between the families of orientation and procreation was significant.

4. *Downward vertical occupational mobility.* The prestige ratings of occupations were obtained from the North and Hatt scale.[19] Ratings of occupations not included in their scale were extrapolated on the basis of their situs and related jobs whose score was known. The precise value of these prestige ratings, however was not a decisive factor in establishing downward movement since comparisons were made only in their gross form. Disparities greater than five points in the prestige scores of the scale in a downward direction were counted as downward mobility of son over father. A significant amount of downward vertical occupational mobility was found between the families of orientation and procrea

[19] Reprinted in Reinhard Bendix and Seymour Martin Lipset, eds., *Class, Status, and Power* (Glencoe, Ill.; The Free Press, 1953), pp. 412–414.

ion for both husbands and wives in the high- and low-rate psy-
hotic areas (P = .001). Thus, both parents residing in the high-rate
ommunities were found to have lost more prestige in moving from
heir families of orientation to that of procreation than those living
n the low-rate areas. These results are consistent with the findings
oncerning shifts in situses of both parents in the high-rate com-
nunities. Less shifting into the professional and business situses by
ccupants of the high-rate psychotic areas seems congruous with
he significantly greater amount of downward vertical mobility of
he inhabitants of these communities. These findings become espe-
ially important in view of the fact that these same subjects had
ignificantly less spatial mobility than their counterparts in the
ow-rate psychotic areas. The so-called "drift hypothesis" attempts
o explain high rates of psychosis as the product of in-migration of
sychotic or potentially psychotic persons, especially those who are
ownwardly mobile, into areas exhibiting high incidence of these
isorders. These data, however, reveal an extreme lack of correlation
etween spatial and social mobility.

5. *Economic instability.*   Inhabitants of the high-rate psychotic
ommunities were found to have significantly more unemployment
nd a higher frequency of job-changing than those in the low-rate
reas (P = .001). While the connection between these findings and
he existence of downward mobility is not certain, it is likely that
he two factors are related.

6. *Family dislocation.*   The prevalence of stepbrothers or step-
isters was postulated as an indication of disruption in the family of
rientation, while the existence of stepchildren was assumed to be
n index of dislocation in the family of procreation. Significantly
nore families of orientation and procreation possessed children of
lifferent parents in the high-rate than in the low-rate psychotic
reas (P = .001). Also significantly more women were employed in
he high-rate than in the low-rate communities (P = .001).

UMMARY AND CONCLUSIONS

The existence of six spheres or clusters of social conditions,
ostulated as conducive to stress among the inhabitants of areas
xhibiting high- and low-rates of functional psychoses were tested

by twenty-five null hypotheses. With the rejection of twenty-one (84 per cent) of these propositions, doubt was cast upon only two of these areas. High spatial and horizontal occupational mobility were not found to be significant social traits of the occupants of high-rate functional psychotic areas. However, social isolation, downward vertical mobility, economic instability, and family dislocation were found to be significantly associated with the living circumstances of persons residing in high-rate psychotic communities in contrast to those inhabiting low-rate areas.

The conclusion that persons living in communities with high rates of mental disorder encounter more stressful life-conditions than those who reside in areas with low rates seems warranted by these findings. In terms of the conceptualization proposed in this chapter, these circumstances are regarded as predisposing factors in the social etiology of these mental disorders. Furthermore, while there may be differences in ecological factors between areas of different rates of mental disease, unless such ecological data can be supported by associated social and interpersonal conditions, their possible influence upon the social etiology of mental disorders seems limited.[20]

Communities whose inhabitants have little social interaction are inclined to be downwardly mobile, economically unstable, and are characterized by disrupted families. They can conceivably be viewed as predisposing their residents to stress. The forces in the community that bring about these stressful social conditions are still in need of further investigation, however. Such inquiries, accompanied by the findings of this study, would be useful in mental health action programs in the community. The application of social etiological research is particularly strategic in the realm of prevention. If stress is found to be induced by certain social conditions in a community, then the eradication or reduction of such conditions would be the major objective of a sound mental hygiene program. If the forces in the community that bring about social isolation, downward vertical mobility, economic instability, and family dislocation are alleviated, then, in terms of the conceptualization and

---

[20] For a discussion of this problem, see E. G. Jaco, *Some Factors in the Social Etiology of Mental Disorders* (Ann Arbor, Mich.: University Microfilms 1954), chap. 1.

findings of this inquiry, the incidence of the functional psychoses might also be expected to be concomitantly reduced. Specific research to test this outcome, however, is still needed, since other social conditions not included herein may also be involved in the social and personal etiology of these psychiatric disorders.

Although this inquiry has revealed significant stress factors in the social environment of persons living in communities of high incidence of mental disorder, the specific connection between these factors and personal etiology of functionally psychotic patients is still undetermined. At least three major factors must be taken into account before the prediction of an individual's becoming functionally psychotic under these circumstances can be accurately made: (1) degree of differential exposure of individuals to these life-conditions, (2) the differential modes of reaction to these conditions, and (3) degree of susceptibility of persons to mental breakdown under these stressful circumstances. These factors of *individual* prediction involving personal etiology were beyond the province of this particular inquiry. However, if one assumes, theoretically at least, that these three individual factors are constant in the population of an area, then those communities whose inhabitants possess a high degree of social isolation, downward social mobility, economic instability, and family dislocation should exhibit higher incidence rates of the functional psychoses than those communities where these conditions exist to a significantly lesser extent.

Community Change

* 20. Urban Impact on a Rural Township

Vincent H. Whitney

Introduction   Two basic approaches used in community analysis are the aggregate and the particularistic. The first approach utilizes census type data such as those on sex, age, race, ethnicity, and mobility, which usually can be quantified. The collection of data from a number of communities permits a summarizing view of community structure and population characteristics. Professor Bell in chapter 3 utilizes such a method (social area analysis) in the study of Los Angeles communities.

The particularistic approach is similar to a case study. While lacking the standardized indices of the aggregate approach, it has the definite advantage of permitting the observer to probe into the workings of a single community and to search for an explanation of recorded events. The community structure, people, and problems become alive, and an intensive analysis of community processes becomes possible. Both approaches are necessary in the building of community theory. The accumulation of particularistic studies results in a more detailed comparative analysis of communities which can be shown to fit into the same general categories. Taken with the aggregate studies, it will allow some measurement of the range of variation of a given type of community such as the industrial village or residential suburb.

Professor Whitney's study of Smithfield, five miles from the mall of Providence, Rhode Island, is a particularistic analysis of a township in transition from a farm area to a limited-industry community to a bedroom extension of urban Providence. What effect do the newcomers to Smith-

413

field have upon the rural way of life? Is the transition producing conflict between individuals and between groups? Under what conditions? Professor James showed in chapter 8 that many residents in Riverville, a community suffering from a flood, became dissatisfied with their town and their neighbors. Where crisis is not present as in Smithfield, but where rapid change and unstable conditions do exist, will there be widespread discontent with the community as a place to live and raise a family? These are a few of the questions Dr. Whitney asks about the town he has studied.

Professor Whitney's paper includes the history of the community, its industrial activity and changes since 1900 and the commercial, business, and residential use of the area. He has interviewed a random sample of newcomers to Smithfield on why they settled in Smithfield and how they feel about their location, services, and neighbors. What reasons do you think Smithfield in-movers gave for settling in that community? What would you suppose was their age, place of work, place for shopping, and source for medical services? What were their major complaints?

This case study has many important and valuable observations. One in particular is that the degree of conflict between newcomers and oldtimers in a community is related to the size of the in-moving group. If the group is homogeneous, *e.g.* in terms of class and the sharing of similar ideologies and values, and if it is relatively large, then its members are likely to act in concert in order to obtain desired goals. Then again, the old-time residents of towns and suburbs may not be completely opposed to aims of the in-migrants, especially if both share to some extent values related to the improvement of the community.

Smithfield is an example of a common type, the specialized residential suburb in a metropolitan area. It has become what it is because of population growth and mobility, the continuous specialization of industrial processes, personal services, and business and commercial operations, and the development of enlarged networks of communication and transportation—all features of the age of specialization. Thus Smithfield's residents are dependent upon others for the very necessities of survival. Smithfield's experience is probably a prototype of changes and adjustments other towns are undergoing on the fringes of our cities known as suburbia.

✳ SUBURBANIZATION can be studied either as an aggregate or as a particularistic phenomenon. The first approach makes it possible to describe suburbs as a whole or a broad sample of them at a fixed moment over a long time span in terms of available quantitative data. As in any other approach, the degree to which the data procurable can provide insight into the problem under analysis is limited by the research design.

The aggregate approach is capable of providing an overall view of such average or grouped characteristics of suburbs as population size, migration patterns, or numbers of formal associations, items which can be expressed in quantitative terms. Major limitations lie in (1) the relatively small number of characteristics for which data are readily available, especially for a series of communities, and (2) the inability of the investigator to derive from such data more than a partial understanding of the nature and mechanics of the suburbanization process.[1]

Limitations inherent in this method are, of course, equally real for the particularistic approach. Here the emphasis is on a comprehensive description and analysis of one, or, at best, of a limited number of units which are taken arbitrarily from the total units of the given type. In this kind of study of suburbanization, conclusions can seldom be generalized, since it is rarely possible to specify the degree to which the communities analyzed are representative of the universe of communities to which they belong. Even a standardized typology of communities is lacking. Thus, the individual deviation which is depicted in the particularistic study cannot be spelled out; there is no existing norm or pattern to which variation can be related. In any strict sense the findings are valid only for the isolated unit described since differences in method, in the form in which the data are presented, or in the character of the units investigated usually make rigid comparisons impossible. Moreover, where the cases observed are only a minute fraction of all possible cases, coincidence of findings may reflect merely chance observation of units which deviate similarly from the majority of existing units.[2]

[1] This is clearly demonstrated by the kinds of conclusions I was able to reach in another paper which employs the aggregate approach in utilizing data for the more than three thousand separate counties in the United States. See Vincent Whitney, "Rural-Urban People," *American Journal of Sociology*, vol. 54 (July, 1948), pp. 48–54.

[2] In the present study two findings, not reported on further, were (1) that residents of Smithfield are, with few exceptions, well satisfied with their place of residence (except for rising tax rates) and that (2) lack of a home vegetable garden is not significantly associated with a less satisfactory adjustment to the

In order to understand a structure, like a community, or a process, like suburbanization, studies of both average tendencies and of individual variation are required. The two approaches compliment one another. The particularistic approach has the advantage of permitting a more intensive study and analysis of a local area by utilizing wider sources of data such as unpublished local reports or field interviews. Because the research worker gains familiarity with the community as a whole, he is less likely to fail to interpret his data or to interpret them erroneously. Ultimately, accumulation of such particularistic studies is necessary to the construction and modification of adequate theoretical statements.

The materials presented in this chapter are particularistic. They are strictly applicable to a single town (Smithfield, Rhode Island) in a single Standard Metropolitan Area (Providence).[3] The advantages and disadvantages of concentrating on one suburban community are those already indicated for the particularistic approach. Conceptually, it is assumed that the metropolitan area and the suburb surveyed are described by generally accepted definitions of the "metropolitan community," which emphasize the interdependence of functionally specialized communities grouped around an integrative and adminstrative center.[4] The general assumption

---

local community. The first conclusion agrees, the second disagrees, with the carefully established findings of Martin in his studies of the Eugene-Springfield fringe area. (Walter T. Martin, *The Rural-Urban Fringe, A Study of Adjustment to Residence Location* [Eugene: University of Oregon Press, 1953], pp. 67–68, 74, 77.) It is only guesswork whether either the agreement or the disagreement is related to similarities or differences in the methods employed or in the size or internal characteristics of the areas involved. We do not know how much the likes and dislikes of people in the fringe of two small Pacific Coast cities correlate with those of people in a suburban township in a middle-sized New England metropolitan community.

[3] The process of suburbanization in several other towns in or adjacent to the Providence Standard Metropolitan Area is being studied. Initially it appears that differences between Smithfield and these other communities are principally related to the degree and rapidity of suburbanization. The impact on local social organization of persons moving in from central cities has been described elsewhere and is in general correspondence with the findings for Smithfield. *Cf.* N. L. Whetten and others, *Studies of Suburbanization in Connecticut* (Storrs: Connecticut Agricultural Experiment Station, 1936–1939).

[4] Amos Hawley, *Human Ecology* (New York: The Ronald Press Company, 1950), chap. 13.

underlying the study was that over time specific local events alter the structure of a community and the needs of residents. Specifically, it seemed likely that the shifts in population and in employment which have occurred in Smithfield in recent years had altered the ability of the town to operate according to traditional "rural" patterns and had required adjustments to a conception of the town as a suburb and as an integral part of a metropolitan area. The study began with the hypothesis that such a transitional stage would produce identifiable conflict between individuals and between groups of residents and that rapidly changing and unstable local conditions would yield widespread dissatisfaction with the town as a place of residence.[5] One final assumption was made—that the patterns of change and of adjustment to change found in Smithfield would broadly characterize many other towns on the periphery of metropolitan areas, smaller communities which have in the last decade or two experienced a substantial increase in residents moving from urban centers.[6]

HISTORICAL DEVELOPMENT

Smithfield is a township of 28 square miles located 5 miles northwest of the business center of Providence at its nearest point and 12 miles at its most distant. Its shape is roughly that of a square with its southeastern corner closest to Providence, the state's largest

[5] See Martin, *op. cit.*, pp. 15–20, for a discussion of the hypotheses of accessibility and of sociocultural influences tested in his study of the Eugene-Springfield fringe.

[6] Something of the rapidity of growth in such areas is indicated by the following figures. In the five years from April 1950 to April 1955 the civilian population of the United States grew by an estimated 11.8 million persons. Of this number 11.5 million were added within Standard Metropolitan Areas. The rate of growth in the central cities was only 3.8 per cent compared with a rate of 27.8 per cent for the remainder of the area. That part of the metropolitan population classified as urban grew 19.1 per cent while the rural sector increased by 46.5 per cent. (*Current Population Reports*, "Civilian Population of the United States, by Type of Residence, April 1955 and 1950," Department of Commerce, Bureau of the Census, Washington, D.C., Series P-20, no. 63 [November 2, 1955], p. 1.) Several studies have emphasized the tendency for more rapid growth to occur in the communities and fringe areas on the periphery of the metropolitan areas than in the central cities or in the communities immediately adjacent to them.

city and capital, which has a population of approximately 250,000 persons. About 4 per cent of the land area is sufficiently built up to be included in the Providence Urbanized Area as defined by the 1950 Census. The entire township is included in the Providence Standard Metropolitan Area, which in 1950 had a total population of 737,203.

Historically, general farming has been the mainstay of the town's economy and the principal source of employment for its

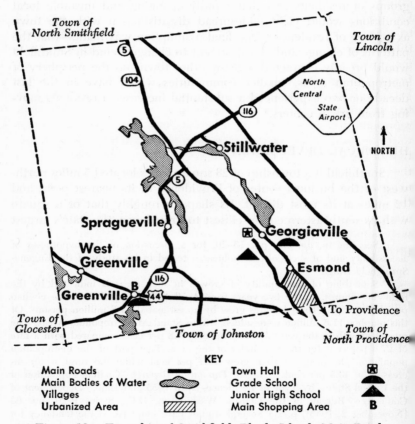

KEY

Main Roads	▬	Town Hall	⊞
Main Bodies of Water	◌	Grade School	◣
Villages	○	Junior High School	▲
Urbanized Area	▨	Main Shopping Area	B

Figure 19.   Township of Smithfield, Rhode Island: Main Roads
and Built-Up Areas

esidents. As early as the period of the American Revolution some f this farm produce was sold in Providence and in the mill communities of the Blackstone Valley. Another source of income, of increasing importance after the first part of the nineteenth century was employment in the mills, principally textile, which developed rapidly throughout the northern part of the state. As early as the 820's a small minority of the town's residents were industrial workers living in mill villages. But far more common was the practice of one or more sons or daughters of farmers taking jobs in the mills.[7] This served as a means of reducing underemployment on arms where the number of children was greater than that required to continue farm operations. And undoubtedly the cash wage and the relative independence it implied appealed to many farm youth more than work on the farm under family direction and with its rewards largely in kind.[8]

The early importance of industry in Smithfield [9] is indicated by two actions of its citizens. In 1827 the town's voters instructed their representatives in the General Assembly (*i.e.*, the state legislature) to try to obtain a law taxing cotton and woolen machinery in operation in the various towns of the state.[10] And ten years later in 1837, they presented a petition to the Assembly to take note of their population growth (then estimated locally at 8,000 persons) by allotting the town additional representatives. In this petition they called attention to the fact that "in the early settlement of the town we were almost exclusively an agricultural people" but argued "at the present time the pursuits of the citizens are extended to a greater

[7] *Cf.* Hannah Josephson, *The Golden Threads* (New York: Duell, Sloan and Pearce, Inc., 1949), p. 62; and Thomas Russell Smith, *The Cotton Textile Industry of Fall River, Massachusetts* (New York: King's Crown Press, 1944), . 36.

[8] Percy Wells Bidwell, "The Agricultural Revolution in New England," *American Historical Review*, vol. 21 (July, 1921), p. 700.

[9] At this period (1820–1840), the township of Smithfield included what are now the townships of Lincoln and North Smithfield and a portion of the city of Woonsocket. Industry was of greatest importance in territory now included in these other townships but was not lacking in the area which is present-day Smithfield.

[10] Thomas Steere, *History of the Town of Smithfield* (Providence: E. L. Freeman and Company, 1881), p. 65.

variety of occupations than almost any other town in this state." [11]

The first mill within the limits of present-day Smithfield was the plant of the Georgia Cotton Manufacturing Company, which developed the village of Georgiaville and began operation in 1813. In nearby Stillwater Village a small cotton mill was in operation in 1824. Although it burned several times, it was always rebuilt and a contemporary observer speaks in 1867 of the "fine woolen mill and model village" there.[12] In the same year, in addition to these two plants, a textile mill and a hosiery mill were operating in Sprague-ville, and there were four mills in Greenville in the southwestern corner of the town. One of these was a "large manufacturing plant" for heavy team wagons. The other three were textile mills. Two of these were woolen mills employing 200 persons and manufacturing 420,000 yards of cloth annually.[13]

Around the mills a group of small villages developed. Here the principal services, public and private, ultimately located. By the third quarter of the nineteenth century an estimated 20 to 25 per cent of the population lived in them and was employed in the mills. Other workers settled nearby both to service the mill workers and to gain easier access to the facilities developing in some of the villages. Still, Smithfield remained primarily a farm community although sales to the nearby cities were inducing specialization, particularly in dairy products and fruits and vegetables. The greater part of the town was in woods or farms.

Until after World War I, Smithfield remained a semi-independent community whose people were for the most part farm operators or hands or who were employed in local mills or in those in adjacent communities. And it was only after World War II that Smithfield became aware of problems growing out of an influx of new residents from the metropolitan centers of the state.

CONTEMPORARY CONDITIONS

Today Smithfield consists of three separate small villages with limited industrial and local commercial functions, and of open

---

[11] Petition of the Citizens of the Town of Smithfield to the General Assembly of the State of Rhode Island and Providence Plantations (1837). State Library, Providence.

[12] Steere, *op. cit.*, p. 131.   [13] *Ibid.*, p. 130.

country dwellings. Most of the latter are the nonfarm homes of commuters to urban jobs in Providence and, to a lesser extent, in other satellite communities in the metropolitan area. These homes are located principally along the main highways in continuous ribbons with lesser concentrations along the secondary roads. About 4 per cent of the land area, nearest Providence, as mentioned before, is sufficiently built up to be included in the Providence Urbanized Area as defined by the 1950 Census. Extensive platting is occurring in the southwest corner of the town on open land much of which was formerly used for farming. Farms have declined steadily in number in recent decades but a few are still being operated, chiefly as dairy farms or as apple orchards. These are almost entirely in the hands of long-established local families. Part-time farming is not common, and only an estimated 20 per cent of the nonfarms homes have vegetable gardens despite the fact that outside the village clusters there is ordinarily sufficient room. Much of the land area in the eastern and northern sections of the town is in woods, but lumber operations are few and products are mostly for home use.

The economic base of the town has undergone a radical change. Agriculture has experienced a long-range decline. Its present importance in the town's economy is negligible despite the fact that a small number of highly successful commercial farm operations still are maintained.

Less well understood is the parallel but more recent decline in the importance of industry within the town. In the nineteenth century the hilly topography and numerous small streams were inducements for the location of textile plants, which were sizeable in comparison with the local population and which offered employment to a considerable fraction of the local labor force.[14] The decline of the textile industry in the Northeast has had a drastic impact in Smithfield. Only two mills are still operating. One is a finishing plant and the other a yarn mill. Both are long-established but small plants hiring fewer than 500 and fewer than 100 workers respectively.[15] Over half their employees are residents of other communities. There are a few other small enterprises engaged in the production of such items as machine tools and mine safety ap-

[14] Kurt B. Mayer, *Economic Development and Population Growth in Rhode Island* (Providence: Brown University, 1953), p. 33.

[15] In 1951 the Rhode Island Department of Labor reported that one textile

pliances. But in terms of the total of local employment they provide and the proportion of town taxes which they pay, Smithfield's industries are of negligible importance.

Until the late 1940's Smithfield retained one relatively large textile plant, the Esmond Mill, manufacturing the nationally-known Esmond blankets. For many years this single plant accounted for one-third of the tax revenues of the town. Since its liquidation its building has been partly vacant and partly occupied by a succession of small operations yielding relatively little in the way of taxes. Meanwhile, a rapidly increasing population and an equally rapid rise in town expenditures have produced a situation in which even the establishment of another plant comparable in size to the Esmond Mill would produce at best only an estimated five to seven per cent of needed tax revenues rather than the 33⅓ per cent of the 1920's and 1930's. At the time the Esmond Mill closed, the total taxable property in the town was valued at $8,000,000. In 1955 it was approximately $20,000,000. So only a large plant, employing a minimum of a thousand workers, would be capable of providing any sizeable share of the new tax needs.

Retail establishments are increasing steadily in response to the growing population and through traffic. Along the main highways a variety of businesses have appeared, the majority since 1948. These range from ice-cream stands, restaurants, and filling stations to drive-in theatres, TV and electric sales and repair shops, marine supply stores, and lumber yards. The major shopping center at Greenville has become too small in area and zoning changes have made possible the erection of a new business block and the breaking of ground for a large chain supermarket to replace a small store of the same firm.

Such changes, however, are only reflections of the basic change influencing the function and character of the town, that is, the rapid increase in population which has taken place since the war. In 1930 the population of Smithfield was 3,967. By 1940 it had increased moderately to 4,611. By 1950 it had risen far more sharply to 6,690, with the greatest gains in the second half of the decade.

---

plant operating in Smithfield employed over 1,000 workers. See Earl C. Tanner, *An Introduction to the Economy of Rhode Island* (Providence: Rhode Island Development Council, 1953), p. 127.

By 1955 the population was estimated at between 8,500 and 9,000 persons. If this rate of increase is maintained through the decade, the annual rate of increase will fall between 5.4 and 6.9 per cent in comparison with an annual rate of increase of 4.5 per cent between 1940 and 1949 and of 1.6 per cent from 1930 to 1939.

This rapid increase in population is primarily attributable to in-movement associated with the outward extension of the urban-industrial nucleus centered in Providence and the suburban drift of urban-oriented persons. This in turn is a movement which has been facilitated by speculative real estate operations involving moderate-priced houses. Since the early 1940's housing construction has boomed in the town. There were over five times as many residential building permits for the years 1945 to 1954 as for 1935 to 1944.[16] The movers have for the most part been young married people. This has contributed to a moderately high rate of natural increase which has constituted an important but secondary factor in the population growth of the town.[17]

THE IN-MOVERS

To supplement town records and interviews with 11 town officials, a sample of 104 households, randomly drawn within each of 4 arbitrarily designated areas covering the entire township, was established. Each residence shown on the most recent Geological Survey map was numbered, and Tippett's table of random sampling numbers applied.[18] To provide an opportunity to include residences built since publication of the map, the dwellings drawn were not the ones at which interviews were carried out. Rather, following a pattern, interviews were conducted at the house next to the one drawn, or the fifth next house, or the tenth next house, on or off

[16] Compiled from town records.

[17] The number of births to town residents in 1945 was 102 and in 1954 was 152. The crude birth rate thus actually declined from 18.2 to 17.7. The number of deaths in 1945 was 44 (a crude rate of 7.9) and in 1954 was 88 (a crude rate of 10.2). Deaths in 1954, however, include those of persons in three convalescent homes, many of whom are non-residents.

[18] *Tracts for Computers,* arranged by L. H. C. Tippett (London: Cambridge University Press, 1927), no. 15.

the same side of the road, in rotation. This made it possible to sample houses within the newer plats.[19] By conducting interviews at various hours of the day and evening, it proved possible to obtain the information on the household schedule for 101 of the families. The consistency of the responses suggests that some confidence can be placed in the replies as general indications of the characteristics of the town's residents, their reasons for settling in Smithfield, and their response to their location. Unfortunately, there can be only a partial summarization here, and these data are for only a portion of the items on the schedule. Moreover, they are only for the 69 families which have moved to Smithfield within the last ten years. Consequently, these replies must be considered as suggestive rather than as definitive.

Of the 69 families moving in, the mean age of the husbands was 32 years and that of the wives 29 years. The group averaged 1.9 children. Slightly over 80 per cent had moved into an available house, either new or used, rather than building their own. All of the in-movers were nonfarm families. Over three-fourths of the husbands and wives had been born in the Providence Standard Metropolitan Area, and the majority of these (nearly 75 per cent) were at birth residents of what is now the Providence Urbanized Area. The remainder had come from other parts of Rhode Island, New England, and as far as New Orleans, Chicago, and England. Almost all had lived in the Providence Urbanized Area before resettling in Smithfield.

Only one of the in-movers was employed in the town. The remainder worked overwhelmingly in Providence, with a scattering among other cities and towns in the metropolitan area. There was a tendency for a higher proportion of in-movers in the northern, southern, and eastern parts of town to come from communities in those directions, although this trend was weakened by the location of the principal urban areas to the southeast.[20] Towns to the

[19] Additional interviews were conducted in these plats to check trends, but these households were not included in the sample.

[20] Dewey found that in Milwaukee County, Wisconsin, "migration to unincorporated towns comes from urban areas which are nearest to them rather than from any single area." Richard S. Dewey, *Residential Development in the Unincorporated Areas of Milwaukee County, Wisconsin* (Milwaukee: Milwaukee County Regional Planning Department, n.d.), p. 9.

west are less urban than Smithfield and apparently provided few in-movers.

Because they are not judged to be sufficiently accurate, income figures for the in-movers will not be given here. However, both the occupations of the husbands [21] and the types of residence suggest that the middle-income range predominates overwhelmingly. Many husbands are skilled factory workers, salesmen, or office workers. There are a few young professional men and a few who operate their own businesses. Almost all drive to work in private cars. For most parts of town this is a necessity because public transportation is either limited or non-existent. No one reported such commuting to be objectionable.[22] Some wives expressed a desire for bus service to give them increased personal mobility.

The reasons given for moving to Smithfield were similar to those found by other observers for suburban moves but were more concentrated.[23] Respondents mentioned chiefly a desire for country living and room for both adults and children. Typical replies were "We wanted peace and quiet"; "to get away from noisy neighbors"; "to have a nice yard and a flower garden"; and "to bring up the kids right." In contrast to some previous reports, neither lower taxes nor better schools was cited as a reason for moving. Many families did want a single-family dwelling, however, and found it hard to locate one in Providence where only 18 per cent of the dwelling units are detached houses.[24] The principal reason given for selecting the specific house in which the family now lived was its availability at the time the family wanted to move and the fact that it fitted the family's generalized conception of what was desirable. In eight

[21] In 85 per cent of the families interviewed, only the husband was employed. In two families the husband was not living and the wife was employed full time.

[22] Actually, the majority of the respondents were wives who necessarily were reporting here on what they believed to be the attitudes of their husbands.

[23] William R. Gordon and Gilbert S. Meldrum, *Land, People, and Farming in a Rurban Zone* (Kingston: Rhode Island State College AES Bulletin 285, 1942), pp. 23–24; Earl L. Koos and Edmund deS. Brunner, *Suburbanization in Webster, New York* (Rochester: Department of Sociology, University of Rochester, 1945), p. 35; Dewey, *op. cit.*, pp. 16–17, and Martin, *op. cit.*, pp. 37–38.

[24] *Census of Housing, 1950,* Department of Commerce, Bureau of the Census, Washington, D.C.: vol. 1, part 5, pp. 39–45, table 17.

cases land was already in the family and was given to younger members for building.

Smithfield offers only a limited range of services, and most families indicated that they ordinarily went out of town to shop, even for groceries.[25] Providence was the overwhelming choice for items other than groceries, including recreation. Smithfield has a doctor and a dentist, but the in-movers preferred to use the services of men to whom they went "in the city." As one woman put it, "Smithfield is a perfect place to live, but only because we can get everything we need nearby."

No respondent expressed any plan nor desire to leave Smithfield. There was general satisfaction both with specific neighbors and with "the kind of people who live in town." Association occurred primarily with other persons in the immediate vicinity and was largely informal in character as well as severely restricted in numbers. This arrangement appeared highly acceptable to the great majority of families interviewed. More formal participation occurred principally through the local Parent-Teacher Associations and in occasional membership in service clubs or fraternal orders.

The major complaint of all residents, whether newcomers or not, was the steady rise in the tax rate. In-movers frequently had an additional complaint, that their properties were over-valued in relation to those of residents of longer standing. There appear to be some objective grounds for such a charge since it is easier to enter new properties on the tax rolls at relatively higher valuations than to raise the valuations of properties which for some time have enjoyed comparatively low estimates of worth. On the other hand, in-movers do not always understand that woodland and pasture and even orchards and grazing land cannot be valued at the same level as their small lots and houses. Additional complications are introduced by the fact that the assessors, as in other towns, are politically appointed and lack special training for their jobs. They were occasionally accused of feeling that property was less valuable when it was owned by a friend or a man known to vote right. Moreover, valuations are made by "driving down the road," a method which can produce wholly equitable results only by accident. Here is an area where both actual inequalities and misunderstanding are

[25] A large chain supermarket was about to have been erected in the southwestern part of town and may have altered grocery-buying habits there.

producing some degree of conflict between older and newer residents. This is aggravated by the feeling of some older residents, reported also in other studies,[26] that the newcomers are out to bankrupt them by insisting on services which they view as unnecessary—school improvements, sewer systems, town-wide street lighting, improved roads, and so on.

Aside from the tax-services question, no important areas of conflict were found between longer-time and newer residents. The presence of in-movers as PTA officers and on town boards is now apparently accepted although some resistance is reported to have occurred in the war and immediate postwar years. This is probably inevitable in view of the increasing numerical dominance of the newer residents. There are still individuals who grumble and attempt ineffectually to resist any transformation of the town's centers from "old New England villages" to more efficient planned service areas.[27] The existence of planning and zoning boards are in themselves indications of a new order. On the other hand, antiquated plumbing and building codes and the lack of authority for the town to control plat development are indications that Smithfield is far from adequately prepared for the influx of population it is receiving.

CHANGES IN SERVICES AND COSTS

The rapid increase in the population of Smithfield in recent years has had its most pronounced effect on the fiscal level. Both new services and the provision of existing services for larger numbers of persons has been costly. In 1943 the town appropriated $142,730 for its total operations. In 1954 the amount had risen to $399,065. Total appropriations for 1955 exceeded $490,000.[28]

On nearly every budgetary item the upward curve of expend-

[26] Henry W. Riecken, Jr. and Nathan L. Whetten, *Rural Social Organization in Litchfield County, Connecticut* (Storrs: University of Connecticut AES Bulletin 261, 1948), pp. 65–66.

[27] Cf. N. L. Whetten and E. C. Devereux, Jr., *Windsor: A Highly Developed Agricultural Area* (Storrs: Connecticut State College AES Bulletin 212, 1936), pp. 134–138.

[28] All figures in this section are from the *Town of Smithfield Year Book* for the years referred to except for 1955 data, which were obtained from town officers.

itures shows a close parallel with the curve of population growth.[29]
One illustration, which directly reflects changing demands for service, involves expenditures for police protection. Prior to 1938 Smithfield was content to appropriate the modest amount of $500 a year
for this service. This was used to pay a part-time officer, who was
available on a catch-as-catch-can basis. In 1938 the town placed
this man on full-time duty and bought him a car, which he also used
to peddle eggs and vegetables according to one informant. Police
appropriations jumped to about $2,500 where they remained through
1947. Since then they have risen steadily, and in 1954 police service
cost the town $19,080. A chief and three other full-time officers,
assisted by a number of trained part-time officers, maintain twenty-
four hour coverage throughout the town. Two radio-equipped
cars are owned and operated, and headquarters are maintained in
the town hall.

Similarly, appropriations for the volunteer fire department,
which averaged $3,000 a year up to 1940, amounted to $13,500 in
1954 and $15,400 in 1955. Highway costs have shown a similar
trend, skyrocketing since 1944. Road and bridge work in 1954 cost
slightly under $42,000, of which $5,000 represented state aid. An
elected highway commissioner was paid $3,800, and other expenses
of the Highway Department amounted to an additional $17,222.
The total cost to the town of the Highway Department for the year
was therefore over $58,000, which represented an increase of sev-
eral hundred per cent over average annual costs before World
War II.

As in other communities, the largest single item in the town's
expenses is for schools. Rounded appropriations for the School Department are shown in table 34.[30] Increased salaries for teachers
and other department employees, higher out-of-town tuition for
high school students, and a rise in transportation costs and in the
cost of supplies have all contributed to the need for ever-larger
appropriations. The single most important contributing factor,
however, is the rise in school population.

[29] Part of the increase is, of course, attributable to a rising price level.

[30] Total expenditures are higher than the appropriation for any given year
because state assistance and certain other revenues are allowed for. In 1954
state aid to Smithfield for schools was $34,418.69.

Changing enrollments are shown in table 35. For the postwar years the impact of in-movers on the town's schools is clearly revealed. What is not shown is the demand for more and better schools which has been widespread since the number of in-movers from the city has mushroomed. This demand has resulted in the construction of a modern but already overcrowded junior high school and the purchase of land for a high school. Until 1955 Smithfield had neither type of school. The impetus for building has come directly from in-mover families, but the junior high school, at least, has received general community support as an obvious need.

Table 34. Town Appropriations for Schools, Smithfield, Rhode Island

YEAR	APPROPRIATION (ROUNDED) *
1930	$ 48,000
1945	75,000
1950	160,000
1954	211,000
1955	240,000

Source: Town records, Smithfield, Rhode Island.
* These are operating figures and exclude all costs for school construction.

Table 35. School Enrollments, Smithfield, Rhode Island, 1930–1954

	ENROLLMENT			PERCENT CHANGE IN ENROLLMENT FROM PREVIOUS DATE		
YEAR	GRADES 1–8	GRADES 9–12	ALL GRADES	GRADES 1–8	GRADES 9–12	ALL GRADES
1930	875	99	974	..	..	..
1940	764	186	950	−12.7	+87.9	−2.5
1945	523	192	715	−31.5	+3.0	−24.7
1950	696	231	927	+33.1	+20.4	+29.7
1954	1,048	322	1,370	+50.6	+39.4	+47.8

Source: School Department records, Smithfield, Rhode Island.

If there had been little or no in-movement to Smithfield in the last decade, costs of government would necessarily have risen. At the same time, it is clear that the magnitude of the increases in all major categories reflects the pressure of rapidly rising numbers and the expectations of the majority of in-movers whose urban orientation has accustomed them to a kind or quality of service which longer-time Smithfield residents do not view as essential or, in some cases, as even desirable. At the same time, the decreasing importance of agricultural and industrial functions and the rise of the residential role of the town make it a foregone conclusion that the town's residents must increasingly pay their own way. Persisting dreams of industrial development and continued expressions of shock at the steady rise in taxes on personal property indicate that this is not clearly understood by all townspeople.

CONCLUSIONS

Ecologically, Smithfield's changing function is made possible—perhaps inevitable—by its position as one of a network of interdependent urbanized communities integrated within a metropolitan pattern. As the friction of space has been minimized by efficient transportation and communication,[31] the specialization which is a corollary of interdependence has become accentuated. Such local specialization is itself a function of complimentary specialization, that is, of the presence of nearby communities which emphasize industrial and commercial activities and offer services and employment to Smithfield residents. The changing character of the town is a reflection of its altered relations with its urban neighbors.

In a general way Smithfield has its counterparts in every metropolitan area. The impact of the urban center upon each can be measured in part in terms of the rapidity of in-movement and the homogeneity of the in-movers, particularly as the latter characteristic suggests the existence or lack of certain dominant attitudes and behavior patterns. The aggregate size of the in-movers relative to that of the group of longer settlement appears to affect adjustment by speeding up or delaying acceptance of the newer residents and their life-style. If the new group is relatively large and fairly homogeneous, it will presumably be more capable of concerted action to implement its wants. Its power is thus a political reality,

[31] Hawley, *op. cit.*, p. 237.

and realities demand ultimate acceptance. That the newcomers to Smithfield were a large group and homogenous appears to be one important factor in promoting the working adjustment of the old and new groups and in minimizing lengthy conflict.

Another factor has been the long-time influence of the urban centers on the thinking and behavior of the town's residents. The gap between the attitudes of the newer and older residents is hardly profound. In other words, the wants of the in-movers are entirely comprehensible to the older residents. That similar or even identical wants can be created for many of the latter group is demonstrated by their rapidly increasing support for the junior high school project, an innovation first sought by the in-movers.

Smithfield's experience suggests that the provision of urban-level services and conveniences for largely residential suburban communities will inevitably increase living costs for local residents. Greater understanding of this economic reality may possibly promote the movement for integrating local areas into larger legally defined metropolitan cities with a broader tax base and avoidance of duplicating municipal offices.

In summary, the story of Smithfield is one variation on a common American pattern, the transition of a rural town into an urban one. Originally it was a relatively independent farming community. At an early period industry supplanted agriculture as the principal economic function. Now declines in the textile industry and, more importantly, the growth and spread of a metropolitan population, have again shifted the function of the town. It is important only as a specialized residential suburb dependent upon adjacent communities for jobs and services. In the process of transition the newer residents have brought urban conceptions of what the community requires for "the good life." These are altering traditional, more conservative, patterns of community action. But as the small town becomes increasingly absorbed in the wider urban community, there is litttle lasting conflict apparent. Similarly there is little indication of dissatisfaction with the new suburb as a place of residence. What differences of opinion there are are mostly economic—how fast to try to tax for services that most residents apparently concede are at least desirable. A few older residents, of course, resent the physical changes that have followed the growth of population—the end of village tranquillity, the development of plats, the closing of lands that used to be open for hunting and fishing. It seems likely that the newcomers' urban trait of avoiding too close relations with their townsfolk and preferring to continue their association with old acquaintances in the city may itself have contributed to an orderly transition.

✳ 21. Urban Personality— Reconsidered

Svend Riemer

Introduction   Are contacts between urban residents principally of a primary or secondary nature? Can human relationships in the city be introduced by the fostering of primary group relations (ultimate face-to-face relationships)? Are primary group relations sought out by the urban dweller? Does cohesion between people increase or decrease with degree of urbanization? Are there differences between men and women in the number of neighborhood contacts each group has? These are a few of the questions raised, studied, and discussed by Professor Svend Riemer in the chapter which follows.

Professor Riemer's basic approach was to measure "neighboring." Neighboring is the number of social contacts a person has in his neighborhood, and in this research the neighborhood is the city block. Measures of neighborhood cohesion were obtained for various city blocks scattered in different sections of the urban area.

Dr. Riemer's analyses indicate variation of the neighboring process. Women tend to neighbor more than men, and children neighbored even more than women. Men on the other hand have extensive contacts outside the neighborhood. Professor Riemer also finds that the number of social and commercial contacts decrease as the distance from the family home increases. The availability of good transportation such as family automobiles affects the rate and magnitude of social contacts beyond the neighborhood.

Professor Riemer rejects the distinction between primary and secondary group life to explain the differences between urban and rural personality. In its place he offers the concept of "tertiary group." The tertiary group is related to social processes and institutions. Persons in the urban environment become loyal to and identified with some on-going social process or institution. Thus, a person may favor a bond issue or support a reform government movement; he may be loyal to a shopping center although he may not know a single person in it or very few. The attachment is emotional rather than rational. Thus, the tertiary group meets an individual need for identification but does so anonymously and not intimately as required in the primary group relationship. Tertiary groups may be a "middle road" between primary and secondary group relations. They minimize the necessary commitment in the latter and avoid the small group of the former. They offer the participant a feeling of identity with a community or neighborhood and interaction with others on a "take it or leave it alone" basis. How useful the concept of the tertiary groups will be in explaining group relations of the urban community awaits empirical verification.

❋ IT HAS BEEN ASSUMED that rural social contacts are mainly made up of primary group contacts, while urban contacts involve secondary group affiliation. Social reality—particularly as far as urban living is concerned—is far more complicated than that. Secondary contacts in the strict sense of the definition do not prevail in the city, but neither have primary group contacts reached sufficient numerical importance to place their stamp upon the personality of the city dweller.

Since the beginning of urban sociology in this country, it was often shown that the personality of the city dweller deviates from that of the person living on the farm or in the village.[1] The difference has been explained, though only plausibly by different patterns of social contacts prevailing in the city and the country. Primary contacts were said to prevail where the relationships between people were intimate and of the "face-to-face" variety. Secondary contacts, on the other hand, were of a very different nature and concerned only with the segmentalized social roles of a personality involved in a specific purpose and that purpose only. These contacts were of a more rational but also of a more segmentalized nature. Only part of the personality of the city dweller, it was assumed, was ever engaged in the social contacts characteristic for him. A

[1] Robert E. Park, et al., editor, *The City* (Chicago: University of Chicago Press, 1925).

peculiar kind of urban "freedom" seemed to come into its own wherever the city dweller was involved mainly with social contacts of the secondary type.[2]

Sociologists have often maintained that the more undesirable features of social organization were found more frequently in the city than in the country, because the behavior of the city dweller is characterized by segmentalization and prevailing secondary group contacts.[3] Informal means of social control break down that work anywhere else. People do not keep each other in line where they do not know each other well. They cannot know each other well in the city because of numbers. How many people it takes for urban anonymity to prevail is difficult to determine.[4] Greater numbers, however, are more frequently found in the large, dense, permanent and heterogeneous settlements which we have come to view as characteristic of all cities.

Under the circumstances, it has often been assumed that the city dweller is more prone to divorce or delinquency because of his peculiar contact pattern. He is left alone by friends and neighbors who do not keep him well in line and who do not exert social controls upon him meticulously and stringently as would be the case in an open-country environment. The remedy for social disorganization in the city has been seen as the transfer of village living to the metropolis. More exactly, improved social controls were expected by a transfer of primary group relations to the city environment.[5]

Early exaggerations, to be sure, have been sloughed off. Of late, however, there has been considerable curiosity among sociologists about primary group relations in the city and secondary group

[2] About the new kind of "urban freedom" in the modern city, different from that granted in the Middle Ages, see Svend Riemer, *The Modern City* (New York: Prentice-Hall, Inc., 1952), pp. 228–229.

[3] Rural and urban differences of social control are discussed by Joseph S. Roucek, *Social Control* (Princeton: D. Van Nostrand Co., Inc., 1947), pp. 68–73.

[4] For reasons hard to explain the adequate number of people among which primary group pressures can still be exerted is considered five thousand people in the United States and ten thousand in Great Britain.

[5] For a discussion of primary group controls in the city, see Judith Tannenbaum, "The Neighborhood: A Socio-Psychological Analysis," *Journal of Land Economics,* vol. 24 (November, 1948), pp. 58–369.

relations in the country. There have been careful investigations of whether secondary group relations predominate in the city or whether primary group relations tend to predominate in the country. In neither case is a 100 per cent relationship found to exist of just secondary group contacts in the city and primary group contacts in the country.

This chapter maintains that the undesirable features of city living cannot be modified by the introduction of primary group contacts into the city and by strengthening them. City living invites a behavior more fugitive than that induced by secondary group relationships only. In the city it is easy to escape from too close a social supervision. If the city dweller does not like it in a cohesive neighborhood characterized by close "primary" group relationships, he has only to move away from the neighborhood. As we know, he could not do so in the country, in the small town, or in the middle-sized town. We observe, in the country, a compulsion toward primary group relationships completely missing in the social environment of the modern city.[6]

Our research has the purpose of showing that primary group relations are not sought out by the city dweller. In fact, while he may come to the city for economic reasons, he may also want to escape the close social controls imposed upon him in a farm or small-town environment. Sometimes he comes to the city for very definite reasons if a case of divorce or delinquency has occurred; but more often he comes because he aspires to a free urban way of life. There has been no attempt in the following to demonstrate motivation. This could be done with an opinion poll. These studies have been concerned entirely with the manner of urban association where all the constraints of "planning" are entirely missing, where, as in the business world, laisser-faire dominates the relationships between people who, under free competition, are allowed to shift for themselves.

RESEARCH

Following a tradition of old standing, the attempt was made to establish behavioral facts about the "personality" of the city dweller

[6] See Svend Riemer, "Villagers in Metropolis," *The British Journal of Sociology,* vol. 2, no. 1 (March, 1951), pp. 31–43.

and to draw inferences from them about his personality. In this manner, it became unnecessary to find out anything about the "typical" motivation for people as a whole in the city. Such motivation might not be found relevant to a particular personality type at all. It is far more objective to deal with observable facts. It is certainly more valid if the facts of group life are given, and if it is then left to the investigating scientist to infer the "personality" of the city dweller.

The investigations tried to show that the city dweller—even in modern times—shows no inclination to limit his social or commercial contacts to a walking-distance area surrounding his family residence. He strays far beyond the locality of his own home for social contacts outside the family. The investigations were an attempt to ascertain empirically what, without empirical proof, has long been accepted as indubitable truth.[7]

The investigators became interested in establishing the pattern of social and commercial contacts in the city. Study of these contacts has so far been neglected in empirical research, but the subject is important, especially since the re-establishment of the primary group in the city is often looked upon as a remedy for all the typical urban evils. The question has arisen whether city dwellers—left to themselves in an era of free movement—show any propensity at all to make the walking-distance area around their home an area of neighboring surmounting in importance for them the rest of the city.

Our research proceeded, then, from actual group behavior to inferences about urban personality. The latter represented the goal of our research, but this research in itself was concerned only with the establishment of urban group behavior and the establishment of the pattern of social contacts at a distance from the family home. From the establishment of social contacts and their pattern, then, proceed statements about urban personality as far as this reveals itself in group life.

Two arbitrary decisions were necessary at the outset of our investigations: the definition to be made of the *neighborhood* and the definition of *neighborhood cohesion*. Less important was the

[7] Frequently the city dweller is admonished to limit his contacts to walking distance, as in *Planning the Neighborhood,* Committee on the Hygiene of Housing, American Public Health Association, Chicago, Ill. (1948).

term *social contact,* which we defined as a situation in which the individual interviewed had visited the home of another individual.

The concept of neighborhood was pragmatically approached by dealing with the city block. This choice does not indicate that the entire city is subdivided into blocks of residential housing. There are many exceptions to this rule. Particularly at the urban fringe, there are many long roads with houses strung out on either side of them. Yet, in general, the urban fabric is made up of the grid-iron pattern about which many scientists of the city complain. We chose the block as a unit of research. It prevails in the residential belt of the city environment and thus challenged us to find out what "neighboring" behavior occurred here.

Neighborhood cohesion was expressed as $\dfrac{A}{A \text{ plus } B}$ where A comprises all social contacts in the neighborhood, and B all social contacts taking place outside the neighborhood proper. This choice was made to avoid measuring sociability separately in different parts of the city environment. "Sociability" would be expressed by A plus B, namely all contacts occurring either inside or outside the neighborhood. The ratio upon which we have focussed our attention provides an estimate for neighborhood cohesion. The city block, to be sure, presented us with a somewhat arbitrary and artificial unit as far as actual neighboring activities are concerned. At the beginning of this explorative research, however, a somewhat arbitrary choice of definition was unavoidable, but this was mitigated by some additions to the basic definition.[8] For every urban residence, the opposite side of the street was also considered part of its neighborhood. So were the two first houses at the crossroads adjacent to the original city block. Once this was decided upon, various city areas were advantageously investigated with regard to the size of neighborhood cohesion.

SCOPE OF INDIVIDUAL CONTACTS

We have been convinced by individual examples that the city dweller spreads his contacts over the entire region he inhabits—

[8] The purpose of explorative research is often the gaining of an interrelated system of hypotheses rather than the proof of a single hypothesis.

certainly beyond walking distance of his residence. While very few studies have been made of this, it is probably because any investigation would merely establish an obvious point. Everybody is aware of the fact that city dwellers do not contain their social contacts within walking distance of their residence. We have not made an extensive study of individual urban contacts, but our isolated empirical cases have confirmed the general opinion and these cases are certainly more valid than hypothetical ones. We must hope, however, that the cases were not typical.

TEST OF MEASUREMENT OF NEIGHBORHOOD COHESION

Reliability of the measurement was established by using a different series of questions regarding the propensity to neighbor and by applying the measurement to different environments in the same city. The measure was confirmed, for example, when it was found, just as should be expected, that neighboring was more pronounced in a city block built up of houses constructed by a cooperative housing development than in fringe-area housing built up by private realtors. The measure also showed that neighboring was at a minimum on a city block which, on the basis of other knowledge, could be assigned to the "single men's" district in the same city. In this environment we could expect the relations between different people to be relatively unimportant as compared to contacts which tied them to other parts of the city, and thus there was again validation for the measurement.

DETERMINATION OF NEIGHBORING OF MEN, WOMEN, AND CHILDREN

After being confident that we used a sound measurement of neighborhood-cohesion, we applied this measure in a different city with the intention of finding out whether men, women, or children neighbored more or less. We did so to find out if there were a difference and also because we could then limit further investigations to the particular member of the family with highest neighborhood cohesion.

*Table 36.   Index of Neighborhood Cohesion by Age and Sex
Status (Lakewood Area)*

	WITHIN LAKEWOOD	OUTSIDE LAKEWOOD	NEIGHBORHOOD COHESION INDEX
	(A)	(B)	(C) *
Men	216	1380	0.14
Women	564	1074	0.34
Children	894	1167	0.43

$$* (C) = \frac{A}{A + B}$$

We found that women tended to neighbor more than men. This was proved statistically, and the difference in Lakewood, Los Angeles, was so startling as to let us assume that it would repeat itself elsewhere. We also found that men tended to neighbor where their womenfolk had neighbored previously. There was no reason to assume that conditions in another community would be different, since the margin by which the neighboring activities of women exceeded that of men was very large.[9]

Children neighbored even more than women. They, of course, tend not to leave their own neighborhood too often. Consequently, they show a high neighborhood coefficient, but inasmuch as it has to be explained by a lack of mobility, this was dismissed as unimportant to any discussion of neighborliness.

In consequence, we learned from this study the following: if only the women are asked with regard to their own neighborhood cohesion, a valid index is probably obtained. The men follow in their wake and have a much lower coefficient for neighborhood cohesion anyway. The children can also be disregarded because they are predisposed to neighbor where their mothers neighbor and to stay away from other districts.

MASS STUDY OF SOCIAL CONTACTS

It was of interest, finally, to establish the pattern of social contacts of the city dweller on a mass basis. This gave us a more reliable empirical proof of the existing neighboring patterns. After

[9] See table 36 above.

all, the single cases mentioned above could have been selected in a one-sided manner, giving us one-sided results which would have supported our own prejudice instead of being reliable and valid.

Table 37. Distance of Contacts from the Residence (Mean Distance for all Contacts)
P < .001 *

	(N)	COMMERCIAL	SOCIAL	MEAN TOTAL
West	(77)	2.10	5.10	3.05
Center	(223)	1.90	4.40	2.62
Both	(300)	1.95 **	4.58 ***	2.73

* The difference between the mean commercial contact distance and the mean social contact distance is significant beyond the .001 level for both the distance from the residence and the distance from the center of the city.
** standard deviation: 1.43   *** standard deviation: 4.61

Table 38. Distance of Contacts from the City Center (Mean Distance for all Contacts)
P < .001 *

	(N)	COMMERCIAL	SOCIAL	MEAN TOTAL
West	(77)	10.70	10.65	10.67
Center	(223)	5.09	6.78	5.76
Both	(300)	6.53 **	7.77 ***	7.02

* The difference between the mean commercial contact distance and the mean social contact distance is significant beyond the .001 level for both the distance from the residence and the distance from the center of the city.
** standard deviation: 3.38   *** standard deviation: 4.45

In collecting this material, we interviewed only family mothers. To get a random sample, the telephone directories of Los Angeles were used. Three hundred families were selected, and of these 223 addresses were investigated in the central section and 77 families in the western section of the city.

The findings were that the number of commercial and social contacts in the city increases at closer distance to the family home and that social and commercial contacts become rarer as the distance to the family home is increased. It is quite plausible that the city dweller is willing to travel farther for social than for commercial contacts. His friends and relatives may live far away in the same town, while he must know of commercial services before he utilizes them, and he is probably more familiar with those near to his own residence (see table 37).

It was substantiated that available means of transportation are somewhat related to the distance of all social and commercial contacts. These differences were found related mainly to different numbers and kinds of the family car. To be sure, it is possible that these differences were tantamount only to differences in income about which we did not ask directly. However, it is also possible that these cars, differing in both kind and number, were bought at the expense of other consumer items. Whatever the reason for such ownership, the more cars available in the family and the more expensive these cars were, the more distant was the average social and commercial contact from the family residence (see table 38).

FINDINGS

1. Neighborhood cohesion as a ratio between all contacts and contacts within the neighborhood is measurable.

2. Children neighbor more than their mothers, and the mothers tend to neighbor more than the men in the family. In other words, neighboring is women's business, and we are justified in limiting our investigation to the mother in a family only.

3. The social contacts of the city dweller are found at greater distance from his family home than the commercial contacts.

4. Under the era of laisser-faire the average family contact is found beyond walking distance from the family residence.

5. The number of family contacts—both social and commercial —decreases in number as the distance from the family residence increases.

6. Family contacts—both social and commercial—are more frequent where more and better cars are available for the housewife.

CHALLENGE TO FURTHER RESEARCH

The frequently used dichotomy of primary and secondary group no longer suffices as a description of urban, as opposed to rural, personality, and it is hopeless to try to reintroduce the primary group in the city.

The social contacts of the city dweller are of an entirely different order. They cannot be entirely primary group contacts because the total number of city dwellers is far too great. No individual can know all people living in the same city. Nor will the city dweller limit his social and commercial contacts to the walking-distance area surrounding his residence. If he wants to indulge in crime or delinquency, if he wants to ask for a divorce, he tends to withdraw from the social environment srurounding his residence where means of social control are relatively effective.

Primary group relations do, however, exist in the city. They exist in the urban family, and they also develop to some extent at the men's places of work. They certainly take place where the child goes to school and establishes his associations with school friends. Still, primary group relations tend to be numerically a small minority in the city environment, and, as stated above, the city dweller and his personality are characterized by different patterns of contact.

But the city dweller is not entirely preoccupied by secondary group relations. Those that exist are of a highly specialized nature. They are temporary also and easily terminated when the goal of the secondary group has been attained. We find them in the school where a motley crowd may gather to take one and the same course or on the job where different people get together to do the same kind of work for the same wages as the next fellow.

The city dweller is not free from other allegiances of his own. They are far from specialized and dedicated to one particular pursuit only like the secondary contact, nor are they based upon the intimate acquaintance characteristic of primary groups. The city dweller establishes his social and commercial contacts in an entirely unique manner.

In want of a better word, we talk about tertiary group affiliations of the city dweller. Although their existence has not been proved empirically, it is sound to hypothesize the existence in the city of this unique tertiary group which can be defined as a group consisting of all those individuals who are loyal anonymously and in mass to a current, existing social process.

The tertiary group, then, consists of all those individuals who

are loyal to some on-going social process in general and anonymously.

The above definition covers such processes as the cheering at
a football game, the loyalty to a shopping district even after many
years have gone by since the individual's presence; it covers pa-
triotism where knowledge of individual people is not involved, and
it covers the many social movements for which the modern city
provides such great opportunities.

However plausible the usefulness of the proposed concept may
be, its usefulness awaits empirical verification. Only if the tertiary
group exists in the city to a preponderant extent will its usefulness
be empirically proven. The primary and secondary group may then
be ruled out in its favor as the most important of urban associations.

✳ Biographical Notes

Marvin B. Sussman, general editor, is Associate Professor of Sociology, Western Reserve University. His major fields of research and publication are the community, family, and medical sociology. He is editor of *Sourcebook in Marriage and The Family* and co-author, *Social Class, Maternal Health, and Child Care* and *Hough, Cleveland, Ohio: A Study of Social Life and Change.* He is co-director of the Hough area and Ludlow community studies in Cleveland.

The numbers in parentheses refer to chapters in this book.

Wendell Bell (3) is Associate Professor of Sociology at the University of California in Los Angeles. His theoretical writings and empirical research are in the community field. He is an exponent of social area analysis methodology and his original work with Eshref Shevky, *Social Area Analysis,* marks an advance in community research methodology.

William W. Biddle (5) is Director, Community Dynamics, Earlham College. An expert on community structure and development, Dr. Biddle has two well-known books, *Cultivation of Community Leaders* and *Growth Toward Freedom.*

Russell R. Dynes (13) is Assistant Professor of Sociology and Anthropology at the Ohio State University. He has done research on the community in the areas of religious and family institutions. He has written two chapters, "The Urban Class System" and "The Urban Religions," for the volume *Dynamic Urban Sociology.*

Allen D. Edwards (2) is head of the Department of Sociology, Winthrop College, South Carolina. As a rural sociologist he has completed extensive research on farm families and rural communities and his published reports appear in the scientific journals.

John M. Foskett (16) is Professor of Sociology at the University of Oregon. His major fields of interest are social structure and social participation. Currently he is working on a research project concerned with decision making processes at the community level.

Ella Kube (4) is a Research Associate in the Laboratory in Urban Culture at Occidental College. She is co-author (with George Lehner) of *Dynamics of Personal Adjustment.*

Scott A. Geer (4) is Associate Professor of Sociology at Northwestern University and formerly Chief-Sociologist of the Metropolitan St. Louis Survey. He has done research on social structure and social area analysis of communities and is author of a monograph, *Social Organization.*

Saxon Graham (17) is Director of Community Epidemiological Surveys at Rosewell Park Memorial Institute and Assistant Professor of Medical Sociology, University of Buffalo. His numerous researches on community behavior appear in the scientific journals, and he is the author of *American Culture.*

Otto G. Hoiberg (6) is Associate Professor of Sociology and Coordinator of Community Service, University Extension Division, University of Nebraska. He is the author of two volumes on the community: *Exploring the Small Community* and *Missouri River Basin Development Program.*

Arthur Hillman (7) is Dean of the College of Arts and Sciences and Professor of Sociology at Roosevelt University. *Community Organization and Planning, To-morrow's Chicago* (co-author), and *Sociology and Social Work* are three of his published works.

E. Gartly Jaco (19) is Director of Social Research, Cleveland Psychiatric Institute, and Visiting Associate Professor, Department of Sociology, and Associate, Division of Psychiatry, Western Reserve University. Dr. Jaco specializes in mental health research and his many published papers appear in the scientific journals.

Robert W. Janes (8) is Associate Professor of Sociology at the University of Illinois and is doing longitudinal research on community organization and change. During 1958 he served as chairman of the Community Development and Research Committee of the Society for the Study of Social Problems.

Christien T. Jonassen (1) is Associate Professor of Sociology at the Ohio State University and an active researcher in the area of community theory and analysis. From 1953–1956 he served as editor of *The Ohio Valley Sociologist* and was Chief Investigator for the National Research Council research projects on urban decentralization in Columbus, Seattle, and Houston from 1952 to 1954. *Shopper Attitudes* is one of Dr. Jonassen's numerous publications.

Fred Massarik (12) is Director of the Research Service Bureau, Los Angeles Jewish Community Council and Acting Assistant Professor, School of Business Administration, University of California. Dr. Massarik is a psychologist and has made numerous studies on Jewish life in Los Angeles.

J. D. Mezirow (15) is Training Advisor to the Government of Pakistan's Village Agricultural and Industrial Development Program. Dr. Mezirow, an education specialist, was formerly with the University of California at Riverside and his studies on school-community relations and adult education appear in the scientific journals.

Mhyra S. Minnis (14) is Assistant Professor of Sociology and Social Work at the University of Idaho. Her papers on women's organizations have appeared in numerous journals.

Lawrence K. Northwood (18) is Assistant Professor of Sociology in the New York School of Social Work, Columbia University. Dr. Northwood has done research on community methodology and opinion. He is the author of *Citizens' Self Study*, a publication of the Council of Social Agencies of Grand Rapids, Michigan.

Louis H. Orzack (11) is Assistant Professor of Sociology at the University of Wisconsin. He is doing research in the areas of social organization and the sociology of occupations and professions.

Mel J. Ravitz (9) is Assistant Professor of Sociology at the Wayne State University. Since 1953 he has been working on the problems of community organization for the Detroit Committee for Neighborhood Conservation and Improved Housing. His many reports on urban renewal, citizens participation and social organization are in housing, planning, and sociological journals.

Svend H. Riemer (21) is Professor of Sociology at the University of California in Los Angeles. A one-time Rockefeller Fellow, Professor Riemer is the author of *The Modern City*.

Morton Rubin (11) is Assistant Professor of Sociology at Northeastern University in Boston. Dr. Rubin is the author of *Plantation County* and was a Visiting Fellow at the Center of International Studies, Princeton University. He is engaged in research on community factors in the migration and adjustment of Southern rural Negroes to Northern industrial cities.

Frank L. Sweetser (10) has served as Director of Area Research for the Urban Renewal Demonstration Project in Boston, Massachusetts and is currently Associate Professor of Sociology at Boston University a specialist in community organization and change.

Ralph Thomlinson (11) is Instructor in Sociology at Denison University, Granville, Ohio. His current research is on the measurement of migration through the use of a mathematical model.

Vincent H. Whitney (20) is Chairman of the Sociology Department at the University of Pennsylvania and past president of the Eastern Sociological Society. He has done extensive research on population and metropolitan community structure. He is co-author (with W. Isard) of *Atomic Power: An Economic and Social Analysis*.

✳ Subject Index

449

* Author Index

453